WAR AND PEACE AND WAR

The Life Cycles of Imperial Nations

Peter Turchin

Pi Press
New York

PI PRESS

An Imprint of Pearson Education, Inc.
1185 Avenue of the Americas, New York, New York 10036

Pi Press offers discounts for bulk purchases. For more information,
please contact U.S. Corporate and Government Sales, 1-800-382-
3419, corpsales@pearsontechgroup.com. For sales outside the U.S.,
please contact International Sales at international@pearsoned.com.

Printed in the United States of America

First Printing

Library of Congress Catalog Number: 2005926903

Pi Press books are listed at www.pipress.net

ISBN 0-13-149996-3

Pearson Education LTD.
Pearson Education Australia PTY, Limited
Pearson Education Singapore, Pte. Ltd.
Pearson Education North Asia Ltd.
Pearson Education Canada, Ltd.
Pearson Educación de Mexico, S.A. de C.V.
Pearson Education—Japan
Pearson Education Malaysia, Pte. Ltd.

To Olga.

Contents

Maps

Introduction

"So Peace Brings Warre and Warre Brings Peace"

The empire has unified all the civilizations at last. After generations of battles, the last enemies have been defeated. Citizens of the empire can, it seems, look forward to permanent peace and prosperity. But a maverick mathematician named Hari Seldon has disturbing news. His new science of psychohistory, built from equations that integrate the actions of myriads of individuals, predicts large-scale social trends. When the equations are run forward, they foretell the decay and eventual collapse of the central power, rebellions by regional barons and rogue generals, and finally a bitter civil war that will transform the capital of the empire from a teeming metropolis of hundreds of billions into a ghost town with a few thousand survivors eking out a miserable living among the ruins. The decline and fall of the empire over the ensuing centuries unfolds precisely as the humble mathematician said it would.

This scenario from the *Foundation* trilogy of Isaac Asimov occurs in the future on the planet Trantor, the capital of a mighty galactic empire. In Asimov's fantasy, human history can be understood and predicted in the same way that physicists understand and predict the trajectories of planets, or biologists the expression of the gene. The key to the prediction of human societies is psychohistory, the "branch of mathematics which deals with the reactions of human conglomerates to fixed social and economic stimuli." The ability of psychohistorians to make accurate forecasts, however, is not absolute. Psychohistory cannot accurately predict actions of a single individual. Furthermore, the knowledge of the prediction must be withheld from the people whose collective behavior is predicted. As Hari Seldon explains, "By knowledge, your freedom of action would be expanded and the number of additional variables introduced would become greater than our psychology could handle." Prediction of human societies might also prove impossible for another reason: Complex dynamic systems are inherently unpredictable in the long run because of "the butterfly effect." Small causes might produce large effects. For example, a butterfly fluttering its wings in Australia might cause a hurricane in the Atlantic. Or, as a children's rhyme has it, "For want of a nail... the kingdom was lost." Asimov, however, could not know about the butterfly effect because he wrote the trilogy in the early 1950s, before the discovery of mathematical chaos.

Asimov's trilogy captured the imagination of millions of readers, among them quite a few scientists and historians. However, his vision flies in the face of the view held by most professional historians and scientists, a view generally accepted in our culture. For centuries, philosophers have mulled over the prospects of a scientific study of history. Despite some dissenting voices, the consensus has been that scientific study of human societies is impossible because they differ too much from physical and biological systems. They are too complex. They consist not of simple identical particles, such as atoms and molecules, but of human individuals, each unique, endowed with free will, and capable of purposeful action. The verdict has been that any sort of scientific history must remain science fiction rather than a real science. And some might believe that this is for the best.

A science of history sounds cold and hard—wouldn't it destroy our enjoyment of the wonderfully rich tapestry of the past? On a darker side, might not such a science enable some shadowy cabal to manipulate societies to a nefarious purpose? But have we ceased to enjoy the blue sky of a brilliant summer day, or the play of colors in a glorious sunset? After all, the physicists, beginning with Newton and ending with Einstein, worked out exactly how colors of the sky result from the interaction of sunlight with the atmosphere. As to the nefarious uses of a science of history, it is true that any knowledge can be turned to good or bad ends. But Asimov's notion of a Second Foundation—a group of psychohistorians pulling the strings from some secret center—was always the least credible part of his vision.

War and Peace and War addresses the question raised by Asimov (and many other people before him, including Marx and Tolstoy): Is a science of history possible? Can we design a theory for the collapse of mighty empires that would be no worse than, say, our understanding of why earthquakes happen? Seismologists have made great strides in understanding earthquakes. They can even make some limited predictions as to which areas of the earth are likely to be hit next by an earthquake. However, forecasting the precise timing and magnitude of an earthquake eludes them. Can a science of history, similarly, explain why states crumble, and perhaps predict which societies are in the danger of collapse?

THIS BOOK FOCUSES ON EMPIRES. Why did some—initially small and insignificant—nations go on to build mighty empires, whereas other nations failed to do so? And why do the successful empire builders invariably, given enough time, lose their empires? Can we understand how imperial powers rise and why they fall?

An empire is a large, multiethnic territorial state with a complex power structure. The key variable is the size. When large enough, states invariably encompass ethnically diverse people; this makes them into multiethnic states. And given the difficulties of communication in pre-industrial times, large states had to come up with a variety of ad hoc ways to bind far-flung territories to the center. One of the typical expedients was to incorporate smaller neighbors as self-contained units, imposing tribute on them and taking over their foreign relations, but otherwise leaving their internal functioning alone. Such a process of piecemeal accumulation usually leads to complicated chains of command and the coexistence of heterogeneous territories within one state.

Empires are not the only objects of study for a science of history. Historians such as Arnold Toynbee wrote volumes on the rise and fall of whole civilizations. Others have been fascinated with the spread of world religions, evolution of art styles, progress in science and technology, or economic and demographic changes. All of these subjects are worthy. However, it is impossible to encompass them all in one book. The rise and fall of empires is a fine place to start.

Unlike such entities as civilizations, territorial states are easier to define and demarcate from each other, as well as from other comparable units (city states, tribal confederations, and so on). Historians continue to argue about how to distinguish one civilization from another. Different authorities place Achaemenid Persia as part of the Syriac, Iranian, or Mesopotamian civilization. In contrast to this multitude of contending notions, were you to consult any historical atlas, you would find the boundaries of the Achaemenid Empire drawn in pretty much the same places.

Although the doings of empires dominate the historical records, we should not conclude that they are the norm in human history. Prior to the nineteenth century most (and until six thousand years ago all) of the habitable space on Earth was divided among small-scale, stateless societies, not empires. Historical empires themselves, as often as not, were in the state of decline or even disintegration. A large stable empire, internally at peace, is a rarity in history. Looked at from this point of view, the most fundamental question requiring an explanation is not why empires decline and collapse, but how they manage to get going in the first place. How are empires possible?

The stories of empire are irresistible. Imagine the feelings of an eighteenth-century Englishman, on his world tour, standing among the fairly well-preserved 2,000-year-old ruins of ancient Rome (before the modern metropolis engulfed them). Today one can have a similar experience in Chichen Itza in Mexico. (Be sure to get there early in the day before the tourist buses arrive.) Who were the people who built these magnificent temples and pyramids? Why aren't they around anymore? From Shelley's "Ozymandias" to Darth Vader, stories of empires fascinate us.

As a road map to what follows, here is a very terse outline of the central theoretical argument of the book.

Many historical processes are dynamic—empires rise and fall, populations and economies boom and bust, world religions spread or wither. The field of historical dynamics investigates such dynamic processes in history. Most research has been done on agrarian societies, those in which the majority (and often more than 90 percent) of people are involved in producing food.

The theoretical framework I have been developing for several years focuses not on human individuals, but on social groups through time. Ultimately, the behavior of a group is determined by the actions of its individual members. However, social groups are not simple collections of identical particles, readily described by statistical physics; they have complex internal structures.

One important aspect of group structure is that different people have access to differing amounts of power and wealth. A small number of members of an agrarian society (typically around 1 or 2 percent) concentrates in its hands most of the power and wealth; this group consists of the elites or aristocracy. Commoners make up the rest of the population.

Another important aspect of social structure is ethnicity. Ethnicity is the group use of any aspect of culture to create internal cohesion and differentiation from other groups. An imaginary boundary separates the members of the ethnic group from the rest of humanity. For example, Greeks drew a boundary between themselves and barbarians, non-Greek speakers. The ethnic boundary can use a variety of *symbolic markers*—language and dialect, religion and ritualistic behaviors, race, clothing, behavioral mannerisms, hairstyles, ornaments, and tattoos. The important thing is not which markers are used, but the distinction between in-group and out-group members, between "us" and "them."

People usually have multiple ethnic identities nested within each other. An inhabitant of Dallas can be simultaneously a Texan, an American, and a participant in Western civilization. The broadest groupings of people that unite many nations are usually called civilizations, but I prefer to call such entities *metaethnic communities* (from the Greek *meta*, "beyond," and *ethnos*, "ethnic group" or "nation"). My definition includes not only the usual civilizations—the Western, Islamic, and Sinic—but also such broad cultural groupings as the Celts and Turco-Mongolian steppe nomads. Typically, cultural difference is greatest between people belonging to different metaethnic communities; sometimes this gap is so extreme that people deny the very humanity of those who are on the other side of the metaethnic fault line.

Historical dynamics can be understood as a result of competition and conflict between groups, some of which dominate others. Domination, however, is made possible only because groups are integrated at the micro level by cooperation among their members. Within-group cooperation is the basis of inter-group conflict, including its extreme versions such as war and even genocide.

Different groups have different degrees of cooperation among their members, and therefore different degrees of cohesiveness and solidarity. Following the fourteenth-century Arab thinker Ibn Khaldun, I call this property of groups *asabiya*. Asabiya refers to the capacity of a social group for concerted collective action. Asabiya is a dynamic quantity; it can increase or decrease with time. Like many theoretical constructs, such as force in Newtonian physics, the capacity for collective action cannot be observed directly, but it can be measured from observable consequences.

Each empire has at its core an *imperial nation*. (Some empires had more than one imperial nation for a time, but this structure appears to be unstable.) The ability of an empire to expand territory and to defend itself against external and internal enemies is determined largely by the characteristics of its imperial nation, especially its asabiya. Because only groups possessing high levels of asabiya can construct large empires, the question is how do they gain it, and why do they eventually lose it?

Groups with high asabiya arise on metaethnic frontiers. A *metaethnic frontier* is an area where an imperial boundary coincides with a fault line between two metaethnic communities. metaethnic frontiers are places where between-group competition is very intense. Expansionist empires exert enormous military pressure on the peoples beyond their boundaries. However, the frontier populations are also attracted to the imperial wealth, which they attempt to obtain by trading or raiding. Both the external threat and the prospect of gain are powerful integrative forces that nurture asabiya. In the pressure cooker of a metaethnic frontier, poorly integrated groups crumble and disappear, whereas groups based on strong cooperation thrive and expand.

To match the power of the old empire, a frontier group with high asabiya—an incipient imperial nation—needs to expand by incorporating other groups. On a metaethnic frontier, integration of ethnically similar groups on the same side of the fault line is made easier by the presence of a very different "other"—the metaethnic community on the other side. The huge cultural gap across the frontier dwarfs the relatively minor differences between ethnic groups on the same side. Empirical evidence shows that large aggressive empires do not arise in areas where political boundaries separate culturally similar peoples.

My main argument, therefore, is that people originating on fault-line frontiers become characterized by cooperation and a high capacity for collective action, which in turn enables them to build large and powerful territorial states. I develop this argument in Part I and illustrate it with examples of Russia and America (Chapters 1 and 2), the Germans and Arabs on the Roman frontier (Chapters 3 and 4), the origins of Rome (Chapter 6), and the rise of the European great powers (Chapter 7).

The critical assumption in my argument is that cooperation provides the basis for imperial power. This assumption is at odds with the fundamental postulates of the dominant theories in social and biological sciences: the rational choice in economics and the selfish gene in evolutionary biology. However, recent developments in the nascent fields of experimental economics and multilevel selection show that the standard model, based on the self-interest hypothesis, is deeply flawed. It cannot explain the puzzle of human ultrasociality—our ability to combine into cooperating groups consisting of millions of unrelated individuals. Moreover, it is refuted by behavioral experiments.

Two key adaptations enabled the evolution of ultrasociality. The first one was the *moralist* strategy: cooperate when enough members in the group are also cooperating and punish those who do not cooperate. A band that had enough moralists to tip its collective behavior to the cooperative equilibrium outcompeted, or even exterminated, bands that failed to cooperate. The second adaptation, the human ability to use symbolic markers to define cooperating groups, allowed evolution of sociality to break through the limits of face-to-face interaction. The scale of human societies increased in a series of leaps, from the village and clan to the tribe and tribal confederation, and then to the state, empire, and civilization. Chapter 5 examines this new science of cooperation.

WHEREAS PART I IS DEVOTED TO *IMPERIOGENESIS*—the factors that explain the rise of empires—Part II switches focus to *imperiopathosis*—why empires decline.

The very stability and internal peace that strong empires impose contain within them the seeds of future chaos. Stability and internal peace bring prosperity, and prosperity causes population increase. Demographic growth leads to overpopulation, overpopulation causes lower wages, higher land rents, and falling per capita incomes for the commoners. At first, low wages and high rents bring unparalleled wealth to the upper classes, but as their numbers and appetites grow, they also begin to suffer from falling incomes. Declining standards of life breed discontent and strife. The elites turn to the state for employment and additional income, and drive up its expenditures at the same time that the tax revenues decline because of the growing misery of the population. When the state's finances collapse, it loses the control of the army and police. Freed from all restraints, strife among the elites escalates into civil war, while the discontent among the poor explodes into popular rebellions.

The collapse of order brings in its wake the four horsemen of the apocalypse—famine, war, pestilence, and death. Population declines and wages increase, while rents decrease. As incomes of commoners recover, the fortunes of the upper classes hit bottom. Economic distress of the elites and lack of effective government feed the continuing internecine wars. However, civil wars thin the ranks of the elites. Some die in factional fighting, others succumb to feuds with neighbors, and many simply stop trying to maintain their aristocratic status and quietly slip into the ranks of commoners. Intra-elite competition subsides, allowing the restoration of order. Stability and internal peace bring prosperity, and another cycle begins. As a sixteenth-century commentator put it, "So peace brings warre and warre brings peace."

The typical period of a complete cycle, which consists of a benign *integrative phase* and the troubled *disintegrative phase*, is around two or three centuries. I call these majestic oscillations in demographic, economic, and social structures of agrarian societies *secular cycles*. The demographic-structural theory that explains secular cycles is developed in Chapters 8 and 9, in which it is illustrated with French and English history during the medieval and early modern times.

The phase of a secular cycle affects a trend in economic and social inequality, which in turn affects the dynamics of asabiya. Incipient imperial nations are relatively egalitarian. Great differences in wealth among group members undermine cooperation, and such groups succumb to rivals with higher levels of asabiya. In addition, metaethnic frontiers tend to be underpopulated, so there is enough land (the main form of wealth in agrarian societies) for all who are willing to work it. The success of an imperial nation at territorial expansion, however, results in the movement of frontiers far away from its core, thus removing an important force holding up the growth of inequality. Imposition of peace results in population growth, and overpopulation brings with it the impoverishment of peasant masses. As the poor grow poorer, the rich grow richer—this process is called the *Matthew principle*. The growing disparity between the rich and the poor puts the social consensus under strain. At the same time, the gap in the distribution of wealth grows not only between the aristocrats and commoners, but also within each social group. Intra-elite competition for diminishing resources results in faction and undermines national solidarity. During the disintegrative phase of the secular cycle, regional and sectarian identities acquire greater saliency than the national or empire-wide identity, and the asabiya of the imperial nation is corroded. Thus, the Matthew principle plays an important role in imperiopathosis, the decline of empires.

Decline of asabiya is not linearly uniform. During the integrative phases of secular cycles when inequality is moderate, intra-elite competition and conflict between elites and commoners subside; the empire-wide identity regains its strength, for a time. As discussed further in Chapter 10, it takes the cumulative effect of several disintegrative phases to reduce asabiya of a great imperial nation to the point where it cannot hold together its empire.

A life cycle of a typical imperial nation extends over the course of two, three, or even four secular cycles. Every time the empire enters a disintegrative secular phase, the asabiya of its core nation is significantly degraded. Thus, several secular cycles are nested within the great cycle of the rise and decline of asabiya. However, disintegrative phases are also not uniformly grim. A civil war begins like a forest fire or an epidemic—violence leads to more violence in an escalating spiral of murder and revenge. Eventually, however, people become fed up with constant fighting, and a civil war "burns out." Both the survivors of the civil war and their children, who had direct experience of conflict, are reluctant to allow the hostilities to escalate again. They are, thus, "immunized" against internecine violence. The next generation, the grandchildren of the civil warriors who did not experience its horrors at first hand, is not immunized. If the social conditions leading to conflict (the main one being elite overproduction) are still operational, the grandchildren will fight another civil war. As a result, civil war tends to recur during the disintegrative phase with a period of 40 to 60 years. I call such dynamics the *fathers-and-sons cycles*. The fathers-and-sons cycles are nested within secular cycles, which in turn are nested within asabiya cycles. I illustrate these "wheels within wheels within wheels" dynamics with the decline of the Roman Empire in Chapter 11.

In this book, therefore, I discuss three central concepts: the meta-ethnic frontier theory, which explains asabiya cycles; the demographic-structural theory, which explains secular cycles; and the social-psychology theory, which explains the fathers-and-sons cycles. These theories comprise part of a new science of historical dynamics, or as I prefer to call it *cliodynamics* (from *Clio*, "muse of history," and *dynamics*, "the study of processes that change with time").

Cliodynamics borrows heavily from two disciplines in the natural sciences. The focus on groups rather than individuals is akin to the approach of statistical mechanics, which integrates over motions of myriads of particles to predict such properties of the ensemble as temperature or pressure. However, the study and prediction of human groups is a much more challenging task because people vary (among other things, for example, in power and ethnic identity). Humans also possess free will. I discuss the implications of these complicating factors for the study of human societies in Chapter 12.

Cliodynamics owes an even greater debt to the discipline of nonlinear dynamics. Human societies and states can be modeled as dynamic systems, consisting of parts that interact with each other. Furthermore, states are part of an international system, which adds another level of complexity. The key concept here is *dynamic feedback*. A change in the state of one component of the system has an effect on another, but the change in the second might in turn affect—feedback on—the first. When a dynamic system contains within it such circular nonlinear feedback, it becomes highly susceptible to oscillation. Stated succinctly, "So peace brings warre and warre brings peace."

Cycles exhibited by historical societies and states, however, are not the same as highly periodic, repeatable phenomena in physics, such as planetary motions or pendulum oscillation. Social systems are much more complex. It is well known from the science of nonlinear dynamics that two or more perfectly cyclic behaviors superimposed on each other may combine to produce noncyclic dynamics—in other words, chaos. Interactions between the asabiya, secular, and fathers-and-sons cycles can lead to such complex, chaotic dynamics. In a chaotic system, a small action of one of its elements—a human being exercising his or her free will—can have huge consequences. External sources also play a role—for example, variations in climate leading to crop failure, random mutations giving rise to new frightful epidemics, and cataclysmic volcano eruptions. The dynamics of real human societies cannot be accurately predicted far in the future because of the nature of chaotic behavior, free will, and natural disasters. Hari Seldon was wrong.

Although prediction far in the future is impossible, given what we know about societies and nonlinear dynamics, it does not mean that improved understanding of how societies function is purely academic knowledge. An understanding of the processes that bring a society to the brink of civil war might suggest policies to avert such a war. Such social engineering, of course, is still far in the future. Our understanding of the dynamics of even agrarian societies is far from perfect, and highly complex modern industrial and postindustrial societies present an even greater challenge for sociologists. Many processes that played a determining role in the functioning of agrarian societies are of much less or even no importance in modern societies. For example, famine has been largely eliminated in modern Western societies. On the other hand, human nature has not been completely changed by the Industrial Revolution. In the last two chapters of this book, I speculate on what lessons cliodynamics might have for us and our future times of war and peace and war.

Part I

IMPERIOGENESIS

The Rise of Empires

Chapter 1

A Band of Adventurers Defeats a Kingdom

Ermak's Conquering Cossacks

On October 22, 1581, the warrior Ermak Timofeev, an ataman leading several hundred Cossacks, decided to make camp on the banks of the Irtysh River. The Cossacks were deep in the hostile territory on the far side of the Urals, surrounded by savage hordes on every side. Night had already fallen, so they lit a ring of fires to guard themselves against stealthy attack and to keep warm their wounded comrades. After making camp, Ermak gathered together the unwounded and those not keeping watch to discuss what they must do next. They had few options, and none looked good.

The chain of events that brought these Russian warriors to the Irtysh began a couple of decades before in 1558, when Tsar Ivan IV granted to Jacob and Gregory Stroganov a huge territory in the wild Upper Kama region just west of the Ural Mountains. The Stroganovs were the Russian counterparts of the Dutch and English merchant-adventurers and empire builders who founded trading companies in the East and West Indies. Earlier in the sixteenth century, the Stroganov family had developed large-scale industries on the northeastern frontier of Russia—salt extraction, fur trade, and fisheries—and therefore they had the necessary experience and capital to develop new territories. The Stroganov brothers immediately started attracting colonists and establishing settlements and military garrisons. The land was sparsely inhabited by indigenous tribes of various Finno-Ugric peoples who, although resentful of the invasion, were unable to offer effective resistance. A more serious threat came from the Tatars inhabiting the steppe and forest-steppe regions beyond the Urals. The *Tatars* was the generic name used by the Russians for Turko-Mongolic steppe nomads. These particular nomads were ruled by Kuchum, a descendant of Chinggis (more familiarly, but inaccurately, spelled Genghis) Khan, who styled himself as the khan of Sibir (whence the name *Siberia*). When Kuchum Khan realized that Russians were in the process of establishing a firm grip on the Upper Kama region, he sent some Tatars and their native allies under his nephew Mahmet-Kul to raid the new settlements. The Tatars massacred the Russians (and the native allies of the Russians), captured many of their women and children, and then retired with this booty across the mountains.

Map 1   *Russia and the Tatars in the sixteenth century*

The Stroganovs' response was that the best defense is offense. The first step was to obtain a formal permission from the tsar to extend their territory across the Urals. The tsar granted permission, but with a stipulation that the Stroganovs were strictly on their own—they could not count on the government for either funds or soldiers. Fortunately, they had an alternative source of recruits—the Cossacks. The Cossacks were rough-and-ready Russian frontiersmen inhabiting the lawless steppe regions between the borders of the Russian state and the territories controlled by the Crimean, Kazan, and Astrakhan Tatars. Their precise origins are obscure, but by the sixteenth century their ranks consisted mainly of runaway peasants, impoverished noble servitors, and other fugitives from central Russia, as well as their descendants. Cossack relations with the Russian state were uneven. Being Christian Orthodox in religion, the Cossacks usually warred against the tsar's enemies, and often entered government service. However, the Cossacks valued freedom above all else, and were known to lead rebellions against the central government. Furthermore, opportunities for peaceful trade were quite limited on the steppe frontier, and many Cossack bands made their living by brigandage.

When the Stroganovs started casting about for recruits, they learned about one such band of outlaws based on the Volga, whose leaders included Ermak Timofeev and Ivan Koltso. Koltso ("the Ring") achieved international notoriety when he led a successful raid on the capital of the Nogay Horde. The Nogays were at the time allied with Russia, and when they complained to Ivan IV, he condemned Koltso to death in absentia. The Stroganovs sent a letter to the Cossacks, offering the company a chance to defend the eastern frontier of Christendom against the "heathens" and, at the same time, earn the tsar's pardon. The Cossacks accepted.

In 1579, Ermak's company arrived in the Stroganov territory, where they first served as the military garrison. In the summer of 1581, for example, they defeated a raiding foray by the 680 Voguls (a warlike Ugric tribe from across the Urals) and captured their leader. However, their main job was to take the war to the enemy. The contemporary *Stroganov Chronicle* relates how the subsequent events unfolded.

"On September 1, 1582, on the feast day of our Holy Father Simeon Stylite, Semen, Maxim, and Nikita Stroganov sent out the Volga *atamans* and Cossacks, Ermak Timofeev and his men, from their town, against the

Siberian sultan [Kuchum Khan]. With these men, they sent 300 of their own troops mustered from the towns and *Litva* [these were some Lithuanian and German prisoners, who were promised freedom upon successful completion of the enterprise], Tatars and Russians, all bold and brave. They set forth as one, together with the Volga atamans and Cossacks. In all, the total was 840 bold and brave men. They sang prayers to the all-merciful God of the Holy Trinity and to the Virgin Mother and all the heavenly powers and saints." The Cossacks loaded boats with supplies and weapons, which included arquebuses and light cannon, and started rowing up the Chusovaya River toward the Ural Mountains. After traveling as far up the river as they could go, they portaged across the Urals (the mountains being gentle in this region), and then floated down the tributaries of the Irtysh.

"On September 9 of the year 1582, of the feast day of the Holy Father Ioachim and of Anna, the intrepid warriors reached the land of Siberia and attacked many Tatar and native settlements down the Tura River. They valiantly made their way to the Tavda River and captured Tatar prisoners at its mouth. One of them, named Tauzak, was a member of the court of the tsar [here meaning Kuchum Khan, not the Russian tsar]; he told them all about the Siberian tsars and princes and horsemen and about Tsar Kuchum. When they learned everything from Tauzak, they set him free to inform Sultan Kuchum about their arrival and their strength and bravery. ...

"The evil Tsar Kuchum sent his son [actually, nephew] Mahmet-Kul with a great multitude of warriors and ordered them to stand bravely against the invading Russians. Kuchum ordered them to fell trees and build an abatis on the Irtysh River at Chuvash, and to reinforce it with earth, and fortify it with defense weapons. This was to be a substantial fortification.

"Mahmet-Kul and his multitudinous warriors reached the place called Babasan. The Russian warriors, atamans, and Cossacks were considerably alarmed to see such a great assemblage of the heathens, but they put their trust in God and set forth from their forts and fell upon the heathens. The heathens attacked the invading forces mercilessly from horseback and wounded the Cossacks with their lances and sharp arrows. The Russian warriors fired back [with their arquebuses and light cannon] and killed a vast multitude of the heathen. There was a fierce struggle with the

Tatar warriors, and both sides suffered a great number of casualties. The heathens, seeing so many of their warriors fall before the Russians, took flight. ...

"When the Cossacks reached the domain of Karacha, a second battle took place against this councillor of Tsar [Kuchum]. They captured his domain and plundered his honey and other property and loaded it into their boats. The heathens, on horseback and foot, pursued them to the Irtysh River. The atamans and Cossacks advanced bravely against the heathens massed on the riverbank, and both sides lost many men killed in this great battle. Then the heathens, seeing so many of their men killed by the Russian warriors, took final flight. In that battle, Ermak's army lost only a few men, but almost everyone was wounded.

"When Tsar Kuchum saw his warriors overwhelmed, he retired with some survivors and camped on the top of a hill called Chuvash. His son Mahmet-Kul remained at the abatis with a large rearguard, while the Cossacks proceeded up the Irtysh River.

"When the Russian forces came upon a small settlement which belonged to Atik-murza, they took it and set up their camp there, because night had already fallen and it was dark. The Cossacks saw an immense gathering of the heathen at their abatis and were in great consternation. They said to one another, 'How can we stand against such a multitude?' They pondered this, then formed a circle and took counsel together [this was the traditional way of reaching a decision in the Cossack democracy]. They debated. 'Should we retreat, or stand together as one?' Some brooded and were of the opinion, 'It would be best for us to retreat.' But others were firm and resolute and proclaimed, 'Oh, brother comrades in arms, how can we retreat? Autumn has already set in. Ice is freezing in the rivers. We cannot take to flight and bring reproach and disgrace on ourselves. Rather let us place our trust in God, for victory does not come from having a great mass of warriors, but from the help of God on high. It is possible that God will help even the helpless. Brothers, have we ourselves not heard what evil this godless and cursed heathen of the Siberian land, Sultan Kuchum, has brought on our Russian land of Perm, how he has laid waste the towns of our Sovereign [the Russian tsar], and murdered and enslaved Orthodox Christians? Do we not know of the number of the Stroganovs' forts he has destroyed? Almighty God will punish the cursed one for shedding

Christian blood. Brothers, let us recall our oath, which we swore before God in the presence of honest men [the Stroganovs]. We gave our word and promised, kissing the cross, that if Almighty God helped us, we would not retreat, even though we might die to the last man. We cannot turn back. We cannot dishonor ourselves and break the oath we have sworn. If the Almighty Glorious God of the Trinity will help us, then even if we fall, our memory will not die in these lands, and our glory will be eternal!'

"Hearing this, the atamans and Cossacks were emboldened in spirit, and their courage was renewed. They all shouted an oath in one voice. 'We are ready to die for the holy church of God. We will suffer for the true Orthodox faith. We will serve the devout Sovereign Tsar and Grand Prince Ivan Vasilevich of all Russia [Ivan IV]. We will stand firm against the heathens to the last drop of our blood, unto death itself. Brothers, we will not violate oaths, we will stand as one, steadfast!' …

"They set out from their camp to go to battle on October 23, the feast day of the Holy Apostle James, brother of our Lord. All together, in one voice, they gave tongue, shouting, 'God be with us! Lord, help us, your humble servants!'

"They advanced on the abatis bravely and fearlessly, and there was a fierce battle with the heathens. The heathens fired countless arrows from the top of the abatis and from embrasures. They wounded many of Ermak's brave men and killed others. And when they saw these brave men fall, the heathens rushed out in sorties through the abatis in three places, hoping to force the Cossacks into flight. During these they fought ferociously, in hand-to-hand combat.

"The Cossacks advanced against the heathens as one man and proved their bravery and ferocity before the dishonored and godless heathen. At length, the heathens' strength weakened, and God gave the Cossacks victory over them. The Cossacks gained ground, overpowered the heathens, and killed a multitude. They forced them back from the abatis and placed their own battle standard on it. They wounded Mahmet-Kul, and his warriors carried him off in a small boat across the Irtysh River.

"Tsar Kuchum, who was encamped on the hill, saw the defeat of his Tatars and the wounding and flight of his son Mahmet-Kul. He ordered his mullahs to call out their wretched Muslim prayers. He called on his foul gods to aid him, but received not the slightest assistance. At the same time the Ostiak princes [the native allies of the Tatars] fell back with their men, however they could. ...

"The wretched tsar galloped off to his town of Sibir, taking a small part of his wealth, and then continued his flight, leaving the town of Sibir deserted. Brave Ermak and his men came to Sibir, later called Tobolsk, on October 26, the feast day of the Holy Martyr Demetrios of Salonika. They gave thanks to God for having given them victory over the godless and cursed heathens, and rejoiced mightily. They seized a great amount of gold and silver, cloth of gold, precious stones, sables, martens and valuable foxes, and divided these among themselves.

"This is splendid to relate, and truly it glorifies the Almighty God of the Trinity who had given the small but strong Russian warriors victory over the heathens, and defeat of the boastful Tsar Kuchum. Tsar Kuchum had assembled an army that outnumbered the Cossacks by 10 to 20 or even 30 to 1. The cursed one lamented the great number of his warriors who had fallen. Thus God brings down the haughty and favors the humble Christians."

THIS STORY OF ERMAK'S CONQUEST of Siberia, as told by the contemporary chronicler, is interesting not only because of the events that it relates, but also in *how* it is told. The ideological spin that the chronicler puts on the story provides a glimpse into how the Russians viewed their conflict with the Tatars, and what were the motivations of the people who advanced the Russian frontier. But let us first focus on the basic outline of the events. A band of a few hundred intrepid European adventurers defeats hordes of natives, conquers a kingdom, and captures an enormous booty. The parallel between Ermak's Cossacks and Cortés' or Pizarro's conquistadors in the New World is striking (although, to be sure, the amount of loot captured by Pizarro dwarfes anything that Ermak could possibly have found in Sibir).

How did they do it? Jared Diamond recently explained the spectacular feats of Cortés and Pizarro by arguing that the Spaniards had guns, germs, and steel, whereas Native Americans, who had no communications with the continent of Eurasia before 1492, did not. This explanation makes sense for the Spanish conquest of America, but it does not help us to understand the Russian conquest of Siberia. We can immediately dismiss two thirds of Diamond's triad, because both sides had been exposed to the same germs and steel for centuries. As for guns, the Russians employed them with great effect against the bow-and-arrow-wielding nomads. But why were the Russians able to equip themselves with guns, and the Tatars not? Neither of these peoples was the inventor of firearms. (If anything, the Tatars were in a much better position than the Russians to get gunpowder directly from its inventors, the Chinese.) A racist explanation, stressing the difference between the Europeans and non-Europeans, is unsatisfactory because other Turkic people—the Ottomans and the Mughals—eagerly adopted firearms and used them with great effect to build huge empires. The Crimean Tatars a thousand miles to the southwest of their Siberian cousins started using siege and handheld guns around 1530. In any case, the role of firearms in the decisive battle of Sibir was quite minimal. The primitive matchlock arquebuses of the Cossacks were slow to fire, lacked accuracy, and could not be used in damp weather. The main impact of the gunpowder revolution in the fifteenth and sixteenth centuries, after all, was the ability of artillery to knock down medieval fortifications. Handheld guns started becoming truly effective only after the seventeenth century, with the invention of the flintlock musket.

The mystery deepens when we consider what happened in eastern Europe three centuries before Ermak. In 1236, a great army of steppe invaders led by Batu, one of Chinggis Khan's grandsons, gathered in the steppes west of the Irtysh, in the same area that three centuries later was to become the khanate of Sibir. Although we call them the *Mongols*, the ethnic Mongols comprised perhaps a tenth of the host's number; the rest were a tribal mixture dominated by various Turkic peoples: Keraits, Tatars (whose name was expanded by the Russians to cover all kinds of Turko-Mongolic steppe people), Uigurs, Khwarizmians, Turkomans, and so on. The Mongol subjugation of eastern Europe began with the destruction of the realm of the Volga Bulgars. Starting in 1237, and for the next three years, the Mongols systematically conquered practically all of Russia. (Only Novgorod in the northwest escaped direct attack, but nevertheless had to submit to Batu and agree to pay tribute.) One of the most remarkable aspects of this conquest was that although each principality fought bravely against the invaders, the Russians were unable to unite against the

Mongol threat. This inability to work together is most graphically illustrated by the tale of two brothers, Yurii and Roman, who ruled the Ryazan principality southeast of Moscow. When the Mongol army approached, Yurii shut himself up in the principality's capital, Ryazan, while Roman, instead of coming to the aid of his brother, stayed in a smaller town, Kolomna, some 50 miles to the northwest of Ryazan. The Mongols first took Ryzan, killed Yurii, and slaughtered the entire population. Then they went to Kolomna, defeated and killed Roman before the fortress, and captured Kolomna itself.

The same story repeated itself over and over again. Fragmentation of Russia into dozens of tiny principalities and the inability of the Russians to unite against the external threat were one of the main reasons (perhaps the main one) why the Mongols were able to conquer Russia in the thirteenth century. This shortcoming was obvious to the Russians themselves, as made very clear in the *Ode on the Downfall of the Russian Land*, written shortly after the Mongol conquest.

The Mongols, by contrast, excelled at teamwork. Historians generally agree that the ability of the Mongols to crush all their opponents was not due to any technical advantage in weaponry, nor to their numbers. (They often fought against and destroyed numerically superior enemies.) The explanation for the Mongol success must be sought elsewhere.

The Mongol army was a well-oiled social mechanism, capable of discipline and internal cohesion to the degree unknown in Europe since the Roman times. The Mongol armies deployed, advanced, and maneuvered in eerie silence. There were not even shouts of command because movements of the blocks of cavalry were governed by the flag signals from the standard bearers. At the right moment, the whole army suddenly charged, yelling and shrieking like demons. Such tactics were extremely unnerving to their adversaries.

One of the favorite tricks used by the Mongols was the fake retreat, luring the unwary enemy into ambush and annihilation. Performing such maneuvers with a host of 100,000 called for precision timing and frictionless cooperation. Another tactic, described by the papal envoy Plano Carpini, was as follows. "They meet the first cavalry onset with a front consisting of prisoners and foreign auxiliaries, while the bulk of their forces take up their positions on the wings in order to encompass the enemy.

They do this so effectively that he fancies them far more numerous than they are. If the adversary defends himself stoutly, they open their ranks and allow him to escape, whereupon they dash in pursuit and slay as many of the fugitives as they can." The world historian William McNeill noted that "the Mongols were capable of moving in widely dispersed columns over all sorts of terrain, while maintaining communication between the separate columns so as to assure concentration of all forces at the decisive time and place. Subotai, the general in charge of the invasion of Europe in 1241, thought nothing of coordinating columns operating in Poland with others pressing into Hungary, despite the Carpathian barrier between them. No comparable feats of coordination over such distances were achieved by European armies until the late nineteenth century."

The Mongol unity of purpose extended from the movements of large-scale military units all the way down to interpersonal relations. As the ambassador from the French court William of Rubruck reported, "In the whole world, there are no more obedient subjects than the Tatars, neither among lay people nor among the monks; they pay their lords more respect than any other people and would hardly dare lie to them. Rarely if ever do they revile each other, but if they should, the dispute never leads to blows. Wars, quarrels, the infliction of bodily harm, and manslaughter do not occur among them, and there are no large-scale thieves or robbers among them." It was this remarkable social cohesion that explains the spectacular successes of the Mongols against all other Eurasian armies from Korea to Hungary.

THE CHARACTERIZATION OF THE MONGOLS that stresses their ability to cooperate will probably sound strange to many readers. *Cooperation* is a "nice" word, and the Mongols of Chinggis Khan were most definitely not nice people. They slaughtered literally millions of men, women, and children, and enslaved millions of survivors. They turned dozens of wealthy and beautiful cities into ruins and piled pyramids of hundreds of thousands of skulls as grisly monuments to their achievements. They practiced cruel executions and unspeakable tortures on those unlucky to fall into their hands. And wasn't the empire of Chinggis Khan a typical "oriental despotism"? So how is it possible to speak about the spirit of cooperation in such a society?

This is a very important question because, as discussed in subsequent chapters, cooperation, or more generally the capacity for collective action, is a key factor in the rise of empires. It must be noted immediately that the concept of *oriental despotism*, if it means the absolute power of one individual over the whole society, is a sociological nonsense. A single person, no matter how physically impressive, cannot rule against the wishes of *all* of his subjects. As soon as he falls asleep, one of the people he has oppressed will end his tyranny by sticking a knife in him. In real life, tyrants could rule only because they had the support of a certain group of people—the palace guard, the aristocracy, perhaps the top bureaucrats. Only groups can oppress other groups and whole societies, and to do that the "oppressor" group must be internally cohesive. In other words, oppression can only be accomplished from the basis of cooperation, paradoxical as it sounds.

The social matrix of Western societies (weaved from such things as education, mass media, and even cocktail-party chitchat) conditions us to think that the only legitimate source of social power is "we the people." As a corollary, we tend to assume that nondemocratic societies are held together by force alone. A recent illustration of this pervasive cultural bias is the implicit assumption by the American planners of the Iraq invasion in 2003 that as soon as Saddam Hussein was overthrown by American troops, the Iraqi people would work together with the occupation authorities in building a democratic society.

There is no question that the Ba'athist regime of Saddam Hussein used violence and intimidation to keep down dissident groups, and the many atrocities committed by Saddam's henchmen are well documented. However, this was not the whole story. In addition to force, the regime relied on cooperation from certain other groups: the core support came from Saddam's clan, with the wider power base provided by the Sunni Arabs of Iraq. In addition, a more diffuse group, originating from other ethnic segments of the Iraqi population (the Shiite Arabs and the Sunni Kurds and Turkmen), had come to think of themselves as "Iraqis" first and members of their ethnic group second. Although this group, let us loosely call them nationalists, did not actively support the Ba'athist regime, they *acquiesced* to its rule. Although perhaps not holding the legitimacy of Saddam's government terribly high, many of them consider the legitimacy of the occupying powers to be even lower.

We now know empirically that Saddam's regime was not based solely on force, because many members of the groups that supported him when he was in power are still willing to sacrifice their lives attacking his captors (even after Saddam himself has become powerless). An even greater number participates in demonstrations and other acts of nonviolent resistance, an activity that, although not as suicidal as direct attacks against the well-armed American troops, is by no means risk-free. Finally, the majority of Iraqis have just chosen to have as little to do with the American authorities as possible. During the first months of the occupation, various commentators attributed this aloofness to the residual fear that Saddam could yet return to power and punish those who cooperated with the Americans. However, the capture of Saddam in late 2003 did not change Iraqi attitudes in any significant way.

The case of Ba'athist Iraq, thus, serves as an excellent illustration of the idea that oppression and cooperation are not mutually exclusive—to oppress the dissidents, Saddam had to have cooperation within his social power base. To the Bush administration, Saddam was a murderous thug, a tin-pot dictator, a failed and incompetent Hitler wannabe. But he can also be seen as a stern and wily tribal leader, who bestowed rich rewards on his people, while meting out harsh punishment to their enemies. The brutality of his secret service, of his sons, and of his very own actions can be seen as strength. Certainly this is how a significant minority of Iraqis saw him. And they were prepared to cooperate with him.

HOW WELL DID THE TATARS COOPERATE on the Eurasian steppes of the sixteenth century? Remember that the Tatars of the Sibir khanate were direct descendants of the Turco-Mongolian horde that was led by Batu to conquer eastern Europe three centuries before. Kuchum Khan, for example, was a Chinggisid, tracing his ancestry to Batu's brother Shayban. Yet these later day Tatars were a very different people from their ancestors. Although enjoying a great numeric superiority, they could not defeat Ermak's Cossacks.

Even more importantly, in the sixteenth century various Tatar principalities were unable to unite in their struggle against resurgent Russia. When the Mongol Empire was divided among the four branches of the Chinggisids, Batu and his descendants received the westernmost part and made their capital in Sarai on the Lower Volga. The Golden Horde, as Batu's realm became known to historians, maintained its unity for 200 years, except for a period of civil war during the late fourteenth century. In the middle of the fifteenth century, it fragmented into a number of independent principalities: the khanates of Kazan, Astrakhan, Crimea, and Sibir, and the Nogay Horde. These successor states of the Golden Horde were none too stable, and continued to be wracked by civil wars into the sixteenth century. Noble factions in Kazan went through one coup after another. One of the contending princes, Shah Ali, went through the process of first gaining the throne and then losing it three times! The khanate of Sibir also went through a series of its civil wars. The last civil war, of 1563–9, in which Kuchum Khan defeated and killed the previous khan of Sibir, concluded only 12 years before the Russian invasion. What we see here, then, is a complete reversal of the situation that pertained three centuries before. Now it was the turn of the Tatars to experience social dissolution in the face of the Russian monolith.

At the same time that the Golden Horde was fragmenting, the Russian lands were slowly but inexorably "gathered," as the Russian chronicles put it, under the leadership of Moscow. The process was largely completed in 1485 with the annexation by Moscow of the last independent Russian principality of Tver. The tendency toward disintegration, characteristic of the pre-Mongol conquest Russia, was completely reversed. When a piece of territory was added to the principality of Moscow, there it would stay. This centralizing, integrative trend persisted even after the principality expanded beyond the core Russian lands with the conquest of Kazan and Astrakhan khanates (1552–56). The tenacity of territorial acquisition can be illustrated with the course of events that followed the battle of Sibir.

After wintering in Sibir, Ermak sent his lieutenant, Ivan Koltso, "the Ring," with the report of their great victory back across the Urals. The news that another kingdom was added to the Russian Empire was met with great popular jubilation. Koltso received a pardon for his crimes and rich gifts from the hands of the tsar himself, and left to Sibir accompanied by a company of government troops. Although the conquest of Sibir started as a private action, neither Ermak nor the Stroganovs considered establishing an independent princedom in Siberia for themselves. Whether their offering of Siberia to the tsar was born of loyalty or calculation, the subsequent course of events showed the wisdom of this course of action.

Although he lost the battle of Sibir, Kuchum Khan did not give up the struggle. The Tatars, however, were plagued by dissent. Several Tatar nobles and their following deserted Kuchum and went over to the son of the previous khan (whom Kuchum had killed in the civil war). Lacking strong forces to dislodge the Cossacks, Kuchum shifted to guerilla tactics. His nephew Mahmet-Kul succeeded in inflicting some casualties on the Russians, but was eventually captured and sent to Moscow. During the second winter, however, the Cossacks ran out of supplies and began suffering from scurvy and starvation. Then disaster struck in the summer of 1584: At night, the Tatars attacked the camp where Ermak and his comrades slept. Most of the Cossacks were killed, and Ermak himself drowned while attempting to swim to the boats in the river. News of Ermak's death was the final straw for the defenders of Sibir. Their numbers had been whittled down by constant Tatar attacks, and it was clear that they could not survive a third winter. The Russians were forced to retreat across the Urals to the Stroganov lands, and Kuchum reoccupied Sibir.

Unfortunately for the Tatars, their ultimate defeat was only postponed. Two years later, the Russians entered Siberia again. They proceeded in a systematic fashion, first building the fortified town of Tyumen (1586); then Tobolsk (1587), near the site of recaptured Sibir; Tara (1594); and, finally, Surgut, on the Ob River (also in 1594). Kuchum fought on for years, but was defeated in a final battle on the Ob in 1598. He took refuge with the Nogay, where he was assassinated in 1600.

THE OVERARCHING QUESTION OF THIS BOOK is why do large empires rise and fall? Therefore, it is only proper to start with the struggle between the people who built the two largest territorial empires ever seen in world history. When we stand back and take a long view at the course of this struggle, we are struck by the complete reversal in the fortunes of these two nations. In the thirteenth century, Russia, fragmented into a multitude of bickering principalities, had no chance against the Mongol steamroller. In the sixteenth century, it was the turn of the Russian monolith to roll over the squabbling Tatar khanates. Why did the Tatars lose their social cohesion? How did the Russians acquire it?

Social cohesion, of course, is not the only factor we will need to explain the rise and fall of empires. History is too complex for single-factor explanations. It is clear, however, that social cohesion, or lack of it, played a large role in the stunning reversal of fortune in the centuries-long Russian-Tatar struggle. What made Russia evolve from a collection of bickering principalities to a highly centralized state?

Chapter 2

Life on the Edge

The Transformation of Russia—and America

One of the most important forces that has shaped Russian history is its location on the great steppe frontier of Europe. For many centuries, the line running from Kiev in the southwest to Kazan in the northeast separated two sharply different worlds. To the north and west of the line were the woodlands inhabited by the Slavic, Baltic, and Ugric peoples who practiced agriculture, supplemented by hunting and gathering. To the south and east lie the grasslands inhabited by the pastoralist nomads and their herds. The first pastoralists—the Cimmerians, Scythians, and Sarmatians—were speakers of Indo-European languages. Beginning in the third century, however, these Indo-European nomads were replaced by repeated waves of Turkic and Mongolian peoples originating in Central Asia.

The woodland farmers and the steppe nomads were divided by a deep cultural chasm. To the nomads, farmers were dirt-grubbers, doers of women's work, clumsy riders, and weak and cowardly opponents in battle. Farmers, however, possessed many things that the nomads coveted—grain, which the nomads could not grow themselves, wealth accumulated by their aristocrats and priests, and last, but not least, their very bodies, which could be sold at the Black Sea slave markets.

From the farmers' point of view, the nomads were the devil horsemen, uncivilized and unlettered barbarians, murderers, slavers, and despoilers. The antagonism between the farmer and the herder goes back to the very beginnings of human history, as exemplified by the biblical parable about the conflict between Cain with his fields and Abel with his flocks. (Because the early Hebrews were herders, naturally the evil guy in the story was Cain.) In eastern Europe, from the tenth century on, the cultural chasm was further deepened by the tendency of the settled cultivators to adopt Christianity opposed by the inclination of the nomads to Islam. The most frequent terms describing the steppe nomads in the Russian chronicles, such as the *godless* or the *pagans,* reflected this religious boundary. Incidentally, in the modern Russian language, the word *pagan* has lost its original religious meaning and now just means "bad" or "evil." As discussed in the preceding chapter, the religious aspect of the conflict between the Russians and the Tatars is evident in the language used by the *Stroganov Chronicle* in its description of battles between Ermak's Cossacks and the Siberian Tatars.

The climatic and ecological boundary between the steppe and forest anchored a significant fault line between two very different civilizations. The interactions across the fault line were shaped by two basic facts of steppe life. First, the nomads had an abundance of animal products, but a scarcity of plant products. And man cannot live on meat alone. Second, their martial skills were strong. Riding and archery were highly developed due to daily practice while following the herds and protecting them against predators, and so the nomads enjoyed a substantial military advantage over the settled people. The need of the nomads for grain and their greater ability to take it by force could not help but create antagonistic relations between them and the farmers. This fact does not mean that herder-farmer interactions were uniformly bellicose. Under certain conditions, the nomads could get what they needed by peaceful trading (especially if the farmers were protected by a strong state). The dealings between the agrarian and nomadic civilizations took a variety of forms. Some intermarriage even occurred, usually at the aristocratic level.

On the fault line between the eastern Slavs and their steppe neighbors, however, the dominant factor was conflict. The intensity of the conflict fluctuated across the centuries, but periodically it reached the level of genocide. One of the relatively peaceful periods was the first half of the eleventh century, when the principality of Kiev was at the height of its power. The strong and unified state was able to reduce the threat from the steppe to a minimum. Unfortunately, toward the end of the eleventh century, the principality began fragmenting, a process that coincided with the arrival of a new wave of Turkic nomads in the Russian steppes, the Cumans. The Russian chronicles record 46 Cuman invasions into the principality between 1061 and 1200. During the twelfth century, as a result of internecine fighting and the Cuman raids, the population of Kiev and the surrounding territories collapsed. The Mongol sack in 1240 struck the deathblow. From that time until the seventeenth century, the core territory of the Kievan state was virtually a desert. Any Ukrainian peasant foolish enough to move in was immediately killed, and his family taken to the Crimean slave markets, by the first marauding Tatar band that would chance upon them.

The thirteenth century depopulation affected not only Kiev, but also the entire forest-steppe transition zone. As a result of increased pressure from the steppe, the cultural fault line was pushed a hundred miles or more to the northwest. In the Russian principality of Ryazan (where the two brothers, Yurii and Roman, would not work together to repel the Mongols), the capital city of Ryazan was too close to the steppe and had to be abandoned. The princely seat was moved to Pereyaslavl-Ryazansky in the northwest corner of the principality.

Life settled down a bit under the Golden Horde, whose rulers were more interested in getting tribute than in murder and rapine. The population of northern Russia enjoyed a substantial recovery, despite the effects of a few punitive expeditions by the Tatars in response to urban uprisings against their tax collectors. As the Golden Horde began fragmenting during the fifteenth century, however, the ability of its rulers to restrain raiding by lower-level chieftains waned. When the Golden Horde experienced its ultimate collapse around 1500, Muscovite lands faced an increasing number of raids from the Tatar successor states. (*Muscovy* is what historians call Russia during the period after the independence from the Golden Horde, but before the reign of Peter the Great, which started the Imperial period.) The greatest danger came from the Kazan khanate, until it was conquered in 1552, and from the Crimean Tatars, who were to remain a thorn in Russia's side until the end of the eighteenth century.

The devastation caused by the Tatar attacks was huge. In 1521, the Crimean Khan Mohammad-Girey, with a 100,000-man army, broke through the Russian defenses along the Oka River and invaded the Muscovite heartland. He did not attempt to assault the fortified cities, but instead laid waste to the countryside. The worst damage resulted from the enormous number of people the Tatars carried away. According to one chronicle, captives numbered 300,000; the imperial envoy Sigismund von Herberstein reported that total losses numbered 800,000 people, some slain, others sold to the Turks in Caffa (in Crimea). Herberstein's report must be greatly exaggerated, but the loss of even 200,000 or 300,000 people was a very serious blow to a country whose total population at the time was only 7 million. In 1533, the Crimean Tatars failed to break through the Oka defenses and had to content themselves with devastating the Ryazan lands. Nevertheless, the Tatars again carried away a multitude of captives. In a letter to the tsar, the khan boasted that Russia lost no fewer than 100,000 of its people: Every Tatar noble acquired 15 to 20 captives; the common warriors each held 5 or 6 "heads."

These two invasions were not unique, only the more successful of many other raids. Few were the years during the first half of the sixteenth century when Muscovy was not assaulted by the Crimeans from the south and the Kazan Tatars from the east. Just during the 1530s, for example, no fewer than 13 Crimean and 20 Kazan raids occurred. Added to that were raids from the Nogay Horde, and on the western frontier Muscovy was embroiled in a long and exhausting conflict with Lithuania.

Muscovy could resist the onslaught from the steppe only by a concerted effort of the whole people, from the mighty boyar to the lowest peasant. A characteristic example of how the external threat helped to unify the society was the construction of the fortified town of Lyubim on the frontier facing Kazan, in an area that did not have a stronghold where peasants could shelter during the Tatar raids. The central government had no resources to spare, and therefore gave permission to build using local resources. Everybody pitched in to help quarry the stone, raise the walls, dig the moat, and make the defensive stakes against the cavalry. Another sign of the willingness of people to sacrifice for the sake of the larger community was the periodic collections of money needed to buy out the Russian captives. Enormous sums of money were gathered in this way, and as a result many thousands of captives were able to return home.

The main role in organizing the defense, however, fell to the state. The government first fortified the southern frontier along the Oka, which faced the Crimean raids. Stone fortresses were constructed at key defensive points. All fords and other places where the Tatar cavalry could cross the river were blocked with wooden stockades manned by soldiers and artillery. Every summer, large bodies of armed men gathered at several designated places, from where they could be rushed to any threatened segment of the frontier. The Cossacks patrolled the lands beyond the Oka to give an early warning of the approaching raiders. By the mid-1520s, the system of defenses was in place and all of its elements well coordinated. In 1527, the campaign of the whole Crimean army in Russia failed completely because the Tatars were unable to penetrate the Oka barrier.

The eastern frontier enjoyed no natural defensive feature such as the Oka, and therefore the defenses against Kazan were ineffective. The Tatars just bypassed the fortresses and devastated the fields and villages, killing or carrying off those souls who were caught in the open. Many of the survivors migrated west to escape the constant danger. Tatar raiding was systematically depopulating the broad band of territory between Moscow and Kazan. It was clear that the only way to avoid the fate of Kiev three centuries before was to solve the problem at its source. Therefore, after the defenses of the southern frontier began functioning properly, the government directed all of its resources to the east. It took two decades of constant war, and a final lengthy siege, but Muscovy succeeded in annexing the khanate of Kazan in 1552.

Although the annexation of Kazan, followed by Astrakhan in 1556, resolved the issue of the eastern frontier, the Oka defense line provided only a temporary solution in the south. The first problem was that the defensive line passed only 50 miles south of Moscow, so any breakthrough by the steppe raiders immediately exposed the heartland to pillaging and devastation. Second, two former principalities of the Kievan Russia, Ryazan and Novgorod-Severski, which were now part of Muscovy, remained beyond the defensive line and vulnerable to the Tatar raids. The third problem, a recurrent one, was that as soon as a secure defense line was established, Russian peasants started moving into the area just in front of it (even though the authorities attempted to prevent such spontaneous colonization because they could not effectively protect these pioneers). Such population movement beyond the defensive line created many challenges for the authorities without yielding a direct profit in terms of taxes (at least, initially). However, the efforts to stem colonization were ineffective. As the population beyond the defenses increased, it attracted raiding Tatar parties, and the cry went up to protect the "Christian souls." The government was forced to come up with resources to construct a new defensive line to the south that would protect the newly colonized territory. Upon securing the territory, government officials could count the population and assign each head of household his share of tax and service in the frontier defense forces, so ultimately the colonization movement worked to the government's advantage. However, then the process would start again as peasants began to trickle across the new line. The result was a curiously self-propelling dynamic, in which the common people and the state collaborated (without necessarily meaning to do so) in extending the Muscovite territory south into the steppe in a series of steps. The process ended only with the final conquest of Crimea, two and a half centuries later.

WHAT WAS LIFE LIKE ON THE STEPPE FRONTIER? Documentary sources provide a good glimpse, and those sources became progressively better during the sixteenth and seventeenth centuries. We are also lucky to have a book by Guillaume le Vasseur, Sieur de Beauplan, who spent the years 1630 to 1647 in the Ukrainian area of the frontier (which was at that time part of Poland-Lithuania). Beauplan left us with much valuable information about the adversary against whom the Russians and the Ukrainians carried out their grueling centuries-long struggle.

The khanate of Crimea enjoyed an advantageous geopolitical situation, which explains why the contest between it and Muscovy took three centuries to resolve. Its capital, Bakhchisarai, was located on the Crimean Peninsula, which could be attacked only after crossing an easily defended Isthmus of Perekop. Even more important was the control by the Crimeans of the huge steppe territory of southern Russia. These steppes created a buffer zone hundreds of miles deep, a zone easily crossed by the Tatar cavalry, but extremely difficult to penetrate with a European-style army composed primarily of foot soldiers and burdened by heavy supply carts.

Although Bakhchisarai was the political capital of the Crimean khanate, the most economically important city in Crimea was Caffa. Caffa is associated with some of the darkest pages of European history. In 1346, when Caffa was in Genoese hands, the Mongols besieged it. When the besiegers started to die from a new disease recently arrived from Central Asia, they catapulted several of the diseased corpses into the town, and then departed. Within a year, the disease traveled from Caffa to all major Mediterranean ports. During the next three years, half of the European population died in the pandemic of the Bubonic Plague, also known as the Black Death.

The Ukrainians referred to Caffa as "the vampire that drinks the blood of Russia" because both under the Genoese and after its conquest by the Turks this port city was the main entrepôt for the slave trade on the Black Sea. Over the centuries, literally millions of eastern Slavs and other peoples inhabiting the forest region north of the steppe were sold in Caffa and shipped to a variety of destinations in the Mediterranean. Most male slaves sold in Caffa probably ended up rowing the galleys. At any given time during the seventeenth century, the city had 30,000 or more slaves. The supply of slaves was so plentiful that there were no free domestic servants in Caffa.

In the second half of the fifteenth century, the Genoese lost Caffa to the Ottoman Empire. The Turks governed Caffa directly, and also exercised an indirect control over the rest of the peninsula, because in 1475 the khan of Crimea became the vassal of the sultan. However, the Turkish-supplied artillery and janissaries became involved only in large-scale military operations against Russia and Poland-Lithuania, leaving the usual steppe raiding entirely in the hands of the Tatars. The Crimean army consisted of 40,000 to 50,000 horse warriors. When allies from other hordes and various other volunteer predators joined this army, its size could swell to 100,000 and more. However, a more typical raid was conducted with "only" 15,000 to 20,000 horsemen led by one of the khan's murzas (a Tatar princeling).

Beauplan records that each Tatar warrior had two spare horses; so, a force of 80,000 was accompanied by more than 200,000 horses. "Trees are no thicker in a forest than horses at such times on the plain, and, seen from afar, they resemble a cloud rising from the horizon, growing larger and larger as it rises, striking terror into the hearts of even the most daring, if they are not used to seeing such multitudes together." On the Ukrainian frontier of Poland-Lithuania, which lacked the systematic defenses constructed by the Muscovites, the typical tactic of the Tatar army was first to rapidly penetrate deep into the settled territory. After reaching 60 or 80 leagues (1 league equals 3 miles) in the interior, the army turned around, extended the flanks 8 to 12 leagues to the right and to the left, and began a systematic sweep of the territory for booty. All those who resisted were killed; everybody else was captured and taken away (including the livestock, except for pigs).

After a successful operation, when the Tatars were far enough in the steppes from the frontier not to worry about pursuit, they stopped to rest and reorganize. "During the interval of this week-long stop, they bring together all their booty, consisting of slaves and livestock, and divide the entire quantity among themselves. The most inhuman of hearts would be touched to see the separation of a husband from his wife, of a mother from her daughter, there being no hope of their ever seeing each other again. They are to become wretched slaves of Mohammedan pagans, who abuse them atrociously. The brutality [of these Tatars] causes them to commit an infinite number of filthy acts, such as ravaging young girls, raping women in the presences of their fathers and husbands, and even circumcising children before their parents' very eyes, so that they may be offered to Mohammed."

When the Tatar host encountered the Polish forces, they avoided fighting, because "these brigands (and so the Tatars should be named) never raid [Ukraine] for the purpose of fighting, but rather to pillage and steal by surprise." The great advantages enjoyed by the steppe horsemen were stealth, mobility, and surprise. It was extremely hard to defend against their depredations and, in fact, the Ukrainians and the Poles, unlike the Russians, were unable to make headway against the Crimeans. When the Tatar pressure intensified in the late sixteenth century, the Ukrainians even lost some ground. For example, one third of all villages in the province of Podolia (situated between the Dniester and Dnieper rivers) were devastated or abandoned between 1578 and 1583.

The key feature of the Muscovite frontier strategy was the construction of fortified defensive lines that extended across hundreds of miles of the steppe. I have already discussed the first defensive line along the Oka River. The need to protect Ryazan and Novgorod-Severski, as well as territories newly colonized by peasants moving from the north, was addressed by the construction of the second defensive line in the 1560s and 1570s. The line ran through a chain of fortified towns, whose function was not economic, but purely defensive. In forested areas between the fortresses, obstacles were constructed by felling trees. Trees were cut at two yards above the ground, and placed with their crowns pointing south.

Interweaved trunks and branches, backed up by two-yard tree stumps, presented an impenetrable barrier to mounted men. Dismantling this barrier would take hours, giving the Cossacks and soldiers more time to organize a proper "reception" for the unwanted guests. The main purpose of such *abatis* was not to prevent entry, but to negate the raiders' advantage in mobility. The obstacles also impeded rapid retreat of the Tatars laden with loot, cattle, and captives. Slowing their flight even by a few hours could allow the pursuit to catch up, spelling the difference between freedom and slavery for the unfortunates who were caught out in the open during the raid.

In areas without forests, the Russians pounded logs into the ground to construct palisades. Wherever possible, rivers were utilized to serve as obstacles. (Unfortunately, no convenient large river ran from west to east, such as the Oka, on which the old defensive line was based.) The forests growing along the defensive lines were strictly protected against cutting. All measures, no matter how petty, were taken to impede the raiders. For example, the grass south of the line was burned after the frost in late fall to deny fodder to the Tatar horses.

The length of the second defensive line was more than 600 miles, a Russian equivalent of the Great Wall of China, fulfilling the same function albeit with very different construction methods. The investment of labor was enormous. Tens of thousands of people, mostly drawn from the frontier population, worked on the construction. The frontiersmen expended a remarkable effort, but it could not have happened without the full backing of the central government, which founded fortified towns on the steppe, recruited the garrisons from the central areas of Muscovy, and provided overall organization. The key role of the central government is highlighted by the occasions when the defenses failed, which always happened either when the authorities were preoccupied with the war on the western frontier or during the Time of Troubles (when the central government collapsed). In 1571, the Tatars broke through the defenses and succeeded in burning Moscow. The last time the Tatars managed to reach Moscow and burn its suburbs was in 1592. Successful raids reached the Muscovite heartland in the first half of the seventeenth century, but after the 1650s the Tatar raids were no longer able to penetrate the defense lines, which by that time had moved even farther south.

The organization of the frontier service was perfected during the sixteenth century. The first line of defenses consisted of Cossack patrols deep into the steppe. In one typical technique, a pair of sentries stationed themselves near a tall tree in the steppe. One Cossack climbed the tree to kept watch, while the other remained ready to ride back immediately upon sight of the enemy. The watchman, after climbing down, followed the Tatars to determine the direction of their movement. This work was very dangerous, because the Tatars hunted the sentries, both to prevent them from raising the alarm and to gain information about the current state of defenses. A surviving letter to the garrison commander at Novgorod-Seversky tells about the misadventures of one such lookout, Yakush, a Cossack from Putivl. In the fall of 1523, Yakush was ordered to guide a company of gentry servitors pursuing some Tatars escaping with loot and captives after a raid. The Russian detachment caught up with the Tatars and succeeded in freeing the captives. Yakush then guided everybody back to the frontier, after which he returned to his lookout station on the steppe. Unfortunately, the Tatars, annoyed at having to return empty-handed, decided to go back and search the area where the Cossacks kept watch. They caught Yakush and carried him away to the khan in Crimea. The subsequent fate of Yakush is unknown, but this little bit of recorded history gives us a glimpse of the everyday life on the edge, with its constant threat of the Tatar raids, the "posses" organized to pursue the robbers, and the precarious existence of the Cossacks serving as the frontier lookouts and guides.

IN CHAPTER 1 I ASKED, HOW did a nation, Russia, transform itself from victim to empire? The outlines of an answer begin to emerge. The whole Russian people from the Cossacks patrolling the steppes to the farmers on the frontier and then on to the boyars in Moscow instinctively knew that they must cooperate against the threat posed by the nomads. This was not a rational calculation, but the result of a slow, centuries-long cultural change resulting from the life on the line where civilizations clashed. After all, the same calculation could have been made back in 1237 in the face of the imminent Mongol threat. The Kiev-period Russians had already had direct experience with Mongol warfare in 1223, when an expeditionary corps under two of Chinggis Khan's generals, Jebe and Subotai, annihilated the joint Russian-Cuman army in the battle of the Kalka. The destruction of the Volga Bulgars in 1236 made it abundantly clear that the Mongols planned a systematic conquest; however, the Russians did not unite. Paradoxically, every principality, when taken individually, behaved in a completely rational manner. Each prince waited for others to unite and defeat the Mongols. Because each prince controlled only a small army, his contribution was not crucial to the common success. His potential costs, on the other hand, could be enormous. (For example, he could be killed.) Unfortunately, the same logic governed the actions of all his peers, with the result that no collective effort attempted to defend against Batu's army. Such an individually rational, but collectively foolish, response is well known to sociologists and economists; it has been dubbed the "tragedy of the commons."

The long exposure to the frontier conditions resulted in a profound change in the Russian culture. The general social mechanism responsible for this change is discussed later; for now, I only want to establish the reality of the cultural shift. Unlike their predecessors, the Moscow-period Russians behaved in a collectively astute way, even though acting so caused individual hardship or worse. As mentioned previously, the sense of solidarity and willingness to sacrifice for the common good were not based on a rational calculation; they had much deeper foundations. The frontier logic of "us versus them" molded the view that divided the world into the opposing camps of good and evil. On one side sat the Christian community that represented all that was decent in the world. On the other side sat the devil horsemen who worshiped their foul gods and committed unspeakable atrocities on the Christians. This black-and-white view of the conflict is wonderfully captured in the long quotation from the *Stroganov Chronicle* excerpted in Chapter 1 and in the painting "Ermak Conquers Siberia" by the nineteenth-century Russian artist Vasily Surikov. (Note that I have related in some detail how the Russians perceived the situation; the Tatars naturally had their own distinct view.)

Religion was the glue that held the Muscovite society together. Certain norms, such as the willingness "to suffer for the faith"—that is, to sacrifice one's comfort and even life itself, to endure hardship for the sake of doing the right thing—were deeply ingrained in the people. Although acts inspired by faith did not have the ostensible function of community survival, indirectly they always contributed to it. Let's turn again to the *Stroganov Chronicle*, which describes how before the critical battle the atamans exhorted the Cossacks to "suffer for the true Orthodox faith." Laying down one's life in the fight against the heathen was an act of piety. The Muscovites cooperated not because it was the rational thing to do, but because it was the *right* thing to do.

Selfless cooperation was not the only motive urging Ermak's Cossacks to battle the Tatars. Rather, they had a variety of motivations, among which the hope for the loot was clearly neither last nor least. In general, people's actions are influenced by a combination of self-interest, the fear of punishment, and *norms*—socially determined rules of behavior. Much of the time people behave in a self-serving manner, but sometimes they do things not to gain a material reward or to avoid punishment, but simply because it is right. The rewards for doing the right thing are nonmaterial— for example, internal satisfaction and perhaps social approval.

Now think of two armies of the same size. The soldiers in both armies are paid the same amount, and are subject to the same system of punishments for dereliction of duty. In the first army, however, soldiers are motivated only by these material inducements, whereas in the second army they believe that fighting the enemy is the right thing to do. For example, they might fight for their faith and country, or they might believe that their goal in life is extermination of the evil enemy. What will happen when these two armies clash in a battle? Unless a miracle occurs, the first one will fall apart and will be trounced by the second. Generally, in a struggle between two groups of people, the group with stronger norms promoting cooperation and the most people following such norms has a greater chance of winning.

To come back to the Muscovite frontier, I am not suggesting at all that its defenders were motivated solely by nonmaterial rewards. On the contrary, the servitors on the Russian frontier received cash, grain, and land in return for their service. Those who failed to serve were punished. For example, if anybody left his watch post, and there was no Tatar breakthrough as a result, he was whipped. If the Tatars got through the defenses during this abrogation of duty, the derelict watchman was executed. Although reward and punishment stimuli were certainly present, the motivations of the Russian frontiersmen cannot be reduced to these purely material incentives. They were also inspired to fight for the tsar and the Motherland, and above all for the Faith.

As all complex agrarian civilizations, Muscovite society was organized as a hierarchy. From the point of view of the state, two main categories of people existed: those who paid taxes (peasants and townspeople) and those who rendered military service. The service category included the hereditary landed gentry who supplied the cavalry for the Muscovite army, and the nonhereditary service class of musketeers, artillery personnel, and Cossacks. During the sixteenth and seventeenth centuries, the core regions of Muscovy developed a substantial degree of socioeconomic inequality. Large landowners occupied the top of society, slaves and landless peasants peopled the bottom.

The frontier, by contrast, had a much flatter social hierarchy, because it lacked both the top of the pyramid and its bottom. Large estates were present only in the northern areas of the frontier, and were greatly outnumbered by petty servicemen living closer to the defensive lines. The frontier areas suffered from a chronic lack of population, so land was plentiful. There were no landless peasants, and anybody could cultivate as much land as needed. Sparse population also meant that military commanders had great difficulties in finding enough men for the garrisons guarding the frontier. The need for troops was so desperate that they were willing to enroll persons from any social background. Over time, there was a transfer of manpower from the category of taxpaying peasants to the category of hereditary servicemen. Most of the servicemen cultivated their land themselves; few of them had any significant number of peasants. The central government did not like that there were so few peasants on the frontier and so many servicemen because it meant receiving less in taxes, but the necessity of maintaining the defenses against the Tatars was paramount. During the 1640s, the authorities confiscated the magnate-owned land within the frontier, freed the peasants, and enlisted them in dragoon regiments for garrison service. The new servicemen supported themselves on the land confiscated from the previous owners. At the same time, the government also invited all impoverished servicemen from the central regions to move south, where they were given land and enlisted in the frontier defense forces.

The unusual social composition, dominated by small landowners liable to military service, was another significant factor promoting a cooperative spirit in the frontier territories. Great differences in rank and wealth are divisive. It is much easier for equals to achieve the unity of purpose and to develop a common course of action. Egalitarianism enables cooperation.

ONCE AGAIN, SOME READERS, ESPECIALLY THOSE who have read books on Russian history, might ask whether I am painting too rosy a picture of the Russian frontier society. Don't the history books tell us that Muscovy was an "oriental despotism"? That peasants were harshly oppressed? That even nobles had no rights, and could be whipped with the *knout* ("leather whip") or even executed at the tsar's slightest whim? Is it really possible to speak about cooperation, and especially egalitarianism, in such a society?

Perceptions of historical processes are often affected by our cultural and ideological biases, and Russian history is one illustration of this. Much of what we know about early modern Russia came to us transmitted through the eyes of western Europeans, such as the envoy from the Austrian Empire, Sigismund von Herberstein, mentioned previously. These individuals were not trained anthropologists, and when we read their descriptions we must consider their various cultural preconceptions. For example, western European visitors made disapproving comments about the weird habit of the Russians to wash every week, on Sunday, even in winter. (Everybody knows that bathing is bad for your health!) Westerners also complained that Russians were not gentlemen. When insulted, instead of challenging to a duel, they sue in court! (This, unfortunately changed with time, and the dueling epidemic of the nineteenth century was to claim thousands of Russian noblemen's lives, among them two of the language's best poets, Pushkin and Lermontov.)

Russian history continued to suffer from observer biases even during the twentieth century. During the Cold War era, American writers often invoked the inherent predisposition of the Russians to autocratic rule to explain Stalin-era totalitarianism. Surprisingly, the Soviet historians concurred, although for a diametrically opposed reason. They contrasted the tsarist oppression with the workers paradise constructed by the Communists after the revolution. Only since the mid-1980s, and especially after 1990 and the end of the Cold War, have the archives become freely accessible to both Russian and Western historians, such that we have started to witness a new and much more impartial scholarship. In the "Notes and Further Readings" at the end of the book, I list several of these works.

Peasants were certainly oppressed in Russia, as in any other premodern state, including western European countries. However, the degree of oppression of the lower classes varied in space and with time. I have already pointed out that the frontier society was much more egalitarian than the central regions of Russia. In the central regions, however, the overall quality of the relations between lords and peasants changed quite dramatically from the fifteenth to the eighteenth century.

Enserfment was a relatively late development in Russia. The right of peasants to leave their landlords was taken away by degrees during the first half of the seventeenth century. The process culminated in the Law Code of 1649, which put together the legal framework of enserfment. The economic oppression of the peasantry gradually increased, and reached its peak toward the end of the eighteenth century. Thus, there was a great difference between the free farmers of the fifteenth century, when Muscovy was a frontier society, and the unfree serfs of eighteenth-century imperial Russia, who could be sold like cattle by their owners. I should not, however, leave the reader with the impression that the location on the frontier is the only factor that determined the degree of oppression endured by the lower classes. The situation is far more complicated, and I shall return to this issue in Part II, "Imperiopathosis," where we will see that the degree of inequality and oppression in any particular society is a dynamic variable that tends to wax and wane in centuries-long cycles.

Finally, it is important to point out that cooperation is not all "sweetness and light." Human beings are capable both of incredible self-sacrifice and of breathtaking selfishness. Cooperation in real societies, therefore, cannot be based solely on the "*Kumbayah* spirit" (in the words of the political scientist Robert Putnam), and has to involve such unpleasantness as communal policing and punishment. Earlier I mentioned that if a watch-man abandoned his post, he was either flogged or executed, depending on the consequences of his dereliction. Human life was as cheap in Russia as in any other premodern society, so torture and cruel and degrading pun-ishments, such as impalement, were widespread. Although during the long struggle between Crimea and Muscovy the overwhelming majority of atrocities were committed by the Tatars against the Russians, to a large degree this was due to the asymmetry of opportunity. After a territory was annexed, certainly any rebellion against the central government was harshly suppressed. No contradiction inherently exists between coopera-tion and cruelty. In fact, large-scale brutality, such as genocide, could be achieved in premodern societies, and perhaps even in modern times, only by internally cohesive groups. Think, for example, about the clockwork precision of the Nazi-organized genocide against the Jews, the Gypsies, and the Serbs.

I HAVE ATTEMPTED TO SHOW THAT the dominant factor in the development of the Muscovite society was the frontier. The pressure from the steppe nomads molded Muscovy's institutions and culture. I propose that a causal connection exists between the frontier position of Muscovy and its trans-formation into a strongly centralizing state, in which different social classes cooperated in territorial defense and expansion. This is a hypothe-sis, because a well-developed theory cannot be based on a single case, but let us continue the exploration of this idea for a while yet, before a more comprehensive test is taken.

So far my focus has been on cooperation at the local level. Cossacks, gentry servitors, peasants, and government officials worked together to defend a particular segment of the steppe frontier. Incidentally, given this social background, it is easier to see why Ermak's Cossacks were able to withstand the Tatar onslaught at the battle of Sibir without breaking down. However, our ultimate goal is to understand how large territorial empires can be assembled and held together. Certainly, coercion from the center is one aspect of the answer. But, again, willing cooperation between the peripheries and the center makes it much easier for an empire to extend its sway. It is a mistake to think that empires are based solely on force—the largest ones always involved some degree of cooperation (and when coop-eration declined, the empires crumbled). The Russian Empire was not an exception.

Whereas the forest-steppe fault line in eastern Europe divided the nomads and the farmers from each other, it integrated people located on the *same* side of the frontier. Farming people inhabiting the territory of the former Kievan Russia spoke very similar eastern Slavic languages (dialects, really) and belonged to the same branch of Christianity. Small cultural dif-ferences resulting from slight dialectal dissimilarities were dwarfed by the presence of the very different "other" on the other side of the frontier: Turkic, nomadic, Muslim. Cooperation is much easier to achieve among culturally similar people with similar goals, values, and behaviors.

In fact, conquest played a less-important role in Moscow's expansion within the eastern Slavic lands than such nonviolent measures as dynastic inheritance, purchase, and even the patent from the khan of the Golden Horde. Of particular interest are the occasions when rulers of various principalities voluntarily entered the Moscow service. For example, in 1500, the princes of Novgorod-Severski, Chernigov, and Starodub deserted Lithuania and joined their lands to Muscovy. It is noteworthy that all of these principalities lie to the southwest of Moscow, right along the steppe frontier. By contrast, the strongest resistance to the expanding Muscovite power came from the principality of Tver and the free city of Novgorod the Great, which lie to Moscow's northwest and were not as exposed to the Tatar raids. Both Novgorod and Tver were subdued by Moscow only after a long armed struggle.

History repeated itself in 1654 with the defection of Ukraine from Poland-Lithuania to Russia. When Poland and Lithuania merged in 1569, its aristocracy rapidly assimilated to the Polish language and Catholic reli-gion, causing unrest among the Orthodox peasantry inhabiting the for-merly Lithuanian lands (what is now Ukraine and Belarus). Resistance against the Polish authorities was spearheaded by the Dnieper Cossacks. These Ukrainian Cossacks established their headquarters, called the *Sech*, on an island below the Dnieper cataracts. They made a living very much like their Russian counterparts, alternating between service to the Polish state and raids against the Crimean Tatars and Turkey. The Sech Cossacks organized themselves as a military democracy, in which officials were elected, and all the important decisions were made at a gathering of all the Cossacks. This is yet another example of the tendency to egalitarianism on the frontier.

In the early seventeenth century, the pressure to convert to Catholicism intensified, while the Polish landlords imposed harsh economic oppression on Ukrainian peasants. Beginning in 1624, a series of peasant rebellions led by the Cossacks swept Ukraine. The Poles kept putting these revolts down, but with great difficulty. Finally, in 1653, the Ukrainians sent representatives to Moscow to ask to be taken under the tsar's protection. The Muscovite government at first hesitated, because accepting this proposal would entail a war with Poland, for which Russia was not ready, but eventually the decision was made. The final step for the union was taken at a *rada*, or "general assembly," in Pereiaslavl in 1654. The delegates to the rada debated at length their course of action. Previous struggle against Poland made clear to the Ukrainians that they were not strong enough to establish an independent state, so their only options were to submit to Poland or to transfer allegiance to either Turkey or Russia. The decisive factor in the final decision was the religious compatibility, and the Ukrainian assembly voted to submit to the Orthodox tsar.

To an American, the words *frontier* and *frontiersman* immediately conjure the visions of the Wild West, the Indians, the cowboys … But are there any parallels between the American and Russian frontiers? What was the impact of the frontier on the European settlers who made their little homes on the American prairie?

The first European settlers to America arrived in Jamestown, Virginia, in 1607, followed shortly by the Dutch on Manhattan Island and the Pilgrims at Cape Cod. The frontier was a true fault line, on which two very different civilizations came in contact, soon to become conflict. On one side were the European farmers originating from urbanized literate societies with a monotheistic religion (mostly, assorted Protestant sects of Christianity). The various Indian societies, on the other side of the fault line, were almost a perfect opposite, except some Indians also practiced farming. Given such deep cultural differences, it was inevitable that the two groups of people would come into conflict. Indeed, the first war between the settlers and the Indians broke out in 1622, and the cross–fault line hostilities went on with few interruptions until the western frontier was officially declared closed in 1890. The conflict, therefore, was almost three centuries in duration.

Modern histories do not emphasize this aspect of the conflict, but it was very intense, at times genocidal. The history of the massacres that the U.S. Army inflicted on the Indians during the last 30 years of the conflict was powerfully told in 1970 by Dee Brown in *Bury My Heart at Wounded Knee*. However, both the Indians and Europeans committed genocide and atrocities. The Indians were more inventive in coming up with horrible tortures, but the settlers were ultimately more successful at exterminating the Indians.

We also tend to forget that the Indian Wars inflicted higher casualties in proportional terms than any other wars in American history. On the very first day of the first Indian War, between the Virginian settlers and the Powhattan Confederacy in 1622, the Indians massacred 347 men, women, and children out of the population of only 1,200. This is a casualty rate of 30 percent! By contrast, the American losses in the World Wars I and II were only 0.1 and 0.3 percent of the total U.S. population, respectively. In the Second Powhattan War, the Indians killed 500 out of 8,000 settlers. In the King Philip's War of 1675–76, about 800 Puritans were killed out of the total population of 52,000. More than half of New England's 90 towns suffered from Indian attacks. As Nathaniel Saltonstall wrote in 1676, "in Narranganset not one House [was] left standing. At Warwick, but one. At Providence, not above three." It took years for the area to recover.

The violent acts committed by the Indians on the Whites were not limited to indiscriminant killing and property damage. During the King Philip's War, the Indian atrocities included "the raping and scalping of women, the cutting off of fingers and feet of men, the skinning of White captives, the ripping open the bellies of pregnant women, the cutting off of penises of the males," and so on. In 1675, the Wampanoag Indians raided the town of Lancaster, Massachusetts, where they killed 12 and captured 24 of its inhabitants. One of the captives, Mary Rowlandson, was the wife of a minister and later wrote a book about her experiences. During the raid, the Indians set her house on fire, forcing its occupants to leave even this inadequate shelter: "No sooner were we out of the house, but my brother-in-law (being before wounded, in defending the house, in or near the throat) fell down dead; whereat the Indians scornfully shouted, halloed, and were presently upon him, stripping his clothes. The bullets flying thick, one went through my side, and the same (as would seem) through the bowels and hand of my dear child in my arms. One of my elder sister's children, named William, had then his leg broken, which the Indians perceiving, they knocked him on the head [that is, killed him]. Thus were we butchered by those merciless heathens, standing amazed, with the blood running down to our heels." During the raid, Rowlandson's baby, sister, brother-in-law, and nephew were killed, and another child died during the forced march after the attack. She was sold by her captors into slavery to another Indian, but eventually was ransomed out, after spending three months in captivity. Her book, published in 1682, became a bestseller.

One characteristic of the Indian warfare that was particularly repellent to the Whites was the torture of captives. Here's one account of Shawnee torture published by Benjamin Franklin in the *Pennsylvania Gazette* in 1729: "They made the Prisoner Sing and Dance for some Time, while six Gun Barrels were heating red hot in the Fire; after which they began to burn the Soals of the poor Wretches Feet until the Bones appeared, and they continued burning him by slow Degrees up to his Privites, where they took much Pains ... This Barbarity they continued about six Hours, and then, notwithstanding his Feet were in such a Condition, they drove him to a Stake ... and stuck Splinters of Pine all over his Body, and put fire to them ... In the next Place they scalp'd him and threw hot Embers on his Head ... At last they ran two Gun Barrels, one after the other, red hot up his Fundament, upon which [he] expired."

The settlers themselves were certainly no shrinking violets, and often conducted themselves in a manner as merciless as that shown by their adversaries. During the Powhattan War, Governor Wyatt invited several hundred Indians to a peace conference, where he attempted to poison them all. About 200 became violently ill and were slaughtered by the Virginians, the rest (including the Indian leader) escaped. During King Philip's War, the Puritans conducted wholesale massacres of noncombatants. When they captured the wife and nine-year old son of King Philip (the leader of the Indian forces), they sold them and hundreds of other captives into slavery.

The Dutch also perpetrated their share of atrocities. In 1643, the Dutch soldiers attacked a village of Wappinger Indians, situated near the site of present-day Albany. The village had already endured a raid of the Mohawks, who killed and enslaved many males but spared the women and children. The Dutch slaughtered all remaining inhabitants, including women and children. They returned to New Amsterdam with the severed heads of 80 Indians, to be used in a grisly game of football on the streets of the town. In addition, 30 prisoners were tortured to death for public amusement.

These are just a few of the stories out of many illustrating the extraordinary intensity of the Indian-settler conflict in North America. A recent compilation counted more than 16,000 recorded atrocities committed by the Whites on the Indians, the Indians on the Whites, and the Indians on other Indians during the 268 years of conflict. This works out to an average of more than one atrocity a week! Actually, there were many more, because not every incident left a historical record. The impact of these incidents on the settler community when they were reported in newspapers (such as the torture story described in Benjamin Franklin's newspaper) and books (such as Mary Rowlandson's bestseller) was much greater than it would be in a preliterate society. It is hard for us to envisage the psychological impact that the continuing barrage of such reports would have on the collective psyche of the settler population. Imagine hearing on CNN that yesterday yet another American town was wiped out by the "Reds." (Let's leave the precise identity of the enemy unspecified.) All men were killed, women raped and then also slain, and those children who were not slaughtered immediately were instead carried away to be sold on the organ black market. Or that the Reds again tortured a U.S. serviceman to death, videotaped it, and showed it repeatedly on the Al Reddiyyah channel. Or perhaps an interview with a ransomed captive about her horrible experiences at the hands of the Reds. You would hear a story of this kind once a week throughout your life; and the same state of affairs was in place when your parents and grandparents grew up. Without doubt, any society subjected to such pressures for generations would be transformed.

One consequence of the life on the North American fault line was the famous American melting pot. Indeed, when confronted with such obvious aliens as painted, bloodthirsty, heathen redskins, two European settlers, even if they came from different countries, could not help but feel that they were kin. Thus, in the old Europe, although the Irish hated the English, and the French fought against the Germans, in the New World all these people cooperated with each other and fought together against the Indians. As a result of the shared feeling that they belonged together, they and their descendants rapidly assimilated to a common American culture and language. Note also the limits of the melting pot. Because the fault line was defined in racial terms, immigrants belonging to non-White races, such as the Negroes and the Chinese, were not accepted as the "Americans." (This pattern began to change in the twentieth century.)

Another characteristic of the Americans, which was commented upon at length by that astute Frenchman Alexis de Tocqueville, was their exceptional ability to form voluntary associations. "Americans of all ages, all stations in life, and all types of disposition are forever forming associations. There are not only commercial and industrial associations in which all take part, but others of a thousand different types—religious, moral, serious, futile, very general and very limited, immensely large and very minute." As a result of this proclivity to associate, the Americans could rapidly and effectively organize concerted collective action. "If some obstacle blocks the public road halting the circulation of traffic, the neighbors at once form a deliberative body; this improvised assembly produces an executive authority which remedies the trouble ... Public security, trade and industry, and morals and religion all provide the aims for associations in the United States. There is no end which the human will despairs of attaining by the free action of the collective power of individuals." Or: "As soon as several Americans have conceived a sentiment or an idea that they want to produce before the world, they seek each other out, and when found, they unite. Thenceforth they are no longer isolated individuals, but a power conspicuous from the distance whose actions serve as an example; when it speaks, men listen."

FROM THE MONGOLS IN THE THIRTEENTH CENTURY, to the Muscovites in the sixteenth and seventeenth centuries, and then on to the Americans in the seventeenth through nineteenth centuries, we have romped through time and space. It is surprising how many things these societies have in common. The first and most obvious one is that they all were empire builders. It would not be an exaggeration to say that they built the three most powerful empires in world history. Less obviously, each of these three societies, although in its own culturally unique way, had a high capacity for concerted collective action. In fact, such a capacity seems to be a necessary condition for successful empire building. The society-level capacity for concerted action was, in turn, based on the ability of individuals to cooperate. Finally, all three peoples originated from intense and prolonged fault-line frontiers. (I have not yet presented the frontier origins of the Mongols, so for now you will have to take my word for it.)

Although each society achieved high capacity for concerted action, it is important to stress that specific cultural mechanisms employed to accomplish this were completely unique to each society. Fault-line frontiers have a strong influence on some aspects of societies, while leaving others indeterminate. Let us, for example, compare the Americans and the Muscovites. The basis for cooperation among the Americans was the voluntary civil association. The political organization of the Americans, accordingly, was democratic, and after they became independent of the British, they immediately set up a republic to govern their affairs. The ideological source of social power was solidly rooted in the popular will (the famous "we the people"). Whereas the Americans were deeply suspicious of the central government, the Muscovites, in contrast, embraced it as the fundamental organizing principle of their society. The form of government was a monarchy, or autocracy. The source of social power was not the people, but God's will. Therefore, in theory, the tsar was not responsible to the common people for his actions, or even to the boyars. He answered for his deeds before God alone (at least this was how power was legitimated in Muscovy; in practice, of course, no ruler can last long if he does not take into account the wishes of his subjects).

It is natural for us to think that the American way is "good" and the Muscovite way is "bad." Indeed, life is much more pleasant under a secular democracy than under an autocracy with strong theocratic elements. However, our ideological biases should not blind us to the basic fact that both societies, in their own ways, were extremely effective at solving the problems that they faced.

Another big difference between the Russian and the American societies was in the main method with which they distinguished "us" from "them." In general, deep cultural differences can be manifested by a variety of "markers," including the differences of language or dialect, religion, external appearance (race, clothing, visual symbols, or emblems). However, often a dominant indicator distinguishes the two peoples on the opposite sides of the fault line. In the Russian case, this marker was religion, so the conflict was primarily between the Christian Orthodox and the Muslims. The heavily religion-laden language in which Russian chronicles describe the conflict is one indication of this. Thus, the integrative role of the frontier worked only on those groups who were Orthodox. The Muscovites experienced a strong feeling of kinship toward the Orthodox inhabitants of Poland-Lithuania (Ukrainians, Belorussians) but not toward the Catholics (the Poles). Actually, the Orthodox Ugric people were more "us" to the Muscovites than the Catholic Slavs. One interesting corollary of using the religion as the principal marker was that it was possible for people originating in other civilizations to join the Muscovite society—by converting. Examples abound of Tatars of all ranks converting to the Orthodox Christianity and becoming "us" as far as the Muscovites were concerned. Many Cossacks originated from the baptized Tatars, and 17 percent of the Muscovite gentry in the seventeenth century were ethnically Tatars or descendants of the Tatars.

The American society distinguished itself from the Indians by using the race marker; it was not important whether the Indian was Christian or pagan, he still remained an outsider. A fair number of intermarriages occurred between those of European origin and Indians, but individuals marrying across the fault line often found themselves ostracized. The feeling against interracial marriages was the strongest when a White woman married, or had sexual relations, with an Indian male. Such a woman was excluded from the community, and in most cases would not be able to find a mate if she became unattached. The integrative role of the frontier was limited to the people of European descent. At this point, one might be tempted to condemn the racist Americans and praise the more broadminded Muscovites, but such value judgments do not help us understand why empires rise and fall. For the purposes of this investigation, we will not be sorting historical peoples into the good guys versus bad guys.

Returning to the main question of the book, we have hit upon a powerful macrohistorical generalization. People originating on fault-line frontiers become characterized by cooperation and high capacity for collective action, which in turn allows them to build large and powerful territorial states. In other words, we have the beginnings of the theory explaining how imperial nations rise to power. But could the association between fault lines and mighty states arising from them be a fluke? After all, so far we have only three examples. The next order of business is to find out whether the postulated relation holds generally. To do that, we travel to the banks of the Rhine and Danube during the first few centuries A.D.

Chapter 3

Slaughter in the Forest

At the Limites of the Roman Empire

E urope and the Mediterranean during the first millennium A.D. is a good place to begin testing the frontier theory, because at the start of the period this part of the world was completely dominated by a single large state: the Roman Empire (see Map 2). Therefore, we have only one set of relatively stationary imperial frontiers to consider, which simplifies the task of tracing their influence on the subsequent development of successor states during the latter half of the millennium. If the generalization proposed in the previous chapters proves correct, all large states inhabiting the post-Roman landscape should have been established by peoples originating from the Roman frontier. We predict that neither the inhabitants of the core area of the old empire nor those living in the non-imperial "hinterland" far away from the frontiers should succeed in founding large states.

The various frontier peoples with whom the Roman Empire had to deal can be roughly categorized as follows. First, there were the inhabitants of the northern European forests, mainly the Germans and (later) the Slavs. Second, the southern frontiers were threatened by inhabitants of the African and Arabian deserts (the Berbers and the Arabs). A third category was the nomadic invaders from Eurasian steppes (the Huns, the Avars, and so on). Fourth, there was a civilized state on the Roman eastern frontier—the Parthian Empire (later replaced by the Sassanian Persia).

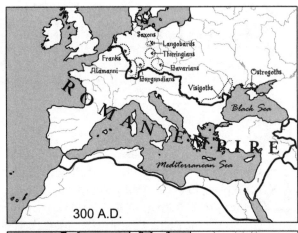

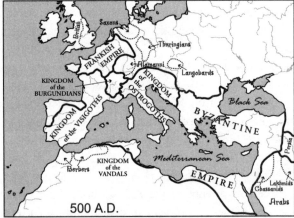

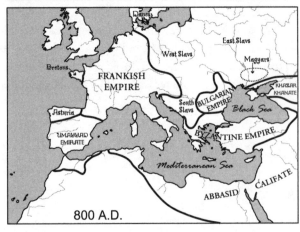

Map 2

The Roman Empire and its successors: (a) A.D. *300, (b)* A.D. *500, and (c)* A.D. *800*

After the Roman Empire collapsed (traditionally in A.D. 476, with the deposition of the last Roman emperor in the West, Romulus Augustus), it was replaced in Europe by a number of states. We are interested in large territorial states, so I only list those Roman successors that had more than roughly 100,000 square miles (0.3 million square kilometers) of territory at their peak. To put this threshold in perspective, this is equivalent to the territory of middle-sized modern European countries such as Italy or Poland.

Between 476 and 1000, Europe had seven large states: the empire of the Franks (reached the maximum area in A.D. 800 under the emperor Charlemagne), the kingdoms of the Ostrogoths (peak in 500) and the Visigoths (600), the khanates of the Avars (600) and the Bulgars (1000), the kingdom of Hungary (1000), and the Byzantine Empire (1000). In addition to the seven European states, two large states arose in the desert belt of North Africa and the Arabian Peninsula: the caliphate of the Arabs (750), and the Fatimid caliphate (960). Finally, three other states deserve mention: the kingdoms of Burgundians (600) and Langobards (600), whose size was smaller than the cut-off point of 100,000 square miles (and which were eventually annexed by the Frankish Empire), and the huge but very short-lived empire of the Huns (peak in 440), which collapsed soon after the death of its founder, Attila. In all of these cases, even the three borderline ones, frontier peoples established the empires: the Germans (Franks, Ostrogoths, Visigoths, Burgundians, and Langobards), the desert nomads (the Arabs and the Berbers), and the steppe nomads (Huns, Avars, Bulgars, and Magyars). In other words, the macrohistorical generalization proposed in Chapter 2 is splendidly confirmed. The only apparent exception is the Byzantines, but as we discuss later in this chapter, the Byzantine Empire in actuality fits the predictions of the theory quite well.

Let us now take a closer look at the ethnic groups that lived on the Roman frontier, and trace their fortunes after the Roman Empire collapsed. It is not enough to know that a strong correlation exists between location on the frontier and the rise of imperial nations; we also need to examine the specific techniques that these nations used in building empires, and what role (if any) cooperation played in this process. This chapter focuses on the northern frontier, running along the Rhine and Danube rivers; Chapter 4 covers the developments on the southern—desert—frontier.

THE ROMANS CALLED THEIR FRONTIERS *limites* (singular, *limes*). The Latin word *limes*, from which the English word "limit" is derived, originally meant a path between the fields, not a wall or an edge, as might be imagined. During the early empire, the frontiers were just that—frontier roads that made the movements of troops easy. With time, legionary encampments turned into defensive forts, and some segments of the frontier acquired walls. (The most famous example is the Wall of Hadrian in northern Britain.) However, the roads remained and played an important integrative role for movements of peoples, goods, and ideas along the frontiers. The European frontier of the Roman Empire, furthermore, ran most of its length along two rivers, the Rhine and the Danube, which further facilitated communications.

The Roman frontier along the Rhine began to take shape during the first century B.C., after the Roman legions led by Julius Caesar conquered Gaul in a series of annual campaigns starting in 58 B.C. With the suppression of the Gallic rebellion led by Vercingetorix in 51 B.C., the Romans acquired a firm control of the whole territory west and south of the Rhine. At first, the Romans probably did not intend to create a permanent frontier along the Rhine. Caesar himself used the river as a forward defense line, and he made two incursions into the lands beyond, which were inhabited by the Germanic tribes. Toward the end of the first century B.C., the Roman legions again campaigned against the German tribes, and it is likely that the emperor Augustus planned to move the border east to the Elbe. These plans came to an abrupt end in A.D. 9, when the Germans led by a chieftain named Arminius ambushed and annihilated a Roman army of 20,000 under the legate Publius Quinctilius Varus. After this disaster— called the battle of the Teutoburg Forest—Augustus decided to construct a series of permanent defensive forts along the Rhine, thus establishing the Rhine frontier. It was to remain largely stationary (with minor fluctuations back and forth) during the next four centuries.

The Romans used the collective name *the Germans* for all nonstate peoples living east of the Rhine, but the Germans themselves did not think of themselves as a single people. Their ethnic identity instead centered on smaller tribal units, such as the Cherusci, the Chatti, the Bructeri, the Sugambri, and so on. A tribe united many villages and farms. Larger tribes could field armies consisting of a few thousand warriors. Each tribe was governed by an assembly of free adult men, called the "Thing," which met regularly to make decisions for the tribe. The German society, however, was not egalitarian—individuals belonging to noble lineages had more power and wealth than the commoners. As the Roman historian Cornelius Tacitus wrote in his treatise on the Germans, "The leading men take counsel over minor issues, the major ones involve them all; yet even these decisions that lie with the commons are considered in advance by the elite." At times of war, the tribal council designated a war leader, usually a member of one of the noble lineages, who had distinguished himself in previous battles and shown leadership qualities. The war leader had considerable authority in wartime, but relinquished political power after the war was over. Another kind of leader, called the *thiudans*, served largely a religious role. The thiudans was associated with the god Tiwaz, the head of the German pantheon (before the rise of Odin, as discussed later in this chapter). Tiwaz was a typical Indo-European Skyfather (equivalent to Zeus in the Greek mythology), the god of creation, order, justice, and the natural cycles of the world. He was also the god of the Thing, and in addition to their other religious duties, the thiudans presided at assemblies.

The Romans used the same term *rex* ("king") for both military and religious leaders of the Germans. However, neither type had the permanent and extensive powers of the monarchs we find among them a few centuries later. Tacitus noted that "the king or a leading man is given a hearing, more through his influence in persuasion than his power in command."

The events associated with the battle of the Teutoburg Forest provide a good illustration of the German political organization, and how it was beginning to be affected by their clash with the Roman Empire. The Greek historian Cassius Dio relates the basic outline of the events. When Varus became *legate* ("governor") of the Rhineland, "besides issuing orders to them [the Germans] as if they were actually slaves of the Romans, he exacted money as he would from subject nations. To this they were in no mood to submit, for their leaders longed for their former ascendancy, and the masses preferred their accustomed condition to foreign domination. Now they did not openly revolt, since they saw that there were many Roman troops near the Rhine and many within their own borders; instead, they received Varus, pretending that they would do all he demanded of them, and thus they drew him far away from the Rhine into the land of the Cherusci, toward the Weser, and there by behaving in a most peaceful and friendly manner led him to believe that they would live submissively without the presence of soldiers. ...

"Among those deepest in the conspiracy and leaders of the plot were Arminius and Segimerus, who were his constant companions and often shared his mess. He accordingly became confident, and, expecting no harm, not only refused to believe all those who suspected what was going on and advised him to be on his guard, but actually rebuked them for being needlessly excited and slandering his friends. Then there came an uprising, first on the part of those who lived at a distance from him, deliberately so arranged, in order that Varus should march against them and so be more easily overpowered while proceeding through what was supposed to be friendly country, instead of putting himself on his guard as he would do in case all became hostile to him at once. And it came to pass. They escorted him as he set out, and then begged to be excused from further attendance, in order, as they claimed, to assemble their allied forces, after which they would quickly come to his aid. Then they took charge of their troops, which were already in waiting somewhere, and after the men in each community had put to death the detachments of soldiers for which they had previously asked, they came upon Varus in the midst of the forests by this time almost impenetrable. And there, at the very moment of revealing themselves as enemies instead of subjects, they wrought great and dire havoc.

"The mountains had an uneven surface broken by ravines, and the trees grew close together and very high. Hence the Romans, even before the enemy assailed them, were having hard time of it felling trees, building roads, and bridging places that required it. They had with them many wagons and many beasts of burden as in time of peace; moreover, not a few women and children and a large retinue of servants were following them— one more reason for their advancing in scattered groups. Meanwhile a violent rain and wind came up that separated them still further, while the ground, that had become slippery around the roots and logs, made walking very treacherous for them, and the tops of the trees kept breaking off and falling down, causing much confusion. While the Romans were in such difficulties, the barbarians suddenly surrounded them on all sides at once, coming through the densest thickets, as they were acquainted with the paths. At first they hurled their volleys from a distance; then, as no one defended himself and many were wounded, they approached close to them. For the Romans were not proceeding in any regular order, but were mixed in helter-skelter with the wagons and the unarmed, and so, being unable to form readily anywhere in a body, and being fewer at any point than their assailants, they suffered greatly and could offer no resistance at all.

"Accordingly they encamped on the spot, after securing a suitable place, so far as that was possible on a wooded mountain; and afterward they either burned or abandoned most of their wagons and everything else that was not absolutely necessary to them. The next day they advanced in a little better order, and even reached an open country, though they did not get off without loss. Upon setting out from there, they plunged into woods again, where they defended themselves against their assailants, but suffered their heaviest losses while doing so. For since they had to form their lines in a narrow space, in order that the cavalry and infantry together might run down the enemy, they collided frequently with one another and with the trees. They were still advancing when the fourth day dawned, and again a heavy downpour and violent wind assailed them, preventing them from going forward, and moreover depriving them of the use of their weapons. For they could not handle their bows and their javelins with any success, nor, for that matter, their shields, which were thoroughly soaked. Their opponents, on the other hand, being for the most part lightly equipped, and able to approach and retire freely, suffered less from the storm. Furthermore, the enemy's forces had greatly increased, as many of those who had at first wavered now joined them, largely in the hope of plunder, and thus they could more easily encircle and strike down the Romans, whose ranks were now thinned, many having perished in the earlier fighting."

Seeing no hope and unwilling to fall into the hands of their enemies alive, Varus and most of his officers took their lives, while the remaining soldiers lost their will to fight (and were either slaughtered on the field, or sacrificed later to German gods). The Roman army was obliterated.

We have a fair amount of information about the war leader of the Germans who destroyed Varus and his three legions in the Teutoburg Forest. Arminius belonged to the most illustrious family of the Cherusci, which itself was one of the largest and most powerful tribes inhabiting the

Weser region. Prior to the events described by Cassius Dio, he had served with the Romans as a leader of auxiliary troops. Most likely, he commanded a contingent of his own Cherusci during the war between the Romans and the Suebi, a Germanic tribal confederation led by Maroboduus. (This war took place in A.D. 6 in the Danubian region of Pannonia.) Noble lineage and military experience made him a natural candidate for war leader of the Cherusci. His first-hand knowledge of the effect of the Roman conquest on the defeated tribes probably provided a motivation to resist the Roman subjugation of his homeland. Arminius was also an accomplished politician and a charismatic leader, an important factor because the military power of the Cherusci alone was, at best, a match for a single Roman legion (and at one point during the wars, the Romans campaigned in Germany with 11 legions). Arminius persuaded several other tribes to join his anti-Roman confederation. (As in the account of Cassius Dio, some of the waverers joined Arminius only when they saw that the Germans were winning.)

Confederations uniting many tribes under a charismatic leader such as Arminius or Maroboduus were a novel form of political organization for the Germans, which arose only when they came in direct contact with the Roman Empire. The first encounter between the Romans and the Germans occurred when the Cimbri, Teutones, and other tribes invaded the Roman territory about a century before the time of Arminius and were defeated by the great Roman general Marius (105–101 B.C.). This incursion had the character of multiple marauding bands rather than a powerful unified confederation of latter times. The first Germanic leader called *rex* in the Roman sources was Caesar's opponent Ariovistus, the leader of a Germanic migration into Gaul in 59 B.C.

The Suebi led by Maroboduus was specifically a name for a tribal confederation rather than a tribe. Tacitus wrote that "the Suebi, unlike the Chatti or Tencteri, do not constitute an individual tribe: They occupy the greater part of Germania, divided among the nations with names of their own, although all are called Suebi in common. It is characteristic of the tribe to dress their hair on the side and bind it up tight in a knot. This distinguishes the Suebi from the other Germani, and their free-born from their slaves." The distinctive hairstyle of the Suebi is found in numerous Roman representations (for example, on Trajan's column in Rome). It is also present on some of the bodies found by archaeologists in bogs. The best preserved is the head of a Germanic warrior found at Osterby in Schleswig-Holstein. The hair knot is a wonderful example of how people use appearance to declare the symbolic boundary between "us" and "them." In fact, the very name *Suebi* basically means "us" ("those belonging to our group"). Incidentally, the names of such modern nations as the Swedes and the Swiss have precisely the same origin. The name of the later Alamanni also expressed the same idea, but with a different means. *Alamanni* means "the (true, real) people," clearly a variation on the "us" versus "them" theme. The origin of the name the *Goths* is more obscure, but some authorities think it simply meant "people." The name for the other great confederation, the *Franks*, however, had a different logic: it means "the fierce," "the brave."

A tribal confederation, such as the Suebi, was still a fragile form of political organization during the time of Maroboduus and Arminius. The individual tribes could easily switch their allegiance from one leader to another. For example, the Langobards (who later played such an important role in Italian history) were initially part of Maroboduus's confederation. After the battle of the Teutoburg Forest, however, with Arminius's reputation at its height, they switched their allegiance to him. Furthermore, the institution of kingship was not yet rooted in the culture of the Germans. Individual tribesmen were suspicious of the royal pretensions of their war leaders, and wary of giving them too much power, which they might use to oppress the commons. Tacitus describes the process by which the tribal confederations fell apart and their leaders perished as follows.

"Now that the Romans had gone and there was no external threat, national custom and rivalry had turned the Germans against one another. The two nations [the Cherusci with allies led by Arminius and the Suebi led by Maroboduus] were well matched in strength, and their leaders equally capable. But the Suebi did not like the royal title of their leader Maroboduus, whereas Arminius was popular as champion of freedom. So in addition to his old soldiers—the Cherusci and their allies—two Suebian tribes from the kingdom of Maroboduus also entered the war on Arminius's side [these were the Semnones and Langobards]. These additions looked like turning the scale. However, Inguiomerus and a group of his followers deserted to the Suebi, merely because the old man was too proud to serve under his young nephew.

"Each army had high hopes as it drew up for battle. The old German unsystematic battle-order and chaotic charges were things of the past. Their long wars against Rome taught them to follow the standards, keep troops in reserve, and obey commands." Tacitus then describes the speeches that Arminius and Maroboduus gave to inspire their troops for the fight.

"Besides these speeches, the armies had motives of their own to excite them. The Cherusci had the glorious past to fight for, and their new allies [the Langobards] their freshly acquired freedom from the Suebi. Their enemy's aim was expansion. Never had a result been so unpredictable. Both right wings were routed. However, instead of renewing the battle, as was expected, Maroboduus transferred his camp to the hills. This showed that he was beaten. Then, weakened by a series of desertions, he retreated. ..."

A year or two later, Maroboduus, deserted by all, crossed the Danube and requested asylum from his old enemies. The Romans kept him in Ravenna, "and whenever the Suebi became disorderly they were threatened with his restoration. But for 18 years he never left Italy, growing old, his reputation dimmed by excessive fondness for life."

Arminius's triumph was short-lived. "The Roman evacuation of Germany and the fall of Maroboduus had induced Arminius to aim at kingship. But his freedom-loving compatriots forcibly resisted. The fortunes of the fight fluctuated, but finally Arminius succumbed to treachery from his own relations."

These passages from Tacitus are extremely telling (not to mention the poetry of "his reputation dimmed by excessive fondness for life"). As long as a powerful external force threatened the Germans, the tribes were capable of uniting and inflicting defeats on it. When the immediate threat went, however, so did the unity. Individual tribes (such as the Langobards) or even parts of tribes (such as Inguiomerus and his Cherusci followers) shifted from one leader to another. Individual tribesmen were wary of enormous power gathered by the leader, and when war was over, desired to limit this power or even to get rid of the leader himself.

THE BATTLE OF THE TEUTOBURG FOREST was, without question, a spectacular success for the Germans. One historian even called it "the battle that stopped Rome." Yet, the Romans lost many battles in their long and illustrious career as imperialists, while always prevailing in the end. (That is, before they went into decline starting in the third century.) It is hard to avoid the feeling that, were the Romans really interested in annexing Germania, they would have been able to do so despite the German resistance. After all, the Romans had just won their "Four Hundred Years' War" against the Gauls (discussed in Chapter 6), whose individual military prowess and social organization were very similar to that of the Germans. Beginning in A.D. 14, the Roman general Germanicus, with eight legions, conducted a series of campaigns into the lands east of the Rhine that culminated in a battle where Arminius and the Cherusci were soundly defeated. In A.D. 74, when the emperor Vespasian decided to optimize the frontier defenses, he annexed the territory east of the Rhine and south of the Main without any significant resistance from its inhabitants. The Romans, consciously or unconsciously, decided that northern Europe was not worth the trouble of conquering it. Children of the sunny Mediterranean, they heartily disliked the cold and humid climate of northern Europe. They could never be comfortable in a land of bogs and impenetrable forests in which "the trees grew close together and very high." (This aversion comes through very clear in Cassius Dio's description of the landscape through which Varus's doomed legions struggled.) Very little profit could be extracted from this land, inhabited by backward and tumultuous people. The main thing the Romans wanted from it was security, and they gradually realized that it was easier to obtain it by means of a forward frontier policy rather than by outright annexation. Accordingly, the Romans began to "domesticate" the Germanic tribes. Their decision to pension off Maroboduus was just one element of this policy. As a result, the Rhine frontier became stationary.

Ironically, the decision to establish a stationary frontier was disastrous in the long run. During the next three or four centuries, the frontier transformed the social and political organization of the Germans. Small-scale tribes of the first century B.C., such as the Cherusci and the Chatti, gave way to powerful tribal confederations of the third and fourth centuries, such as the Franks, Alamanni, and Goths, who began expanding at the expense of the aging Roman Empire. Eventually one of these confederations, the Franks, evolved into the only state in European history that managed to unify most of western Europe—the Carolingian Empire.

The forces that the Roman frontier exerted on the incipient German nations were of several different kinds. The first, and most obvious, was the military pressure, which was particularly strong during the early centuries of the frontier's existence. When Caesar led his forces into the territory of the Sugambri in 55 B.C., the Romans burned the villages and destroyed the crops in the territory they passed through. The inhabitants saved themselves by fleeing before the advancing Roman troops. The Chatti were less lucky when they were attacked by Germanicus in A.D. 15. "Germanicus completely surprised the Chatti. Helpless women, children, and old people were at once slaughtered or captured. The younger men swam across the river Eder ...." As Germanicus advanced into their territory, the tribesmen "evacuated their towns and villages, dispersed and took to the woods. Germanicus burnt their capital, and, ravaging the open country, started back for the Rhine." The atrocities committed by the Romans were reciprocated. For example, after the battle of the Teutoburg Forest, the Germans selected 500 prisoners to be sacrificed to the gods. According to a reconstruction by Peter Wells, these unfortunates were killed in a variety of ways: Some were hanged from oak trees; others had their heads cut off and nailed to tree trunks. Yet others were taken to the marshes, their throats cut in such a way that their blood poured into the water. Their lifeless bodies were then flung into the pool.

The wealthy and civilized society on the Roman side of the frontier produced many things that were coveted by the "barbarians": bronze, silver, and gold ornaments and vessels; fine weapons and cloths; coins; pottery; and wine and olive oil. These items were prized not only for their intrinsic value, but also for the prestige they bestowed on the owner. Thus, drinking wine was not only pleasurable because wine tastes good—it was also an act of "conspicuous consumption" that demonstrated the high status of the wine drinker. A beautiful golden wine cup reinforced the message. Anthropologists postulate that prestige goods played an extremely important role in state formation. Of course, a chieftain aiming to become king could reward his loyal retinue with, say, cattle. Taking care of a cow, however, is a pain in the neck for a professional warrior (and not a particularly prestigious occupation), whereas a golden arm-ring of the same value is portable, maintenance-free, and a visible symbol of status.

Whereas military pressure is a "push" factor, obliterating the weak and further strengthening the strong, a source of prestige goods is a "pull" factor. Its effect, however, is the same: to increase the selective pressure for increased military strength. The Germans could obtain prestige goods from the Roman Empire by raiding, trading, or subsidies (rewards for good behavior). Raiding was an increasingly feasible option beginning in the third century, as the Roman Empire started declining. Even then, only very large tribal confederations had any chance at securing a significant amount of booty. Trading was a peaceful way to obtain goods, but it also led to increased conflict. Tribes that controlled the cross-frontier trade (because they were better situated on the frontier, or perhaps secured a trading agreement with the Romans) were resented by those who were cut off from directly dealing with the Roman traders. The obvious remedy was to defeat and displace the lucky intermediaries. Imperial subsidies caused conflict by the same logic. As a result, both push and pull factors worked to establish a highly conflict-prone band of territory extending 100 miles from the frontier in both directions. Within this band, it was a "dog-eat-dog" morality, and the strong dogs became even stronger as they ate the small ones.

The frontier also exerted more subtle influences on the Germanic societies. The Empire was not only the source of prestige goods, but also of ideas, techniques, and other kinds of cultural elements. Recollect the comment of Tacitus about how rapidly the Germans learned from the Romans the value of discipline. By the time the Franks began expanding into the Roman territory in the fifth century, they already realized the value of records and bureaucracy, so they employed the Roman administrators and accepted them as members of the nascent imperial aristocracy.

It is interesting that the Romans sometimes inadvertently helped the process that eventually resulted in their succumbing to the Germanic conquest. Roman frontier administrators encouraged several small tribes to band together under one leader. It was much simpler to control (by gifts or intimidation) one "kinglet" than a bunch of chieftains or, worse, to deal with many tribal councils. The side effect of this policy, however, was to acculturate the Germans to the institution of kingship, with dire consequences for the later empire. Another mechanism that inadvertently promoted cooperation among Germanic chieftains was their frequent meetings with each other in the capitals of frontier provinces, such as Cologne, Mainz, or Augsburg.

Although the Germans learned a lot from the Romans and adopted many Roman cultural practices, the cultural difference between them and the Romans did not become blurred. If anything, it actually intensified with time. The clearest evidence for this polarization comes from the religious changes on each side of the frontier. During the first centuries of contact, both peoples followed polytheistic religions that were fairly tolerant of other peoples' beliefs. However, beginning with the reign of Constantine (306–337), the Romans converted to Christianity—a monotheistic religion that treated all other beliefs as (at best) an error, and (at worst) devil worship. The religion of the Germans also evolved, and in a direction that increased the distance between them and the Romans.

At the time of the contact with the Romans, the head of the German pantheon was Tiwaz, an Indo-European deity of creation, order, justice, and natural cycles—an appropriate god to worship for an agricultural population. The conditions of the frontier with their heightened insecurity and incessant military conflict, however, favored the rise of war leaders and their retinues. War increasingly became the occupation of adult free men, whereas subsistence tasks were left to women and slaves. (The latter were constantly replenished from the pool of war captives.) As a result, the cult of Tiwaz declined, and many Germanic tribes turned to Odin (Wodan). Odin had probably been a minor wind god and perhaps, like Mercury, he conducted the souls to the other world. (At least, the Romans usually identified Odin with Mercury, although this could be due to the fact that both were depicted wearing wide-brimmed hats and carrying a staff or a spear.) Between A.D. 50 and 200, Odin was transformed into Allfather, the king of gods, and became the patron deity of the new warlords and their retinues. According to the new mythology, Odin sacrificed himself—to himself—

for knowledge and power. In *The Words of the High One*, a poem from the Elder Edda, Odin says:

> *I know that I hung*
> *on the wind-swept tree*
> *nine entire nights,*
> *wounded with a spear,*
> *given to Odin,*
> *myself to myself,*
> *on that tree,*
> *of which no man knows*
> *of what roots it runs.*

The "wind-swept tree" is the world tree, Yggdrasil. During his nine-day ordeal, Odin learned rune magic; later he sacrificed an eye to drink from the Well of Mimir, which bestowed great knowledge. These experiences transformed a minor deity into the god of war, death, wisdom, and magic, and the chief among the gods. Although interesting parallels exist between the ordeal of Odin and the passion of the Christ, it is difficult to imagine two more different religions than Christianity and the cult of Odin. Jesus of Nazareth sacrificed himself to save humanity, whereas Odin sought wisdom and power for himself. Odin's message was not one of mercy or hope. Human sacrifices were frequently offered to Odin, especially prisoners taken in battle. The skalds (poets) called Odin the "God of Hanged Men" or the "Lord of Gallows," because the usual method of sacrifice was hanging the victim on a tree. The eleventh-century historian Adam of Bremen recounts that in the sacred grove in Uppsala, Sweden, many human bodies hung from the branches of the sacred trees.

Odin thrived on war, and could even cause one where none existed. He was a dour, merciless, and deceitful god. Odin was destined to die at Ragnarok, the last battle between the gods and the giants. Even knowing his doom, Odin nevertheless prepared for Ragnarok by gathering to himself the souls of heroes slain in battle. Awaiting the final battle, the heroes whiled their time away at Odin's hall, Valhalla, by alternatively feasting and fighting each other to the death. Valhalla was the idealized version of the lifestyle of real Germanic warriors.

The cult of Odin was suited to the violent, unsettled, and treacherous conditions that existed in the Rhineland. Survival required banding together with trusted comrades to follow a war leader who could deliver an assured victory. The development of the new institution of sacral kingship, thus, paralleled the growth of the cult of Odin. The new warlords worshipped Odin as the giver of victory on the battlefield, and legitimated their political power by claiming direct descent from him. For example, all Anglo-Saxon royal lines claimed direct descent from Odin.

To recapitulate, when they first came in direct contact in the first century B.C., the religions of the Romans and the Germans were not widely dissimilar variations on the basic Indo-European theme. By A.D. 400, however, the cultural divide deepened into a chasm between civilizations. The two religions stood in sharp ideological opposition to each other. Both provided symbolic "markers" for delineating "us" versus "them." The cult of Odin, additionally, legitimated the military and political power of the Germanic sacral kings, solidifying previously loose tribal confederations into highly cohesive warrior nations. The frontier between the Romans and the Germans, thus, became a major fault line, similar in its intensity to the Russian-Tatar and American settler-Indian frontiers.

The concept of a "civilizational fault line" was popularized by the political scientist Samuel P. Huntington in his 1996 book *The Clash of Civilizations*. Huntington argued that after the collapse of the Soviet Union, different countries began aligning themselves not along the ideological divide between communism and liberalism, but reverted to older sources of large-scale identity, based on belonging to various world civilizations. Huntington's thesis provoked a storm of controversy, and I myself could quibble with many of the points that he raised. Nevertheless, the decade since he wrote the book has amply demonstrated that his main insight is correct. The events of 9/11 and the wars that the United States subsequently waged in Afghanistan and Iraq are precisely the kind of a "fault-line war" that he predicted.

Huntington was concerned exclusively with contemporary politics, but the concept of the "clash of civilizations" proves to be illuminating when we analyze the past. The word *civilization*, however, does not sit well as a description of such historical groups as the Germans or Eurasian nomads. I prefer to use *metaethnic community* (from the Greek *meta*, "beyond," and *ethnos*, "ethnic group" or "nation") for large-scale supranational entities of this kind; this term includes both the traditional civilizations and cultural groupings that are not usually included in the standard lists of civilizations. Another example of a metaethnic community, which is not usually treated as a civilization, is the Celtic world of the first millennium B.C. Each metaethnic community is unified by some sort of shared identity, which is usually based on religion or another form of ideology (for example, Confucianism). However, the most important aspect of the metaethnic identity is the dividing line between "us" and "them." A metaethnic community cannot coalesce until it is confronted with a significantly different other. The rise of Germania on the Roman frontier is one example of that. A modern example is the formation of the "African civilization." Prior to the conquest of the sub-Saharan Africa by Western powers in the nineteenth century, the Africans had no sense of shared identity. But shared experience of first colonization, then decolonization, and now the tendency of the rest of the world to lump them together created the conditions for a gradual emergence of the African community. This metaethnic identity is still quite fragile (and not all authorities agree that sub-Saharan Africa qualifies as a separate civilization), but it seems to be slowly strengthening.

IF WE DATE THE FIRST CLOSE encounter between the Romans and the Germans to be the conquest of Gaul by Caesar (the middle of the first century B.C.), then the frontier remained stationary and exerted its tranformative influence on the German tribes for roughly three centuries before detectable signs of the interaction emerged—large and powerful tribal confederations led by sacral kings. The Alamanni, situated along the Upper Rhine, appear in the historical record in A.D. 231, the Goths (on the Lower Danube) in 238. The first mention of the Franks (the Lower Rhine region) is in 257. Saxons east and north of the Franks are mentioned from 286. The Saxons were situated in the "second tier"—not directly on the frontier, but behind the Franks. Similarly, the Vandals (first appeared on the Middle Danube in 270) backed the Goths and the Burgundians deployed behind the Alamanni.

The appearance of these confederations coincided with (or, more likely, was triggered by) a period of political instability in the Roman Empire that followed the assassination of the emperor Severus Alexander in 235. For 50 years, internecine fighting between multiple pretenders was riving the empire apart. The period between 259 and 268 was the age of the "Thirty Tyrants" (or pretenders). The pretenders stripped the legions from the frontiers to be used in the civil war, and the German war parties poured across the frontier. The Franks raided deep into Gaul and even crossed the Pyrenees into Spain. The Goths started to raid the Balkans and Asia Minor. In 251, they wiped out the Roman army and killed the emperor Decius (not the last emperor to be killed by the Goths). Lands east of the Rhine and south of the Main were conquered and settled by the Alamanni, and the Romans had to permanently abandon the trans-Danubian province of Dacia.

In 285, Diocletian reunited the empire, and for almost a century it was able to defend its frontiers against the pressing Germans. But the arrival of the Huns on the European steppes in the mid-fourth century set in motion a chain of events that led to a battle of Adrianople (in 378) between the Romans and the Visigoths. (By this time, the Goths had broken up into two confederations, called the Visigoths and the Ostrogoths.) The Goths again defeated the Roman army, and another emperor was slain. The battle of Adrianople signaled the final decline of the Roman Empire in the West. During the fifth century, Germans overran the Latin provinces of the Roman Empire and divided them up in a number of tribal kingdoms—the Visigoths in southern Gaul and Spain, the Vandals in North Africa, the Ostrogoths in Italy, and the Burgundians in eastern Gaul.

THE MOST SUCCESSFUL GERMANIC EMPIRE was the Frankish. Whereas the Germanic invaders of the first wave (the Vandals and the Goths) dashed around in search of easy pickings within the dying empire, the second wave of invasions (the Franks, the Alamanni, and the Bavarians) involved masses of farmers quietly colonizing frontier regions in a much more lasting way. Under the Merovingian king Childeric and his son Clovis, the Franks expanded from the Rhineland into northern Gaul. In 497, the Franks decisively defeated the Alamanni, and over the next decade subjected the Alamanni to Frankish control. The territory of the Alamanni was reorganized as a duchy within the Frankish Empire.

It is interesting to note that the Romans were unable to subdue the Alamanni, despite repeatedly defeating them in battle. By contrast, after they were forcibly joined to the Frankish Empire, the Alamanni served it quite loyally. The most likely explanation is that the ethnic gap between the Franks and Alamanni was fairly trivial compared to that between the Alamanni and the Romans. Both Franks and Alamanni spoke dialects of German that were recognizably related, and probably mutually comprehensible. Both peoples followed Odin (before they converted to Christianity) and had similar political organization. It appears that being situated on the same side of the frontier for centuries exerted its usual integrative effect (as discussed in Chapter 2). This integrative process was, without doubt, facilitated by the ease of communication between the two ethnic groups—both of them were situated along the Rhine, which was an important trading route.

However, it would be incorrect to say that the Alamanni assimilated and became Franks. These two related but distinct peoples continued speaking distinct dialects throughout the centuries. Thus, the direct descendant of Alamannic is the Alsatian dialect of German, still spoken today, whereas the direct descendant of the Frankish language is Flemish.

After annexing Alamannia, Clovis swiftly dealt with two other Germanic kingdoms in Gaul, the Burgundian and the Visigothic. By the death of Clovis in 511, the Franks had annexed Burgundia and deprived the Visigoths of Aquitaine. With the exception of the Bretagne Peninsula and Provence, retained by the Visigoths, the Franks now controlled the whole Gaul. During the Carolingian period (the eight and ninth centuries), the Franks further expanded their empire (see Map 2). At its peak, the Frankish Empire included all Germanic peoples, with the exception of the Scandinavians and English. The most notable addition made by the emperor Charlemagne was the annexation of the territories of the Saxons and the Bavarians. The political unification of the Germanic peoples under the Carolingian emperors laid the foundations for the modern German nation, although not all constituent elements of the Frankish Empire ended up within modern Germany. (By a twist of fate, the direct descendants of the Franks—the Flemish—are now in a separate state of their own.) But coexistence within the empire of Charlemagne clearly created the basis for the pan-Germanic identity. Although the Carolingian Empire fell apart during the ninth century, the Saxon emperors reconstituted it a century later along pretty much the same lines as the Frankish realm (but without France).

The integrative process that created the medieval German identity, which took expression in the so-called Holy Roman Empire of the German Nation, was a direct result of life on the Roman frontier and developed in three phases. During the first phase (100 B.C.—A.D. 100), war chiefs such as Arminius or Maroboduus banded the independent Germanic tribes together in loose confederations. These confederations were very unstable, and their leaders faced severe problems of legitimacy. During the second phase, associated with the rise of the Odin cult and sacral kingship, the confederations became much more tightly integrated and evolved a high capacity for concerted action. In the third phase, one of the confederations, the Franks, united most of the others within a single territorial state. The other tribes were added primarily by force, but upon annexation they apparently transferred their allegiance to the imperial level of political organization (while not necessarily losing their lower-level identity as the Alamanni, the Saxons, or the Bavarians; both identities coexisted).

THE BULK OF THIS CHAPTER HAS FOCUSED on tracing the development of empires in northwestern Europe. The Roman frontier along the Rhine provides a very clear case of frontier *ethnogenesis* ("the birth of a nation") and *imperiogenesis* ("the birth of empire"). It was the interface along which two very distinct civilizations (actually, metaethnic communities) clashed and at the same time influenced each other: Romance-speaking Christian citizens of the Roman Empire against Germanic pagan, stateless societies. The Danubian frontier was more complex, and disentangling various interactions across it takes correspondingly more effort. On the imperial side, there were Latin speakers in the West and Greeks in the East. On the "barbarian" side, there were, first, peoples who originated in Europe's forest zone (first the Germans and later the Slavs), and, second, various nomadic invaders from the great Eurasian steppe (the Sarmatians, the Huns, the Avars, the Bulgars, and so on). These two kinds of peoples mixed together in a bewildering variety of ways, so it was often hard to tell which one was which. Thus, the Ostrogoths adopted so many of the steppe ways that the Romans called them the "Scythians," although they were not at all related to the historic people of the same name. The Hun confederation of the fifth century was extremely heterogeneous in its ethnic composition. It is interesting that Attila "the Hun" had a Gothic name. (*Attila* means "daddy" in Gothic.) The location of the Middle and Lower Danube, within the westernmost extension of the great steppe, significantly complicated its ethnic history. Chapter 7 considers this issue again, because the history of this region cannot be understood without taking into account the events that took place thousands of miles to the east, at the interface between the steppe and *Sinic* ("Chinese") metaethnic communities.

What we can do here, however, is address one of the greatest puzzles of medieval European history: why the eastern Roman Empire (which we call *Byzantine*), survived the fall of Rome by a thousand years. (The traditional end of the Roman Empire in the West is 476, whereas the Byzantine Empire ended with the fall of Constantinople to the Turks in 1453.)

The first step in resolving this puzzle is to realize that the question is *ill-posed*—it does not make sense as formulated. The history of the Byzantine Empire is not well known even among the well-educated Western public, and what is known is heavily mythologized—the Byzantine Empire is portrayed as an oriental despotism in a permanent state of decadence. To qualify something as "Byzantine" is certainly not a compliment! The roots of the negative attitude toward Byzantium go all the way back to the times of the Crusades. In 1204, the Western knights, instead of attacking the Muslims, treacherously attacked and sacked Constantinople. Then, to add insult to injury, they spread tales about "perfidious Greeks." The intellectual tradition of dumping on the Byzantines began in the eighteenth century with Edward Gibbon's *The Decline and Fall of the Roman Empire*. Gibbon begins his tale with the golden age of the Antonine emperors (the second century A.D.) and, according to him, it was all downhill from that point on—for more than 12 centuries! A "decline" of such long duration loses any utility as an analytical concept. As the historian of Byzantium Warren Treadgold noted, even nowadays most historians tend to concentrate on the first and last third of Byzantine history, the periods that fit the best idea of decline. The middle third, when the internally cohesive and militarily strong Byzantine Empire expanded its territory over three centuries from 230,000 to 460,000 square miles (0.6 to 1.2 million square kilometers), gets much less attention. Gibbon raced through this period in one chapter, and devoted the rest of his three fat volumes to the "decadent" periods.

No, it does not make sense to ask why one part of the Roman Empire lingered on for more than a millennium after the heartland collapsed. Instead, we should ask why a new imperial nation was born in the Balkans-Anatolia area when the old one collapsed. Confusion arises because the nation at the core of the Byzantine Empire called themselves "the Romans" (*Romaioi* in Greek), and their state the "Roman Empire." A little reflection, however, makes it clear that the medieval Byzantines were an entirely separate people from the Romans of antiquity. (This is why modern historians invented the name Byzantine—from *Byzantion*, the name of the Greek town on which site Constantinople, the capital of the Byzantine Empire, was built in the fourth century.) Just designating themselves as "the Romans," however, is not a sufficient reason to equate this later people with the Romans. For example, there is a modern country whose citizens still call themselves "the Romans": Romania. In general, an appropriation of an old and glorious *ethnonym* ("a name of a nation") is a common thing in history. The French call themselves the "Franks," but Germans also lay a claim to the Frankish legacy. (There is a province in Germany called Frankonia.) The Russians think of themselves as direct descendants of the Kievan Rus, a claim that is hotly contested by the Ukrainian nationalists.

Apart from the name, the Romans and the nation that we now call the Byzantines had almost nothing in common. They spoke different languages (Latin versus Greek), practiced different religions (paganism versus Christianity), and their core territories were in different parts of Europe. They also had a different political organization—the Byzantines were ruled by an *avtokrator* who, at least in theory, had a total power over all matters of life and death, whereas the Romans were a republican people. (Even during the imperial period, the legal fiction was that the emperor was only a *princeps*—"the first among the senatorial class.") The substance of power might not have changed a lot, but its external trappings and the ideological basis did. Princeps was legitimized via election by the senate, whereas the avtokrator's legitimacy stemmed from the divine mandate.

The Byzantines and the Romans even dressed differently—by A.D. 500, the Roman toga was replaced in the Empire with oriental-style long brocaded coats.

The collective psyche of the two nations also could not be more different. The Romans were a worldly and eminently practical people, whereas the Byzantine culture had very strong otherworldly and deeply mystical elements. Indeed, during the fifth and sixth centuries, the whole Mediterranean world was transformed from the naturalism and rationalism of the ancient Hellenistic civilization to the transcendentalism and mysticism of medieval Christianity. Were a medieval Byzantine and the Roman of classical antiquity to be brought together by a time machine, their meeting would be one of mutual incomprehension, akin to the encounter between Pontius Pilate and Jesus of Nazareth. In short, it seems incontrovertible that the Byzantines were an entirely new people, and therefore their empire was a new thing, not a lingering splinter of the Roman Empire. How did the Byzantine nation arise, then?

The birth of a nation—ethnogenesis—is not an instantaneous event, but a process that usually takes many centuries. For the Byzantines, the beginning of the process can be traced to the first century, when the swath of northern Balkans south of the Lower Danube (Roman provinces of Illyria/Dalmatia, Moesia, and Thracia—roughly modern Serbia, Bulgaria, and European Turkey) became part of the Roman frontier. Just as the pressure by the Romans molded the nations north of the frontier, the pressure from the "barbarians" molded the frontier society on the "civilization" side. We can measure this social evolution with a variety of metrics, but perhaps the most striking one follows the geographic origin of recruits for the Roman legions. In the first century A.D., Italy contributed roughly 10 times as many troops as came from the Lower Danube provinces. By the third century, the situation had completely reversed—there were 10 times as many recruits coming from the Balkans as from Italy. While Italians lost taste for the army service, the hardy Danubian frontiersmen took up the slack. In fact, as the historian Ramsay MacMullen wrote in *Corruption and Decline of Rome*, the longer a population enjoyed security, the less likely its youth would be enrolled in the legions. Other frontier areas—the Upper Danube, the Rhineland, northern Africa, and Syria—also heavily contributed troops, while Italy and such nonfrontier provinces as Spain contributed fewer and fewer. The inevitable end result of this process was the leakage of power from the center toward the peripheries.

During the third century, the Roman Empire went through a catastrophic phase of political decentralization, marked by decades-long civil war between various aristocratic factions, popular uprisings, devastating epidemics, and barbarian invasions. Earlier in this chapter, I described how the Germanic invaders were able to break through the Rhine frontier and pillage the Gaul and even penetrate as far south as Spain. In the East during the 250s, 260s, and 270s, the Goths crossed the Danube and pillaged Moesia and Thrace (including the area of the future capital of the Byzantine empire). They then took to boats, broke through the Bosporus and Dardanelles into the Aegean Sea, and pillaged the shores of Greece and Asia Minor.

With the collapse of the authority in the center, the frontier provinces were left to pick up the pieces and look toward their own defense. To legitimize their power, army commanders had their troops declare them as emperors. The process of social dissolution reached the peak during the reign of the emperor Gallienus (253–268), "the age of Thirty Tyrants." We know of at least 18 of these usurpers; history did not preserve the names of the other 12. Most of the pretenders were killed soon after assuming power, often by their own troops. The longest lasting were usually those whose base was in the frontier provinces, partly as a result of the location of legions, but, more importantly, because the population inhabiting frontier areas had higher group solidarity than the central areas. For example, in 260, Gallienus controlled only the middle third of the empire (see Map 3). The western third was controlled by the Gallic Empire of Postumus, with the capital in Trier on the Rhine. The eastern third was part of the Palmyrene Empire of Odenathus, and after his death, Queen Zenobia. This was also an incipient frontier state, because Palmyra was a trading city on the frontier with Parthia/Persia.

Gallienus was a representative of the Italian senatorial class, and by all accounts not a bad emperor. By the third century, however, the Italians had become a weak reed upon which to build a power base. In 268, a cabal of his own officers, all originating from the Danubian frontier provinces, assassinated Gallienus and produced a string of capable emperors (the so-called "Illyrian soldier-emperors") from their ranks who were gradually able to bring order to the empire. The best known of them is the emperor Diocletian, who was born in 245 to a poor peasant family in Dalmatia, served on the Danubian frontier, and rose through the ranks to high military command. In 284, Diocletian was proclaimed by the legions as emperor. During the next 10 years, he and his generals defeated all other pretenders and reunified the Roman Empire. However, when Diocletian retired in 305, the empire was again thrown into civil war, and the task of putting it together, yet again, was left to Diocletian's successor, Constantine the Great.

Constantine was born in Naissus (modern Nish in Serbia) in 285, a son of Helena, an innkeeper's daughter, and Constantius Chlorus ("the pale"). His father, like Diocletian, was born in a poor Danubian family, served in the army, became a trusted associate of Diocletian and then was named "Augustus" (one of two co-rulers of the empire) upon the abdication of Diocletian in 305 until his own death in 306. Thus, Constantine the Great was a second-generation Illyrian emperor-soldier. Apart from reunifying the empire, Constantine left two lasting accomplishments that shaped the course of Byzantine history: He adopted Christianity as the state religion and built Constantinople, the Byzantine capital.

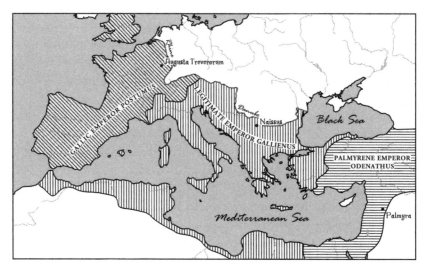

Map 3   *Roman Empire divided:* A.D. *260*

The importance of Christianity in Byzantine history cannot be over-stressed. It permeated the whole society, philosophy, and art. Most importantly, it provided the glue that kept together the heterogeneous ethnic elements of which the Byzantine state was initially composed: Latin-speaking inhabitants of the Balkan and North African provinces; Greek-speaking inhabitants of Greece, Anatolia, and all the large cities of the eastern half of the Roman Empire, such as Alexandria and Antioch; and Coptic and Aramaic speakers of Egypt and the Levant.

The founding of Constantinople (modern Istanbul) in 324 was a stroke of genius, and played not the least role in the subsequent survival and flowering of the Byzantine Empire. The geographic location on the Straits of Bosporus, where the Black Sea flows into the Sea of Marmara and then through the Dardanelles into the Mediterranean, made Constantinople a crossroads of North-South and East-West traffic, and ensured that it would be an important trading center for centuries to come. It also allowed the Byzantines to conduct military campaigns both in Europe and in Asia. At the same time, it was relatively easy to make Constantinople virtually impregnable. It was situated on a promontory protected by the sea from two sides and by strong land fortifications on the third side. So long as the Byzantines controlled the seas, Constantinople could not be starved by a siege. Even more important, however, was the move of the capital from central Italy, which was dominated by selfish and fractious Roman nobility, who by the fourth century had lost all ability for cooperative action. Establishment of the capital in Thracia on the Danubian frontier moved the empire's center of power close to the areas where it recruited its military strength.

The key factor in understanding the Mediterranean world in the fourth through sixth centuries is the "imperiopathosis" of the Roman nation, and its displacement by a new and yet incompletely formed imperial nation, gradually crystallizing along the Lower Danube frontier. This period is a sort of transitional phase between Rome, which really fell in the third century, and Byzantium, which fully formed only after the shock of the Arabic conquests. Like most transitional phases, this was a period of much instability. First, the incipient Byzantine nation was still in the process of formation. Second, similar processes to those operating along the Danube frontier were affecting other frontier areas, most notably northern Gaul and Syria. Any empire that has more than one imperial nation is unstable, because each power group is unwilling to submit to the others, and if it has the necessary degree of internal cohesion it will have the means to resist. As a result, late antiquity was a period of endemic civil war, in which rival centers of power contended for the command of the empire. Third, new imperial nations arose outside the Roman frontiers—the Franks, Goths, and others. Now that internal divisions weakened the empire, these new aggressive nations looked to expand at its expense.

The fragile equilibrium established by Constantine was upset when the Visigoths wiped out the emperor Valens and his army at the battle of Adrianople (A.D. 378). This catastrophe set in motion a chain of events that resulted in the failure of frontier defenses in Europe and the inundation of the western empire by the barbarian hordes. In 476, when the last Roman emperor in the West was deposed, the only area in the western empire remaining in Roman hands was northern Gaul under the Roman patrician Syagrius. If left alone, perhaps the kingdom of Syagrius would have eventually grown into a Gallic empire, just like the Lower Danubian frontier was transformed into the Byzantine Empire, but the new Germanic nations proved to be too strong for it. In 486, Clovis defeated Syagrius and incorporated his fledgling kingdom into the Frankish Empire. The ultimate fate of the Romance-speaking inhabitants of northern Gaul was to be ethnically fused with the Germanic-speaking Frankish colonists and to give birth to the kingdom of France five centuries later (as discussed in Chapter 7).

The eastern empire, on the other hand, was able to withstand the barbarian pressure, although its emperors for a while fell under the sway of barbarian strongmen. Nevertheless, under the emperors Justin (518–527) and especially his son Justinian (527–565), the Byzantine Empire reconquered the majority of the western Mediterranean lands: North Africa, southern Iberia, and Italy. At the same time, Justinian was able to hold his own against the Sassanian Persia, which was trying to expand west at the expense of the Byzantines. Despite these impressive feats, religious controversy was one structural problem that plagued the late Roman Empire and eventually played the key role in its loss of African and Middle Eastern possessions.

The religious controversies centered on the two natures of Christ. The Nestorians argued that Christ had two separate natures, one human and one divine, in the same person, but not commingled. Monophysites, by contrast, claimed that Christ's two natures were fully combined into one. Finally, the Chalcedonians maintained a middle-of-the road position that Christ was completely human and completely divine, one and the same Christ having two natures without confusion or change, division, or separation. This probably sounds like complete gibberish to many readers, and it does to me. It is hard to believe that anyone other than a handful of theologians steeped in their arcane lore could make any sense of this distinction. How could a soldier, a peasant, or a boot maker get passionate about this question? Yet, when in 457 a pro-Chalcedonian bishop was imposed on Monophysite Alexandria, the Alexandrians rioted, lynched him, and installed a Monophysite in his place.

One way to make sense of this is to remember that religion often provides a *symbolic marker* that is used by people to distinguish "us" from "them." A modern example of such a usage is the war in Yugoslavia between the Orthodox Serbs, the Catholic Croats, and the Muslim Bosnians—ethnically closely related peoples who, in fact, speak essentially the same language (Serbo-Croatian), yet are willing to commit genocide against each other. In the Byzantine Empire, the Aramaic-speaking Syrians, for example, and the Greek-speaking Anatolians both professed the same religion. However, they must have felt that they were distinct peoples, and did not want to "belong together." It is doubtful that a Syrian boot maker in Antioch understood the fine points of distinction between the Chalcedonian and Monophysite creeds, but he knew very well that the Greeks were "them," not "us," and he wanted to emphasize the difference. Monophysite Christianity provided a source of identity distinct from the dominant imperial one. The struggle over the nature of Christ was an external manifestation of deep centrifugal tendencies tearing apart the social fabric of the empire. The geographic distribution of the sects confirms this conclusion. Monophysite and Chalcedonian bishoprics were not intermixed—the Balkans, Greece, and Anatolia were solidly Chalcedonian; Syria, Palestine, and Egypt were Monophysite. The separate state of Sassanian Persia was the stronghold of Nestorianism.

In the second half of the sixth century, the Byzantine Empire went into a secular disintegrative phase. Internal civil war coupled with repeated invasions by Persians, who at one point conquered all of the Levant and Egypt, removed the last restraint on the centrifugal forces forcing Chalcedonian and Monophysite areas apart. Even though Byzantium was able to regain Egypt and the Levant from Persia in 630, these territories stayed within the empire less than a decade. In 636, the Arabs defeated the Byzantine army at the battle of Yarmuk, and Syria fell to the caliphate. The next year, Jerusalem surrendered, and between 640 and 642 the Arabs conquered Egypt. Hundreds of thousands of committed Christians (mainly of Chalcedonian persuasion) immigrated to Byzantium rather than submit to Islam. The majority of the Monophysite population did not have any particular loyalty to the Byzantine Empire and acquiesced to the Muslim rule. The Byzantine loss of Egypt and the Levant was to be permanent.

The Arab conquests reduced the Byzantine Empire to its core on the Balkan and Anatolian peninsulas (plus some territory in southern Italy), inhabited by Greek-speaking people following the Chalcedonian creed. The whole empire, or what was left of it, became a frontier zone (see Map 4). From the east, it was pressed by the Arabs, and from the west by the steppe nomads—Avars and Bulgars, as well as by the Slavs migrating from eastern Europe. The invading armies reached Constantinople on numerous occasions. For example, the Arabs besieged Constantinople by land and sea in 678 and again in 717. These repeated hammer strokes forged the Byzantine nation. When the pressure abated at the end of the eighth century, the Byzantines resumed their empire building. During the next three centuries, the Byzantine Empire doubled its territory. When the Carolingian Empire fragmented in the ninth century, Byzantium became Europe's most powerful state. With half a million inhabitants, Constantinople was the largest city in Europe. The wealth of the Byzantine rulers was fabulous, and attracted mercenaries from as far away as Norway to serve in the elite Varangian Guard. By 1025, the Byzantine treasury had accumulated an enormous surplus of 14.4 million nomismata—which is more than 60 tons of gold, a cool $1 billion at today's prices! The cultural brilliance of the Byzantines rivaled that of the contemporary Islamic and Chinese civilizations, and dazzled the Westerners who saw it. In *Chronicle of the First Crusade,* Fulcher of Chartres wrote, "Oh, what an excellent and beautiful city! How many monasteries, and how many places there are in it, of wonderful work skillfully fashioned! How many marvelous works are to be seen in the streets and districts of the town! It's a great nuisance to recite what an opulence of all kinds of goods are found there; of gold, of silver ... and of holy relics."

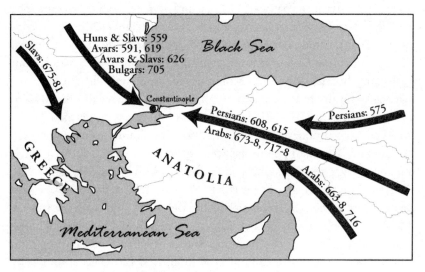

Map 4   *Byzantium encircled:* A.D. *559–718.*

OUR TEST OF THE EFFECT OF the Roman frontier on the political development in post-Roman Europe yields a resounding confirmation of the hypothesis advanced in Chapter 2. All new states of the second half of the first millennium arose in the Roman frontier zone. Consider that observation in quantitative terms. The total area of Europe is 3.8 million square miles. The length of the Roman frontier, from the mouth of the Rhine to the mouth of the Danube, is a bit longer than 1,200 miles. Assuming that the frontier influence extended 100 miles to each side, the total area of the frontier zone is 240,000 square miles, or less than 7 percent of the total area of Europe. All of the seven large European states of the post-Roman period (and the three smaller-sized or shorter in duration) arose within this narrow band of territory.

None of the nonfrontier regions of the Roman Empire—Italy, Greece, Spain, and southern Gaul—showed any signs of incipient empire formation. This is contrasted with the frontier areas. In northern Gaul south of the Rhine, there were two attempts at empire building, the Gallic Empire of Postumus in the third century, and the kingdom of Syagrius in the fifth, both of which, however, proved to be abortive (destroyed by stronger rivals). In the Balkan area south of the Danube, the empire-building effort was successful and produced the magnificent and long-lived Byzantine Empire.

Similarly, the only non-Roman territories that generated empires were those within the frontier zone. Rhineland was where the Frankish empire was born, profoundly affecting the whole subsequent course of European history. The people of other less-successful German states, such as the Alamanni and the Burgundians, were absorbed by the Franks. The Danube frontier produced an even greater number of empires. The Hungarian plain north and east of the Middle Danube generated a succession of states: Dacia, the short-lived Hunnish empire; the mighty Avar khanate; and, finally, the kingdom of Hungary. To the east, along the Lower Danube and in the Black Sea steppes was where the Goths coalesced as a nation, before splitting into Visigoths and Ostrogoths. Ostrogoths established a short-lived empire with the center in Italy, but succumbed to the Byzantines. Visigoths traveled farther, crossing the whole Roman Empire to establish a kingdom in southern Gaul and Spain, which they held for more than two centuries before falling to the invading Muslim hordes of Arabs and Berbers.

Contrast this feverish empire-building activity by frontier peoples to the complete absence of such efforts in the non-Roman Europe away from the frontier. We know very little about the northeastern quadrant of Europe, inhabited by Finnish and Baltic peoples, but we can be certain that they lived in small-scale communities. There were no hints of any incipient states there in the first millennium. Interesting developments, with great consequences for the future, began to happen in the wide band of territory located between the frontier zone and the sleepy northeastern quadrant (roughly modern Denmark, northern Germany, Poland, Belarus, and western Ukraine). This territory was not subjected to the direct impact of the Roman frontier, but indirectly it felt its influence (primarily through the trade). No state-building activity occurred here (before the tenth century), but the tribes were on the move. The Saxon pirates terrorized the shores of Britain and Gaul. Soon after the Roman Empire abandoned Britain, bands of Saxons, Jutes, Angles, and Frisians invaded it from the east and south, and began to settle there. In a similar fashion, small but numerous bands of Slavs began pushing south into the Balkan territories of the former Roman Empire, where they settled down as far as southern Greece. Other Slavic tribes expanded in all other compass directions—west, east, and north. All these movements would gradually reshape the ethnic landscape of Europe, but their real impact was starting to be felt only toward the end of the millennium.

Chapter 4

Asabiya in the Desert

Ibn Khaldun Discovers the Key to History

When Ibn Khaldun was 17 years old, the Black Death struck North Africa and carried away both his parents. His full name was Abd-ar-Rahman Abu Zaid ibn Muhammad ibn Khaldun, and he was born in Tunis on May 27, 1332. He belonged to an aristocratic family of statesmen and scholars. Until the early thirteenth century, the Khalduns lived in Seville in Muslim Andalusia. When it became clear that Seville was about to fall to the Christian *reconquista*, they removed themselves and their wealth from Andalusia to the Maghreb, a region of northwest Africa (modern Morocco, Algeria, and Tunisia). Born into extraordinary privilege, Ibn Khaldun led a life of high drama, amazing intellectual creativity, and swashbuckling adventure. During the second half of the 1300s, the Maghreb region was constantly in turmoil resulting from the struggle for supremacy between two dynasties, the Marinids and the Hafsids. Ibn Khaldun's career mirrored the unsettled times he lived in. He was entertained by kings in palaces and by rats in dungeon cells. Personal misfortune continued to dog him. In the winter of 1384, Ibn Khaldun's wife and five daughters, sailing from Tunis to join him in Cairo, were lost in a shipwreck. But Ibn Khaldun was not a man to resign himself to despair.

As a young scion of the prominent family, Ibn Khaldun was expected to enter the government service, which he did at the age of 20. However, instead of working for the ruler of his native Tunis, he moved to Fez and took up service with Sultan Abu Inan, the head of the Marinid State of Morocco. Unfortunately, in 1357, Abu Inan became suspicious of Ibn Khaldun's loyalty and threw him into prison, from which he was freed only a year and half later, when Abu Inan died. Ibn Khaldun served the next Marinid sultan for a while, and then emigrated to Granada, which was the last Muslim principality left in Spain at that time. In 1364, he was put in charge of the diplomatic mission sent to Pedro the Cruel of Castile. The king was so impressed with the Tunisian that he offered to take Ibn Khaldun in his service and restore his ancestral property in Seville, but the philosopher turned him down. In 1365, Ibn Khaldun is back in the Maghreb, serving as prime minister in the court of Abu Abdallah, the new Hafsid ruler of Bougie. The next decade North Africa was torn apart as a result of conflict between the Marinids and Hafsids, and it is a miracle that Ibn Khaldun survived. When Abu Abdallah fell, Ibn Khaldun raised a large force of the desert Arabs and entered the service of the sultan of Tlemcen. However, a few years later, Tlemcen was also conquered by the Marinids, and Ibn Khaldun was captured by the forces of the new Marinid Sultan Abd-al-Aziz. Fortunately, this time he spent only a night in captivity, and was allowed to retire to a monastery.

After many further vicissitudes and turns of fortune, Ibn Khaldun left the Maghreb on pilgrimage to Mecca. By that time, his fame as a scholar was widespread, so when he was passing through Cairo, the ruler of Egypt offered him a chief justice position, which Ibn Khaldun accepted. He lived most of the rest of his life in Cairo, except for some travel to complete the Hajj, and trips to Jerusalem and other cities in Palestine and Syria. In 1400, he was in Damascus when the city was placed under siege by the Central Asian empire builder Timur (Tamerlane). Timur was eager to meet with Ibn Khaldun, the famous thinker who understood the inner workings of societies. Ibn Khaldun was soon lowered in a large basket from the wall of the besieged city. He spent seven weeks in Timur's camp, where he gave a series of lectures on the theory of history to the famous tyrant.

THE SOUTHERN FRONTIER OF THE Roman Empire extended from the province of Mauritania Tingitana (modern Morocco) in the west to Palestine and Syria in the east. The location of this frontier was determined almost entirely by environmental influences. Nonirrigated agriculture in North Africa and the Arabian Peninsula requires a minimum of 25 centimeters (10 inches) of rain annually, and the Roman frontier followed almost exactly the transitional line between areas where agriculture is possible and the desert. The only exception to this rule was Egypt, where the Roman territory cut deep into the desert thanks to the Nile.

The "barbarian" people south of the frontier were the Berbers of North Africa and the Arabs of the Middle East. Incidentally, the origin of the word *Berber* is the same as *barbarian* (because to the Greeks and Romans, the incomprehensible languages of these aliens sounded like "bar-bar-bar"). During the post-Roman period, these *Bedouins* (from Arabic "desert dwellers") built a number of empires, of which the most spectacular was, without any doubt, the caliphate of the Arabs. The Berbers provided the manpower for the Islamic conquest of Spain, and also founded the Fatimid, Almoravid, and Almohad empires, as well as a host of smaller states.

Chapter 3 examined agrarian societies that derived their subsistence from growing crops. But what if wealth comes not from a field of wheat, but from a factory, or a herd of camels? How does the economic infrastructure influence the character of empire building? The best authority to ask regarding the nomadic pastoralist life is Ibn Khaldun, a practical politician and a theoretical sociologist, the author of a remarkable theory of group solidarity that explained the rise and fall of states.

The concept of collective solidarity, or *asabiya* in Arabic, was Ibn Khaldun's most important contribution to our understanding of human history. The theory is described in his monumental *The Muqaddimah: An Introduction to History*. Asabiya of a group is the ability of its members to stick together, to cooperate; it allows a group to protect itself against the enemies, and to impose its will on others. A group with high asabiya will generally win when pitched against a group of lesser asabiya. Moreover, "royal authority and general dynastic power are attained only through a group and asabiya. This is because aggressive and defensive strength is obtained only through ... mutual affection and willingness to fight and die for each other." In other words, a state can be organized only around a core group with high asabiya. By acting in a solidary fashion, the members of the core group impose their collective will on other constituents of the state and thus prevent the state from falling apart.

But it is not enough to identify group solidarity as the main factor responsible for the strength of the state. Why do some groups have it in abundance, whereas others do not? Ibn Khaldun's theory provides an explanation. It focuses specifically on the situation in the Maghreb, but its genius lies in how well it translates across time and space.

As a result of the distribution of rainfall, which was discussed previously, the Maghreb is divided by an environmental frontier into two zones. In the north, there is a band of territory, running along the Mediterranean shore, where rain is sufficient for agriculture. This zone (which was part of the Roman Empire) is where all cities and towns of North Africa are found. It was also where all states and empires were located. Ibn Khaldun referred to it as "civilization." South of the civilization zone lies the semi-desert and desert inhabited by the Bedouin tribes. This distinction between the "civilized" (we would now say urbanized) and Bedouin societies is absolutely crucial for the theory of Ibn Khaldun.

In the desert, each tribe can rely only on itself for survival against the harsh environment and depredations of other tribes. Ibn Khaldun stressed that "only tribes held together by asabiya can live in the desert." A kind of natural-selection mechanism operates in the desert that eliminates any tribe that lacks internal solidarity. By contrast, cities are defended by walls against the external enemies, and internal peace is imposed by the state. As a result, unlike in the desert, no constant struggle occurs for survival within the civilization zone that would nurture and maintain high asabiya.

Furthermore, as discussed in Chapter 2, the life of a nomadic pastoralist provides a much better martial training. A shoe maker in the city who spends hours every day hunched over his work will make a lousy warrior—weak, clumsy, and nearsighted. Therefore, any Bedouin is a better warrior than your average city slicker. When you add to this individual superiority the high group solidarity of the desert dwellers, their military advantage becomes overwhelming.

The civilization zone is divided into states and empires, which are, in any case, normally quite good at defending themselves against nonstate societies. For one thing, the civilization supports much greater population densities than the desert, so the civilized armies tend to be larger than the "barbarian" ones. Civilizations also have technological advantages, such as fortifications, catapults, better arms, and armor. As long as the state keeps its internal cohesion, it is capable of defending itself against the nomads. (There are exceptions—nobody could stand against the Mongols of Chinggis Khan.) When the state loses its unity and falls into civil strife, however, it immediately becomes easy prey for Bedouins.

Ibn Khaldun noticed that political dynamics in the Maghreb tend to move in cycles. When a state in the civilization zone falls into internal strife, it becomes vulnerable to conquest from the desert. Sooner or later, a coalition of Bedouin tribes is organized around one group with a particularly high asabiya. When this coalition conquers the civilization zone, it founds a new state there. The leading group establishes the ruling dynasty, while other Bedouins become the ruling class—the new aristocracy.

The members of the conquering generation and even their children preserve their desert ways. They keep their military skills honed, and, most importantly, their group solidarity high. As generations succeed generations, however, the conditions of the civilized life begin to erode the high asabiya of the former Bedouins. Generally speaking, by the fourth generation the descendants of the founders become indistinguishable from their city-dweller subjects. At this point, the dynasty goes into a permanent decline. It can persist in the "degenerate" state for a few more generations, but sooner or later another Bedouin coalition arises in the desert, and the cycle repeats itself. The members of the degenerated dynasty are dispossessed of their wealth, some killed, and others driven into exile.

An important element of Ibn Khaldun's theory is the corrosive effect of "luxury" on group solidarity. He argues that as the former tribesmen forget the rude ways of the desert, and become accustomed to the new luxurious life, they somehow become "enervated." This aspect is actually the weakest component of the theory. It is not clear at all why "luxury" should be detrimental to the military effectiveness of a group. Such "luxurious" habits as good food, sound shelter from the elements, and bathing should promote good health, and thus have a positive effect on military prowess. Even obvious "excesses," such as immoderate drinking and feasting, did not seem to impair the military effectiveness of, for example, barbarian Franks or the later Vikings. On the contrary, collective feasting creates the feeling of camaraderie that strengthens group cohesion. Ancient writers frequently inveighed against the supposedly enervating effect of luxury. But it does not seem to be good sociology. Interestingly, Ibn Khaldun, who also devotes a lot of space to this theme, nevertheless hedges his message. He says, "luxury will at first give additional strength to a dynasty. The reason for this is that a tribe that has acquired royal authority and luxury is prolific and produces many children, so that the community grows. Thus, the group grows. Furthermore, a great number of clients and followers is acquired. The new generation grows up in a climate of prosperity and luxury." Luxury begins to play a negative role only "when the first and second generations are gone, and the dynasty starts to become senile." Ibn Khaldun's explanation of how the ruling dynasty loses its asabiya is weak, because he relies too much on inappropriate biological analogies: "Dynasties have a natural span like individuals." We need to do better to explain the process of social dissolution, but this is a large task, and I do not fully develop my explanation until Part II.

The last element of Ibn Khaldun's theory that will be useful to us is the role of religion. Ibn Khaldun points out that religion gives a dynasty another power in addition to that of asabiya. It "does away with mutual jealousy and envy among people who share in an asabiya." When people are united by religion, "nothing can withstand them, because their outlook is one and their object is one of common accord. They are willing to die for their objective." Although Ibn Khaldun does not say it directly, it seems that the religious feeling is a sort of asabiya, but one that can unite broader groups than tribal-level asabiya. This is a very important insight, especially for the Bedouin societies of North Africa and Arabia, where religion played a particularly important role in empire building.

The insights from Ibn Khaldun's theory can help us to understand better the history of societies on Rome's desert frontier during the first millennium A.D.

DURING THE FIRST SIX CENTURIES AFTER the birth of Christ, the geopolitical configuration of the Middle East stayed relatively stable, with the political landscape dominated by two huge empires. In the west, the Mediterranean littoral (roughly, modern Israel, Lebanon, and Syria) was part of the Roman Empire and then of its successor, the Byzantine Empire. Until the early third century, the territory east of the Euphrates belonged to the Parthians; after that date, to the successor state of Sassanian Persia. Between the two imperial frontiers was wedged a huge area of dry steppe and desert, which extends south into the Arabian Peninsula. The northern part of this arid zone is called the Syrian desert, but there is no physical barrier between it and the Arabian desert to the south. The people who inhabited this region then (and still do so now) were the Arabs. The main adaptation that allowed the Arabs to live in the desert was domestication of the camel and the invention of the camel riding saddle. Camels could survive and thrive in areas where sheep and goats could not. They provided their owners with milk, meat, leather, and wool. But their most important advantage over other domesticated animals was their ability to carry people and goods through waterless wastes of Syria and Arabia. The camel was the critical "technology" that allowed the Arabs to expand over the whole Syrian and Arabian deserts during the first millennium B.C.

Not all Arabs were nomadic pastoralists. Some made a living from long-distance trade. (Several lucrative caravan routes ran through the desert.) Others penetrated into the borderlands of the Roman and Persian empires, and switched to a semi-nomadic way of life, or even settled down to agriculture. (Agriculture was also practiced in the oases of the Arabian Peninsula.) Finally, a number of cities in the Fertile Crescent, such as Palmyra, Edessa, and Hira, were ruled by Arab dynasties that arose in the Ibn Khaldunian fashion.

Although sharing common language and culture, before Muhammad the Arabs were never politically unified. The desert was divided up among a multitude of tribes who continuously warred against each other. (Most of the warfare took the form of livestock raiding and counter-raiding.) The constant state of conflict served to keep tribal asabiya high, but also prevented the tribes from uniting into a powerful confederation. If left alone, the nomads would never unite, and the state of intertribal warfare could persist indefinitely. In fact, this is precisely what happened to Arabia after the Islamic conquest exploded the imperial frontiers away from it—the desert again fragmented into a multitude of warring tribes. During the first six centuries of the common era, however, the Bedouins were not left alone. Their society was powerfully molded by two imperial frontiers—the Roman-Byzantine in the northwest and the Parthian-Persian in the northeast (and southeast, when the Persians annexed southern Arabia). In addition, there was a third imperial power, the Ethiopian kingdom of Axum, which impinged on the Arabs during the sixth century when it conquered Yemen. In 570, the year when Muhammad was born, an Ethiopian army even made an unsuccessful attempt to conquer his hometown, Mecca. As a result, the Arabs were "squeezed" by empires from all directions.

Imperial pressures took many of the same forms that we saw on the Rhine frontier. For example, using diplomacy and generous subsidies, the Byzantines engineered the rise of a powerful tribal confederation, the Ghassanids, on their Palestinian frontier (in the area corresponding, roughly, to the modern Jordan and Syria). The Ghassanid Kingdom protected the Byzantine frontier from desert raiders, and provided mounted auxiliary troops for the Byzantine-Persian wars. But the side effect, just as happened in northwest Europe, was to introduce into Arabia the political techniques for putting together and holding together a supra-tribal organization. Similar developments took place along the Euphrates, where Persians encouraged the formation of the frontier Lakhmid state with the capital in Hira. Another imperial influence was the demand for luxury trade generated by the affluent civilized societies. Two products of southern Arabia in particular were much in demand, frankincense and myrrh. Profits from the caravan trade could be taxed, generating cash—"the sinews of state," as the ancient Greeks were fond of saying. The final ingredient in the geopolitical matrix surrounding Arabia was that each of the neighboring empires possessed its own brand of monotheistic religion: Christianity for the Byzantines and Ethiopians, and Zoroastrianism for the Persians. Within Arabia, the influence of Judaism was strong. Many Arabs in Syria converted to Nestorian Christianity, and some tribes practiced Judaism, although many Bedouins during Muhammad's time still followed polytheistic tribal cults.

Similar to the Germans, the pre-Islamic Arab tribes had two kinds of leaders, military and religious. Different noble lineages specialized in one or the other function, but usually not both. The chiefs that ruled the Ghassanid tribal confederation on the Byzantine frontier were one example of an aristocratic warrior lineage. On the other hand, the Quraysh (to whom the future prophet of Islam Muhammad belonged) were a clan of religious leaders associated with the holy pre-Islamic shrine of Mecca. For a leader to become a powerful unifying force that would enable his followers to found an empire, he had to concentrate all forms of power—religious, military, and economic—in his hands. Both the Germanic and Arabic society eventually developed such leaders under the influence of frontier conditions. However, whereas in Germania the evolution took the route of investing the military chiefs with sacral legitimacy, in Arabia it was the religious leaders who acquired military power. The endpoint was the same, but the route taken there was culture-specific.

While the evolutionary processes slowly changed the Arab society, thus creating the conditions for their eruption from Arabia during the seventh century, the triggering event occurred during the decades around A.D. 600. During the second half of the sixth century, both the Byzantine and the Sassanian empires fell prey to secular disintegrative tendencies. Their aristocracies broke into factions, each following their own pretender for the throne. The resulting civil wars weakened both empires. To make matters worse, each empire meddled in the civil wars of the rival, adding international conflict to internal war. The whole area between Constantinople, Alexandria, and Ctesiphon (the Sassanian capital) was convulsed in a series of wars. Armies plundered their ways back and forth and cities were sacked, sometimes repeatedly. Lesser states, such as the Ghassanids and the Lakhmids, also collapsed. Starting with the great epidemic of 540, the plague carried away at least a third of the agricultural and urban population of the area (but, as far as we know, the nomadic Arabs largely escaped its effects).

The chaotic conditions in the Middle East aided the rise of Islam in two ways. First, there was no powerful empire in the vicinity, practicing a forward frontier strategy, that would be able to squash the early Islamic movement led by Muhammad when it was still small and weak. A century before, it would have been easy for the Byzantines to send their clients Ghassanids to deal with the new dangerous cult in Medina. Although the Arabian Peninsula is huge, camel transport allowed desert armies to strike across distances of hundreds of miles. During their heyday, the Ghassanids conducted successful military operations against powerful tribes located 500 miles or more away. Second, when people are exposed to years and decades of chaos, they begin to yearn for stability. Any message of hope, even if it only offers a better afterlife, becomes attractive. Monotheistic religions effectively address that deeply seated human need. The new monotheistic religion that was preached by Muhammad offered hope for this world also, so it is no surprise Muhammad was able to unify the tribes and stop their internecine fighting.

Islam seems to be a peculiarly attractive religion to societies that had recently experienced chaos and calamity. This quality of Islam continues to aid its spread even today. Ten years after experiencing the horror of civil war and genocide, many Rwandans are turning to Islam. During the decade since 1995, the number of mosques in Rwanda doubled to 500, and the existing mosques cannot accommodate all those who want to pray—many faithful have to spread their prayer mats on the dirt outside the mosques. It is estimated that 15 percent of the population now practices Islam.

It is a little known fact that Muhammad was just one (albeit the most successful) of at least half a dozen monotheistic prophets active in Arabia in the early seventh century. Naturally, the other five religious leaders are now considered "false prophets," because they lost out to Islam. But such a sudden appearance of comparable religious movements all over Arabia is indicative of sociopolitical conditions that were ripe for something such as Islam to happen.

As mentioned previously, Muhammad was a member of the tribe of Quraysh, who tended the polytheistic shrine in Mecca. During the sixth century, Mecca gradually became the center of the west-Arabian religio-political association. The Arab tribes journeyed to Mecca during truce months to worship at the shrine, and to conduct various kinds of business, such as trade deals or resolution of blood feuds. Mecca offered a neutral place where even enemies could meet without worrying about a sudden attack. As a result, Mecca became an important trading nexus, and the Quraysh derived a large part of their livelihood from trade. Note that there was not enough water at Mecca for agriculture.

We know the main events of Muhammad's life—divine revelation (in A.D. 610), emigration to Medina (622), the struggle with the Meccans and their capitulation (630), and the subjugation of the tribes of the Arabian peninsula just before Muhammad's death (632). But how did he manage to forge the tribes into an Islamic "meta-tribe"? The answer appears to lie in the nature of Muhammad's religious message. The old polytheistic religion of the Arabs was an integrative force only at the level of a tribe, but could not serve as the basis for a confederation of all tribes. Accepting the religion of any particular tribe would mean for the rest to subjugate them-selves to the aristocracy of the lucky tribe, something that freedom-loving nomads were extremely reluctant to do. Not that the tribesmen were particularly interested in proselytizing their brand of religion. After all, one of the main functions that it served was to distinguish "us" from "them." Islam, by contrast, was a new, monotheistic, and proselytizing religion. Converting to Islam meant submitting to God, rather than any particular earthly ruler. In fact, most flavors of Islam to this day retain their aversion to "kings." Because Islam was a monotheistic religion, submitting to a single God automatically united all Muslims into a single state with a single army. Finally, Islam welcomed converts from all tribes (and even from non-Arabs). It did not matter which tribe the convert belonged to, all were now brothers under a universal, unique God. An important part of Muhammad's message was that all Muslims belonged to one closely knit community, the *umma*. No one was excluded from the umma for reasons of social status or tribal origin. The universality of Islam marked a radical break with traditions of pre-Islamic pagan cults, and was crucial to its ultimate success.

The umma concept had a powerful grip on individual believers. Leaving umma was much more difficult than abandoning a tribal confederation put together for whatever materialistic reasons. Breaking with the Muslim community was apostasy. Not only was a Muslim required to kill an apostate, but the apostate also damned his or her very soul to burn in hell.

Thus, Muhammad was able to take a multitude of tribes, each internally solidary but unable to work together, and forge them into a metatribe, the umma. In the process, the former tribesmen, now Muslims, transferred their identity and allegiance to the new supra-tribal level of political organization. The new cohesion enabled the Muslims to prevail over their enemies. Between 622 and 630, when Muhammad was the ruler of only a small oasis community of Medina, the Muslims were much weaker than their chief enemies, the Meccans. For example, at the battle of the Trench (627), 10,000 Meccan troops confronted 3,000 Muslims. Muslims were also constantly suffering from the shortage of military equipment such as armor, and particularly horses for cavalry. Nevertheless, they prevailed, and in 630 Mecca capitulated and was annexed to Muhammad's incipient Islamic Empire. The Meccans lost because they confronted Muhammad with the typical loose tribal federation, made up of tribesmen with intense loyalty only to their own clan. As a result, a member tribe could decide not to join battle at a critical juncture, or even be bought over to the other side. By contrast, for Muslims tribal origin did not matter. Of paramount importance was belonging to the single Islamic commune, the umma. Toward the end of Muhammad's career, he could put a tribal cavalry unit under the command of a lieutenant, who was not a member of the tribe he commanded—something that was unthinkable in a traditional tribal confederation.

The remarkable discipline of the new Islamic army is illustrated by the last episode in the struggle between the Muslims and the Meccans. In 630, Muhammad unexpectedly appeared in front of Mecca with a large army. It was clear to the Meccans that they had a very little chance of resisting the Prophet. They attempted to negotiate, but Muhammad only promised the envoys that all those who stayed within their houses would be spared. On the next day, Muhammad's troops entered Mecca in four columns from all directions simultaneously. Only one column encountered resistance from some die-hard anti-Muhammad forces, which was speedily suppressed. Not a single house was broken into, and no Meccan was assaulted. Somebody stole the silver necklace of the sister of Abu Bakr (who later was to become the first caliph), but this happened because she left the house with her father to watch Muhammad's entrance into Mecca. No pillage occurred. Muhammad's order against entering Meccan houses was carried out to the letter. This degree of obedience is particularly remarkable given the origins of Muhammad's army—robbing strangers was always part of the Bedouin's lifestyle.

DURING THE LAST TWO YEARS OF his life (630–632), Muhammad expanded his political influence throughout Arabia. When Muhammad died, however, many Arab tribes rebelled against his successor, the first caliph Abu Bakr (in Arabic *khalifa* means "successor"). On his accession in 632, Abu Bakr could count on perhaps 6,000 committed Muslim troops. Although the tribal troops vastly outnumbered the Muslims, they were fragmented, and Abu Bakr was able to rapidly subdue all rebels. Such a quick success was, of course, taken as another proof that the new faith was genuine. However, the unification of the Arabian Peninsula created some unanticipated problems.

As far as we know, Abu Bakr originally intended only to unify all Arabs within the new faith, and did not plan any conquests of the great empires to the west and east. Therefore, he sent two armies to Syria and Iraq to spread Islam to the Arab communities inhabiting the frontier lands of the Byzantine and Persian empires. However, after all of the Arabs were brought within the Islamic community, they could no longer attack each other, and their military energies had to be directed elsewhere. Furthermore, the better pickings were to be found in not robbing other nomads, but in attacking the wealthy Byzantine and Persian cities. Thus, the Islamic unification of Arabia almost necessarily, without any intervention of human purpose, had to lead to an attempt at world conquest. The logic of the situation was such that the Arabs had to either conquer a great empire, or fragment back into the multitude of warring tribes. Speaking in terms of nonlinear dynamics, the unification of Arabia only was an unstable cusp from which the trajectory had to go either in one or the other direction.

The army sent to convert the Arabs of Iraq to Islam was led by Khalid ibn al-Walid, one of the best early Islamic military leaders, later called "the sword of Allah." He started from Medina in 633 with 2,000 troops. As he was traveling toward Iraq, however, his army was gradually increasing by absorbing tribal Bedouins, who accepted Islam. One of the participants of the conquest of Ubullah in southern Iraq later recounted: "Khalid ibn al-Walid with his cavalry attacked us, but we told him, 'We are Muslims!' So he left us in peace, and we went with him to Ubullah and conquered it." By the time Khalid reached Iraq, his army already had 10,000 warriors. The Persian governor of the Lower Euphrates, worried by the appearance of this great army, gathered his troops and advanced into the desert to bar Khalid's way. According to later chroniclers, Khalid sent a message to the Persians offering them to either become Muslim, or to keep their faith and pay tribute. "If not, blame yourself. I lead those who love death as you love life."

Khalid, traveling through waterless desert, had to take one of two routes, either going by the well of Al Casima, or by the well of Al Khafir. The Persian commander first blocked Khalid's route at Al Casima. Khalid, therefore, changed the direction and went to Al Khafir instead. The experienced Persian commander learned about this maneuver and got to

Al Khafir first. Khalid's troops were in desperate straits—their horses were tired and, if they were not given water soon, they would perish. Throwing caution to the winds, Khalid left behind all of his baggage, dismounted his troops, and advanced against the enemy on foot. Fortunately for the Arabs, it rained, which allowed them to slake their thirst (and was taken as sign that Allah was with them). The resulting battle was extremely fierce, with the Arabs fighting as men who had nothing to lose. When Khalid killed their commander, the Persians ran, leaving all their baggage behind.

It is remarkable how many parallels there are between this battle and the battle of Sibir. A band of desperate warriors deep in the enemy territory prevails against overwhelming odds. But the similarities between Khalid's Arabs and Ermak's Cossacks run even deeper. Both groups were the product of life on a fault-line frontier and, as a result, enjoyed a preponderance of asabiya over their enemies. A crucial component of their asabiyas, the potent "glue" that made each group highly cohesive, was a powerful monotheistic religion.

THE SPECTACULAR ARABIC CONQUESTS OF the seventh century continue to cause wonder. Many explanations have been offered, but most of them do not make sense. The Arabs did not have a numeric or technological advantage over their adversaries; in fact, quite the reverse. The conquest of Byzantine Syria was accomplished with only about 24,000 men, whereas the Byzantine Empire had 10 times as many soldiers. The only technological advantage that the Arabs had was the camel, which gave them enhanced mobility in desert or semi-desert environments. Camels were used primarily as transportation; prior to the battle, the Arabs dismounted and then fought on foot. Early Islamic armies also suffered from the lack of horses. In fact, at the battle of Uhud (625), Muhammad had no cavalry of his own. Two years later, he had only 30 horsemen. The problem was that under arid conditions of the Arabian Peninsula, keeping and breeding horses was very expensive, and only wealthy people could afford it. The Arabs encountered similar problems in attempting to find enough armor. Only a fraction of warriors possessed chain mail. Early victories over the Byzantines and Sassanians were not accomplished by employing cavalry, either as mounted archers or by charging, as one might think. Instead, the

Arabs fought on foot. The single advantage that the Arabs had was their fighting spirit and willingness to fight to the death.

The Arabs defeated the Byzantines and the Persians because the Arab asabiya was much greater than the asabiya of their opponents. Centuries of life squeezed between two imperial frontiers changed the Arab society in ways that made it possible for Muhammad to forge them into a unified powerful entity. By contrast, the Byzantine and Persian empires were going through decentralization phases right at the time when Muhammad was unifying the Arab tribes. For example, between 630 and 633, Persia saw seven emperors (shah-in-shahs) and one empress, none of whom managed to survive for more than half a year, and one just a few days. Success in war is a result of relative strengths of asabiyas of the opponents. A nation with high collective solidarity can lose many battles and still prevail in the end. This is what happened to the Romans during the Hannibalic wars (discussed in Chapter 6). Hannibal smashed one Roman army after another, but Rome always raised a new one. Romans lost one third of their population before they ground Hannibal up and won the war. By contrast, the Byzantines lost one major battle, and the whole of Palestine and Syria fell before the Arabs. Similarly, it took only one major defeat at Qadisiyya (637) for the Persians to surrender their capital, Ctesiphon, and all of Iraq to the Arabs.

THE WILLINGNESS TO SACRIFICE LIFE in the name of the faith has been one of the enduring strands in the history of Islam. One of the best-known examples is the Hashishim sect, which existed from the eighth century until its suppression by the Mongols. The name Hashishim ("Assassins"), actually was what their enemies called them, because they allegedly used drugs to indoctrinate sect members. Their own name for themselves was *fedayeen*, which in Arabic means "one who is ready to sacrifice life for the cause." The Hashishim were opposed to the Abbasid caliphs, whom they thought to be impious usurpers. They conducted a campaign of assassination directed mainly against the Sunni Muslim rulers (but they also murdered at least one crusader king in Jerusalem). Because the Hashishim disdained the use of poison or long-range weapons, and relied on the dagger, assassination attempts usually ended in the death of the assassin; these were suicide missions. The parallels with the suicide bombings happening in the Middle East today are palpable. Earlier I cited the words of Khalid ibn al-Walid, "I lead those who love death as you love life." Fourteen centuries later, perpetrators of terrorist acts in Palestine, Madrid, Moscow, and Baghdad have used precisely the same words.

THE LAST TWO CHAPTERS SURVEYED all large states within a defined area (Europe and the Mediterranean) during a defined period of time (the first millennium A.D.). We found that the empirical generalization, proposed in Chapter 2, that future empires are born in areas where the frontiers of the empires of yore coincide with civilizational fault lines is supported by empirical evidence. In fact, the hypothesis works very well—on the European frontier of Rome, where the situation is particularly clear-cut, *all* large states originated within a narrow band of the frontier zone (that is, from less than 7 percent of the total of the area of Europe). *No* large states were born either in the interior of the Roman Empire, or in the nonimperial hinterland of northern and eastern Europe. We obtain the same result when we examine the southern—desert—frontier. Clearly such a striking pattern could not happen by chance alone.

Here then a powerful general principle of world history is uncovered: A close connection exists between fault-line frontiers and new, expansionist states. However, what about the specific mechanism that I proposed to account for this empirical generalization—the role of frontier in nurturing high degree of cooperation, or asabiya, to use Ibn Khaldun's term? This explanation runs counter to the "received wisdom" of social science in the twentieth century, when the main current was to downplay the importance of cooperation and altruism while putting on the pedestal self-interested, "rational" motives of behavior. Influential thinkers, such as Carrol Quigley in his *The Evolution of Civilizations: An Introduction to Historical Analysis*, or Joseph Tainter in *The Collapse of Complex Societies*, contemptuously dismissed theories, such as Ibn Khaldun's, as "the softening of the fiber" or "mystical" explanations. The majority of social scientists perceived cooperation and collective solidarity as somehow "soft" and unscientific, while (and this was particularly true for the economists) extolling the virtues of the "rational-choice theory" that explained the collective behaviors of human masses by assuming that all people behave in a purely self-interested manner.

If the prevailing wisdom is correct, and theories explaining historical processes by postulating an important role for solidarity and cooperation are without scientific merit, we need to look for the explanation of the relationship between frontiers and empires elsewhere. However, the prevailing paradigm has been recently challenged in such a vigorous way that it is crumbling right before our eyes. We are in the process of a major scientific revolution, which will ensure that the social science of the twenty-first century will differ significantly from that of the last century. The next chapter reviews some of these recent developments that allow us finally to put cooperation on a firm scientific basis.

Chapter 5

The Myth of Self-Interest

And the Science of Cooperation

On June 28, 1914, in Sarajevo, Bosnia, the Serbian nationalist Gavrilo Princip rushed to a car in which sat Archduke Franz Ferdinand, heir to the Austro-Hungarian throne, and his wife, Countess Sophie. Princip shot two times, hitting Sophie in the stomach and Franz Ferdinand in the neck. Both died shortly thereafter of their wounds. After accomplishing his mission, Princip swallowed a capsule of cyanide, but the poison was defective and only made him vomit. He then tried to shoot himself with his gun, but it was wrestled from his hand. Princip was tried, sentenced to a life in prison (he was too young for the death penalty), and died four years later in prison from tuberculosis.

One month after the assassination of Franz Ferdinand, and using it as a pretext, Austria-Hungary declared war on Serbia. Russia, who was tied by a defensive treaty to Serbia, began mobilizing, which was treated as a hostile act by Germany. On August 1, Germany declared war on Russia, which dragged into the war Russian allies France and England. World War I had begun.

We know of the carnage and social trauma that ensued, but little is usually made of how overwhelmingly the European populace supported its various governments' decisions to go to war. Patriotic crowds demonstrated for war in Vienna, Berlin, and London. More tellingly, all over Europe hundreds of thousands volunteered for the army. In the British Empire, for example, there was no need to introduce conscription until 1916. Three hundred thousand men enlisted during the first month of the war, and more than 450,000 in the next month. Even on the other side of the world, Australians rode for days to get to towns where they could enlist and begin the long voyage to Europe.

By the end of war, more than 8.5 million were dead from bullet, artillery shell, poison gas, or trench sickness. In France, every sixth soldier mobilized for war was killed. More than half were wounded. Only one soldier in three escaped the meat grinder unscathed in body (if not in soul).

The willingness of the British, the French, and the Germans to fight for their country is only one of the many striking examples of the human capacity to sacrifice self-interest for the sake of a very broad common good. Less dramatically, we pay taxes, take time to vote, and participate in unions and demonstrations. On a darker side, the willingness of Gavrilo Princip to murder Franz Ferdinand even at the expense of his life, or the eagerness with which Palestinian suicide bombers sacrifice themselves to inflict horror on the Israelis, falls into the same category. The "common good" does not refer to the whole humanity, but only to a part of it, the group for which the sacrifice is made, be it the Serbian, Palestinian, or English nations.

The capacity to sacrifice self-interest for the sake of common good is the necessary condition for cooperation. Without it, concerted collective action is impossible, as I have stressed in the previous chapters. To ancient and medieval thinkers such as Aristotle, Thomas Aquinas, and, above all, Ibn Khaldun, it was obvious that it was cooperation that provided the basis of social life. Beginning in the early modern period, however, this certainty was gradually abandoned by most influential social thinkers. By the end of the twentieth century, the "rational-choice theory," which postulated that people behave in entirely self-interested manner, became the dominant paradigm in the social sciences. Any theories that invoked cooperation as moving force of history were ridiculed as unscientific. If people are motivated entirely by self-interest, the only forces that matter are rewards and punishments.

To trace the development of this shift of paradigms, we might begin with the life and work of that brilliant Florentine political philosopher and statesman Niccolo Machiavelli (1469–1527). In his best work, *The Prince*, Machiavelli famously asked whether for a ruler "it is better to be loved than feared, or the reverse. The answer is, of course, that it would be best to be both loved and feared. But since the two rarely come together, anyone compelled to choose will find greater security in being feared than in being loved. For this can be said about the generality of men: that they are ungrateful, fickle, dissembling, anxious to flee danger, and covetous of gain. So long as you promote their advantage, they are all yours, as I said before, and will offer you their blood, their goods, their lives, and their children when the need for these is remote. When the need arises, however, they will turn against you. The prince who bases his security upon their word, lacking other provision, is doomed ... Men are less concerned about offending someone they have cause to love than someone they have cause to fear. Love endures by a bond which men, being scoundrels, may break whenever it serves their advantage to do so; but fear is supported by the dread of pain, which is ever present."

Machiavelli's ideas were completely at odds with the prevailing political ideology, and his contemporaries rejected them with horror. A much more conventional wisdom was uttered by the French king Louis IX (1226–70) before his death. When he fell ill, he said to his son and heir, "Fair son, I pray that you make yourself beloved of your people; for truly I would rather that a Scot should come from Scotland and govern the kingdom loyally and well than that you should govern it ill." The people of his time clearly agreed with this sentiment, and Louis was canonized in 1297, but from the perspective of our cynical age, his words sound hopelessly naïve as opposed to the harsh but seamlessly argued case put forward by Machiavelli. On the other hand, although St. Louis was no great shakes as a political thinker, he was a remarkably successful practical politician. Despite some notable setbacks, such as the disastrous crusade in Egypt (1248–50), during his long reign France became the hegemonic power of Europe, famous for the quality (and quantity) of its fighting men, the learning of its university, and the beauty of its Gothic cathedrals. The reign of St. Louis was the golden age of medieval France.

By contrast, Machiavelli was ultimately a failure as politician. He served as secretary to the Second Chancery of the Signoria, and was one of the most trusted associates of Pier Soderini, *gonfalonier* of the republic (the chief magistrate of Florence). Machiavelli's public career spanned 14 years, during which time he represented the republic on several diplomatic missions. He played an important role in the successful subjugation of Pisa by the Florentines in 1509. However, in 1512, the Spanish troops attacked the fortified town of Prato, which guarded the northern approaches to Florence. After only a brief struggle the Florentine militia, recruited by Machiavelli, broke and ran away. Florence surrendered without further resistance, and the Spanish installed the new government headed by the

Medici, who had been chased away from Florence 18 years earlier. Soderini was forced to resign and went into exile, and Machiavelli was dismissed from his post and banished. He withdrew to a small farm that his father left him, and there wrote the book that made him famous. *The Prince* (1513) was addressed to Lorenzo the Magnificent de Medici, and Machiavelli's stated desire was to be reinstated in the government. His plea, however, remained unanswered, and he was forced to rusticate for the rest of his life.

The failure of Machiavelli's political career does not refute his logic. Irrespective of the political success he found in his own life, the truth of any logical construction, no matter how finely reasoned, is only as good as the validity of the premises on which the argument is based. The main premise of the argument in *The Prince* is that all people behave all the time in a completely self-interested manner—they are motivated solely by the desire for gain and fear of punishment. Is this right?

Although the "self-interest axiom" was vehemently rejected by Machiavelli's contemporaries, as the modern period unfolded it gradually gained ground in the thinking of European philosophers, economists, and other social scientists. In *Leviathan*, Thomas Hobbes (1588–1679) assumed that in the "state of nature"—in the absence of the state keeping order—society would fall apart and degenerate into the war of all against all. A century later, the great Scottish philosopher David Hume (1711–76) wrote, "Political writers established it as a maxim, that, in contriving any system of government ... every man ought to be supposed to be a *knave* and to have no other end, in all his actions, than his private interest." And this sad truth (that all are knaves) is perhaps not so sad after all—it may even be good for the society as a whole. At least so argued Bernard Mandeville (1670–1713) in *The Fable of the Bees: Private Vices, Publick Benefits*: "Thus every Part was full of Vice, yet the whole Mass a Paradise." This *does* sound familiar. Wasn't it the motto of the exuberant 1980s and 1990s—"greed is good"?

Back in the eighteenth century, the ideas of Mandeville (as those of Machiavelli before him) were still met with great hostility by the public. Mandeville's book was even convicted as "a nuisance" by the grand jury of Middlesex in 1723. By the end of the century, however, the concept of

"Private Vices, Publick Benefits" became a solid part of scientific mainstream, largely due to the work of Adam Smith (1723–90). In his masterpiece *The Wealth of Nations*, Smith wrote, "It is not from the benevolence of the butcher, or the baker that we expect our dinner, but from their regard to their own interest." The contribution for which Smith is best known is his "invisible hand" argument. "Every individual necessarily labors to render the annual revenue of the society as great as he can. He generally neither intends to promote the public interest, nor knows how much he is promoting it ... He intends only his own gain, and he is in this, as in many other cases, led by an invisible hand to promote an end which was no part of his intention. Nor is it always the worse for society that it was no part of his intention. By pursuing his own interest he frequently promotes that of the society more effectually than when he really intends to promote it."

During the twentieth century, the ideas of Mandeville, Smith, and many others have been developed and systematized into what is now known as "the theory of rational choice." The core of the theory is the postulate that people—"agents"—behave in such a way as to maximize their "utility function." In principle, the utility function could be almost anything, but in practice almost all applications of the theory in the mainstream economics equate utility with material self-interest. In the most basic version, the utility is simply the dollar amount that an agent expects to get as a result of a certain action. The agent then should perform the action that yields the greatest payoff—this is what "maximizing utility" means. Agents that behave in ways that maximize their utility functions are "rational."

The premise that all people are exclusively pursuing their self-interest is a parsimonious assumption with truly astonishing implications. It turns out that the price of a loaf of bread or a used Ford, the salary of a trained nurse, the interest you have to pay on your mortgage, and even divorce rates, or how many people want to get college education—a broad variety of economic and social phenomena can be adequately explained by the rational choice theory. Scientists in all disciplines prize theories that explain a large variety of facts by making the smallest possible number of assumptions, and the theory of rational choice excels at it.

There is, however, one area where the rational choice theory fails utterly—in explaining why people cooperate. Take volunteering for the army when your country is attacked. The cost—the risk of injury or death—is substantial. The benefit—preventing the defeat that might entail paying war reparations, being evicted from your home, enslaved, or even killed—is also substantial. However, the cost of enlisting you bear directly, whereas the benefit is shared equally among everybody (what economists call the public good). Your participation, or not, in the army of millions is not going to make any appreciable difference to the outcome of the war. By failing to join the army, you will reap all the benefits of victory without bearing any of the costs. According to the rational choice theory, this is precisely what a rational agent should do. Of course, if everybody behaves in this rational manner, nobody will volunteer, and the invaders will win. If nobody volunteers, however, you have even more reason not to enlist—a one-person army is certainly going to be defeated. In other words, whatever others do, it is in your interest not to enlist (to "defect"). In a society of rational agents, everybody will defect, with the end result that collective action will always fail. The economist Mancur Olson called this logical deduction the "collective-action problem."

What about forcing people to cooperate? For example, we might establish firing squads that would go to towns and villages and shoot everybody who fails to volunteer. When faced with a choice of being shot here and now, or joining the army and taking one's chances, the rational agent would of course "volunteer." But who will constitute the enforcement squads? Certainly not rational agents. Participation in the enforcement squad is personally costly (you might get killed by rioting draft evaders), whereas the benefit (getting an army together and resisting the invaders) is again spread evenly among all. In other words, the same logic applies as with enlisting in the army in the first place. (In the technical jargon, this is known as the "second-order collective-action problem.") Perhaps we should punish those who do not join punishment detail? This is the suggestion of the famous graffiti in Boston scribbled by an opponent of Jay's Treaty in 1795: "Damn John Jay! Damn everyone who won't damn John Jay!! Damn everyone that won't put lights in his windows and sit up all night damning John Jay!!!" But no, forcing self-interested people to join enforcement squads also does not work—it leads to infinite regress, the third-order collective-action problem, then the forth-order one, and so on. It turns out that if everybody is a rational agent, it is impossible to bring about cooperation, even by force.

Rational self-interested agents cannot join together in a functioning society—this could be one of the fundamental theorems in sociology. In a world where all individuals behave strictly rationally, armies would run away at the first shot (or would not even get together in the first place). Nobody would vote or pay taxes. IRS agents would accept bribes not to prosecute tax evaders, and then pass some fraction of that to the members of the Senate overseeing committee, to buy *them* off. The courts would make verdicts in favor of whoever can pay more, or has more power to intimidate the judges and juries. The police would let criminals go in exchange for part of their loot. Actually, I am painting too rosy a picture—when all behave in a purely self-interested manner, there will be no IRS, courts, or police. There could only be a Hobbesian war of all against all.

AT THE SAME TIME THAT THE social scientists were perfecting the theory of rational choice, biologists were doing the same for the theory of evolution by natural selection, reaching very similar conclusions. The biological counterpart of utility is "fitness"—the expected number of viable offspring contributed by an organism to future generations. Just as rational agents maximize utility, evolution maximizes fitness: The genes that endow their carriers with greater ability to survive and reproduce increase in the population by virtue of the inevitable fact that they make more copies of themselves than their competitors.

The theory of evolution by natural selection is *the* most successful theory in biological sciences; in fact, modern biology is unimaginable without it. Yet for a long time, beginning with Charles Darwin himself, there was one puzzle that bothered evolutionary biologists—how could sociality evolve. Take the beehive. If you try to plunder its honey, you will be immediately confronted with an angrily buzzing swarm of bees. If you do not have protective clothing, you will be stung many times. A bee cannot withdraw its barbed sting from the skin of the victim, so the inevitable result of its attack is that the sting is torn out of its abdomen, and the bee dies. Thus, its defense of the hive is a true act of self-sacrifice, and herein lies the puzzle. Natural selection should weed out such "altruistic" genes—when you sacrifice yourself, you reduce your fitness to zero.

Sacrificial defense of the hive is a highly visible feature of bees, but in a quieter way they, and other social insects such as wasps, ants, and termites, do something even more puzzling—they give up their ability to reproduce. Only one individual produces offspring in a hive, the queen. All workers are sterile female. (The hive also produces male drones, but these do not participate in hive's functioning.) By giving up their ability to reproduce, worker bees reduce their fitness to zero. Again, on the face of it, such traits should be weeded out in the process of evolution.

The decisive breakthrough in our understanding of the evolution of sociality in nonhuman organisms came in 1964 when the British biologist William D. Hamilton advanced the theory of kin selection. We know that all bees in a hive are sisters and, due to a quirky genetic makeup of Hymenoptera (a group that includes wasps and ants), a bee shares three quarters of her genes with any of her hive mates. (In most other animals, including humans, the siblings share only 50 percent of genes with each other.) Now suppose that by a selfless act of hive defense a bee, at the expense of her life, will save enough honey on which to raise, say, four new sisters. An altruistic gene programming the bee for this behavior will be favored in the process of evolution, because by sacrificing one copy of itself in the defender bee it will produce three more copies in the new bees. Expending one copy to get three is an excellent deal from the point of view of natural selection, and such altruistic genes will spread in the population.

The second important strand in evolutionary research that has a bearing on human sociality is the idea of "reciprocal altruism" developed by the biologist Robert Trivers and the political scientist Robert Axelrod. Consider the following situation. Giovanni, a merchant of Venice, entrusts Lorenzo, the captain of a ship, with a certain sum of money. Lorenzo promises to travel to Cairo, purchase oriental spice there, and carry it back to Giovanni, who will sell it at a profit and pay Lorenzo a handsome fee. Suppose also that there is no way to write an enforceable contract (maybe the Venetian Republic has imposed a blockade on Cairo, and therefore the deal is illegal). If Lorenzo is a rational agent, he should accept the money from Giovanni, but upon return simply sell the spice himself and pocket the proceeds. But Giovanni is also a rational agent, so he will figure out that Lorenzo will cheat him, and therefore Giovanni will keep his money. No business is transacted, and both "agents" are the poorer for it. If the interaction between Giovanni and Lorenzo is a one-shot affair, the rational strategy for both is to "defect" (fail to cooperate). This failure to cooperate is really a special case of the collective action problem, but instead of a large group, just two individuals are involved.

If Giovanni and Lorenzo have a long-term relationship, however, in which they have an opportunity for repeated deals over the years, the logic of the situation is completely transformed. Now Giovanni can do much better by adopting the strategy known as "tit-for-tat": cooperate on the first round, and then do as the partner does. Accordingly, Giovanni entrusts Lorenzo with the money, and if Lorenzo fulfils his part, next year Giovanni does it again (and again, and again). If Lorenzo cheats Giovanni, Giovanni cuts him off and takes his business elsewhere. But Lorenzo will not cheat, because he calculates that he will derive more profit from many future deals than he would from cheating in a single one. Therefore, in the situation where interactions are repeated, a pair of rational agents can sustain cooperation via the mechanism of reciprocity. Many examples exist of reciprocal altruism among animals, such as the mutual grooming in monkeys. You scratch my back, I'll scratch yours.

The theories of kin selection and reciprocal altruism transformed our understanding of how animal societies evolved. But what about humans? In the 1970s, evolutionary biologists, of whom the most notable was Edward O. Wilson of Harvard University, flushed with success in understanding nonhuman sociality, decided to invade the traditional turf of social scientists and created the new science of "sociobiology." Richard Dawkins, the author of the wildly popular and influential book *The Selfish Gene* proclaimed in 1976: "We are survival machines—robot vehicles blindly programmed to preserve the selfish molecules known as genes." And it is true that kin selection, for example, helps us understand many human behaviors, such as nepotism. Kin selection and reciprocal altruism, undoubtedly, played an important role in the early phase of the evolution of human sociality. But even "primitive" human societies, like bands of hunters and gatherers, are not composed of relatives only. There are too many nonrelatives for kin selection to explain their behavior. When meat of a large animal is meticulously shared out among the band members, many recipients are very distantly related to the hunter who brought in the game, or even not related at all. At the other extreme of social complexity, when a Frenchman enlisted in the army in 1914, the vast majority of his 40 million countrymen and women had no blood relation to him whatsoever. Hamilton's insight does not really help us understand human "ultrasociality"—extensive cooperation among large numbers of unrelated individuals. Humans, among all living creatures, appear to be unique in the extent to which they cooperate with nonrelatives.

What about reciprocal altruism? Does this help us understand how we can solve the collective-action problem involving many people? Unfortunately not, as David Hume saw in the eighteenth century: "Two neighbors agree to drain a meadow, which they possess in common; because 'tis easy for them to know each other's mind; and each must perceive, that the immediate consequence of his failing in his part is abandoning of the whole project. But 'tis very difficult and indeed impossible, that a thousand persons shou'd agree in any such action; it being difficult for them to concert so complicated a design, and still more difficult for them to execute; while each seeks a pretext to free himself of the trouble and expense, and wou'd lay the whole burden on others." Modern research using formal mathematical models confirmed this intuition. When the group size becomes large enough, cooperation among rational agents unravels as free-loading becomes rampant. The collective-action problem strikes again.

In the final analysis, although they made valuable contributions to the debate, sociobiologists failed to explain human ultrasociality. In the last chapter of *The Selfish Gene*, Dawkins himself acknowledged, "Kin selection and selection in favor of reciprocal altruism may have acted on human genes to produce many of our basic psychological attributes and tendencies. These ideas are plausible as far as they go, but I find that they do not begin to square up to the formidable challenge of explaining culture, cultural evolution, and the immense differences between human cultures around the world."

This is where matters stood about a decade ago, during the mid-1990s. Mainstream theories, rational choice in social sciences and natural selection in biological sciences, could not explain cooperation among large numbers of unrelated individuals. According to the scientific understanding of the time, human ultrasociality was, we're sorry, impossible. Anomalies such as, for example, World War I were generally ignored. Some scientists tried to explain such instance of mass cooperation away. Perhaps enlisting in the army was an atavistic cooperative impulse, which evolved by means of kin selection when primordial humans lived in bands of relatives, and now was somehow triggered by nationalistic war propaganda. In other words, volunteers behaved in truly irrational fashion, both in the technical and common senses of the word; they were somehow "fooled." Or perhaps they were purposefully fooled—manipulated by the Machiavellian elites into spending their blood for the sake of the capitalists' profits.

Another group of scientists neither ignored nor tried to explain away such anomalies. Working in a truly interdisciplinary fashion, these biologists, anthropologists, sociologists, and economists finally cracked the puzzle of human ultrasociality. Not all of the loose ends have been tidied up yet, but the general outlines of the answer are becoming quite clear.

BEFORE WE TRY TO EXPLAIN SOMETHING, we need to assure ourselves that the phenomenon to be explained is real. The wave of volunteering at the beginning of World War I is a striking example of human capacity to sacrifice self-interest, but it is a single and highly complex event, open for diverse interpretations. The best way to proceed in science is through experiment—a study performed to verify or falsify a hypothesis while controlling or even manipulating external conditions. During the 1990s, several economists, most notably Ernst Fehr at the University of Zürich and his colleagues, decided to test the assumptions of the rational choice theory experimentally. This was a significant break within the scientific culture of economics, where most researchers had either constructed abstract and rigorous mathematical models or applied statistical methods to huge data sets on things such as inflation and economic growth.

One kind of experiment, which has now been conducted by a number of investigative teams, is called "the public goods game." Subjects are divided up in groups of four and given an initial endowment of $10 each.

The game is played in 10 rounds. Every round each participant can contribute any part, from 0 to 10 dollars, to the group project. The experimenters first double the total amount contributed to the common account, and then divide it up equally among all participants. Thus, for each dollar contributed to the common pot, a participant gains back only 50 cents. On the other hand, he or she also gains 50 cents for each dollar contributed by others. If all participants contribute the maximum amount ($10), they would end up with $20 each, doubling their initial endowment.

Clearly a rational, self-interested player will contribute nothing to the common pot, keeping the initial stake plus whatever gains come from the cooperative behavior of the others. In the best case, when the other three all contribute the maximum, the "free-rider" would get $15 in addition to the initial stake, for a total of $25. However, others will make the same calculation and also contribute nothing, so everybody is left with $10, instead of the maximum cooperative payoff of $20. Thus, the rational choice theory predicts that there will be no cooperation.

Real people did not behave in the way predicted by the self-interest hypothesis. The average contribution to the common pot in the early rounds was about half the endowment. In other words, people started halfway between the fully cooperative and fully self-interested positions. In subsequent rounds, however, cooperation gradually unraveled, and on the last round three quarters did not contribute anything at all, while most of the rest contributed just a dollar or two. Did this happen because the participants were stupid, so that it took many rounds for them to figure out the rational strategy? No, because in the post-experiment interviews many subjects told the researchers that they grew increasingly angry at those who did not contribute and punished them the only way they could—by curtailing their contributions to the common pot.

To test whether this was the real reason, the researchers added a modification to the basic game. Now, after each round, the participants were told how much other group members contributed, and they could punish free-riders at a cost to themselves. For every dollar forked out by the punisher, the punished was fined three. As discussed previously, punishment cannot force rational agents to cooperate, because it is the second-order collective good. In the context of the public goods game with punishment it is downright irrational to pay out punishment dollars for no personal gain. Therefore, the self-interest hypothesis predicts that the punishment option should not change the outcome of the game in any way. Yet adding punishment completely reversed the trend to declining cooperation. As before, participants started by contributing on average a half of their endowment. But this time there was a significant amount of punishing activity directed against the free-riders, and after a few rounds the average contribution to the common pot climbed up to nearly the maximum, and stayed there to the last round.

What these experiments, and many others like them, reveal is that the society consists of several types of people. Some of them—perhaps a quarter in experiments with American students—are self-interested, rational agents—"the knaves." These will never contribute to the common good and will choose free-riding, unless forced to do so by fines imposed on them. The opposite type, also about a quarter, are the unconditional cooperators, or "the saints." The saints continue to contribute to the common pool, and lose money, even when it is obvious to everybody that cooperation failed (although most of them reduce the amount of their contribution). The largest group (40 to 60 percent in most experiments) is the conditional cooperators or "the moralists." The preference of moralists is to contribute to the pot so that everybody would be better off. However, in the absence of the mechanism to punish noncontributors, free-riding proliferates, the moralists become disgusted by this opportunistic behavior and withdraw their cooperation. On the other hand, when the punishment option is available, they use it to fine the knaves. To avoid the fines, the knaves grudgingly begin contributing. Once free-riding has been eliminated, the saints and the moralists can follow their prosocial preference of contributing the maximum. The group achieves the cooperative equilibrium at which, paradoxically, the moralists do almost as well as the knaves, because they now rarely (if ever) need to spend money on fining the free-riders.

Experiments employing the public goods and similar games have now been conducted by many teams of investigators in many countries. In some studies, stakes were very high—equivalent to three months of salary. The general result is always the same. A substantial proportion of moralistic subjects always behaves in a cooperative, rather than rational fashion, and many people are willing to incur personal costs to punish cheaters.

This is not to say, however, that all social groups are alike in their composition with respect to knaves, saints, and moralists. College students, for example, tend to be more cooperative than subjects coming from less-educated and poorer social strata. Graduate students in economics, on the other hand, tend to behave more selfishly than students from other disciplines (probably because they learn too much about rational choice in their classes!). Most interestingly, the strength of cooperative behavior tends to vary among different countries. Particularly good evidence for cross-cultural variation comes from studies that used the "ultimatum game," which is simpler to set up and cheaper than the public goods game.

The ultimatum game is played between two people, the "proposer" and the "responder." Anonymous subjects are paired for a single interaction (which precludes any possibility of reciprocal altruism based on pre-existing long-term relationships). The task is to divide up "the pot" of $10. The proposer offers a certain proportion of the pot to the responder. (The proposal must be expressed in whole dollars.) If the responder accepts, the proposer keeps the rest of the pot. If the responder rejects the offer, nobody gets anything. If this game is played by purely self-interested agents, the theory predicts that the responder should accept any nonzero offer. Knowing this, the rational proposer will offer the minimum nonzero amount, which is $1. On the other hand, if the responder is a moralist, he will reject any offer deemed unfair. In a society with a strong norm of fairness, the moralistic responders will insist on the 50:50 division of the pot. They will certainly reject offers of one or two dollars. Knowing this, even a knavish proposer will make a fair offer. By now it should come as no surprise that in no real society that has been investigated with the ultimatum game, people behave according to the prediction of the self-interest hypothesis.

When the game is played with university students from industrial societies, cross-cultural variation is not huge, although detectable. For example, one study found that the most frequent offer made by the American and Slovenian students was precisely half the pot, whereas in Israel and Japan the modal offer was lower, 40 percent of the pot. In Israel, there was also a substantial number of low offers (10 to 30 percent of the pot), which were very rare in the other three countries. The probability that a low offer would be rejected was highest in the United States and

Slovenia, intermediate in Japan, and the lowest in Israel. Thus, lower propensity by responders to reject an unfair offer depressed the average offer amount made by proposers.

The researchers went around the world and played the ultimatum game in 15 small-scale traditional societies, which included hunter-gatherers, herders, and farmers. The amount of cross-cultural variation found in these small-scale societies was much greater than in the modernized ones (although in no society did people behave as would be predicted by the self-interest axiom). The Machiguenga of Peru made the lowest offers. Three quarters of proposals were 25 percent of the pot or less, and there was only one case of rejecting a low proposal. The Machiguenga economy is entirely focused on the household; almost no productive activity would require cooperation outside the members of the family. Same story with the Quichua of Ecuador—poorly integrated society, low offers in the ultimatum game. By contrast, the Aché of Paraguay practice widespread meat sharing and cooperation on community projects. "Aché hunters, returning home, quietly leave their kill at the edge of camp, often claiming that the hunt was fruitless; their catch is later discovered and collected by others and then meticulously shared among all in the camp." The average proposal made by the Aché was 51 percent of the stake, almost precisely the 50:50 split predicted by fairness considerations. The Lamelara whale hunters of Indonesia go to sea in large canoes manned by a dozen or more individuals. Close cooperation is critical for a successful hunt. In the ultimatum game the Lamelara are super-fair—the average proposal was 58 percent of the stake.

Generally speaking, the average offer amount among the 15 societies was correlated with the probability of rejecting a low offer. But there was one exception. The overwhelming proportion of offers rejected by the Au and the Gnau of New Guinea were those that were high (greater than half of the pot). Among these groups, accepting a large gift puts the receiver under a strong obligation and into a subordinate position with respect to the giver. As a result, such gifts will be frequently refused, and this cultural quirk was reflected in the way people played the ultimatum game. Another example of how culture can be reflected in the manner with which people behave in the experimental setting is the Orma. This herding people in Kenya practice wide-scale cooperation. When they decide to build a new school or a road, members of the community are asked to contribute, with the wealthier (those who have larger herds) contributing proportionally more. This system is called *harambee*. When the public goods game was explained to the Orma, they quickly dubbed it a *harambee* game. Interestingly, their contributions in the game were strongly correlated with their real-world wealth, as it would be in *harambee*.

THE BEHAVIORAL EXPERIMENTS USING THE public goods and the ultimatum games decisively prove that Machiavelli's self-interest premise was wrong. It is simply not true that *all* people behave in *entirely* self-interested manner. Some people—the knaves—are like that. However, other kinds of people, whom I have called the saints and the moralists, behave in prosocial ways. Furthermore, different societies have different mixtures of self-interested and cooperative individuals. Cultural practices (for example, the *harambee* system) and social institutions have a strong effect on whether and how collective action can be sustained.

The experiments also point to the key role of the moralists. Kindly saints are completely ineffectual in preventing cooperation from unraveling. In the absence of effective sanctions against free-riders, opportunistic knaves waste any contributions by the saints to the common good. Self-righteous moralists are not necessarily nice people, and their motivation for the "moralistic punishment" is not necessarily prosocial in intent. They might not be trying to get everybody to cooperate. Instead, they get mad at people who violate social norms. They retaliate against the norm breakers and feel a kind of grim satisfaction from depriving them of their ill-gotten gains. It's emotional, and it's not pretty, but it ensures group cooperation.

A recent experiment, conducted in Zurich by Fehr and colleagues, confirms that emotions play a strong role in moralistic punishment. As in other studies, the experiment involved human subjects playing a variant of the public goods game. The new twist was that the researchers scanned brain activity of the subjects who were contemplating whether to punish a cheater. The brain scan showed that when a player was deciding on punishment, a spike of neural activity occurred in the region of brain known as the caudate nucleus. The stronger the nucleus fired, the greater was the fine imposed by the subject on the norm violator. The caudate nucleus is known to be involved in the processing of rewards. More specifically, it has an important role in integrating reward information with goal-oriented behavior. The implication of the experimental findings, therefore, is that the subjects were anticipating the satisfaction of punishing the cheaters. The individuals who derived more pleasure from revenge (whose caudate nuclei fired particularly intensely) were willing to fork out more dollars to impose a heavier fine on the cheater.

Other groups of researchers in New Jersey, Texas, and California are also busily scanning brains of experimental subjects contemplating social choices—to trust or not? To punish or not? A whole new hot discipline, called neuro-economics, was born in the last few years. The results churned out by different research groups are striking. They indicate that the capacity for trust and moralistic punishment are wired into our brains. At some level, they are as basic as our abilities of obtaining food or finding mates. It does not mean that all humans will always behave in a cooperative manner. People are different—some are knaves, others moralists. Societies differ in their ability to sustain collective action. But the *capacity* for cooperation (even if it is never exercised by many people) is part of what makes us human. Machiavelli was wrong.

WHAT DOES IT MEAN FOR OUR theories of social and economic dynamics? First, there is no need to flush the theory of rational choice down the drain. Science typically advances in an incremental way, by building on earlier successes, and the development of our ideas about cooperation is not an exception to this principle. Remember that the theory assumes that rational agents maximize a "utility function," which in the general case need not be only material self-interest. It is quite straightforward to include in the utility function the prosocial inclinations of some individuals, and in fact theoretical economists have already started doing that. This research shows that in some kinds of circumstances prosocial inclinations do not matter, and we obtain results identical to the classical theory built on the self-interest assumption. Take price formation in the markets, one of the greatest successes of the classical theory, as developed by Adam Smith. Moralistic individuals may bitch and moan about not getting the "fair price," but the invisible hand of the market will inexorably set the price at the level determined by supply and demand.

In other kinds of situations, prosocial norms held by part of the population will result in an outcome completely at variance with the standard theory. Take the example with which this chapter started. From the point of view of the self-interest hypothesis, massive volunteering for the army is incomprehensible. But being familiar with the results from the public goods game and similar experiments, it is easy to understand what went on. The initial surge of volunteers must have been entirely saints and moralists. After enough moralists joined up, they put a lot of pressure on the knaves to do the same. In England during World War I, particularly effective were the female moralists who could not serve themselves but had husbands and sons in the army. Here's an eyewitness account by William Brooks, who joined the army in 1915: "Once war broke out the situation at home became awful, because people did not like to see men or lads of army age walking about in civilian clothing, or not in uniform of some sort, especially in a military town like Woolwich. Women were the worst. They would come up to you in the street and give you a white feather, or stick it in the lapel of your coat. A white feather is the sign of cowardice, so they meant you were a coward and that you should be in the army doing your bit for king and country. It got so bad it wasn't safe to go out. So in 1915 at the age of 17 I volunteered under the Lord Derby scheme. Now that was a thing where once you applied to join you were not called up at once, but were given a blue armband with a red crown to wear. This told people that you were waiting to be called up, and that kept you safe, or fairly safe, because if you were seen to be wearing it for too long the abuse in the street would soon start again."

Lest the import of this quote be misinterpreted, it is worth reiterating that pure coercion is *not* the explanation of why the British enlisted in huge numbers in the World War I. *Some* undoubtedly were forced to enlist by the tactics described in the previous paragraph, but others enlisted out of sheer patriotism; yet others were motivated by a mixture of patriotism and fear of harassment. Furthermore, the harassment of shirkers by the British women is emphatically not a self-interested behavior. By inducing another man to enlist, they did not better the survival chances of their husbands or sons in any appreciable way. These women put pressure on men to enlist not out of self-interest, but because of the expectations of their society at large, or more precisely, social norms.

Cooperative inclinations played a large role in explaining mass volunteering, but it would be simplistic and wrong to say that the whole nation spontaneously and uniformly rose up to smite the enemy. Just as it would be simplistic and wrong to say that all the British enlistees were coerced to join. The explanation requires a more nuanced and dynamic understanding.

EACH SOCIETY CONTAINS A SUBSTANTIAL proportion of people who, in addition to looking out for their material interest, are also motivated, at least in part, by social norms. So how did it come about that adherence to such norms became widespread in humans? Doesn't the theory of natural selection predict that such altruistic behaviors could never evolve? For an explanation, we need to look to some recent developments in evolutionary biology and anthropology.

Actually, Charles Darwin himself was concerned with the apparent problem altruistic behavior presented to his theory of evolution. "Selfish and contentious people will not cohere, and without coherence, nothing can be effected. A tribe possessing ... a greater number of courageous, sympathetic, and faithful members, who were always ready to warn each other of danger, to aid and defend each other ... would spread and be victorious over other tribes." The mechanism, proposed by Darwin, is now known as "group selection"—cooperation within groups evolves as a result of competition between groups. During the twentieth century, group selection went on a dizzying roller coaster, first enjoying wide acceptance, then being completely repudiated, and now on its way back to prominence, although in a different, more mature form. The problem was that during the first stage of uncritical acceptance, a lot of very bad theory was propounded by the adherents of the concept such as the famous Austrian ethologist Konrad Lorenz in his book *On Aggression*.

The main problem with the initial, crude version of the group-selection theory is this. Think about two types, altruistic "saints" and self-interested "knaves." It is true that groups that have many saints will be doing better than groups with lots of knaves. However, in addition to this between-group competition, there is a within-group competition between saints and knaves, which saints inevitably lose. This is the collective-action problem, all over again. The benefits from prosocial actions of the saints are spread evenly among all group members, including the knaves, but the costs are born entirely by the saints. As a result, the saints will suffer higher mortality and lower reproduction rate compared to the knaves. Overall, numbers of saints will change as the result of two opposing tendencies: between-group competition that causes saint numbers to increase, and within-group competition that causes their numbers to decline. It is hard to say which process will prevail without doing calculations. Unfortunately for the group-selection theory, mathematical models show that, except under quite unusual circumstances, the individual (within group) selection will almost always overwhelm group selection.

By the 1970s, this mathematical result was widely known, and it became fashionable to make fun at the expense of the "naïve" proponents of group selection. The said proponents crawled into various holes with their tails between the legs (with a few exceptions, most notably David Sloan Wilson at Binghamton University, who continued to plug on in almost total isolation). The "individual-selectionist" view became the dogma in the field of evolutionary biology as seen in, for example, Richard Dawkins's book *The Selfish Gene*.

Yet, although Dawkins and others pronounced that there is just one dominant unit on which natural selection operates—the individual—in Dawkins' own book he discusses at least three distinct units of selection. These units are the gene (which is reflected in the very title), the individual, and the group of relatives (Hamilton's kin selection). Individuals, after all, are not unitary, structureless "atoms" (despite the name—*individuum*—meaning "undividable"). They are made up of organs, tissues, and cells, and each cell contains many genes. It might be in the common interest for genes to cooperate to ensure the cell's proper functioning, but there could also be incentives for selfish genes to free-ride on this collective effort. Similarly, cells usually cooperate to promote the survival and reproduction of the organism, but at times this cooperation breaks down, and a bunch of knavish cells begins to increase at the expense of the cooperative ones. We know this as cancer. To cut a long story short, things are not quite as simple as Dawkins and other adherents of individual selection imply. In recent years, Wilson and colleagues were able to mount a successful attack on the individual-selectionist dogma. It is now becoming broadly accepted that natural selection operates at all levels simultaneously—genes, cells, organisms, groups of relatives, and simply groups.

It is true that among nonhuman organisms, under most conditions, group-level selection is quite weak. Empirical examples of group selection in nature are rare. Humans, on the other hand, are unique in the biological world in their capacity for thought, communication, and culture, and this makes group-level selection a very powerful force. The best current explanation of how human ultrasociality evolved is the theory of cultural group selection, advanced by the UCLA anthropologists Robert Boyd and Peter Richerson.

Probably the most important difference between humans and other organisms is the unique importance of cultural transmission of behaviors in humans. This is not to say that genes are unimportant in influencing the behavior of people. Studies of twins separated at birth have decisively shown that genetic makeup has a strong effect on behavioral traits, ranging from intelligence to political orientation. In the age-old debate on "nature versus nurture," neither of the extreme positions is right; the truth lies squarely in between. Moreover, nature and nurture collaborate in determining behavior of people. Genes do not really tell people to vote Republican. Rather, certain genetic makeup can predispose people to conservative views, but whether they become card-carrying Republicans, or not, will depend very much on the family upbringing and accidental experiences throughout their life, such as reading a particular book or making a particular friend.

What makes cultural transmission really distinct from genetic inheritance is that people can learn from other people, not only from their parents. Young people adopt certain behaviors by imitating a particularly successful or charismatic individual in their tribe. They are also taught many things by the tribal elders, from catching fish to telling the truth. The point is that behavioral practices can spread rapidly within a group by this process of cultural transmission, much more rapidly than if the transmission process were determined solely by genes. Of course, any kinds of behaviors can spread by imitation and teaching, both beneficial and harmful for the group. That is why the competition between groups is so important—it weeds out groups that have fixated on harmful practices. For example, take the ritual consumption of the brains of deceased relatives among the Fore people of New Guinea. This turned out to be a bad practice because it allowed the transmission of a neurodegenerative disease known as Kuru. Had Shirley Lindenbaum and Daniel Gajdusek not discovered the cause of the disease, the Fore would have eventually succumbed and been replaced by other tribes that did not eat dead relatives.

Humans have large brains and highly developed cognitive abilities. Apparently, people can keep in their minds information about the history of dealings within a group of more than a hundred people, remembering those who keep their word versus the cheaters. Furthermore, evolutionary psychologists Leda Cosmides and John Tooby argue that there are specialized "cheater-detection circuits" that allow a potential cooperator to detect individuals who free-ride. In short, people are very smart when it comes to social interactions. This unique ability of humans enables us to become very efficient moralists. Remember that a moralist not only behaves according to the norms, but also detects and punishes cheaters—people who break such social rules. A "second-order" moralist also keeps track of those who shirk by not punishing cheaters, and punishes *them* ("Damn John Jay! Damn everyone who won't damn John Jay!!").

As far as we can tell, the social organization of our distant evolutionary ancestors was not too different from that of the chimps. Unlike chimps, however, who enjoy eating meat but can capture only small prey, our ancestors learned how to hunt large game in the savannas of Africa. Humans eventually learned (perhaps too well) how to kill large mammals, including the largest ones such as elephants and mammoths. When they spread out of their ancestral Africa to other continents, prehistoric humans wiped out most of the large animals living there. That is why the mammoths of Siberia or giant sloths of South America are no longer with us. Unlike African species, large animals elsewhere did not co-evolve with humans and, as a result, had no defense against their predatory ways. What made primitive humans such fearsome killers? Not their teeth or claws, obviously, but their ability to hunt cooperatively.

Taking up hunting of large game exposed early humans to intense selection at the group level. Not only coordination was key to a successful hunt for large game, but moving to regions where such prey are found exposed humans to formidable predators. Only collective vigilance and cooperative defense could protect humans against saber-tooth tigers and cave bears. Again, humans got so good at dealing with these predators that they eventually exterminated them.

Even more importantly, as humans got better at hunting large game, they also got better at killing other humans. At some point, warfare (that is, any kind of organized fighting, from several chimps waylaying and killing a member of a different band to trench warfare involving millions during World War I) became the most important force of group selection. Several kinds of evidence show that early humans practiced extensive warfare. For example, we know that interband warfare is very common among the chimps, our closest evolutionary relatives. Warfare is also nearly ubiquitous among the small-scale societies of hunter-gatherers and farmers. The anthropologist Lawrence H. Keeley presents evidence that somewhere between 20 percent and 60 percent of males in these societies die in wars. By an argument of "interpolation," therefore, if both chimps and modern pre-state people practiced extensive warfare, so must have our human ancestors. There is also direct evidence—cave paintings depicting lines of warriors shooting at each other, defensive walls around Mesolithic settlements, arrowheads embedded in skeletons, and mass burials of fighting-age males, many of whom were killed by a blow to the head.

It is easy to imagine how prosocial behaviors that benefit the group could evolve in early humans. Consider, for example, the following theoretical scenario of evolution of moralistic punishment. Suppose our apelike ancestors had already evolved the behavior that I will call "familial moralism"—cooperate with close relatives and punish any of them who attempts to free-ride. The punishment part is important, because we know that relatives do not all automatically cooperate. Any family can have a "black sheep" or a prodigal son. Or a daughter who refuses to sacrifice herself for the benefit of the family, when she rejects an old and repulsive but wealthy suitor. Sanctions are needed to keep family members in line, from spanking a naughty child to disinheriting a disobedient daughter or a wild nephew. Evolution of this behavior is noncontroversial because it is driven by kin selection. Kin groups consisting of familial moralists would be able to achieve a higher degree of cooperation, and greater fitness, than groups consisting of those who cooperate with relatives, but do not punish uncooperative ones. As a result, familial moralism will spread through the population.

Now suppose that a cognitive mutation arises in a population of familial moralists. Instead of limiting cooperation (and punishment of noncooperators) to relatives only, these mutants also—"mistakenly"—cooperate with unrelated people they know, friends. Although I am describing here a hypothetical scenario, it is likely that human sociality evolved precisely by this kind of mutation. Just think how readily kinship terms enter our discourse when we want to promote cooperation—a *band of brothers*, the *father of a nation*, or *our motherland*.

Once the true (as opposed to familial) moralistic behavior arose, groups containing moralists acquired the ability to raise larger war bands, because they were not limited to relatives. Cooperation within the enlarged war parties was sustained by moralistic punishment of free-riders, so that they were as cohesive as the smaller parties consisting of familial moralists. Thus, group-level selection favored the spread of true moralistic behaviors. At the same time, within-group (individual) selection against the moralists was extremely weak, because after the moralists tip the group over to a cooperative equilibrium, punishments become so infrequent that they hardly impose any costs on the moralists. Slowly but surely, large bands dominated by moralists displaced smaller groups in which the only basis of cooperation was kinship.

In the scenario of group selection described above, it is not even necessary to assume that all members of defeated bands were physically destroyed. More likely, defeated bands simply disintegrated or disbanded, with their members seeking admittance to other surviving bands. Furthermore, cultural group selection operates on a much faster time scale than genetic group selection. If a moralistic individual turned out to be a very successful hunter or a particularly charismatic person, he or she would be emulated by the young members of the group. The moralistic behavior, then, will rapidly spread within the group. However, other groups are also observing what the successful group is doing, and can imitate its various practices. Moralism in the form, say, of a religious commandment from Muhammad can spread rapidly to other groups. Of course, cultural imitation can spread not only group-beneficial practices, but also harmful practices. A band initially dominated by moralists may happen to include a highly charismatic knave, who will influence people around him. But as knavery spreads through the band by the process of cultural imitation, the group will lose its internal cohesion and succumb to the moralistic bands in the neighborhood. In other words, it is competition between groups that ensures that prosocial behaviors spread and flourish. Cultural transmission facilitates and speeds up the evolution.

Recall the situation on the Roman frontier in northwestern Europe. When they first came in contact, the Romans were clearly superior in their military ability to the various Germanic tribes. The Romans did many things differently; so what should the tribesmen have imitated? The Romans did not wear pants, but any German foolish enough to imitate that aspect of the Roman cultural package would not survive the next winter, never mind the next night out partying with the guys. On the other hand, the Romans had discipline and fought in close ranks. When the Germans imitated this particular cultural practice, they found that it worked for them, too. The point is that we do not even have to assume that imitators know what they are doing. By imitating enough cultural elements of a successful group, they will eventually hit on the ones that bring success. In the process, they will probably also adopt many irrelevant, but harmless practices. (The harmful ones will be eventually weeded out by group selection.) And humans are quite smart, so they will often figure out precisely just what behavior they need to imitate.

Cultural evolution is faster than genetic also because it does not need generations to unfold. Looking again at the Roman frontier, we can see the cultural group selection in action in the rise and fall of charismatic leaders and their retinues, such as Arminius or Maroboduus. Through a process akin to mutation and recombination in genetics, each new warrior group will adopt somewhat different ways of organization and its members will internalize different norms. In the frontier situation, where the pressure of group selection is particularly heavy, groups will rapidly arise and dissolve. Only the most successful ones, those that hit by chance or design on the most advantageous combination of cultural elements, will survive. The cultural elements in question are not only those related to fighting prowess. Military bands that did not treat their women well never became functioning societies, and did not perpetuate themselves.

WHEN HUMANS EVOLVED THE ABILITY to cooperate with unrelated individuals, they relied on face-to-face interactions and memory to distinguish friends and acquaintances from the enemies or untrustworthy individuals in the group. There must have been an intense selection pressure for what science writer Malcolm Gladwell calls the "social channel capacity," the ability to handle the complexities of living in large social groups. After all, to ensure cooperation you need to remember not only what each group member did to you, but also what they all did to each other. If Mary cheated Jane, she might also cheat you. When Bob fell asleep on guard duty, but John did not shun him, as he was supposed to do, it means John is failing to cooperate in a collective sanctioning task. Making a society work is a complicated business.

But social channel capacity cannot be developed beyond a certain point—we cannot remember everyone on Earth, let alone what they have done to one another. As the size of the group increases, the number of relationships to remember explodes. If you belong to a group of 5 people, you only need to keep track of 10 separate relationships. If the group has 20 people, however, you need to remember 190 two-way relationships. The group size increased fourfold, but the number of relationships almost twenty-fold. Among the primates, humans live in the largest groups, and have the largest brains, but a limit is inescapable. "The figure of 150," estimates the British anthropologist Robin Dunbar, "seems to represent the maximum number of individuals with whom we can have a genuinely social relationship, the kind of relationship that goes with knowing who they are and how they relate to us. Putting it another way, it's the number of people you would not feel embarrassed about joining uninvited for a drink if you happened to bump into them in a bar." It turns out that the "magic number" of 150 is very close to the average size of villages in hunter-gatherer societies. Gladwell has cited many other examples of how the magic number crops up again and again—from military units to the maximum size of agricultural settlements allowed in the Hutterite sect, which originated in Central Europe in the sixteenth century, and moved to America in the twentieth.

Although our social channel capacity puts a limit on the number of people with whom we can maintain face-to-face relationships, group selection continued to favor social groups that could put out larger armies (or develop larger and thus more efficient economies) than their rivals. Evolution had to find another way for humans to distinguish between those with whom to cooperate and those who should be killed on the spot. And it did.

One aspect of human cognition that I have not yet touched on is our capacity for symbolic thinking. The distinctly human ability to invent and manipulate symbols was an important aspect of evolution of ultrasociality. In fact, as the Russian psychologist Lev Vygotsky (1896–1934) and his school argued, all higher forms of human cognition have social origins.

Think about the psychological difficulties involved in the idea of cooperating with a group. It is easy to imagine working together with a concrete person such as Bob or Jane, or a small group of people such as a family. (You can visualize it as people sitting around a table eating supper together.) When the group starts running into dozens of people, however, its "thingness" becomes blurred—its composition keeps changing with time, and its precise physical boundaries are unclear. How can it be made more concrete? In the process of evolution, humans developed the ability to represent such fuzzy entities with tangible objects. One example of a symbol representing a social group is the totem of American Indians. As the great French sociologist Emile Durkheim recognized almost a century ago, the totem is "the symbol of the determined society called the clan. It is its flag; it is the sign by which each clan distinguishes itself from the others, the visible mark of its personality." Another example is the standard of a Roman legion, called the Eagle. The Eagle was a sacred emblem of the legion; for most intents and purposes, it *was* the legion. It was better to die to a man than allow the enemy to capture the Eagle.

As a result of our ability to use symbols, the idea of a social group ("us") has a peculiar grip on human imagination. Because of our psychological makeup, we tend to think of social groups, such as nations, as more real than they are "in reality." And because people treat nations as real, they behave accordingly, and, paradoxically, make them real.

To illustrate how we imagine nation as more real than "it really is," think of what images "America" evokes. (Feel free to substitute any country.) What is America? The Stars and Stripes, the national anthem, the White House and the Capitol, the Statue of Liberty, Uncle Sam, the president in the Oval Office, jeans, Coke, apple pie, the American Constitution, the Pledge of Allegiance, "the leader of the free world," "the Manifest Destiny," "the land of opportunity," the visual image of a U.S. map (or just the outline of the lower 48) … and so on. These are all symbols that emphasize the "thingness" of America. The fact that a large minority of inhabitants of the country were born overseas and many do not even speak English very well, or that in recent elections half of the voters loathed the incumbent of the oval office, whereas most of the remainder loathed equally intensely the challenger for the office, is irrelevant. When people are inspired to die for their country, it does not matter that their country is imagined—the act of sacrifice is real enough. As Durkheim put it, "Social life, in all its aspects and in every period of history, is made possible only by a vast symbolism."

The capacity for symbolic thinking was the last great evolutionary innovation that made possible human ultrasociality. People now did not need to know personally another individual in order to determine whether to cooperate with him, or treat him as an enemy. Particularly good diagnostic features are religious observances and ritual actions. However, one could also look at the details of his clothing and ornamentation (including such permanent markings as tattoos or caste marks). One could listen to his dialect and observe his behavior.

"It's 1992 and I am sitting in a bar in Harare, Zimbabwe," wrote Patrick Neate in *Where You're At*, "when a guy walks in wearing a Lakers vest and Chipie jeans, his hair is neatly dreaded and he walks with a rolling ease of the B-boy swagger. He clocks my Karl Kanis and second pair of Air Jordans and comes straight over. 'Yo, my brother, wassup?'" Here were two complete strangers, one a Zimbabwean black kid, another a white kid from Chippenham, U.K., but they instantly recognized each other as being "us," members of the same hip-hop subculture—from they way they dressed, the way they walked or even sat, the way they were "blunted." (I do not even pretend to understand what the last one means—but I am an outsider.)

Symbolic demarcation of the group made possible cooperating with strangers who were clearly marked as "one of us." Symbols made it possible to identify with very large groups of "us," groups that included many more people than the small circle any individual person could meet and get to know personally. In other words, the evolution of symbolic thinking enabled defining as "us" a group of any size.

Large nations of tens of millions of people did not, of course, arise in one fell swoop. The process was gradual and happened in stages. Several villages, threatened by a powerful enemy, could unite in a tribe and invent symbolic ways to mark and emphasize their union. In the next stage, several tribes could unite in a region-sized society; then regional societies into nations, and those, finally into supranational unions, such as large empires and whole civilizations. At each step, new symbols are invented to demarcate ethnic boundaries, or old symbols are stretched to encompass the larger society.

Traces of this stepwise increase in the size and complexity of societies can be detected by observing that people's ethnic identities have many nested layers, like Russian Matryoshka dolls. A person from Indiana (a "Hoosier") is also a Midwesterner, an American, and a member of the Western civilization. New Englanders ("Yankees") and Southerners ("Rebs") are other instantly recognizable subethnic identities. Regional identities can be quite strong. Many Texans take as much pride in the Lone Star state as in their country.

The United States is a modern country that arose as a result of torrents of immigrants entering the melting pot, so the nested nature of ethnicity is not as clear-cut here as in many more traditional societies. In many pastoral societies, by contrast, the nested, hierarchical organization is glaring. (Anthropologists call such societies "segmentary.") The basic principle of segmentary social organization is expressed in the Arab proverb "I against my brothers; I and my brothers against my cousins; I, my brothers, and my cousins against the world."

The Germanic peoples on the Roman frontier also had segmentary social organization. Several village communities together made up a tribe, such as the Chatti. Several tribes united into a tribal confederation, such as the Franks and the Alamanni. Finally, when the Franks constructed an empire, they united within it many Germanic tribal confederations. The presence of an imperial frontier was the key force driving this scaling up of the Germanic society. Tribes located far away from the threat and the opportunity of the Roman frontier would have little need to unite in a tribal confederation. On the Roman frontier, however, the fusion of tribes into a tribal confederation and then the amalgamation of tribal confederations into an imperial confederation was a matter of life and death.

SUMMING UP THE MANY STRANDS of argument followed in this chapter, we started with the puzzle of human ultrasociality—our ability to combine into cooperating groups consisting of millions of individuals. Two key adaptations enabled the evolution of ultrasociality. The first one was the moralist strategy: Cooperate when enough members in the group are also cooperating, and punish those who do not cooperate. A band that had enough moralists to tip its collective behavior to the cooperative equilibrium outcompeted, or even exterminated, bands that failed to cooperate. The second adaptation, the human ability to use symbolic markers for defining cooperating groups, allowed evolution of sociality to break through the limits of face-to-face interactions. The scale of human societies increased in a series of steps, from the village and clan to the tribe and tribal confederation, then to the state, empire, and civilization.

As a new level of social complexity arose, the lower levels of organization were not completely eroded. As a result, people in general have coexisting identities, nested within each other. They can feel attachment and loyalty to their native town, their region, their country, and even to supranational organizations. The degree of identification with, and loyalty felt toward, an identity at any particular level can vary a lot. The attitudes of the modern Germans and the French toward their regional, national, and supranational identities are in stark contrast. The French can be quite attached to their regional identities, but they are first and foremost French. Their supranational identity as members of the European Union also takes a second seat to their Frenchness. By contrast, numerous sociological studies have shown that the post-war Germans identify primarily with their regional and supranational identities, and de-emphasize the national one. Thus, an inhabitant of southern Germany will think of himself or herself as a Bavarian and a European, tending to skip the intermediate level of German. Consequently, the Germans have been the most enthusiastic promoters of the European Union. This example also illustrates how the strength of identification with national identity can change with time. Up to and during World War II, of course, the Germans were fervently nationalistic—"*Deutschland über alles*"—but the shock of defeat and subsequent anti-Nazi propaganda discredited this identity for most of them. A similar de-emphasis of the identity associated with the state, but for a different reason, is observed among such ethnic minorities as the Catalans (many of whom would object strenuously to being called "Spanish") or the Catholic Irish in the United Kingdom. Such ethnic groups also tend to be ardent supporters of the European integration. In sum, different levels of social identity can evoke strong or weak feelings of loyalty, and the intensity of these feelings change as history unfolds.

Although the disposition to moralism or knavery might have a substantial genetic component, it is clear that temporal changes in the intensity of ethnic feeling, such as shifts in the main locus of ethnic feeling from regional to national level, and vice versa, must be culture-based. As noted previously in this chapter, cultural evolution can occur on a much faster time scale than changes in genetic frequencies. After moralists and symbolic thinkers evolved through the process of genetic evolution, the rise (and fall) of identification with and loyalty to higher-level identity could happen much more rapidly. Rapidly, that is, when compared to the glacial pace of genetic evolution. The empirical examples that we examined so far suggest that even cultural evolution needs centuries to produce societies capable of wide-scale cooperation.

Chapter 6

Born to Be Wolves

The Origins of Rome

No theory of imperial rise and fall can avoid the topic of the Roman Empire. The Roman achievement of peace across such a large area—Pax Romana—put an indelible stamp on how the peoples of western Eurasia imagined an ideal state. The very word *empire* comes from the Latin (*imperium* means "military power"). Countless peoples modeled their states, and even named them, after Rome: the Eastern Roman Empire that we now called Byzantine, the Holy Roman Empire of the German peoples (which, according to Karl Marx was neither holy, nor Roman, nor even an empire), Moscow the Third Rome, the Rum Seljuks ("Roman Turks"), and the modern Romanians. Christian theologians imagined their kingdom of God as a better, cleaner, and more just version of the Roman Empire. The "decline and fall" of the Roman Empire is a must for any aspiring theorist of history to explain.

My interest is not in Rome per se, but rather in using it as a case study to test the theory outlined in the previous chapters—that imperial nations arise on metaethnic frontiers. I begin with a bird's eye view of the geopolitical and cultural matrix from which Rome emerged.

A snapshot of Europe and the Mediterranean taken c. 400 B.C. (see Map 5) reveals three general areas. In the eastern Mediterranean, we see the zone of old civilizations, dominated by the brilliant Achaemenid Persian Empire. Asia Minor, the Levant, and Mesopotamia are directly governed by the Achaemenids, Egypt is about to secede and regain its independence, and Greece is the only area that had successfully fought off Persian advances earlier in the century. By the fourth century B.C., this old civilizational core had had states, cities, and literacy for at least a millennium.

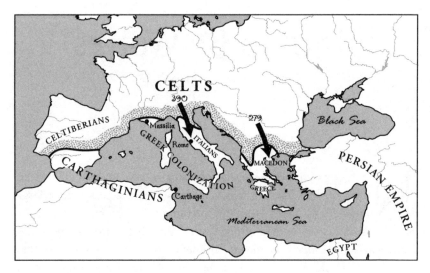

Map 5   *The Mediterranean c. 400 B.C.*

During the first millennium B.C., the civilization also began spreading into the central and western Mediterranean. Some of this spread was accomplished by colonization of new areas by the seafaring peoples—the Greeks and the Phoenicians. In addition, the literate urbanized culture spread by diffusion to several formerly barbarian peoples, the most notable of which were the Etruscans of central Italy.

The bulk of Europe and North Africa, by contrast, was inhabited by stateless and illiterate tribal peoples. A highly aggressive culture, known to archaeologists as the La Tène Celts, had been expanding from its homeland in northern Europe and had come in contact with the civilized areas in several places. The peculiar nature of this expansion was that there was no center directing it. At each point, expansion was accomplished by independent bands of warriors led by their own chieftains. These bands sometimes cooperated and combined their forces against a common enemy, but more often fought among themselves.

The most interesting is the zone of contact between "civilization" and "barbarism" in Europe. It runs along the Mediterranean shore in southeastern Iberia, south France, central Italy, and northern Greece (see Map 5). This zone is a typical metaethnic frontier, where two very different kinds of people come in contact and conflict. The metaethnic frontier theory predicts that new aggressive empires should originate from this contact zone. Indeed, the three "great powers" of the Mediterranean in the next two centuries will be Carthage, Macedon, and Rome. By the end of the first century B.C., one of them, Rome, will have defeated its rivals and unified the whole Mediterranean for the first (and last) time. This chapter traces the rise of Rome, from the modest beginnings in the seventh century B.C. to its peak of power in the second century A.D. Understanding the specific case of Rome is a critical test of the metaethnic frontier theory, its ability to explain the rise of imperial nations in general, as well as how their rise to power carries within it the seeds of their inevitable downfall.

ONE DISTINCTIVE FEATURE OF ROME was that it experienced not one, but two distinct frontiers, one after another. The geography of Italy and the kinds of peoples who inhabited it in the early Iron Age explain much about Rome's formation. The flatlands of Italy suited to intensive agriculture are divided by the Apennines into three distinct areas: the Po Valley in the north, the Tyrrhenian Italy (lying between the Tyrrhenian Sea and the mountains) in the center, and the "heel and toe" of the Italian boot in the south. By the eight century B.C., the Tyrrhenian Italy was divided between the Etruscans in the north and speakers of various Italic languages, including Latin, in the south. The origins of the Etruscans remain one of the unsolved historical puzzles. We know that they spoke a non-Indo-European language and that their religion and culture were distinct from the Latins and other Italic tribes. (Italic languages belong to the Indo-European family.) Also in the eighth century B.C., Greeks were beginning to colonize southern Italy. They and Phoenician traders were spreading an urban and literate culture into the central Mediterranean; Etruscans were eager to adopt it. As far as we know, the Etruscans were never unified under a single central authority, but instead operated as a loosely confederated league of "12 cities," united by common language and a shared religious cult. In the seventh century, the Etruscans dominated central Italy and expanded north into the Po Valley. They also established colonies on the coast of Sardinia and in Campania, where they competed and fought with the Greeks.

The flowering of the Etruscan civilization had a profound effect on the barbarian Italic tribes in the neighborhood, particularly the Latins, whose territory Latium was just south of Etruria across the Tiber. They, like the Etruscans, were not unified politically. Nevertheless, they constituted a distinct ethnic community united by a common name and language. They had similar social and political institutions and worshipped the same gods. Archaeological studies show that a distinctive form of material culture arose in Latium during the early Iron Age. The Latins were a real nation, and they themselves were aware of it.

Along the Tiber River, where the two nations came in contact, a cultural frontier formed between the more advanced civilization of the Etruscans and the Latins. As frontiers go, it was fairly local in character, and thus a mighty empire would not, according to the theory, arise out of it. (The Roman Empire grew on the second frontier.) But the theory does predict the formation of a relatively cohesive regional state. And that is what happened.

Rome began as a frontier town at the interface between the Etruscan and Latin cultures. It was situated on the first ford and easiest landing place on the Tiber. The location on the Tiber was a great bonus for later development of Rome, because this river provides the best route for moving goods inland in Tyrrhenian Italy. But the frontier location was even more important in molding the future empire. From the evidence of the Roman chronicles, supported by archaeological data, it seems the Roman nation arose as a result of a classic process of frontier ethnogenesis. According to the Roman tradition, the population of early Rome was divided into three tribes—*Ramnes*, *Tities*, and *Luceres*. Their names come from Romulus, a Latin; Titus Tatius, a Sabine; and Lucumo, an Etruscan. Clearly a fusion of Latin, Sabine, and Etruscan ethnic elements led up to the rise of the Roman nation. The tale of the Rape of the Sabines, of Romans capturing wives from the Sabines and eventual unification of the two groups, also attests to the multi-ethnic origin of the Romans. The Romans of later times were well aware of their mixed ethnic origins, and actually prided themselves on their ability to accept talented foreigners into their ranks. In 504 B.C., the Sabine leader Appius Claudius migrated to Rome with a private retinue of 5,000 armed clients. He was admitted to the senate as a patrician, and his followers were given land to settle on. The patrician clan of Claudii played a prominent role in later Roman politics, and supplied a number of emperors to the Roman Empire. Another indication of the openness to outsiders is the mottled ethnic origin of the Roman rulers during the Archaic period, who included the Sabine Titus Tatius and Numa Pompilius, and the Etruscan Tarquins. The ability to incorporate groups and individuals of foreign origin into the social fabric of their society served the Romans well when they expanded beyond the boundaries of Latium.

According to Livy and other ancient historians, Rome was founded by Romulus in 753 B.C. Archaeological evidence indicates that the area occupied by the eighth-century settlement was more than 100 acres, suggesting population of a few thousand. Around 625 B.C., the rural settlements on Roman hills were transformed into a city-state. A century later, Rome expanded to cover an area six times the size, which indicates an urban population of more than 30,000. Livy and Dyonisius of Halicarnassus portray Rome under the last king, Tarquinius the Proud (535–510), as a hegemonic power in Latium. Twentieth-century historians dismissed this as a nationalistic fiction that projected the later greatness of Rome to its Archaic period, and insisted that Rome, when ruled by the kings, was instead an insignificant place, and under the domination of the Etruscans to boot. In the last few years, thanks largely to better archaeological data, this view of early Rome has been revised, and it is becoming clear that the ancient historians were not mistaken. One strong indication of the importance of Rome under the kings is its size. Known areas of other Latin towns are an order of magnitude smaller than that of Rome. In fact, around 500 B.C., Rome was already the largest city in Tyrrhenian Italy. The territories of five largest Etruscan cities were around half the size of Rome. The only city on the whole Italian Peninsula whose size exceeded Rome was Tarentum. Another sign of Rome's importance is the treaty that it made with Carthage in 507. The text of the pact treats Rome as the ruling power in Latium and a significant power in the Mediterranean politics.

Note that Rome was located not in the center of Latium, but on its very edge (see Map 6). The rise of Rome from a small town at the edge of Latium to the principal Latin city was a result of the pressures from the Etruscan-Latin frontier. The Romans were at war with the Etruscan city of Veii throughout their whole early history, beginning in the times of Romulus and ending only with the conquest of Veii many centuries later.

Map 6   *Italy, eight century B.C.*

The chief Etruscan rival of Rome, Veii, was situated at the very edge of the Etruscan territory. Although Veii did not unite Etruria, both the archaeological and historical evidence indicate that toward the end of its long struggle with Rome it became the largest, the wealthiest, and the most powerful Etruscan city. Apparently, the Etruscan-Latin frontier molded the development of both rivals in similar ways. Under the influence of the conflict across the ethnic divide, both peoples acquired a high degree of internal cohesion, which allowed them to dominate and integrate smaller ethnically similar communities on the same side of the frontier.

If Rome achieved such preeminence in central Italy at the end of the regal period (509 B.C.), why didn't it continue to expand during the fifth century and unify the Mediterranean centuries before it actually happened? The answer has two parts. First, the Etruscan-Latin frontier does not qualify as a true metaethnic fault line. Both cultures were heavily influenced by the urban Mediterranean civilization, which was transmitted to them by the Greeks and the Phoenicians. The somewhat mild nature of the frontier could produce at best a regional state, not a world-class empire. It was only after the Romans found themselves on the second frontier, facing much more alien and terrifying "others" that they were forged into a truly imperial nation. Second, history usually does not develop linearly; there is also a strong cyclic component to it. What happened was that the long period of growth during the regal period created forces that now promoted decentralization tendencies in the Roman society. Part II examines such forces further; but during the fifth century, Rome experienced a disintegrative phase, a period of internal infighting that periodically threatened to become outright civil war, which brought the Roman state to the brink of destruction. Until such internal pressures subsided, Rome could not resume its expansion.

The time of troubles began with the revolt of a part of aristocracy against the last king of Rome, Tarquin the Proud. They were successful in deposing Tarquin and establishing an oligarchic form of government (somewhat misleadingly called the Republic) that would rule Rome for the next five centuries. Unfortunately, the process of social dissolution did not stop with Rome herself, but spread to Latium. The Latin cities subject to Rome's control revolted and formed the Latin league to resist Rome's power.

Back in Rome, unrest was growing between the commoners and the aristocrats. As a result of population growth during the sixth century, land became scarce and many people were impoverished. To feed their families, they borrowed heavily from the wealthy. Roman laws were very harsh to insolvent debtors. Creditors could enslave a debtor who could not pay what he owed. Scarcity of land and oppression by wealthy creditors resulted in a loss of support among the commoners for the policies of the ruling class. The struggle between patricians and plebs never resulted in outright revolution because Rome was surrounded by enemies on all sides, and this precarious situation ensured a critical level of cooperation. Nevertheless, the plebs periodically "seceded"—that is, they withdrew from the city to the Aventine Hill, at the time outside the city boundary.

These secessions were a kind of blackmail of the upper classes; by denying recruits to the army, the plebs were attempting to force the aristocrats to address issues of concern, reduction of debt and land redistribution.

The fifth century saw that kind of urban class struggle between the wealthy aristocrats and the impoverished commons as well as internecine rivalry among the Roman aristocratic factions, and rebellion of the provincial Latin subjects. The fifth-century crisis, in fact, affected not only Rome, but the whole of Tyrrhenian Italy. The internal weakness also invited attack by the noncivilized tribes inhabiting the Apennines. Rome was subjected to raids and territorial encroachment by the Italic hill tribes of Sabines, Volsci, and Aequi. And the war against the Etruscans continued to flare up periodically. On top of incessant warfare, overpopulation led to recurrent epidemics and subsistence crises.

In 463 B.C., reports Livy, "In both town and country there was a great deal of sickness. Cattle suffered as much as men, and the incidence of disease was increased by overcrowding, as farmers together with their livestock had been taken into the city for fear of raids. The smell of this motley collection of animals and men was distressing to city folk, who were not accustomed to it; the farmers and yokels, packed as they were into inadequate quarters, suffered no less from the heat and lack of sleep, while attendance upon the sick, or mere contact of any kind, continuously spread the infection. The unhappy people were already at the end of their tether, when report suddenly arrived that a combined army of Aequians and Volscians … were overruning the countryside."

The invaders swept into the territory of Rome, "where farmlands needed no enemy to make them desolate. In all the countryside they found not a single man, armed or unarmed; there was no sign of defenders, not a trace of cultivation…. In the city, the consul Aebutius had died; his colleague Servilius was in a lingering state, almost despaired of. Most of the leading men, the majority of the Senate, almost anybody of military age were down with the disease…. Her strength gone and with no one to lead her, Rome lay helpless.

"The Senate despairing of human aid, turned people to their prayers, bidding them to go with their wives and children and supplicate heaven for a remission of their sorrows. It was official command, but no more than what each was impelled to do by his own distress: Every shrine was packed; in every temple women lay prostrate, their hair sweeping the floor, praying for the angry gods to grant them pardon and to put an end to the plague." Dyonisius writes that during the plague of 463 B.C., the corpses of the very poor had to be thrown into the Tiber, and again in 451, when the corpses were thrown into the sewers as well.

As a result of epidemics, famines, and ceaseless warfare, the population declined, freeing land for the landless. The aristocrats became poorer, and after a few generations their descendants became used to the less-ostentatious way of life. Archaeological evidence suggests that luxury imports (mainly brought by the Greek traders) declined drastically. Opulent burials disappeared. Wealth inequality decreased. The social system, so disturbed around 500 B.C., returned slowly and painfully to an equilibrium. Aiding this process was the external pressure from the hill tribes of Aequi and Volsci, and from the Etruscans of Veii, which helped to consolidate different orders by focusing their minds on the task of common survival. Toward the end of the fifth century, Rome largely subdued the hill tribes. After reverses during the first and second wars with Veii, Rome was finally successful in conquering it for good in 396. This was a momentous event, because it signaled the closure of the Etruscan-Latin frontier. However, resting on the laurels was not to be Rome's fate. A short six years later, Rome was subjected to a tremendous shock that would first bring it to the brink of precipice, but in the long run set it on the path to empire. The traumatic event, as terrifying as a Nazi blitzkrieg or a terrorist mass murder, was the Gallic sack of Rome in 390.

THE CELTS, OR GAULS, AS the Romans called them, entered northern Italy sometime during the sixth or fifth century. The Celts did not build a centralized territorial state. Instead, they usually operated as independent bands of warriors who, nevertheless, were capable of uniting under a charismatic leader when they encountered significant opposition. The Etruscan cities in the Po Valley succumbed to the Gallic pressure, and the north of Italy became Gallic (and was henceforth known to the Romans as the Cisalpine Gaul, as distinguished from the Transalpine Gaul—modern

France and Belgium). Thus, during the fifth century, the "barbarism-civilization" frontier shifted south to the Apennine hills dividing the Po Valley from Tyrrhenian Italy. A few towns of the Veneti (near modern Venice) were the only remaining outposts of the Mediterranean civilization north of the Apennines.

The intensity of the new frontier dwarfed ethnic divisions on the Italian Peninsula, such as that between the Etruscans and the Latins. By 400 B.C., these two peoples, although speaking different languages and possessing distinct ethnic identities and religious cults, had acquired similar social and political institutions. Both belonged to the literate and urbanized Mediterranean civilization. After many centuries of conflict, they came to use similar methods of conducting war. The "savage Gauls" were an entirely different kind of people.

In 391, one of the Gallic tribes, the Sennones, crossed the Apennines in search of land and besieged the Etruscan city of Clusium. As Livy describes, "The plight of Clusium was a most alarming one: Strange men in thousands were at the gates, men like of whom the townsfolk had never seen, outlandish warriors armed with strange weapons, who were rumored to have scattered the Etruscan legions on both sides of the Po; it was a terrible situation...." The people of Clusium asked for Rome's help, and the Senate sent as envoys three Fabii brothers (Fabii were one of Rome's most illustrious patrician families) to persuade the Gauls to desist. "The object of the mission was wholly conciliatory; unhappily, however, the envoys themselves behaved more like savage Gauls than civilized Romans." During the negotiations, the Gauls demanded that Clusium cede to them a part of its territory. "When the [Roman] envoys asked by what sort of justice they [the Gauls] demand land, under threat of violence, from their rightful owners, and what business Gauls had to be in Etruria anyway, they received the haughty reply that all things belonged to the brave who carried justice on the point of their swords. Passions were aroused and a fight began." During the melee, "Quintus Fabius, riding ahead of the line straight for the Gallic chieftain as he was making for the Etruscan standards, killed him with a spear-thrust through the side and began to strip him of his armor." This was a serious breach of diplomatic protocol, to say the least. "The quarrel with Clusium was forgotten and the anger of the barbarian army was turned upon Rome."

The Gauls sent their own envoys to Rome to demand the surrender of the Fabii, but the Senate was loath to give up members of one of the most powerful and wealthy families in the ruling oligarchy. As soon as the Gauls learned of the Senate decision, they "flamed into the uncontrollable anger which is so characteristic of their race, and set forward, with terrible speed in the path to Rome. Terrified townships rushed to arms as the avengers went roaring by; men fled from their fields for their lives; and from all the immense host, covering miles of ground with its straggling masses of horse and foot, the cry went up 'To Rome!'

"Rumor had preceded them and messages from Clusium and elsewhere had already reached the City, but in spite of warnings the sheer speed of the Gallic advance was a frightful thing. The Roman army, moving with all the haste of a mass emergency levy, had covered hardly eleven miles before it met the invaders at the spot where the river Allia descends in a deep gully from the hills of Crustumerium and joins the Tiber not far south of the road. The ground in front and on both sides was already swarming with enemy soldiers, and the air was loud with the dreadful din of the fierce war-song and discordant shouts of a people whose very life is wild adventure…."

The war leader of the Gauls, Brennus, first led his troops to attack and drive away the Roman reserves, and then fell on the main body with all his might. "… the main body of the army, at the first sound of the Gallic cry on their flank and in their rear, hardly waited even to see their strange enemy from the ends of the earth; they made no attempt at resistance; they had no courage even to answer his shouted challenge, but fled before they lost a single man. None fell fighting; they were cut down from behind as they struggled through to force a way to safety through the heaving mass of their fellow-fugitives."

After the defeat at the Allia, some of the surviving Romans escaped to Veii; others ran to Rome and locked themselves up in the Citadel on the Capitoline Hill. The Gauls entered Rome unopposed, pillaged it, and besieged the Citadel. One night they almost managed to capture the Capitol by stealth, but fortunately the geese sacred to the goddess Juno raised an alarm, and the Gallic assault was repelled. However, the Roman situation was becoming desperate, and they entered into negotiations with Brennus to buy the Gauls off with gold. During the weighing of the gold,

Brennus flung his sword on the scale saying "Woe to the vanquished!" Meanwhile Marcus Furius Camillus (later esteemed as one of the fathers of the Roman nation) gathered troops from Veii, where a part of the defeated Roman army escaped, and from the Latins. He arrived in Rome just in time to put a stop to the shameful transaction, and drove the Gauls away after inflicting two defeats on them.

Even four centuries after the events that Livy describes, and after the Romans had defeated and subjugated the Gauls, the Gauls still inspired in Romans intense feelings of loathing and terror. The Gauls were an alien and terrifying enemy. In several places, Livy stresses how different they were from people whom Romans knew: "outlandish warriors armed with strange weapons," "strange enemy from the ends of the earth." A Gaul was also physically larger and stronger than a Roman. They were ferocious fighters and sometimes fought naked, which further terrified their civilized enemies. They uttered "cries like the howling of wolves and barbaric songs." They were known to take scalps and heads of their enemies as battle trophies. They were the only enemy who penetrated the city and defiled its sacred places (before the days of the Vandals and the Huns). The whole experience left deep scars on the Roman psyche. The mere threat of a *tumultus Gallicus* evoking disorderly hordes of barbarians fighting against all established rules, was enough to induce the people to extreme panic. On at least three occasions, the menace of a Gallic invasion caused the Romans to carry out human sacrifices in an attempt to avert the danger threatening the city. Speaking in a more dispassionate and analytical manner, the famous orator Cicero said in one of his speeches, "In the opinion of all who have ever deliberated soundly about this Commonwealth of ours, Gaul has always been the greatest threat to this empire, ever since its inception."

Many modern historians tend to overlook the significance of the Gallic frontier during the formative period of the Roman state (which I call Roman ethnogenesis), and for the Roman success in unifying Mediterranean within a single empire. After all, the Gauls were just barbarians, how could they have such an influence on the Romans? To counteract this "civilizational bias," we should pay attention to the historian Polybius (200–118 B.C.). One advantage of Polybius was that he was Greek, and therefore (at least in principle) capable of rising above the Roman-Gallic struggle. On the other hand, he lived for many years in Rome, where he observed the aristocratic politics at first hand. He also made many trips to Spain, Africa, and Gaul. He had first-hand experience of what he was writing about. Moreover, prior to writing his history, he served as an official of the Achaean League, so he had practical political experience.

The importance that Polybius assigns to the formative influence of the Gauls in the rise of the Roman Empire is made clear at the beginning of his history: "The date I have chosen, then, to mark the beginning of the establishment of Roman power in Italy" is the year when "the Gauls captured Rome by storm and were occupying the whole city except for the Capitol." Later he says, "For those who desire a complete and comprehensive account of the development of Rome's present supremacy, ... they must acquaint themselves with the period and the process whereby the Romans began to advance towards better fortunes after the defeat they suffered on their own soil." In a chapter titled "Rome and the Gauls," Polybius describes the almost continuous wars the Romans fought against the Gauls during the fourth and third centuries, and concludes: "There were two great advantages which the Romans gained from these struggles. In the first place, once they become accustomed to suffering great losses at the hands of the Gauls, there was no more terrifying experience than this which they need expect either to undergo or fear. Secondly, by the time they had to meet Pyrrhus they came to contest like trained and seasoned athletes in military operations." Throughout his book, Polybius continues to stress the Gallic-Roman relations. "The Romans ... regarded the threat from the north as by far the most pressing of their problems." And: "The age-old terror inspired by the Gauls had never been altogether dispelled" (at least this was true for the second century B.C., when Polybius wrote these lines).

THE ROMANS WERE FATED TO STRUGGLE against the Gauls for four centuries, finally triumphing over them only with the conquest of the Transalpine Gaul by Julius Caesar. During the fourth and third centuries B.C., the Romans and other peoples of peninsular Italy were subjected to constant small-scale raiding, punctuated by large-scale invasions, from northern Italy. It was only toward the end of the third century, when the

Romans gathered enough strength to mount a sustained effort to "pacify" the Gauls of the Po Valley. The campaign of conquest was successful, but its effect turned out to be short-lived.

In 218 B.C., Hannibal crossed the Alps with his African and Spanish troops and 20 elephants, and for the next 17 years he ravaged central and southern Italy. What is often not appreciated is that the troops that Hannibal brought with him were outnumbered by the Gallic troops he recruited in the Po Valley. In fact, even before entering Italy, he corresponded with the chieftains of Cisalpine Gaul and ascertained that they would join him in his war on Rome. As time went on and battles took their toll on Hannibal's African and Spanish troops, the Gallic element became more and more prevalent. Thus, the Hannibalic war can be thought of as yet another episode in the struggle of Rome against the Gallic hordes. The Roman fear of the Gauls was so ingrained, that although Italy was prostrated at the end of the Hannibalic war in 201 and the resources of Rome almost exhausted, the Romans nevertheless immediately began their reconquest of Cisalpine Gaul as soon as they expelled Hannibal. They campaigned there every year before 190 until they resubjugated the Gauls.

Even in an age when atrocities were regularly committed by all sides, the Roman treatment of the Gauls was especially brutal. Unlike other Italian peoples who were frequently admitted as allies, or even citizens, in the Roman commonwealth after being defeated by the Romans (as discussed earlier in this chapter), this treatment was never extended to the Gauls. On the contrary, when the Romans definitively conquered the Po Valley, they "ethnically cleansed" Gauls from it. Such treatment of the inhabitants of a conquered territory was exceptional in Roman practice. Even in the harsh treatment meted out to the defeated Carthaginians (the other nation that Romans hated with passion), when their beautiful and wealthy city was razed and its ground salted, the Romans left the agricultural population in the Carthaginian territory alone.

The intrusion of the Gauls into Italy and the establishment of the metaethnic frontier running along the Apennines was the decisive factor in the rise of Rome. The first immediate consequence was the sack of Rome, which shocked both the aristocracy and the commons, and convinced them that they must cooperate to overcome the external threat. When the Roman society was confronted with ferocious scalp-collecting howling savages, internal divisions between different orders somehow lost their urgency. The long-standing conflict between two noble factions was resolved within a generation after the sack. These factions were the patricians, the old senatorial nobility, and the so-called "plebeians," new powerful and wealthy families that arose from the ranks of the commons during the fifth century. The Licinio-Sextian Laws of 367 ended all sorts of discrimination against the plebeians (for example, they opened the highest office of the Republic—consulship—to them) and merged the patricians and noble plebeians into a united ruling class. The legislation also probably included some sort of debt relief. The problem of land for the poor was solved partly by the population decrease in the previous century, partly by emigration of citizens to colonies, and mainly by expansion of the Roman territory resulting from successful wars. (The first of which was the annexation of the territory of Veii in 396.) The social transformation of the Roman state in the first half of the fourth century resulted in a highly consolidated and aggressive society geared for territorial expansion. The consensus among the elites came none too soon. The two decades after 367 saw almost continuous Gallic raiding of central Italy, during which time Rome fought no fewer than four wars against the Gauls.

In addition to increasing the internal cohesiveness of the Roman nation, the Gallic frontier also made the job of unifying Italy and eventually the Mediterranean much easier. Other civilized peoples of Italy also feared and detested the Gallic barbarians. Peoples who were directly exposed to the Gallic threat, such as the Etruscans and the Veneti, joined the growing Roman Empire essentially voluntarily. Until 390, the Romans and the Etruscans were almost constantly at war, but after they both found themselves on the Gallic frontier, these wars ceased. In fact, as discussed previously, an Etruscan city of Clusium, when threatened by the Sennones, appealed to Rome for protection, even though there was no preexisting defensive treaty. The Veneti, who were the most exposed to the Gallic pressure, proved to be the staunchest Roman allies. Even during the darkest hour of the Hannibalic war, when Rome was abandoned by many of her allies, the Veneti loyally soldiered on. To a lesser degree, the same logic applied to other Italian peoples who were in a more-protected situation in southern Italy. They undoubtedly would have preferred to keep their independence, but when given a choice between whom to submit to—civilizational aliens (Gallic hordes and other foreign troops lead by a Semitic general) or civilizationally more familiar Rome—they eventually opted for Rome. This was one of the main reasons why the Romans prevailed in the Second Punic War.

Polybius describes integrative effect of the Gallic threat. On learning that a Gallic invasion was imminent, the Roman authorities began to enroll the legions and summon the Italian allies. "Help was readily provided on all sides, for the other inhabitants of Italy were so terror-stricken by the invasion of the Gauls that they no longer thought of themselves as allies of Rome, nor regarded this as a war to uphold the Roman hegemony. On the contrary, every people saw the danger as one which threatened themselves and their own city and territory. For this reason they responded to the orders from Rome without a moment's hesitation."

The logic of metaethnic frontier aided not only Roman unification of Italy, but her expansion into the Mediterranean, too. By the second century B.C., the Celt became the chief kind of barbarian on the European frontier of the Mediterranean civilization. From west to east, the pressure was intense. In Iberia, the invading Celts mixed with local population to give rise to the Celtiberians. In southern France, the Greek cities on the Mediterranean shore (with Massilia—modern Marseille—the chief of them) were under strong pressure from the Celtic tribes. In northern Italy, the threat from the Celts/Gauls was long established. In the Balkans, the Celts moved down the Danube, colonizing the territory along its whole length, and then settled on the western shorelands of the Black Sea. In 279, the Celts poured down into Macedon, Greece, and Thrace. The Macedonians expelled them from Macedon with great difficulty, but in Thrace the invaders founded a robber kingdom. Three tribes crossed into Asia Minor, where they established themselves in central Anatolia, from this point known as Galatia (the land of Celts). Throughout the third century these Gauls periodically plundered other Anatolian kingdoms, such as Bythinia and Pontus.

Lesser civilized states on the Celtic frontier, such as Massilia and Pontus, never needed to be conquered by force. They first sought Rome's protection against their enemies, then became faithful allies, and eventually were incorporated into empire in a consensual, noncoerced manner.

WHAT KIND OF PEOPLE WERE THE ROMANS? What collective qualities enabled them to become one of the greatest imperial nations in history? We are fortunate in that we have a large body of texts, ranging from the multivolume works of historians such as Livy to speeches of Cicero to short inscriptions found by archaeologists. Topics for graffiti have varied little over the millennia. One inscription found in Pompeii reads: "Apollodorus, doctor to the Emperor Titus, had a good crap here." "Yours for a two pence," runs a prostitute's ad. "A copper pot is missing from this shop. 65 sesterces reward if anybody brings it back, 20 sesterces if he reveals the thief so that we can get our property back."

These texts, coming from both the humblest and the most exalted strata of the Roman society, can give us insight into the Roman psyche, but we have to understand the context. The purpose of Cicero's speeches was not to inform us about the Romans; he used them to denounce his political opponents. Livy's history reflects the biases of him and the Romans of his times, first century B.C. During the century between the tribuneship of the reformer Tiberius Gracchus (133 B.C.) and the establishment of the Principate by Augustus (27 B.C.), Rome experienced a period of secular decentralization. It would be difficult for Livy, living as he did during the turbulent and fratricidal civil wars, to avoid painting early Roman history in rosy colors, depicting the Romans of bygone times as more patriotic, virtuous, and moderate in tastes and personal consumption than his contemporaries. Nevertheless, biased as they are, the Roman texts are of great value to anyone who wants to understand world history because they articulate a detailed world view; they describe the Roman ideal of a good citizen. In conjunction with other kinds of data, they can also tell us how societies change with time. Livy often contrasts the rampant luxury and conspicuous consumption of his own times, the first century B.C., with the simpler, less-materialistic mores of the ancestors—and the archaeological record confirms that Roman aristocrats of the fourth and third centuries led very Spartan lives. When we combine the wealth of textual and archaeological data with modern theory, new understandings of the nature of world history can emerge.

The early Romans developed a set of values, called *mos maiorum* (ancestral custom), which governed their private and public lives. Probably the most important value was *virtus* (virtue), which derived from the word *vir* (man) and embodied all the qualities of a true man as a member of society. *Virtus* included the ability to distinguish between good and evil and to act in ways that promoted good, and especially the common good. It also meant the devotion to one's family and community, and heroism in war. Unlike Greeks, Romans did not stress individual prowess, as exhibited by Homeric heroes or Olympic champions. The ideal of hero was one whose courage, wisdom, and self-sacrifice saved his country in time of peril. "Who with the prospect of death, envy, and punishment staring him in the face, does not hesitate to defend the Republic, he truly can be rekoned a *vir*," says Cicero. Young men were taught that it was "sweet and glorious to die for one's country."

Other important Roman virtues included piety, faith, gravity, and constancy. Piety (*pietas*) was a family virtue—devotion and loyalty by men and women to the family group, willing acceptance of parental authority. It also meant reverence to the gods, expressed through performance of required religious rites and ceremonies, such as the sacrifice of a ram to Janus, or a heifer to Jupiter. Even the infamous gladiatorial fights evolved from an ancient religious ritual involving sacrifice of prisoners to the dead.

Faith (*fides*) meant keeping one's word, paying one's debts, and fulfilling obligations toward people and gods. Violation of *fides* was an offense against both community and gods. Gravity (*gravitas*) meant discipline, absolute self-control—a dignified, serious, and calm attitude toward both good and bad fortune. Constancy (*constantia*) was a related virtue of perseverance, doing what was necessary and right, even under the most trying circumstances. Romans greatly prided themselves on moderation, the avoidance of all kinds of extremes and excesses, and remarked on any instances of immoderate behavior in themselves and in other peoples with disapproval. For example, recollect the characterization by Livy of the Gauls above as susceptible to "the uncontrollable anger which is so characteristic of their race." No true Roman would behave in such a way. This contrast between the Roman *gravitas* and barbarian immoderation, at least as perceived by the Romans themselves, is well illustrated on one episode from the Gallic wars. The story, most likely, is a complete invention, but the point is not whether it actually happened, but how the Romans perceived themselves in opposition to the "other." During one of the encounters between the Roman and Gallic forces, "a Gaul of enormous size" challenged the Romans to a single combat. When the challenge was taken up by Titus Manlius (a member of a patrician family), the Gaul "was fatuously delighted and even stuck out his tongue in derision." The two combatants met between the armies. "One was remarkable for his stature, resplendent in multicolored clothing and painted armor inlaid with gold; the other had a moderate physique for a soldier and was nothing special to look at, with armor that was suitable rather than ornate. He did not sing out war cries, or dance about with useless brandishings of weapons, but his breast swelled with courage and silent anger; all his ferocity was held back for the critical moment of the duel...." Needless to say, Roman determination wins over Gallic brute strength.

ROMAN VALUES WERE PART OF *RELIGIONES*—literally, bonds that held the community together. The ancients recognized the importance of religion in strengthening the state. Socrates reportedly said, "Those who honor the gods most finely with choruses are best in war." Polybius, personally skeptical of religious metaphysics, thought that it played an important role in keeping the masses under control. In general, Roman religion extolled the virtues of hard work, discipline, duty, loyalty, and courage. Religion was the glue that cemented the people together and gave the early Roman society an extremely high degree of asabiya. The cohesiveness of the society was so high that until the first century B.C. Romans did not need a police force to keep public order. The internally motivated discipline of early Romans, the formalized and ritualized behaviors of their culture, was enough to maintain public order. Punishment for many transgressions was a public declaration that the perpetrator acted dishonorably. According to Tacitus, for example, the only penalty suffered by a prostitute was the shame of having to profess her name before public magistrates.

One cannot overemphasize the importance of these personal qualities of early Romans to their subsequent rise as an imperial nation. Note how the Roman virtues served to limit individualism (gravity and constancy), strengthened ties within family (piety) and community (faith), and sacrifice for the common good (*virtus*). Romans held no physical or technological advantage over the peoples they conquered. An average Roman was smaller and weaker than an average Gaul. In a one-to-one duel, an average

Roman would most likely lose to an average Gaul. On the other hand, a hundred Romans could hold even against a hundred of Gauls, and ten thousand Romans would easily defeat a Gallic army many times their number.

But even this comparison is somewhat misleading, because curiously enough, the Romans were pretty lousy at winning battles. The typical sequence of any war between the Romans and their numerous opponents was to lose battles early in the war, but then, nevertheless, win the war. As Livy said, "That lot has been given to us by some fate that in all great wars, having been defeated, we prevail." If the first war was lost, the Romans tried again and again, until they won. (This is a reflection of the Roman virtue of constancy, of course.) That is why the history of Rome is full of "the first," "the second," and "the third" wars with Veii, Samnites, Carthage, Macedon, and so forth.

Perhaps the best illustration is the Second Punic War. Hannibal was a brilliant general and inspired leader. With his heterogeneous army, half of which was brave but undisciplined Gauls, he smashed one Roman army after another—at the Ticinus, at the Trebia, at lake Trasimene, and the worst one, at Cannae. Fifty thousand Romans died at Cannae, one third of the senate was wiped out. "No other nation in the world," says Livy, "could have suffered so tremendous a series of disasters and not been over-whelmed."

What distinguished the Romans from their adversaries was that they were able to overcome such disasters. The Romans knew in a culturally rooted subconscious way that life could only be ensured by willingness to die. The Roman general and later dictator Sulla told his troops once, "You will be the safer the less you spare yourself." Cicero proclaimed in one of his speeches, "That which appears most splendid is that done with a great and exalted spirit and in disregard of the concerns of mortal life."

Perhaps the ultimate expression of this sacrificial spirit was the Roman ritual of "devotion." If a battle was going against the Romans, the Roman commander could devote himself and the enemy army to the gods of the underworld. The basic idea was to place a potent curse on oneself and carry it in the midst of the enemy, thus saving the Roman legions. According to Livy, the ritual involved standing on a spear and repeating the following words: "Janus, Jupiter, Father Mars, Quirinus, Bellona, Lares, new gods, native gods, deities who have power over us and other enemies, and gods of the underworld: I supplicate and revere you, I seek your favor and beseech you, that you prosper the might and victory of the Roman people and afflict the enemies of the Roman people with terror, dread, and death." This was the formula pronounced, for example, by Publius Decius Mus in 295 when the Roman army was on the point of breaking before the onslaught of a combined force of Gauls and Samnites. "After ritual prayers he added that he was driving before him dread, slaughter, and bloodshed, the wrath of the gods above and below, and would pollute with a deadly curse the standards, missiles, and arms of the enemy; that the place of his own destruction would mark that of Gauls and Samnites. With these imprecations upon himself and the enemy he galloped his horse into the Gallic lines, where he saw they were thickest, and threw himself on the enemy weapons to meet his death."

Devotion, thus, was a kind of suicide bombing. Not on the model of the Japanese kamikaze pilot in the Second World War but rather the modern Islamic fundamentalist. The effect was intended to be primarily psychic, rather than physical. The main goal of modern suicide bombers, after all, is much more that the destruction of those specific unfortunates caught in the actual blast. The effect on the Roman troops of such acts of selfless sacrifice was electrifying, while the enemy army became dismayed and prone to losing its will to fight. To resume Livy's narrative: "From then on, the battle hardly seemed to depend on human effort. The Romans, after losing their general (which on other occasions is generally a cause for alarm), checked their flight and wanted to renew the fighting; the Gauls, especially those crowding round the body of the consul, kept throwing their javelins without aim or purpose, as if they had lost their wits, while some of them were stupefied and could think of neither fighting or flight. But on the Roman side, the pontiff [chief priest] Livius … cried out that the Romans had won the day, now that they were freed by the consul's fate. The Gauls and Samnites now belonged to Mother Earth and the gods of the underworld; Decius was carrying off the army he had devoted [that is, the Gauls and Samnites], calling on it to follow him, and on the enemy's side all was madness and terror."

VERTICAL INTEGRATION OF A SOCIETY, the degree of solidarity felt between the commons and aristocracy, is one of the most important characteristics explaining its success at empire building. To investigate how Rome stacked up on this score, we need to understand its social structure, which was intimately connected to Rome's military organization. It was no accident that the original meaning of the Latin word "people"—*populus*—was "army." The bulk of the Roman citizen population were small landowners working their own land. Their great importance to the Roman state was that they supplied the recruits to the legions. Citizens with property valued at 50,000 to 100,000 *asses* (an *as* was a bronze coin; during this period Romans did not use silver or gold coinage) served as hoplites—infantrymen armed with helmet, shield, spear, and sword. These heavily armed infantrymen were the mainstay of ancient Mediterranean armies, and are familiar to us from many Greek depictions. Poorer citizens with property valued at 11,000 to 25,000 *asses* served as light infantrymen (armed with a sling or javelin). At the bottom of the social scale were those who did not serve—propertyless citizens (*proletarii*), foreigners, and slaves.

Wealthier citizens served as cavalry, and for this reason the Roman aristocratic class was known as equestrians or knights. The property qualification for a knight was 400,000 *asses*. At the top of the Roman hierarchy were the senatorial families, who served as cavalry and top officers. The senators and their families constituted around 1 percent of the population, and their average wealth was probably close to 1 million *asses*. In other words, the richest 1 percent of the Romans during the early Republic was only 10 to 20 times as wealthy as an average Roman citizen. This is a remarkably low degree of economic inequality for a pre-industrial population, and even for a modern democratic society. To put these numbers in perspective, consider that in 2000 a median household in the United States had wealth of about $60,000. The top 1 percent of households' average worth was $12 million, or 200 times that of the median. We take pride in the U.S. as a country of equal opportunity, but the sad fact is that our society is much less egalitarian than that of the early Roman Republic.

Economic inequality in a typical ancient or medieval state was much greater than in the early Rome, or even in the United States today. By around A.D. 400, just before the collapse of the empire and when the degree of wealth inequality reached its maximum value, an average Roman noble of senatorial class had property valued in the neighborhood of 20,000 Roman pounds of gold. There was no "middle class" comparable to the small landholders of the third century B.C.; the huge majority of the population was made up of landless peasants working land that belonged to nobles. These peasants had hardly any property at all, but if we estimate it (very generously) at one tenth of a pound of gold, the wealth differential would be 200,000! Inequality grew both as a result of the rich getting richer (late imperial senators were 100 times wealthier than their Republican predecessors) and those of middling wealth becoming poor, indeed destitute.

The frugal lifestyle of the senatorial aristocracy in early Rome also did not distinguish them greatly from the common citizens. Overseas trade during the early Republic was at a low ebb, so hardly any oriental luxuries were imported to serve as goods for conspicuous consumption. The only difference in clothing that distinguished senators from the rest of citizens was the broad purple stripe on their toga. Roman historians of the later age stressed the modest way of life, even poverty of the leading citizens. For example, when Cincinnatus was summoned to be dictator, while working at the plow, he reportedly exclaimed: "My land will not be sown this year, and so we shall run the risk of not having enough to eat!" This is not to deny that the Roman society was acutely aware of rank and status. A noble patrician such as a member of the Claudii clan, many of whose ancestors served as consuls, had more wealth, power, and *auctoritas*—prestige and respect—compared to a common citizen. The Roman Republic was no democracy, and the few senatorial families gathered in their hands the bulk of political power. Nevertheless, no huge precipice existed between the wealthy and powerful few on one hand, and the dispossessed masses on the other, which was to develop during the later Republic and, especially, during the golden age of the Roman Empire.

Vertical integration—lack of glaring barriers between the aristocracy and the commons—seems to be a general characteristic of successful imperial nations during their early phase. To cite another example from antiquity, the lifestyle of the royal family of Macedon before the Persian conquests was also very modest. The mothers and sisters of the kings cooked the food and wove the cloth. When Alexander was conquering the Persian Empire, he wore homespun clothes made by his sisters. During the campaigns, Alexander ate the same food and slept under the same conditions as his soldiers.

Unlike the selfish elites of the later periods, the aristocracy of the early Republic did not spare its blood or treasure in the service of the common interest. When 50,000 Romans, a staggering one fifth of Rome's total manpower, perished in the battle of Cannae, as mentioned previously, the senate lost almost one third of its membership. This suggests that the senatorial aristocracy was more likely to be killed in wars than the average citizen. Add this to the peculiarly Roman practice of "devotion," which was always performed by a member of noble lineage, and it is easy to conclude that generally Roman aristocrats led the commoners in battle, and were the first to die.

The wealthy classes were also the first to volunteer extra taxes when they were needed. One of the best examples of such behavior comes again from the Second Punic War, when the internal cohesion of Rome was tested to what would be a breaking point for almost any other state. When the state ran out of money, the propertied classes agreed to pay a surcharge to provide for salaries for galley crews. A graduated scale was used in which the senators paid the most, followed by the knights, and then other citizens. In addition, officers and centurions (but not common soldiers!) served without pay, saving the state 20 percent of a legion's payroll. Finally, the equestrian businessmen who supplied the army and the fleet agreed to accept promissory notes in lieu of actual payments, which the state simply did not have. In short, everybody sacrificed for the sake of victory, but the greatest burden was placed on the wealthy.

When the leaders do not hide behind rank and shoulder their share of the common burden, the common people are much more likely to fall in line. This is perhaps why the plebs and the aristocracy had coexisted in rather harmonious relations with each other during the early and middle Republic. Even during the most class conflict-ridden decades of the fifth century, the commons never revolted outright. Were they to start a revolution, they would have made short work of the nobility. Plebeian infantrymen heavily outnumbered the aristocratic knights (by a factor of more than 10 to 1—a typical legion had 4,200 infantry and 300 cavalry). The great majority of plebeians were veterans. They could easily self-organize into an army by electing centurions and higher officers from among their ranks, and then slaughter all the upper classes. But they never did so, instead relying on a peaceful direct social action, in their refusal to provide recruits, to press their claims. After the social problems were resolved in the fourth century, and until the next period of social instability during the late Republic, the relations between the aristocracy and the commons were quite harmonious.

TWO FACTORS EXPLAIN THE RISE of the Roman Empire: the high degree of internal cohesiveness of the Roman people, or asabiya, which reached a peak c. 200 B.C.; and the remarkable openness of the Romans to the incorporation of other peoples, often recent enemies. Both factors are necessary for building a world empire. Without high asabiya, an incipient imperial nation cannot survive being surrounded by powerful enemies in the early days of its expansion. Without the ability to truly incorporate the conquered people, an imperial nation cannot grow. Theoretically, there is an alternative: genocide or ethnic cleansing of conquered territory followed by colonization. Many imperial nations employed this strategy to some degree, but in practice all successful ones expanded mainly by cultural assimilation, rather than by biological reproduction. Openness to incorporation is a critical factor in explaining the difference between the imperial careers of the Romans and, say, Macedonians, as opposed to the Spartans, or Athenians.

The internal organization of the Spartans shows that the great degree of internal solidarity characterizing Rome was not unique. Of all Greek nations, the Spartans appear to be most similar to the early Romans. The grave demeanor of the Spartans, their abhorrence of excesses and luxury would have met with approval in Rome. More importantly, the two ancient nations had similar ideas about service to the country, up to and including giving up life. One does not need to go further for an example than the sacrifice of the 300 Spartans in the Thermopylae Pass. Some would propose that the Spartans achieved an even higher degree of asabiya than Romans.

The Spartan upbringing was designed to turn each Spartan into an outstanding, but above all loyal, soldier. At the age of seven, Spartan boys were taken away from their family and were brought up by the state. Plutarch, a Greek historian of the first century A.D., wrote of the Spartan education system emphasizing its military toughness. "They learned reading and writing for basic needs, but all the rest of their education was to make them well-disciplined and steadfast in hardship and victorious in battle. For this reason, as boys grew older, the Spartans intensified their training, cutting their hair short and making them used to walking barefoot and for the most part playing naked. When the boys reached the age of 12, they no longer had tunics to wear, but got one cloak a year. Their bodies were tough and unused to baths and lotions. They only enjoyed such luxury only a few special days a year. They slept, in packs, on beds which they got together on their own, made from the tops of the rushes to be found by the river Eurotas. These they broke off with their bare hands, not using knives."

At the age of 20, the Spartan youths made the transition to adulthood by trying to get elected to one of the dining fraternities, a "mess," to which all Spartan citizens belonged. To fail to win election to a mess meant becoming a social outcast. Members of the mess ate all their meals communally, and each man had to contribute a fixed amount of barley, wine, cheese, and figs every month. Although their status had changed, the state's regulation of their life did not. "Their training continued right into manhood, for nobody was free to live as he wished, but the city was like a military camp, and they had a set way of life and routine in the public service. They were fully convinced that they were the property not of themselves but of the state. If they had no other duty assigned to them, they used to watch the boys, either teaching them something useful, or learning themselves from seniors. For indeed one of the fine and enviable things which Lykourgos achieved for his citizens was a great deal of leisure. He forbade them to practice any manual trade at all. There was no need for the troublesome business and efforts of making money, since wealth had become completely without envy and prestige. The helots worked their land for them, supplying the fixed amount of produce."

Their rigorous upbringing and discipline made the Spartans into unbeatable soldiers. Sparta did not lose a single battle between 800 and 371 B.C. In fact, their training was so severe that war was treated as a vacation. "In times of battles, the officers relaxed the harshest aspects of their discipline ... They also had less rigorous exercises, and they allowed the young men a regime in other respects less restricted and supervised, so that for them alone war was a rest from the preparation for war … It was an impressive and frightening sight to see them advancing in time to the flute and leaving no space in the battle line, with no nervousness in their minds, but calmly and cheerfully moving into the dangerous battle to the sound of music. For men in this frame of mind are unlikely to suffer from fear or excessive excitement, but rather to be steady in their purpose and confident and brave as if their gods were there with them."

How did the Spartans develop this unusual but highly effective social organization? In the eight century B.C., when Sparta unified Laconia in the southern Peloponnesus, it was a fairly typical Greek city-state. The turning point occurred toward the end of the eighth century when Sparta conquered the neighboring area of Messenia. The Spartans divided the land into allotments and turned the Messenians into serfs (helots) who were required to work the land. The rent from each allotment supported an individual Spartan household. In other words, the Spartans turned themselves into a ruling class with leisure (if it can be called that) to devote to military training. The helots were not particularly happy with this state of affairs, and during the succeeding centuries periodically revolted in an attempt to free themselves from the Spartan subjugation. The perpetual threat of helot rebellion (who were ready to rise any time Sparta would encounter military difficulties) was a constant reminder to the Spartan masters not to slacken off on their training and relax their discipline. When the Spartans were finally defeated in battle in 371, the Messenians immediately seceded, and that was the end of Sparta as an important player in Greek politics.

Note here the great difference between the arrangements that Sparta made in Messenia and Rome's treatment of her defeated enemies. Through the fourth, third, and second centuries, Rome continued her policy of admitting former adversaries to the commonwealth. At the end of the last Latin war in 338, Rome absorbed all Latin communities. By the end of the fourth century, Latium and Campania were merged together into a Roman-Campanian state, which involved agreement between the Roman and Capuan aristocracies to create a shared army. The great Capuan families were welcomed into the Roman senate. By 264, all peninsular Italy was under Rome's control. The details of incorporation varied. Some communities were closely integrated with Rome. Their aristocrats were full

Roman citizens, and commoners had all rights of a Roman citizen except for voting. Other communities became allied states—they managed their internal affairs, contributed troops to the Roman army, but did not pay taxes. In the last century B.C., all Italian communities were given full citizenship.

There were, however, limits to the Roman willingness to incorporate aliens. Most significantly, their openness did not extend across the metaethnic divide. Although the definition of *Romanitas* ("Romanness") was gradually extended to include Latins, Campanians, Etruscans, and Greeks, the Gauls were most definitely beyond the pale, and were likely to be treated quite harshly. It was only after the conquest of Transalpine Gaul and with assimilation of the Gauls to the Roman culture and language that they were accepted as "us." The appearance of a new and more extreme kind of barbarian, the German, was also instrumental in the Gauls losing their former status of "them." The important point here is that all ethnic differences are relative. When confronted with the barbarian Gaul, a Roman felt that he and a Tarentine (a Greek denizen of Tarentum), both carriers of urban and literate civilization, had something in common, even though those Greeks were really strange fellows, and some of their habits were quite disgusting. Still, compared to a howling, head-collecting savage....

The Spartans treated the Messenians as a race to be enslaved—because Sparta was not located on a metaethnic frontier. The absolute ethnic difference between a Spartan and a Messenian was much less than between a Roman and a Tarentine. Spartans and Messenians were both Greek people, who spoke different, but mutually understandable dialects of the same language. However, all ethnic difference is relative. In the absence of a very alien "other," the Spartans did not perceive the Messenians as "us," and therefore had no compunction in reducing them to the status of slaves.

Indeed, Sparta went even further. Every year, when they took office, the principal magistrates of Sparta, the ephors, made a formal declaration of war on the helots! The helots, thus, were treated as enemies of the state, and could be killed whenever needed, without going through the cumbersome legal process. As the historian G. E. M. de Ste. Croix noted, declaring war on one's own workforce was an action quite unparalleled in history.

The constant tension between the Spartans and helots was both a source of strength for the Spartan state and, ultimately, the cause of its downfall. Being constantly in the state of war nurtured and maintained a powerful asabiya among the Spartans. But lack of solidarity, in fact, acute conflict between the ruling and producing classes, sapped the ability of Sparta to expand. As a result, Sparta was never able to translate its military hegemony in Greece into a large-enough size to achieve some degree of security against its neighbors, and was brought down when it weakened.

ALTHOUGH THE ATHENIANS WERE VERY different in their social organization from the Spartans, a similar logic affected their treatment of their own subject people, and ensured that their short-lived empire (478–404 B.C.) would not be terribly cohesive or extensive. The Athenian Empire started as a cooperative venture—the Delian League, put together by Ionians to better resist the Persian Empire. Note that it was the overwhelming external threat of Persian invasion in the early fifth century B.C. that briefly united the Greeks. One might imagine that if the Persian frontier were to stabilize for an extended period of time right by Athens, instead of Macedonia as was the case, it would be Athens that would build a mighty empire. Instead, however, the Persians withdrew from the Greek heartland after they lost the naval battle of Salamis.

When the external threat was gone, the Athenians proceeded to use the Delian League for their own selfish purposes rather than for the common good. They gradually converted the contributions by the league members from ships and men to money, which they used to build Athenian ships and to man them with Athenians. In other words, the Athenians set themselves up as a warrior upper class, supported by the economic contributions from the lower classes—the non-Athenian members of the Delian League. The parallel with the Spartans is striking, although the degree of subjugation imposed on the Athenian "allies" was not as severe as that imposed by the Spartans on the helots. The Ionians, nevertheless, resented the state of subjugation they found themselves in and looked for ways to throw off the oppressive Athenian yoke. When Athens lost the Peloponnesian War to the Spartans, her allies all escaped, and the Athenian Empire was over.

In contrast to Sparta and Athens, Rome was not abandoned by all her allies when she found herself in desperate straits during the Hannibalic war. Hannibal was able to detach various Italian communities from Rome only by threatening them with overwhelming force. Only the Bruttians, a hill tribe of southern Italy, went over to Hannibal wholeheartedly (and were later brutally punished by Rome for this). Many Italian cities fought loyally for Rome, and suffered greatly from Hannibal as a result. Some cities were internally divided by pro-Punic and pro-Roman factions. Aristocratic factions tended to stand by Rome, because of the inclusive way they were treated by Romans. Their loyalty was later rewarded when they and their descendants participated in the spoils of the spectacular Roman conquests of the second and first centuries B.C.

The final comparison in this chapter is between the Macedonians and other Greeks. Macedon arose as a typical frontier state on the periphery of the Hellenic civilization. The Macedonians were first confronted with the nomadic Thracians, and then they were conquered by the Persians. After a brief stint as the marchland of the Persian Empire, they regained independence, and immediately came under strong pressure from the expanding Celts. These repeated blows and life on the metaethnic divide, in general, forged a strong sense of national unity among the Macedonians. When they were finally conquered by Rome, the Romans divided Macedon into four separate provinces, thus incorporating it piecemeal into the empire. The Macedonians were so incensed about this treatment that they revolted. The revolt was not about gaining independence from Rome (Macedonians realized that this was not in the cards), but they wanted to be incorporated as one unit, because the Macedonians felt they belonged together. The Romans caved in and created a single province of Macedonia.

Unlike classical Greek city-states, Macedon from its inception was a territorial state. It is a telling distinction. When the Athenians acquired the island of Salamis, they did not incorporate it into *Attica* ("Athenian land"). Instead, they planted some colonies of Athenians on the best land and treated the natives of Salamis as inferiors. Salamis continued to be a separate unit from Attica. The Spartans, similarly, did not expand the definition of Laconia when the conquered Messenia, but continued to call the two regions by their old names. By contrast, every time the Macedonians conquered any land, they incorporated it into Macedon. They continued doing so until Philip II, the father of Alexander the Great. Their inclusive policy provided the Macedonians with a strong base from which to begin the conquest of the known world.

WE HAVE NOW TRACED THE FATES of imperial nations in Europe from the first millennium B.C. to the first millennium A.D. At each step, we have seen that the historical record bears out the predictions of the metaethnic frontier theory. World empires arise from regions where civilizations clash. Does the pattern hold for the second millennium A.D., the world into which we were born? This is the question that is addressed in the next chapter.

Chapter 7

A Medieval Black Hole

The Rise of the Great European Powers on Carolingian Marches

E urope experienced three imperial ages. The first was the Roman Empire. As discussed in the preceding chapter, Rome arose on the fault line between Mediterranean civilization and Celtic "barbarism." The geographic core of the Roman Empire was the Mediterranean Sea, which the Romans affectionately called "Our Sea" (*Mare Nostrum*). During the Roman period, the Mediterranean knitted its coastal regions together by permitting rapid communications by ship and cheap transport of troops and bulk goods. For example, Rome was fed by the annual shipment of enormous quantities of grain from North Africa. When Rome imploded, however, its core region (Italy, Greece, and the coastal provinces of Spain and North Africa) became a kind of "asabiya black hole"—an area where social cooperation on a scale large enough to build an empire was impossible to achieve. At the same time, new imperial nations, with the gift for collective action, arose on the Roman frontiers—the Franks, the Arabs and the Berbers, the Byzantines and the Avars. The new powers built their empires and squabbled over the core areas of the former Roman Empire, where capacity for collective action was low and political power was fragmented. As Christianity spread within Europe, and Islam within the Near East and North Africa, the Mediterranean Sea, instead of being a connector, became a dividing moat between two hostile and armed camps.

During the second imperial age, the empire of the Franks and other Germanic peoples dominated the western half of Europe. Like all large pre-industrial states, this medieval German Empire went through secular cycles of alternating integrative–disintegrative phases: the kingdom of the Franks under the Merovingian dynasty (the sixth and seventh centuries), the Frankish Empire under the Carolingians (the eighth and ninth centuries), and the German *Reich* under the Ottonian and Salian emperors (the tenth and eleventh centuries). The core region of this empire was centered on the Rhineland (formerly the Roman frontier in northwest Europe). Beginning in the twelfth century, this core area gradually disintegrated into a hodgepodge of statelets ruled by dukes, counts, and imperial knights; bishops and archbishops; and town councils. This political dissolution marked the development of another asabiya black hole, which ran in a wide band right through the middle of Europe.

During the third imperial age, roughly speaking the last 500 years, no single empire dominated the political landscape of Europe. Instead, there were always several great powers contending for European hegemony. The composition of this exclusive club of nations changed across the centuries, and episodically one of them or another would achieve a hegemonic status, but these hegemonic moments were fleeting, and none of the European imperial nations could match the preponderance of power achieved by the Romans or the Franks. This peculiarity of European history, the failure of all attempts since the Frankish Empire to unify it, has generated much discussion among the scholars. Solving this puzzle will be one of our goals in this chapter. To trace the rise of great powers and to understand how "Europe was made," we need to go back in time to the Franks and even to the Romans. Did the European great powers arise on metaethnic frontiers?

A convenient date to begin tracing the making of Europe is Christmas day in A.D. 800, when Charlemagne was crowned as the new "Roman emperor" by the pope. At this point in time, the Carolingian Empire united the huge territories of modern France, Benelux, West Germany, Switzerland, Austria, the northern and central Italy, and a foothold on the Iberian Peninsula (Catalonia). After the death of Charlemagne in 814, however, internecine dissension began weakening the Frankish Empire. Sensing the internal weakness, the external enemies of the Franks increased raiding pressure on the Frankish borderlands. As the process of internal dissolution gathered momentum within the empire, the predatory forays began reaching beyond the frontiers. The Magyar raids deep into France on Laon in 919 and on Berry in 937 proved that no region was safe anymore.

Enemies surrounded the Frankish Empire: the Saracens in the south-west, the Vikings in the northwest, the western Slavs in the northeast, and the Magyars in the southeast. Frontier regions, which the Franks called "marches," faced each of the invaders. After the Carolingian Empire disintegrated, its successors together with the other Roman Catholic states—collectively called Latin Christendom—continued the centuries-long struggle. The four former Frankish marches were true metaethnic fault lines, where Christians confronted Muslim Saracens, and pagan Vikings, Slavs, and Magyars. We will look at all of them in turn, beginning with the Spanish march, and then moving in clockwise manner from there.

THE CAROLINGIAN FRONTIER WITH ISLAM took shape during the eighth century. In 711, an army of 7,000 Berber infantry and 300 Arab cavalry invaded Spain and destroyed the Christian army in the battle on the Guadalete. The Visigothic kingdom collapsed, and by 719 the Saracens drove the remaining Christians into the mountains of Galicia and Asturia. The Muslims then crossed the Pyrenees and invaded France, but were defeated by Charlemagne's grandfather Charles Martel, "The Hammer," in the battle of Tours in 732. The Muslim wave crested, and after that they began their centuries-long retreat. By 759, they were expelled from France, and in 777 the Franks led by Charlemagne crossed into Spain. This campaign, however, ended in disaster. As Charlemagne's army returned to France through the Pass of Roncesvalles, its rearguard was cut to pieces by the Basques. Despite this disaster, in 801 Charlemagne captured Barcelona and established the Spanish March in Catalonia.

This battle of Roncesvalles inspired the eleventh-century *Song of Roland*, in which Roland, a loyal and courageous, but proud and rash vassal of Charlemagne, is ambushed by demonic Saracens and dies together with 20,000 Franks of the rearguard. But his sacrifice is not in vain because he is fighting for God and Christianity. Charlemagne returns with the main army, defeats the Saracens, forces more than 100,000 "pagans" to convert to Christianity and kills those who refuse. Note the similarities with the *Stroganov Chronicle*: Both texts depict the struggle across the metaethnic frontier in stark black-and-white terms. Both characterize the enemy as "pagan," although Islam, similarly to Christianity, is a monotheistic religion.

When the Muslims destroyed the kingdom of the Visigoths, they settled in the rich southern region of Andalusia with the capital in Córdoba.
The Visigothic remnants hung on by the skin of their teeth in the mountainous north. When the Christians retreated north, they removed the
population and razed the fortifications and settlements. The Muslims kept
pressure on the Christians in the north with annual raids, but did not
attempt to settle the abandoned area. As a result, a wide swath of territory
running through the middle of the Iberian Peninsula between the Muslim
and Christian areas became essentially empty of all population. This was a
classical metaethnic frontier. It separated two monotheistic world religions
utterly opposed to each other. It was also a significant cultural and economic fault line. Andalusia was a wealthy urbanized society with literate
elites. Its capital, Córdoba, was the largest city in Europe after
Constantinople. By contrast, the Christian society in the north was rude,
unlettered, poor, and rural. The populations of its largest "cities" such as
Barcelona or Santiago were a hundred times smaller than Córdoba's.

The Iberian frontier between Muslims and Christians persisted for
almost eight centuries, from the Muslim invasion in 711 to the conquest of
Granada in 1492. During the first three centuries, it was largely stationary—a broad swath of territory running east-west about one third of the
way down the peninsula. There were minor fluctuations back and forth.
The Frankish armies pushed south around A.D. 800, but were driven back
after the death of Charlemagne. During the tenth century, the Asturians
and the Navarrese seized some territory from the Muslims and began settling population there. Toward the end of the century, however, the
Muslim armies under the capable general Al-Mansur inflicted a series of
defeats on the Christians. Al-Mansur sacked Barcelona, Leon, Santiago,
and Pamplona. He leveled the Basilica of Santiago and carried away its
bells to Córdoba where, to add insult to injury, he ordered them upended
and used as braziers in the mosque. The situation looked grim, but fortunately for the Christians, beginning in the 1030s, the caliphate of Córdoba
lost its internal cohesion and began fragmenting into smaller statelets. At
this point, the frontier's nature changed from the "push" to "pull"—there
were empty frontier lands for the settling and much lucrative booty farther
down south, in the wealthy but now weak Andalusia. The *Reconquista*
began.

CAN WE GAIN A GLIMPSE INTO the life on the Iberian frontier? Here is the story of one small episode in this centuries-long conflict from the chronicle of Alphonso VII, as retold by the historian James Powers in *A Society Organized for War.* "In 1132 a small army of Christian soldiers advanced northwest along the road to Córdoba, offering periodic shouts and chants in the manner of armies attempting to keep up their spirits as they proceed through the enemy territory. Outside the Iberian Peninsula in the twelfth century, this force would have to be regarded as remarkable in every respect. The column consisted of both mounted and foot troops, they were situated over four hundred kilometers from their home base, and they consisted largely of the municipal militias of two towns, Segovia and Ávila, operating on a campaign they had chosen to initiate. They had passed three mountain ranges and they moved far from home on a daring raid into the heart of Almoravid Spain. As they ranged over the countryside seeking targets, a scouting party dispatched earlier to search for sources of booty rejoined the main body. It brought sobering intelligence information: a Muslim force commanded by the Almoravid prince Tashfin of Córdoba had been spotted encamped in the vicinity, probably dispatched in pursuit of their own squadrons. A more timorous force of skirmishers and raiders might well have sought the nearest ford in the Guadalquivir River and made its way back to the Trans-Duero region whence it mustered. However, these troops were no panicky amateurs, prone to flight without consideration of the risk of being overtaken and routed. Like trained professionals, they instead sought out the enemy army.

"The leaders demonstrated initiative and combativeness. Frontier warfare in Iberia included taking risks, and sound strategy dictated a direct assault on the opponent's force, especially if any kind of surprise could be achieved. Altering plans and direction and invoking 'the God of Heaven and Earth, Holy Mary, and Saint James' for their protection; the town militia undertook to search out the enemy army with whom they now shared the Campo de Lucena. In time, estimating that they were close to the Almoravid position, the militias encamped and divided into two detachments. The entire cavalry force and approximately one half of its infantry moved out on reconnaissance to locate the Muslims, while the other half of the foot soldiers remained at the campsite to guard the baggage and supplies.

"The breadth of the *campo* proved sufficient to hide the Muslims and Christians from each other for a time. They traveled a half day's journey from their camp and found nothing; afternoon faded into evening and brought no contact. As the darkness of night intensified, the Christians stumbled upon the Almoravid encampment, catching the settled force completely off-guard. The Muslims sounded the alarm, raced for their weapons, and a confused and fierce melee ensued. The Christians pressed the advantage of their surprise attack and cut down many opponents before they could arm themselves. In the darkness and disorder, Christian and Almoravid could barely distinguish each other. Suddenly, Prince Tashfin bursts form his field tent shouting commands in an attempt to rally his men. He was greeted by a Christian lance that pierced his thigh, transforming his determination to sudden panic. Ignoring his wound, Tashfin hobbled to the nearest horse, mounted it bareback, spurred it into action, and galloped from the scene of the struggle, disappearing into the gloom in the direction of Córdoba. The surviving Almoravids soon followed their leader's example, retreating in confused disarray. Tashfin's troops never recovered from their initial surprise to put up a good fight.

"Once the dust settled, the Christian militiamen looked about them at the campsite and the booty left there for the taking. They gathered all that they could carry and marched back to their camp. The raid had been extremely successful: mules, camels, gold, silver, weapons, and even Tashfin's own battle standard were included in the spoils. The warriors of Ávila and Segovia divided the booty on the spot, then began the trek back to their own towns while praising God for their fortune. They would discover that Tashfin had planned a raid against Toledo with the force they had encountered, a raid the militias had terminated. The Muslim soldiers instead straggled back to Córdoba empty-handed. Prince Tashfin … walked with a limp for the remainder of his days."

Although the particular way of organizing frontier warfare, municipal militia, was culture specific, this band of Castilian frontiersmen in most important ways resembled many other forces of frontiersmen, such as the Cossacks of Ermak, for instance. Neither force was a professional army. Both were cohesive self-organized units, for which no orders needed to be issued, because every man was ready to do his share. Both groups used similar religious symbols to maintain their cohesion and demarcate themselves from the enemy. Finally, both were motivated in a large degree by the prospect of the booty.

I am not the first one to draw parallels between the Iberian *Reconquista* and the Russian conquest of the steppe. Several historians, including James Powers, have noted how the similarities of the frontier environment in these two societies resulted in many similar social institutions. Probably the most striking parallel is the remarkable egalitarianism and easy social mobility that characterized each society. As in Muscovy, the frontier warriors served either as cavalry or infantry. The mounted *caballeros* enjoyed a higher social status compared to the *peones* who fought on foot. They also had access to better land and pasturage, and better opportunity for booty in warfare. The *peones* were non-noble peasants, herdsmen, and craftsmen. However, a *peón* who wanted to achieve the status of *caballero* had numerous opportunities to do so. The most direct way, assuming he had the funds, was to purchase a horse and arms and begin serving as cavalry. Not all towns allowed for such upward mobility, so a move closer to the frontier might be necessary. A foot soldier could also move to the area where the king had a particular need for cavalry and obtain the horse and arms from the state. Finally, a foot soldier could gain the needed equipment as booty in combat. For example, a soldier who unseated a Muslim cavalryman in battle was awarded the enemy's horse. The openness of the Castilian elites to those who were willing to provide military service persisted as long as the frontier conditions prevailed. Just as in Muscovy, when the frontier moved away, the opportunities for upward mobility dried up, and the social structure hardened.

The Castilian frontier society also had highly developed norms of fairness. This was reflected in, for example, the strict rules for the division of the profits of war. When a raiding party returned, the town council announced a day on which everyone had to bring to the town plaza whatever booty they captured. All spoils, including livestock, clothing, arms, and precious metals, were auctioned. A portion of the proceeds was used to reward acts of heroism, but the bulk was distributed to everybody who participated in the expedition, with the size of the share dependent on the equipment. (Thus, cavalrymen received greater shares than those who fought on foot.) Anybody who tried to conceal an item was punished. The system curbed self-serving behavior that could be detrimental to the collective effort—all too many battles in history were lost because soldiers were more intent on plundering the captured camp of the enemy instead of nailing down victory. By making sure that each received his fair share, this method of booty division promoted cooperation on the battlefield. Clearly, the system was designed by a bunch of moralists!

Most of the population on the Iberian frontier lived in towns. As on the Russian frontier, the role of towns was not economic, but defensive. The numerous fortified communities dotting the frontier region provided a defense in depth against the Muslim raids. Unlike the Russians, however, the Castilians did not build defensive lines. Whereas the Russians had grain fields to protect, the main economic activity in Castile was sheep herding, and it was easier to bring the sheep flocks inside the walls when a raid threatened. Another difference between the two frontiers was that whereas the Russian frontier was mainly of the "push" type (due to the murderous pressure from the raiding Tatar parties), the Iberian frontier, after the Reconquest gathered steam, was mainly of the "pull" kind. The rich Muslim lands and towns in southern Spain offered opportunities for plunder and were more attractive to Christian raiders than anything offered from other compass points.

The municipal militias played the key role in the Iberian Reconquest. There was no single center orchestrating military operations. Instead various Christian kingdoms (Navarre, Leon, Aragon, Portugal, and Castile) operated independently of each other, and often fought with each other. Eventually, three main pushes developed: the Aragonese down the Mediterranean coast, the Portuguese along the Atlantic littoral, and the Castilians down the middle. Even within each kingdom, such as Castile, advance was achieved not by royal armies winning spectacular victories. In fact, the Christians lost most of the major battles prior to the thirteenth century! (As I have commented before, the ability of winning despite repeated setbacks seems to be one of the talents that high-asabiya nations have.) But groups of frontiersmen, driven by relentless pressure to colonize, won numerous small victories, and that was what powered the advance. "Different men, different regimes, different attainments," wrote the historian of Medieval Spain Claudio Sánchez-Albornoz, "but always, always, century after century, following battle, colonization, and after colonization, battle." The same words could be said about the Cossacks and peasants on the Russia's steppe frontier.

As a result of this decentralized organization, the advance south could only happen when the Muslim states fell prey to internal strife, which they did once every hundred years or so, following Ibn Khaldun cycles. Thus, a tentative push south by the Christians during the tenth century was repelled and reversed by the Córdoban general Al-Mansur. When the caliphate of Córdoba disintegrated in the middle of the eleventh century, a more lasting advance became possible, and Castile conquered the area around Toledo. This push was checked when the Almoravid Berbers entered Spain and crushed the Castilian army at Zallaka (A.D. 1086). In the twelfth century, the Almoravid dynasty went into decline and the Christians pushed the frontier farther south, until stopped by another wave of Berbers, the Almohads, who conquered the Muslim Spain in 1150. The biggest push came in the thirteenth century, after the Almohads were defeated by a Christian coalition in the great battle of Las Navas de Tolosa (A.D. 1212). By the end of the century, the only Muslim state remaining in Spain was Granada. During the fourteenth and most of the fifteenth centuries, however, the Reconquest stalled again, this time because Castile experienced a secular decentralization phase (together with the rest of Western Europe, as discussed in Part II).

This lengthy period of internal instability and civil war finally ended when the forces loyal to Queen Isabella won the War of Succession in 1476. To bring order to the war-torn Castilian countryside, Isabella turned to town militias. She created the *Santa Hermandad* ("Holy Brotherhood"), which unified the town militias, and gave it extensive police and judicial powers. The brotherhood patrolled the roads and suppressed brigandage. When they caught a criminal, they judged him in their own court and meted out swift and savage punishment. They were so effective that they restored order in the countryside in just a few years. Instead of disbanding the brotherhood, however, Isabella and Ferdinand used it in their war against the last Iberian Muslim state. When Granada fell to the Christian armies in 1492, the Iberian frontier ceased to exist. With the end of the frontier, the utility of urban militias also came to an end. The last time they played an important military role was, ironically, in the Comunero uprising against Charles V in 1520–21. However, the militia tradition influenced the subsequent military evolution of the famous Spanish infantry troops, called *tercios*. Spanish *tercios* consisted of a mixture of pikemen and arquebusiers. Pikes were used for defense (especially against a cavalry charge), whereas the fireguns provided the offensive power. Spanish *tercios* were the dominant military force in Europe during the sixteenth century. The division of infantry companies into pikemen and gunners was made obsolete only with the invention of the bayonet in the seventeenth century.

The Anglo-Saxon historiography tends to play down the glory and power of Spain, but in the sixteenth century it was the supreme power in Europe, and it was a great power until the end of the eighteenth century. It is useful to consider what Pierre de Bourdeille, lord of Brântome, wrote in about 1600 about the achievements of the Spaniards: "They have conquered the Indies, East and West, a whole New World. They have beaten us and chased us out of Naples and Milan. They have passed to Flanders and France itself, taken our towns and beaten us in battle. They have beaten the Germans, which no Roman emperor could do since Julius Caesar. They have crossed the seas and taken Africa. Through little groups of men in citadels, rocks and castles, they have given laws to the rulers of Italy and the estates of Flanders." High praise indeed from the enemy.

The imperial nation at the core of the Spanish Empire were the Castilians. They carried the burden of the empire. On a per-capita basis, they paid more taxes and supplied greater numbers of recruits for the *tercios*. They spearheaded the overseas conquests. They also had a knack for cooperating with other peoples within the Spanish Empire. As the historian Henry Kamen recently argued in *Empire: How Spain Became a World Power, 1492–1763*, the Spanish Empire was a collaboration of the Castilians with the Aragonese, Italians, Flemish, Germans, and even Chinese and Aztecs. Italian financiers, German technicians, and Flemish traders were as critical to the imperial success as Castilian military men and administrators.

The Castilians were made as a nation on the Iberian frontier. The bands of adventurers led by Cortés and Pizarro who conquered the New World and the Spanish *tercios* that smashed European armies were direct descendants of the Christian militias that battled the Moors during the Reconquest. The frontier transformed the Castilians into "A Society Organized for War" (as the title of James Powers' book has it). But it not only made Castile into an effective war machine, it also molded the national character of its people—their deep faith, tenacity, sense of honor, and ability to cooperate—all qualities that made them such good imperialists.

THE IBERIAN METAETHNIC FRONTIER HAD a rather simple topology and dynamics—a band of territory extending from east to west, which slowly advanced south (although the advance occurred in fits and starts). The metaethnic interaction zone in northern France had a much more complex history. By "North France" here I mean the territory centered on the Seine River, and extending to the Loire Valley in the south and the Somme in the north. During the Carolingian period, it was called *Francia*.

After the conquest of the Gaul, the Roman frontier was established on the Rhine, leaving North France deep behind the lines. During the crisis of the third century, however, the Rhine frontier collapsed, and North France was subjected to severe raiding pressure from the Germanic tribes. Moreover, at the same time the Franks began pushing south and settling the Low Countries. As a result, North France found itself on a metaethnic frontier. This was a major fault line—between urbanized Romance-speaking Christians and tribal Germanic Odin worshippers—discussed in Chapter 3.

During the fourth century, the Roman Empire regained its internal stability. It was a time of prosperity and population growth, and archaeological data indicates that the population of southern Gaul completely recovered from the troubles of the third century. But in the north, population recovery was feeble, indicating continuing conditions of insecurity associated with an intense frontier. The usual frontier pressures must have been at work, because by the end of the fifth century a reasonably cohesive society emerged in North France. When the western Roman Empire finally collapsed in A.D. 476, its territory was divided among the kingdoms of Visigoths, Ostrogoths, Franks, Burgundians, and Alamanni. The only exception was the area of North France, which was held by the native elites led by the Roman patrician Syagrius.

The kingdom of Syagrius, however, was not a match against the surging power of the Franks. In 486, Clovis defeated Syagrius and incorporated his territory into the Frankish Empire. The Romano-Gallic nobility, however, was not displaced by the Frankish war chieftains. The Merovingian kings realized the value of trained and literate administrators for their budding empire, and the Romano-Gallic patricians were incorporated into the Frankish ruling elite. Several generations later, intermarriage and mutual assimilation made it difficult to tell the Frank from the Roman.

Archaeological and toponymic (place names) evidence suggests that there was a very substantial immigration into North France by Germanic farmers. They were probably the dominant element north of the Seine, becoming sparser as one moved south toward the Loire. Eventually, all these colonizers converted to Christianity and assimilated to the Romance language. Although the contemporary sources called them "the Franks," they were now divided from their brethren living in the Rhine area by language. (The Frankish language, belonging to the Germanic linguistic group was a direct ancestor of the modern Flemish.) The inhabitants of North France, thus, were of very diverse ethnic origin (which is a typical situation on the metaethnic fault line). The Celtic population who inhabited this region when it was conquered by Caesar were already a mongrel people. To this substrate were added Roman legionnaires and their dependents who were brought in to defend the frontier, and the Germanic farmers who moved into the area when it was added to the Frankish realm (and there was to be another infusion of Germanic people from Scandinavia, as discussed shortly). After the empire of Charlemagne broke up in the ninth century, it gradually became clear that, despite their diverse ethnic origins, the people of North France had developed a distinct ethnic identity. When the German Empire was reconstituted under the Ottonian and Salian dynasties, Francia stayed out of it.

The incorporation of the kingdom of Syagrius into the Frankish Empire should have been the end of the frontier in North France, but for a quirk of history. During the fifth century, Roman Britain descended into anarchy and was abandoned by the legions. Internal weakness invited first raiding and then colonization by Picts, Irish, Saxons, Angles, Jutes, and Frisians. Many British (Celtic) chieftains and their dependents fled from the chaos and established themselves across the English Channel in Armorica. British migration to Armorica continued during the sixth century, and the area became known as Brittany ("Little Britain") and its Celtic inhabitants as Bretons. For some reason (perhaps because they detested Germanic invaders who drove them out of Britain), the Bretons conceived an abiding hatred for the Franks, and started raiding into Francia. The Franks attempted to conquer Brittany on several occasions and once managed to occupy the peninsula briefly. But the Franks were never able to sustain their political control over the Bretons, and had to establish the March of Brittany to guard against the Breton pressure.

The Breton identity turned out to be stonily resistant to assimilation by the French. It even survived a rather brutal attack on it by the republican French government during the nineteenth century (when children were severely punished for speaking Breton in schools). It is still alive and kicking today. Nevertheless, the March of Brittany does not qualify as a major fault line, because the Bretons and the Franks were both Christians (although Bretons practiced a somewhat different brand of Christianity). Yet the animosity between the two peoples, and the constant raiding and counter-raiding resulted in a sparsely populated gap in North France. This gap created an opportunity for a different kind of invaders to wedge themselves in—the Vikings.

Viking dragon boats first appeared off the British Isles c. 790, but did not trouble the Frankish Empire while it maintained its internal cohesion. This changed dramatically when the empire was plunged into a series of civil wars among Charlemagne's successors. During the 840s, the Vikings established camps in the mouths of the Loire, Seine, and Somme and used these rivers as highways for raids deep into Francia. One of Charlemagne's grandsons Charles the Bald (843–877) established the March of Neustria and appointed Robert the Strong, the count of Paris, to organize the defense against the Vikings. It became clear to the locals very soon that the crumbling Carolingian Empire, preoccupied with internecine fighting, could not spare forces for the defense of frontiers. If they wanted protection, they had to organize it themselves. This job fell to the capable and energetic counts of Paris, such as Odo, son of Robert the Strong, who in 885 led the heroic defense of Paris against the great Viking attack. The future capital of France during the ninth and tenth centuries was a frontier fortress, and from the line of Robert the Strong and Count Odo would come the Capetian kings of France.

The Scandinavians began their assault on the northwestern margins of the Carolingian Empire with raids, which soon became annual affairs. The next logical step was to establish permanent bases in the mouths of the rivers, such as the Seine and the Loire, which facilitated penetration deep into the Frankish territory. Finally, the bases began attracting land-hungry colonists from Scandinavia who came to settle and work the land. Ultimately, the colonization push into the hinterland succeeded from only one beachhead—from the mouth of the Seine. In 911, the Viking chief of Rouen, Hrolfr (Rollo to the Franks), extorted from Charles III, one of the last Carolingians, a charter granting him the lands that would eventually become Normandy. For these lands, Hrolfr did homage to Charles III, but this act was as much a legal fiction as Hrolfr's conversion to Christianity a year later. A Frankish chronicler wrote that Hrolfr "after having been made Christian, had many captives beheaded before him in honor of the gods he worshipped."

New waves of settlers from Scandinavia arrived during the tenth century, and Normandy was expanded in the western, southern, and eastern directions. The Norman expansion exerted an enormous pressure on the surrounding people. The Bretons, who fought so effectively against the Carolingians, collapsed, and their chieftains escaped across the channel. The Norse war bands continued plundering the Frankish lands. A Frankish chronicler wrote that in 924, "Rögnvald with his Norsemen ... depopulated Hugh's [count of Paris] land between the Loire and the Seine." Another band "devastated the land across the Seine." The Normans themselves were very well aware of the amount of devastation they visited on the Frankish lands, and how much hatred their raids inspired, as the following story shows. When Norse chieftains rebelled against William Longsword (Hrolfr's son and successor in Rouen), William contemplated taking his personal war band with him and fleeing to the Franks. His chief supporter Bernard the Dane demurred, "We will hasten with you as far as the river Epte [the border of Normandy with Francia], but truly we will not go into Francia. For in the past we often raided there with your father, and we cut down many once fighting had begun. Indeed we either killed or took captive the grandfathers and maternal uncles, the fathers and paternal uncles, the maternal aunts and paternal aunts, the cousins and brothers of those living there. And how we hope to survive in the face of such enemies?" As the historian Eleanor Searle noted in her book *Predatory Kinship and the Creation of Norman Power, 840–1066*, the Normans thought of their relationship with the Franks in terms of a blood feud.

DURING THE NINTH AND TENTH CENTURIES, Norse raiding and the establishment of Normandy created a metaethnic frontier in North France. It was remarkably similar to the Roman frontier of half a millennium before, but on a smaller scale. On one side was a Romance-speaking Christian culture with at least some literacy among the elites (mainly, the ecclesiastical ones). On the other side were the "barbarian" Germanic Odin worshippers. Even after A.D. 1000, when the Normans assimilated to the Romance language and Christian religion, they retained a fierce self-identification as Normans, separate from, indeed hostile to, the Franks.

It took only a century or so for the north French to begin organizing effective resistance in the face of Norman pressure. This was an unusually rapid response—generally speaking, around two or three centuries under frontier conditions need to pass before new aggressive nations arise. But the people of North France descended from the Roman frontiersmen and Frankish colonists. Finding themselves on the periphery of the Frankish Empire, they were not subjected to asabiya-corrupting influences that always affect core regions. Thus, already by the middle of the tenth century, we see the first clear signs of political consolidation around the counts of Paris, Anjou, and Blois—and the dukes of Normandy.

After all, when the alien population from Scandinavia settled down within Normandy, surrounded by hostile neighbors on all sides, they came under the same kind of pressure that they exerted on their neighbors. The Viking raiders had very high asabiya, but its social scale was small—they cooperated within small kin-based groups. This was enough for raiding. A Norman war band, faced by an overwhelming army, could get on their ships and row themselves to safety. After the Normans acquired land, however, they had to learn to cooperate on a larger scale to defend it. In her important book on Norman "predatory kinship," Eleanor Searle traced the process by which the Norman community formed out of disparate bands of Nordic raiders and settlers. "By the mid-eleventh century," she writes, "the descendants of the settlers formed the most disciplined, cooperative warrior society in Europe, capable of a communal effort—the conquest and subjugation of England—that was not, and could not have been, mounted by any other European political entity." Searle argues that the tenth century Normans creatively used their notion of kinship to cross-link the whole warrior society in Normandy. Perhaps the most striking example of such a "predatory kinship" group is the Norman conquest of southern Italy and Sicily. It was led by, literally, a band of brothers—the 10 sons of Tancred of Hauteville. The army of William the Conqueror, which invaded England in 1066, was a band of brothers in a less literal sense. It was a band of kinsmen—brothers, first and second cousins, brothers-in-law and sons-in-law, and so on. Kinship links crisscrossed the leadership of William's host and held it together as one cohesive whole.

The specific mechanism for Norman solidarity that Searle proposes, therefore, is particular to the time and place and to the cultural peculiarities of the Normans (for example, their Germanic notions of kinship). More generally, however, the Normans had high asabiya because they coalesced as a nation on a metaethnic frontier. In general, although group solidarity always increases under frontier conditions, the specific means of achieving cohesion depend on the culture and situation.

The Norman conquest of England is especially remarkable because they had to subjugate a nation that itself had achieved a high degree of social cohesion. The English of the eleventh century were descendants of Saxons, Angles, Jutes, Frisians, and other Germanic tribes who began colonizing Britain in 430–440s, taking advantage of the social disintegration that followed the withdrawal of the Roman legions. The British west and north (Cornwall, Wales, Strathclyde, and Scotland) remained Celtic, whereas in the south and east the Germanic invaders largely replaced the native population. There was probably no systematic genocide against the Britons (although this period is very obscure, and almost anything is possible). But when the German farmers took over the agricultural land, the fate of the Romano-British population in towns was sealed. Until modern times, death rates of urban populations always outweighed their birth rates, and Roman towns in England quietly withered.

The metaethnic frontier running between the Christian Celts and pagan Germans existed for more than two centuries, until A.D. 670 when Anglo-Saxons converted to Christianity. The ethnic frontier between the English and Celtic areas, nevertheless, did not go away and the enmity between the two peoples continued. Another metaethnic frontier arose during the ninth and tenth centuries when Britain was inundated by Viking raiders and colonizers. The Norse and Danish settlers inserted themselves in large numbers into Yorkshire and northern East Anglia.

By 1066, the centuries of frontier pressures forged the heterogeneous bands of Germanic invaders into a cohesive English nation. The country was unified and had an effective king in the newly elected Harold Godwinson. Historians agree that the battle of Hastings was a very closely fought affair. If Harold and his army had not needed to dash up to Yorkshire (where they handily defeated the invading Norse at the battle of Stamford Bridge) and then dash back south, arriving tired and under-strength, they probably would have pushed William's army into the sea. As it was, the whole English leadership perished at Hastings. During the next 20 years, the Normans killed or drove away practically all the English nobility, replacing them with new continental elites.

The nearly simultaneous Norman conquests of England and southern Italy gives a rare "experimental" demonstration of the importance of asabiya in the lower classes. The ruler class in both cases was recruited from the same pool of highly cohesive Norman warriors. During the twelfth century, Norman Italy and England were probably the two best-governed states in all of Europe. However, whereas in England the Norman nobility implanted itself on top of a socially tight-knit English peasantry, southern Italy—the core region of the defunct Roman Empire—was an asabiya black hole. After the twelfth century, the trajectories of the two countries diverged in opposite directions. England conquered the whole of the British Isles and half of France, lost this first empire, and then conquered a world empire and became a hegemonic power in the nineteenth century.

By contrast, southern Italy, after its Norman nobility lost its initial solidarity, slipped back into geopolitical backwater. It passed first into the hands of German emperors, and then to a junior branch of the French Capetians (the Angevins). For many centuries, it was part of the Spanish Empire, and finally it was forcibly incorporated into new Italy by the house of Savoy. Many northern Italians feel, even today, that it was a terrible mistake.

NORMANDY WAS ONLY THE FIRST EMPIRE to explode from the metaethnic pressure cooker of North France. New centers of political power crystallized on the French side of the frontier during the tenth century around the counts of Anjou, Blois, and Paris. Blois was the first to succumb, torn apart by the stronger surrounding states. The duel between the remaining two counts, however, was more evenly matched and for a while it was not clear whether France's capital would be Paris or Angers. The counts of Paris gained some advantage by becoming the kings of France in 987, but at this point the royal title was a largely empty honor. The early Capetians barely controlled the area around Paris (Ile-de-France) and some lands around Orléans on the Loire. Even these nominally royal lands were studded by castles owned by unruly and recalcitrant nobles, over whom the king had no real power.

The counts of Anjou expanded their domains by skillfully playing the dynastic game. Henry II Plantagenet (1154–89), inherited Anjou, Touraine, and Maine from his father, and Normandy and England from his mother, the daughter of Henry I, when the latter died without male offspring. Henry married Eleanor of Aquitaine, gaining Poitou, Guyenne, and Gascony. While the French kings puttered about reducing the power of their unruly barons, castle by castle, the Plantagenet domains grew to dwarf the lands of the French crown. It might have seemed that the contest was over. Yet in the end it was the patient and systematic strategy that won the day. The main problem of the Angevin Empire of Henry II was that his ruling class was recruited from two different imperial nations, which is always an unstable situation. The Normans and the French came from the opposite sides of the metaethnic frontier, and even though they both now spoke similar dialects and professed the same religion, they thought of themselves as different and opposed groups. Much more time would have to pass before a merger would be possible. (The Normans of Normandy began to think of themselves as French in the sixteenth century at the earliest.) As a result, the configuration of the Angevin state was unstable, and it had to tip one way or another, with either the French nobility dominating, or Norman, but not both. The issue was resolved when Philip August (1180–1223) conquered all French possessions of the Plantagenets except for Guyenne.

The lasting success of the Capetian state was due to their first unifying their ethnic core, the population of North France, and only then expanding beyond it. After the core was unified, however, the subsequent expansion was rapid. Normandy and Flanders were annexed in the north, while the Albigensian crusade gained for France Languedoc in the south. During the thirteenth century, France became the hegemonic power in Europe. Its large territory and population generated a steady flow of taxes into royal coffers. Its warlike and cohesive nobility dominated the European battlefields. And its brilliant and influential culture was admired throughout Latin Christendom.

UNLIKE THE COMPLEX HISTORY OF THE northwestern marches of Latin Christendom, the dynamics of its northeastern frontier are much easier to trace. In this respect, this frontier is more like that in Iberia, than in North France. In fact, it is remarkable how similar the German *Drang nach Osten* ("drive to the east") was to the Iberian *Reconquista*, as we shall see.

The area of primary interest to us is the region between the rivers Elbe and Oder, which closely corresponds to what was until recently East Germany. During the Roman times, Germanic tribes inhabited this region. During the period of the great migrations after the collapse of the western Roman Empire, however, the Germans abandoned East Germany and were replaced with western Slavs, whom the Germans called the Wends. Historians do not completely understand why this happened. Most likely, local Germanic tribes were weakened when their most active elements migrated toward the former Roman lands, attracted by the opportunities of booty and rich agricultural lands to settle on. At the same time, the Slavic people began their expansion from wherever their homeland was. (The authorities continue to wrangle over this question.) When German tribes, who stayed home, came under stiff raiding pressure from the Slavs expanding westward, they probably decided to join their relatives in warmer and safer climes. This Slavic "drive to the west" started during the fifth or sixth century. By the end of the eight century, the border between the Germanic Saxons and Slavic Wends was located along the Elbe. When Charlemagne conquered the Saxons in 785 and converted them *en mass* to Christianity, the Elbe frontier became a metaethnic fault line.

The German eastward drive occurred in fits and starts, and took centuries to complete. There was a tentative thrust under Charlemagne, which did not amount to anything. When the Carolingian Empire collapsed, the Saxon lands came under stiff raiding pressure from the Wends. Effective resistance against the raids could be organized only in the beginning of the tenth century under the new Ottonian emperors. The Elbe and Weser valleys in Saxony and Thuringia were fortified. Towns, villas, and monasteries were palisaded and garrisoned. After their heartland was protected, the Saxons went on the offensive against the Wends. In 928, they crossed the frozen Havel River and stormed Branibor (Brandenburg). Several years later, the emperor Henry I destroyed a large Slav army at the battle of Lenzen. During the subsequent decades, the Saxon emperors divided East Germany into marks and established several bishoprics under the new archbishopric of Magdeburg to convert the Slavs. However, in 983, a Slav uprising destroyed most of the Saxon gains east of Elbe. The problem was that the emperors were more interested in expanding their influence in Italy than in subduing the wilderness of East Germany, and the marcher lords were not strong enough to make headway against the Wends on their own. For the next century and a half, the *Drang nach Osten* ground to a halt.

The centuries-long German drive to the east put a lot of pressure on the Slavic (and later Baltic) peoples on the other side of the frontier. As it advanced, it triggered formation of the states of Czechs, Poles, and later Lithuanians. Both Czechs and Poles converted to Christianity during the early eleventh century. The Czechs had to accept the vassal status within the empire. The core area of Poland was farther east, which gave the Poles enough of a respite to organize a state large enough to resist the German advance. History showed that the Czech and Polish chieftains who decided to adopt Christianity made a wise decision, because it allowed these nations to preserve their identity and language, survive and even at times thrive.

The other Slavic tribes, such as the Abodrites, Liutizi, and Rugians, persisted in their paganism. Reacting to the Christian pressure, these Slavs developed their own militant and organized form of paganism. For example, the Rugians worshipped the four-headed idol Svantovit, whose shrine was located in Arkona on the island of Rügen. The cult of Svantovit was headed by the high priest, the only Rugian allowed to grow his hair long. Every year the whole nation attended the harvest festival in Arkona, bringing cattle for sacrifice. The cult collected taxes and was guarded by a war band of 300 horsemen.

The intensity of the struggle between the Saxons and Polabians easily qualifies as genocidal. Slav raiding parties routinely massacred men and enslaved women and children. The name of one tribe, *Liutizi* means in Slavic "the Fierce Ones" (which is an interesting parallel with the Franks, whose name meant the same thing). Another tribe was called the *Wilzi*—"the Wolves." The Saxons, on their part, committed a great many atrocities, such as gouging eyes and cutting off tongues, or simply slaughtering hundreds of captives, which their chroniclers report very matter-of-factly. In one episode, Margrave (marcher lord) Gero invited 30 Slavic leaders to a "friendship banquet." After they got drunk, he had them all slaughtered. This anecdote is reminiscent of Virginia Governor Wyatt's "peace conference" with the Powhatan Indians in 1622—different times and different places, but the same murderous quality where civilizations clash. There were no, or very few, kinship ties across the metaethnic divide, which could mitigate the hostility, because Christians were forbidden to marry pagans. When a Slav chieftain proposed that his son marry the niece of the Saxon duke, Margrave Dietrich responded that the duke's kinswoman was not to be given to a dog. The marriage never took place.

The eastward expansion resumed during the reign of Conrad III (1138–52). The pressure for the crusade came from the grass roots, not the emperors. Conrad himself did not get involved in any way. The expansion was orchestrated by the marcher lords, such as Henry the Lion, duke of Saxony, and Albert the Bear, margrave of Brandenburg. The ideological cover was provided by the pope, who authorized the German crusade against the Slavs in 1147. The motivations of the crusaders were the usual mixture of ideology and self-interest. "The pagans are evil," wrote the bishop of Magdeburg in 1108, "but their land is good in meat, honey, flour, and poultry, and when it is tilled, full of rich harvests beyond compare. Thus say those who know it. Therefore, oh you Saxons, Franks, Lorainers, and Flemings, you famous men and conquerors of the world, here you can save your souls and if it pleases you, gain the best land for your dwelling."

This time East Germany was conquered for good, and Henry the Lion began the push into lands east of the Elbe. In 1226, a new player appeared on the scene—the Teutonic Order. The Teutonic knights responded to an appeal from the Polish duke Conrad of Masovia for aid against the pagan

Prussians. Conrad gave them Kulmerland as a base, and promised them whatever territory they conquered from the Prussians. In 1237, the Teutonic Order merged with the Livonian Brothers of the Sword, who were based in Latvia, and the crusading knights pushed away from the Baltic littoral. Prussian resistance was brutally put down. The suppression was marked by a large-scale genocide against the native Balts, followed by forced Christianization and Germanization of the survivors. At the same time, the newly conquered lands received a steady flow of colonists— Westphalian nobles, Cistercian monks, Flemish and German merchants, and peasants from Saxony, the Netherlands, and Denmark.

During the thirteenth century, East Germany became a melting pot that swallowed diverse peoples, from pagan Slavs to Flemish merchants, and turned them all into Germans. Its northern part, the province of Brandenburg with its capital in Berlin, was to become the core from which Germany became unified many centuries later. Other areas that were heavily colonized by Germans were Pomerania along the Baltic shore (western Pomerania is now in Poland), Prussia (now partly in Poland, and partly the Russian region of Kaliningrad), and Silesia, lying along the Upper Oder (now also in Poland). These four areas became the core around which modern Germany crystallized during the seventeenth, eighteenth, and nineteenth centuries. The rise of Brandenburg-Prussia-Germany was rapid. "In 1640, when Fredrick William of Hohenzollern, the Great Elector, came to power in Brandenburg, Prussia was a poor and remote province which he held in fief from the Polish crown, while his other territories lay scattered widely through the Germanies. But when the Great Elector died in 1688, Brandenburg-Prussia had become a garrison state, in which all available resources were concentrated upon the task of sustaining a large and efficient standing army. Frederick William and his officials allowed nothing to stand in the way of this goal. Noble privileges, provincial and town immunities, guild and even village customs all were coordinated, adjusted, and if need be suppressed in order to produce the greatest possible military strength. As a result, what had been poor, weak, and disparate territories were knitted together into an administrative unity which proved capable of not only defending itself, but also providing an effective base from which the authority of the house of Hohenzollern could be extended to new lands" writes William McNeill in *The Rise of the West*. In other words, Prussia was yet another "society organized for war."

Brandenburg, Prussia, Pomerania, and Silesia were all products of the *Drang nach Osten*, and during the seventeenth and eighteenth centuries these former frontier provinces became the core of the resurgent Germany. It is ironic that the greater part of the real core of the modern Germany now lies outside it. A result of the defeat of the Third Reich, it is not an irony Adolf Hitler would have enjoyed.

As a result of conversion and colonization, by the end of the thirteenth century the whole southern Baltic from Denmark and northern Germany through Poland and East Prussia to Latvia and Estonia became an integral part of Latin Christendom. This great thrust ground up and destroyed some Baltic peoples, such as the Prussians, whose very name has now been appropriated by their conquerors. Others, such as Estes and Letts, submerged for many centuries, but persisted as serfs working for their German masters, and emerged as small nations in the twentieth centuries. Finally, one people responded by consolidating its forces, and building its own great empire—the Lithuanians.

When the Sword-Brothers of Riga intruded in the territory of the future Lithuania in 1203, there were no such people as the Lithuanians. Instead, many small Baltic tribes of peasants were governed by a mounted-warrior class. Two centuries before, the Russian lands to the south and east became Christian, and these Baltic pagans found themselves on a metaethnic frontier. They endured raiding pressure from the Principality of Polotsk, and occasionally had to pay tribute. When the Kievan Russia disintegrated during the twelfth century, the Balts themselves began raiding the Polotsk lands, as well as in other directions. Chieftains with their armed retinues went on raids every spring, returning with cattle, slaves, and silver. Each tribe had a fort, where they could take refuge when the neighbors retaliated. Given low population density, dense forests, and extensive marshes, the military pressure on these Balts was not particularly high.

The situation changed dramatically with the arrival of the disciplined and rapacious knights of the Teutonic and Sword-Brother orders. During the thirteenth and fourteenth centuries, the "proto-Lithuanians" were squeezed from the western and northern directions simultaneously.

They saw their Baltic brethren annihilated or subjugated by the German juggernaut. Beginning in the 1240s, they were also assaulted from the east by the Mongols of the Golden Horde. In short, they found themselves in a metaethnic pressure cooker, where they had only two choices—consolidate or go under. The Lithuanians consolidated and founded one of the largest European empires.

In 1219, there were about 20 Lithuanian princes. Forty years later, one of them, Mindaugas, had mobilized the entire population to fight for him, the nobles as cavalry, the peasants as infantry. This first attempt at unification foundered, and in 1263 Mindaugas was murdered by his own brother-in-law. But the pressure from the Teutonic Order continued, and when it intensified in the early fourteenth century, another unifier arose. Under Gediminas (1316–41), Lithuania began expanding into the land of former Kievan Rus, which were at that time under tribute to the Golden Horde. The expansion continued under the next grand duke, Algirdas (1341–77), and Lithuania reached to the Black Sea. The next grand duke, Jogaila (1377–1434), married Jadwiga of Poland. During the fifteenth century, Lithuania-Poland became the largest territorial state in Europe. In 1410, Jogaila defeated the Teutonic Order in a great battle of Grünwald, and in 1466 the Teutonic Order was finally brought to heel. It became a vassal of the Polish crown, and henceforth half of its membership was to be Polish. This triumph of a Slavic-Baltic state over the German crusading order is undoubtedly one of the most spectacular turnarounds in human history. But no triumph is permanent in history. At the end of the eighteenth century, the Hohenzollern kings of Prussia, who started as the vassals of the Polish crown, were busily carving up Poland, squabbling over choice cuts with their fellow predators, the Habsburgs and Romanovs.

To the end of the fourteenth century, Lithuanians remained pagan, because paganism was an inalienable element of their national identity, based as it was on the opposition to the Latin Christianity of the German crusaders. However, after the German threat subsided, the Lithuanians found that they could now dispense with their paganism. Jogaila accepted baptism in 1386 as part of the deal in which he acquired the Polish crown. There was some initial resistance to Christianity, but during the fifteenth century the Lithuanians gradually converted. They were the last European people to become Christian.

THE THREE FRONTIERS DISCUSSED IN this chapter were, in a way, local affairs. Their dynamics were affected by events that occurred, at most, a few hundred kilometers away. The southeastern march of the Latin Christendom, by contrast, responded to pulses that originated many thousands of miles away, on the other side of Eurasia. There, on the interface between Mongolia and northern China, lay arguably the world's greatest metaethnic fault line, "the Mother of all Clashes of Civilizations" (with apologies to Saddam Hussein and Samuel Huntington). This Inner Asian frontier formed during the first millennium B.C. and was responsible for repeated state formation in China across the ages. On the steppe side of the frontier, three great imperial nations were born—the Hsiung-Nu, the Turks, and the Mongols. Each of these nomadic nations built a huge Eurasian empire, subjugating some steppe peoples, and thrusting others out. A nomadic nation, coming under pressure from the powerful neighbor in the east, would gather its fighting men, women, children, and herds and shift westward, putting pressure on the next people down the line, in a kind of a domino effect. As a result, the repeated empire-building pulsations on the frontier with China generated waves of pressure traveling westward across the great steppe. The last stop was the westernmost extension of the Eurasian steppe, the plains of Hungary.

The first nomadic wave from Inner Asia to reach the Hungarian plain were the Huns, who are thought to be the descendants of the Hsiung-Nu. At the very least, they took their name from that imperial nation. (Hsiung-Nu is the modern reading of the Chinese characters; in ancient times the name was probably pronounced something like "Hunnu.") The next wave, the Avars, was an offshoot of the Turkic Empire. The Avars were followed by the Magyars. The last nomadic invasion, the Mongol *tumens* under Batu Khan, wiped out the Hungarian army in 1241, but then left, because Batu wanted to participate in the election of the next great khan, and had to prepare for a trip of several thousand miles to the east.

Every time the Hungarian plain was inundated by the nomadic people from Inner Asia, the area on the Middle Danube just to the west (modern Austria *sans* Tirol) found itself in a very tough neighborhood. This was the region where the southeastern march of Latin Christendom was located. The march dates to the Carolingian times. In 788, Charlemagne deposed Duke Tassilo and incorporated Bavaria into the Frankish Empire. The future Austria was at the time within the Avar Empire. In a series of campaigns over the next eight years, the Franks destroyed the power of the Avars and established the East March (Ostmark in German, which was later changed to Osterreich, Latinized to Austria). Austria became predominantly German as a result of colonization from Bavaria.

For about a century, the Hungarian plains became a sort of no man's land. The power of the Avars was destroyed, but the Frankish Empire did not have enough people to colonize it. In any case, during the ninth century, the Carolingians went into decline, and had more than enough to occupy themselves within the empire. The local people, a farrago of Dacians, Germans, Huns, Avars, and Slavs, were not organized into states. Into this political void the Magyars (also known as Hungarians) thrust themselves. One puzzling thing about the Magyars is their language, related to the Ugro-Finnic dialects of the northern Eurasian forests; some scholars have suggested that that region must be the origin of the group. Most likely, the Magyars arose as a result of some kind of interaction between the forest Ugric and steppe Turkic peoples. In all other ways, the Magyars were a typical nomadic tribal confederation like the Huns or the Turks. Indeed, medieval Europeans simply called them the Turks.

As soon as the Magyars settled down in Hungary, they began preying on the German lands of the former Carolingian Empire. As mentioned earlier, some of their raids reached as far as France. Austria was the natural corridor through which Hungarian raids were channeled, when they wanted to plunder the empire, and it was devastated. In 924, the first Ottonian emperor had to agree to pay tribute to the Magyars to stop their destructive forays. However, as the power of the Ottonian Germany became consolidated (in which the Magyar pressure played not the least role), the Germans gradually shifted to the offensive. In 955, the Emperor Otto I decisively defeated the Magyars at the battle of Lechfeld. Charlemagne's Ostmark was reestablished, and Bavarians were again encouraged to colonize Austria. At the same time, the Hungarians, deprived of easy pickings in Germany, began settling down. As they gradually shifted from nomadism to settled agriculture, the Hungarians became susceptible to conversion to Christianity. The first attempt to convert them was made by St. Stephen (997–1038), but in 1046 Christianity in Hungary was dealt a huge blow, when pagan tribal chiefs overthrew Stephen's successor, massacred the Christians, and destroyed the churches. Hungary finally became a predominantly Christian kingdom only after 1100.

The conversion of Hungary nevertheless was an important turning point. Hungary became part of Latin Christendom, and even though the Hungarians and the Germans fought many wars after 1100, and mutual enmity lingered on all the way to the nineteenth century, a metaethnic divide no longer existed between the two nations. They now belonged to the same civilization.

For three centuries, Austria was the Frankish march against the steppe invaders (and before that, this region was the Roman frontier province of Noricum). The centuries on the metaethnic fault line created a highly solidary nation with its own distinct identity (which is one of the reasons why Austria is still outside Germany). The rise of Austria as a great power was slow but steady. It acquired the status of an independent duchy in 1156, and in 1282 became the core of the budding Habsburg Empire. The Habsburgs acquired Carinthia and Carniola (Slovenia) in 1335 and Tirol in 1368. In 1438, they became emperors of the German ("Holy Roman") Empire, and kept the imperial crown until the dissolution of the empire in 1806. Of course, the Holy Roman Empire was a pretty ramshackle construct, but nevertheless it gave the emperor a good deal of soft power. The big spurt of territorial expansion came in 1526, after the Ottoman Turks smashed the Hungarian army at the battle of Mohacs and conquered two thirds of the Hungarian Empire. The Habsburgs grabbed the unconquered Hungarian possessions of Croatia, Bohemia, Moravia, Slovakia, and Silesia. (Silesia was lost to Prussia in 1742.)

With the arrival of the Turks on the Hungarian plains, Austria again found itself on an intense metaethnic fault line. Vienna became a frontier fortress and was besieged by the Turks twice, in 1529 and 1683. During this period all expansion ceased and the Austrians dug themselves in, repelling one wave of Muslim invaders after another. Finally, after the second siege of Vienna the Austrians went on the offensive. The conquest of Turkish Hungary and Transylvania in 1699 doubled the Austrian territory and made it into a great power of the first rank. During the eighteenth century, Austria took over the Spanish possession in Italy and the Netherlands, participated in the partitions of Poland, and continued to expand at the expense of the Ottoman Empire.

In the nineteenth century, Austria was undoubtedly a member of the great powers club, but it was probably the weakest—not because of lack of territory or manpower, but because of the centrifugal tendencies of various nationalities within the empire. The main problem was the Hungarians. As noted before, any political construction that contains two distinct imperial nations is unstable. Either there must be amalgamation into one ethnic core nation, or separation. During the reign of Charles V (1519–58), the Habsburg Empire had two cores, the Castilians and the Austrians. This arrangement was not workable, and the empire peacefully separated when Charles abdicated. The Spanish part went to Charles's son Philip II, and the German to his brother Ferdinand I. When Hungary was reconquered in 1699, the Habsburg Empire again enfolded two imperial nations. The Hungarians chafed under the Austrian tutelage. Even though the Austrians tried to propitiate them by reformulating the empire as the double monarchy of Austria-Hungary, and assigning such Slavic lands as Slovakia and Croatia to the Hungarian crown, it was not enough to satisfy the Hungarian ruling class, who still dreamed of past imperial glories. That the Austrians and Hungarians were born on the opposite sides of the metaethnic frontier was also a factor, even though that was centuries in the past. Not only did the Hungarians refuse to assimilate to German, as the logical common language of the empire, they embarked on a program of assimilating their subject Slav populations to the Hungarian. The tension between the two nations encouraged centrifugal tendencies on the part of smaller nationalities of the empire. For example, Hungarian persecution of the Slovak language and culture played an important role in feeding the nascent national identity of this small Slavic people. In any case, the nineteenth century was the age of nationalism, and this ideology infected all subject nations of the Habsburg Empire—Italians, Czechs, and South Slavs—with the disastrous consequences for the internal cohesion of the state. The end came when the Habsburgs overextended themselves with the occupation of Bosnia in the late nineteenth century. It was formally annexed in 1908, which led directly to the fateful shots fired by Gavrilo Princip in Sarajevo six years later, World War I, the Austrian defeat, and dismemberment at the hands of the victors.

The collapse of the Habsburg Empire in 1918 should not, however, make us forget the Austrian achievement in the preceding centuries.

All empires collapse, sooner or later. The remarkable thing about the Austrians was that they managed to keep their multinational empire for so long, given that they were only 10 percent of the total population! How did they make it work? For one thing, they sacrificed more than any other people within the empire. The Germans paid heavier taxes than anybody else. Second, and more important, was the arrival of the Turks on the doorstep of Vienna in 1529. For the next three centuries, the struggle against the Muslim Ottomans became the *raison-d'être* of the Habsburg Empire. The Ottoman thrust reawakened the defensive mechanisms engraved on the national psyche when Austria was on the steppe frontier with the Avars and the Magyars. It also enhanced the cohesion of the multinational empire. When confronted with the Muslim threat, Germans, Czechs, Italians, and even Hungarians knew that they were on the same side, and had to hang together.

I NOW RETURN TO THE QUESTION that I asked at the beginning of the chapter. Why did Europe stay disunited in the post-Carolingian period? A current answer to this question, offered by Jared Diamond in *Guns, Germs, and Steel*, is that European geography was not conducive to imperial unification. "Europe has a highly indented coastline," the explanation goes, "with five large peninsulas that approach islands in their isolation, and all of which evolved independent languages, ethnic groups, and governments: Greece, Italy, Iberia, Denmark, and Norway/Sweden." Diamond contrasts Europe with China, whose coastline is much smoother. The geographic unity of East Asia, argues Diamond, was responsible for the longest-running empire in the world—from the Chin unification in 221 B.C. to the present.

But this explanation cannot be correct. Seas are not always moats; they can also unite. The Roman Empire unified three of the peninsulas that Diamond mentions, plus Britain, Anatolia, the rest of the Mediterranean, and half of continental Europe. The Mediterranean Sea knitted together the Roman Empire, instead of isolating its provinces from each other. People are divided by mountain chains, not by internal seas and narrow straights. China has more mountainous terrain than Europe. (Those Chinese landscape paintings are not fantasies!) By contrast, Europe has a broad plain running all the way from Aquitaine through Germany, Poland, Belarus and Ukraine, to Russia. This huge plain offers no significant barriers to expansion. History shows that life there was always precarious—just look at how often the capitals located on the plain have been overrun by enemies. Moscow was destroyed by the Mongols, occupied by the Poles, burnt by the Tatars and the French of Napoleon, and came within a hair of falling to Nazi Germany in 1941. Paris was occupied by the Russians at the end of the Napoleonic wars, and captured twice by the Germans since then. Berlin was captured and burned by the Russians during the Seven Year War, and again stormed in 1945. But the most graphic example of how precarious existence can be on the North European Plain is Poland—dismembered in three stages by Prussia, Russia, and Austria in the eighteenth century, then once again divided between Germany and Soviet Union in 1939. There must be some other reason than geography that would explain why these conquests never took, why the North European Plain was never unified since the days of Charlemagne.

In fact, it is not Europe that is exceptional, it is China. No other region in the world has had such a long history of imperial rule. Perversely enough, the reason, ultimately, is geographic or, more precisely, ecological. The distribution of rainfall within eastern Asia creates a sharp ecological boundary between the drier steppe and wetter agricultural regions. Ever since humans learned predatory nomadism, this ecological boundary coincided with a metaethnic frontier between nomadic pastoralists and settled agriculturalists. Under pressure from the steppe, Chinese agriculturalists built one empire after another. On the steppe side, the nomads united in one imperial confederation after another. The Chinese made forays into the nomad territory, but never could make it their own, because they could not grow crops there. Nomads repeatedly conquered China, but in the process assimilated and merged into the Chinese. The fault line between the Chinese and nomadic civilizations was anchored by the geography of eastern Asia. That is why one universal empire repeatedly followed another in China. A universal empire is a state that unifies all, or virtually all, of a civilization.

The western part of Eurasia also saw two universal empires, that of the Romans and of the Carolingians. Both of these empires arose on metaethnic frontiers. And in that they were similar to China. But unlike China, the

Roman and the Carolingian empires moved the frontiers away from their cores. After centuries away from the frontier, Roman and Carolingian cores became asabiya black holes—regions where people are unable to cooperate on a scale large enough to build functioning states.

After the Carolingian decline, the Frankish core went through another centralization-decentralization cycle (under the Ottonian and Salian emperors), and then disintegrated for good. This configuration of the collapsed core ringed with outward-facing marches predetermined a "centrifugal" orientation of the new centers of power. The rising powers fought over the core area constantly, but their efforts repeatedly stalemated each other. (The Mediterranean was never unified in the post-Roman times for exactly the same reason.) Expansion proved to be much easier in the directions away from the core. Many centuries passed before the great powers finally divided the core among themselves—France getting Lorraine and Alsace, the Habsburgs grabbing the Netherlands, and the Prussians gobbling up most of the rest, leaving just a few fragments such as Luxemburg.

The Carolingian Empire was the embryonic form of what we now call Western civilization. The main bulk of Latin Christendom, that part of medieval Europe that was Roman Catholic, rather than Orthodox or non-Christian, consisted of the Carolingian successor states (for example, France and the German *Reich*). To this core were added regions that were conquered (Spain and Prussia, for example) or proselytized (for example, Denmark and Poland) from the formerly Carolingian lands. Although never united politically, the inhabitants of Latin Christendom knew that they belonged together in a certain, supranational sense. They were unified by their common faith, headed by the pope in Rome, by shared culture, and by the common language of literature, liturgy, and international diplomacy, Latin. As the historian-medievalist Robert Bartlett argued in *The Making of Europe: Conquest, Colonization and Cultural Change, 950–1350*, the outsiders were also aware of this metaethnic identity, and called Latin Christians collectively "the Franks" (*Faranga* in Arabic, *Fraggoi* in Greek). The minstrel Ambroise wrote about the First Crusade, "When Syria was recovered in the other war and Antioch besieged, the great wars and battles against the Turks and miscreants, so many of whom were slaughtered, there was no plotting or squabbling, no one asked who was Norman or French, who Poitevin or Breton, who from Maine or Burgundy, who was Flemish or English … all were called 'Franks', be they brown or bay or sorrel or white." Latin Christendom was the direct predecessor of Western civilization, and even the religious schism of the Reformation, despite the rivers of blood that it undammed, turned out to be a quarrel within family. It did not destroy the metaethnic identity whose roots go back to the Carolingians.

Even today, it is easy to see the traces of this identity. The first members of the European Union were, and the most enthusiastic proponents of the European Union are, France, Germany, the countries of Benelux, and Italy—almost precisely the regions that were part of the Carolingian Empire. Any region that during the Middle Ages was Roman Catholic, whether it is now Catholic or Protestant, is welcome within the European Union. Poles, Croatians, and the Czechs were eagerly encouraged to join, as soon as they freed themselves from Soviet domination. By contrast, Muslim Turkey, even though a part of NATO for more than half a century, is not a member yet, and it is doubtful that it will become one. Formerly Orthodox Ukraine and Belarus are most emphatically not welcome. Even Greece was accepted in the European Union only as a result of heavy-handed American pressure.

Latin Christendom, and its successor, Western civilization, never developed a universal empire. Not because of Europe's indented coastline, its lack of unity was due to the centrifugal orientation of the empires born on the Carolingian marches, away from its fragmented core. There is nothing particularly unusual in Europe's inability to achieve unity. Almost all other regions of comparable size were unified for only a portion of their history. The only exception to this rule is China, in which one universal empire replaced another soon after the previous one collapsed. And the reason for the Chinese exceptionalism is its location on a permanent metaethnic frontier with steppe nomads.

The permanency of the Chinese steppe frontier is unusual, but in other ways the case of China provides yet another confirmation of the macrohistorical regularity that imperial nations are born on intense and prolonged metaethnic frontiers. That is the essential history of the rise of all world empires.

Part II

IMPERIOPATHOSIS

The Fall of Empires

Chapter 8

The Other Side of the Wheel of Fortune

From the Glorious Thirteenth Century into the Abyss of the Fourteenth

"Iam in Paris, in the royal city where abundance of natural wealth not only holds those who live there, but also attracts those from afar. Just as the moon outshines the stars in brilliance, so does this city, the seat of monarchy, lift her head above the rest." Thus wrote Gui de Bazoches, a chronicler from Champagne who visited Paris during the reign of Philip II Augustus (1180–1223).

The thirteenth century was the golden age of medieval France. The territory controlled directly by the French crown tripled between 1200 and 1300. The territorial explosion of France began under Philip Augustus, who took away all French possessions of the Plantagenets, except Aquitaine. Southern France was acquired under his successor Louis IX (St. Louis) as a result of the Albigenisan crusades. By 1300, France came to dominate Western Europe militarily, politically, and culturally. To the east, the once formidable German Empire had disintegrated, leaving a multitude of city-states and tiny principalities. To the south, the resurgent Castile was still preoccupied with its *Reconquista* against the Iberian Moors. Castile's time of greatness was still two centuries in the future. France's only significant rival was England. But the population of England was only one fourth of France's, and the income of the English Plantagenets was a fraction of that of the French Capetians. The population of France was more than 20 million—every third inhabitant of Western Europe owed allegiance to the French king.

The city of Paris with its 230,000 people was by far the largest and most splendid city of Latin Christendom. The cultural predominance of

France during the High Middle Ages cannot be overstated. The Gothic style of architecture, known to the contemporaries as the French style, developed in Ile-de-France and spread from there to England, Germany, Spain, and northern Italy. During the thirteenth century, the University of Paris became the main center of learning and philosophy in Europe, attracting the best thinkers of the age: Albertus Magnus of Germany, Thomas Aquinas of Italy, and Duns Scotus of Scotland. Although Latin still reigned as the language of learning and international diplomacy, French became the most important vernacular language in Europe. It was spoken by the nobilities of England, Flanders, the kingdom of Naples and Sicily, in the remnants of the kingdom of Jerusalem, and, after 1310, in Hungary.

When the fourteenth century opened, wrote the historian Barbara Tuchman in *A Distant Mirror*, the superiority of the French in chivalry, learning, and Christian devotion was taken for granted. Gerald of Wales acknowledged that "the fame of French knights dominates the world." The Spanish knight Don Pero Ninō described the French as "generous and great givers of presents ... very gay, giving themselves up to pleasure and seeking it. They are very amorous, women as well as men, and proud of it." Knights and even monarchs from all over Europe assembled at the royal court of France—"the most chivalrous sojourn in the world," according to the blind King John of Bohemia, who preferred the French court to his own. French monarchs were accorded the formula of "Most Christian Kings."

Yet despite its brilliant opening, the fourteenth century was to plunge France into the depths of wretchedness. During the next 150 years, France would experience famine, pestilence, incessant war, political disintegration, brigandage, and a widespread social mood of pessimism and despair. At the nadir, France was going to find herself without a crowned king and capital, and with most of her territory occupied by foreign troops. When the Italian humanist Francesco Petrarch visited France in 1360, he lamented, "I could scarcely recognize anything I saw. The most opulent of kingdoms is a heap of ashes; there was not a single house standing except those protected by the ramparts of towns and citadels. Where is now Paris that was once such a great city?"

PEOPLE IN THE MIDDLE AGES knew very well that power, riches, and glory were impermanent. A common visual expression of this idea, found in

Gothic cathedrals and illustrated manuscripts, was the "Wheel of Fortune." A typical representation showed a goddess of Fortune standing by a large wheel. At the top a man is seated, his head crowned and a scepter in hand. Little does he know that his moment of power and glory is transient. When Fortune turns the wheel, the king descends and his crown falls off. By the time he reaches the bottom, he is dressed in rags. But then Fortune gives the wheel another crank, and he who was at the bottom is carried high to glory again.

Looking at the history of France and other Western European countries from a bird's eye view, the Wheel of Fortune is clear. Periods of national prosperity and strong states alternate with periods of economic decline and social disintegration in a cyclical fashion. The High Middle Ages were followed by the calamitous fourteenth century. But then Europe experienced the Renaissance, a period of prosperity and cultural brilliance in many ways similar to the High Middle Ages. The Renaissance was followed by the "crisis of the seventeenth century," but again, the times of trouble were eventually over. The last complete cycle began with the Age of Enlightenment and ended with the Age of Revolution (1789–1849). There is a peculiar rhythm of history, forcing societies to alternate between secular (century-long) periods of prosperity and crisis. And such *secular cycles* were not peculiar to the European history—we find them in all agrarian empires about which we know enough to quantify their economic, social, and political changes.

The Wheel of Fortune is simply an allegory for any cyclical process of rise and fall. One problem with this metaphor, however, is that it offers a too mechanical view of history—that rise and fall are somehow imposed by an external force. It is natural for us to think in terms of simple cause-effect explanations of this kind. Thus, the most popular explanation of why the fourteenth century was the time of decline and disintegration in Europe invokes climatic change. During the medieval times, the explanation goes, climate was warm and harvests abundant. In the fourteenth century, however, temperatures fell, crops suffered, and complex societies could not sustain themselves any longer and went into collapse. However, this explanation cannot be right. During the past few years, climatologists made great strides in refining their estimates of how temperatures fluctuated over the last two millennia. With these better data, we now see that there is no correlation between spells of cold weather and times of trouble.

Cooling climate sometimes coincides with crisis periods, but most often not. Climatic change, thus, cannot be the real reason for the secular cycles, although it can contribute to trouble—causing crop failures or aiding the spread of disease.

An alternative way of thinking about rise and fall looks to the internal workings of states and societies, rather than some external agent, be it the goddess of Fortune or climatic change. This way of thinking originated within physical sciences during the days of Newton and Leibnitz and was, in large degree, responsible for the brilliant successes of such fields as classical mechanics and thermodynamics. During the last two or three decades, it spread to biology and social sciences under the guise of "the science of nonlinear dynamics."

The gist of the approach was admirably expressed by George Puttenham in 1589: "Peace makes plentie, plentie makes pride, pride breeds quarrel, and quarrel breeds warre: Warre brings spoile, and spoile povertie, povertie pacience, and pacience peace: So peace brings warre and warre brings peace." What is important here is not the specific details of how one thing leads to another, but the absence of a simple, linear causal relationship. What causes "warre"? Peace. But peace itself is caused by war. So there is no cause and effect, or rather each is both the cause and the effect. War brings peace, and peace brings war, and so on, cycle after cycle, ad infinitum. The causation is not linear, but circular.

How does this insight help us understand why agrarian societies experience periodic crises every two or three centuries? By itself it doesn't, but it points to how we can gain understanding. Measurements of things that change with time need to be done, variables can then be quantified, equations connecting them composed, and then those equations can be tested against the data of historic and current realities. This grand process of the making of the science of world history has begun, and many results are in. Unfortunately, these results do not read like narratives. Only specialists can get excited about technical papers with titles such as "Dynamical Feedbacks Between Population Growth and Sociopolitical Instability in Agrarian States," and I admit to sharing this kind of pleasure. Here, however, I will strip all the mathematical and statistical scaffolding away and focus on the main edifice. Specifically, we will trace economic and social changes in France during the medieval cycle and observe "how one thing led to another," so that in the end a brilliant and powerful state collapsed in ruins.

ONE OF THE MOST STRIKING historical trends in France during the twelfth and thirteenth centuries was massive population growth. In 1100, about six million people inhabited the territory within the modern national borders of France. By 1300, the population more than tripled and reached a level between 20 and 22 million. The rest of Western Europe experienced a similar population buildup. We are on firm ground when it comes to tracing the dynamics of the population of England. In 1086, William the Conqueror, who wanted to know just how many new subjects he had acquired by his conquest of England, conducted a massive census whose results were preserved in the Domesday Book. Using this information, modern historians estimate that there were around two million people in England at the end of the eleventh century. Two centuries later, there were close to six million.

The population increase put the productive means of the medieval society under a colossal strain. All land that could be cultivated was turned into fields. In the process, more than 30 million acres of forests—one quarter of the modern area of France—were destroyed to make room for agriculture. Land was worked more intensively by shifting from the two-field to the three-field system. Instead of letting land rest every other year, each field was cultivated every two years out of three. As a result of increases in cultivated area and the switch to the three-field system, the amount of food produced in France probably doubled during the twelfth and thirteenth centuries. But the number of mouths to be fed increased threefold, with the inevitable result that the per-capita food consumption declined.

In *An Essay on the Principle of Population*, published in 1798, the English economist Thomas Robert Malthus argued that when population increases beyond the means of subsistence food prices increase, real wages (that is, wages expressed in terms of purchasing power) decline, and per-capita consumption, especially among the poorer strata, drops. By the early fourteenth century, France found itself in a classical Malthusian trap. A clear indicator of increased Malthusian pressures was thirteenth-century inflation. The price of the main staple, wheat, more than doubled between 1200 and 1300. Similar price increases took place in England and Italy. Other commodities were also affected. For example, in the twelfth century, an ox could be bought in England for three shillings. By the beginning of the thirteenth century, the average price was already six shillings. Toward the end of the century, the price of oxen doubled yet again.

Wages paid to carpenters and masons or for performing agricultural works, such as threshing, also increased, but did not keep pace with inflation. Scholars in the multivolume compendium *Agricultural History of England and Wales* estimated that during the thirteenth century the real wage of English laborers declined by one third. This means that if in 1200 a worker's daily wage could buy three loaves of bread, by 1300 he had enough money only for two.

These economic trends were the result of an inexorable operation of the laws of economics. The law of supply and demand says that if demand for some commodity increases and is not matched by increased supply, the price of the commodity must go up. Conversely, if the supply goes up, the price declines. Increased population meant greater demand for food, whereas food production lagged—therefore food prices went up. Greater number of people also meant an increased supply of labor, therefore the price of labor (wages) went down. Another commodity in limited supply was agricultural land, and its price was also driven up by the greater demand resulting from population growth. At the beginning of the thirteenth century, an acre of land in Normandy cost 2 livres; a century later it went for 20 livres. Much the same trend was observed in Picardy. Land rents paid by peasants to landowners also increased drastically. Around Lille in Picardy, rents grew fivefold in just 40 years between 1276 and 1316. In England around 1250, a peasant could rent an acre for between 2 and 4 pence. By 1300, he could not find it for less than 12 pence. In the early fourteenth century, land rents in many English shires shot up to 30 pence per acre and above.

Using information on medieval yields, economic historians have calculated that the minimum amount of land needed to a French peasant family for comfortable living was 15 acres; incidentally, working with independent sources of data the English historians arrived at the same estimate. After paying the tithe to the Church and the tax to the crown, and reserving enough seed grain for the next year's planting, the peasant would have enough left to feed and clothe a family of four or five. In a year of a bad harvest, the family would have to tighten their belts, but it did not have to starve. The problem is that by 1300 only one peasant household in five had 15 or more acres. Thus, the majority of rural households did not have enough land to feed themselves, and their very survival critically depended on securing outside employment. The result of this process was a vast and growing rural proletariat. But there was not enough work for everybody. In a vain hope of finding employment, many of the landless peasants migrated to towns, where they swelled the ranks of the urban unemployed, beggars, and vagrants.

By 1300, the massive population increase strained the economic system of France and other Western European countries to the breaking point. The majority of peasants lived on the edge of starvation. Even a mild deficit in the amount of annual crops brought in spelled disaster for a certain segment of population. Unfortunately, during the fourteenth century, the climate began changing for the worse. A series of cold and wet years between 1315 and 1322 brought on disastrous crop failures and livestock epidemics and triggered the kind of famine that Europe had not known for centuries.

"In the year of our Lord 1315," wrote the medieval annalist Johannes de Trokelowe, "apart from the other hardships with which England was afflicted, hunger grew in the land.... Meat and eggs began to run out, capons and fowl could hardly be found, animals died of pest, swine could not be fed because of the excessive price of fodder. A quarter of wheat or beans or peas sold for 20 shillings [four times the price before famine] ... The land was so oppressed with want that when the king came to St. Albans on the feast of St. Laurence [August 10] it was hardly possible to find bread on sale to supply his immediate household....

"The dearth began in the month of May and lasted until the feast of the nativity of the Virgin [September 8]. The summer rains were so heavy that grain could not ripen. It could hardly be gathered and used to bake bread down to the said feast day unless it was first put in vessels to dry. Around the end of autumn the dearth was mitigated in part, but toward Christmas it became as bad as before. Bread did not have its usual nourishing power and strength because the grain was not nourished by the warmth of summer sunshine. Hence those who ate it, even in large quantities, were hungry again after a little while. There can be no doubt that the poor wasted away when even the rich were constantly hungry....

"Considering and understanding these past miseries and those that were still to come, we can see how the prophecy of Jeremiah is fulfilled in the English people: 'If I go forth into the fields, behold those slain with the sword, and if I enter into the city behold them that are consumed with famine' (Jeremiah 14.18). Going 'forth into the fields' when we call to mind the ruin of our people in Scotland and Gascony, Wales and Ireland ... Entering the city we consider 'them that are consumed with famine' when we see the poor and needy, crushed with hunger, lying stiff and dead in the wards and streets....

"Four pennies worth of coarse bread was not enough to feed a common man for one day. The usual kinds of meat, suitable for eating, were too scarce; horse meat was precious; plump dogs were stolen. And, according to many reports, men and women in many places secretly ate their own children.... Thieves who had been imprisoned, but given no food, ferociously attacked new prisoners and devoured them half alive." Cannibalism was widespread everywhere in northern Europe. In Livonia and Estonia, starving mothers ate their children. Another chronicler confirms the stories of cannibalism and also reports that famished men often died on graves while digging up bodies for food. The effects of dearth were particularly terrible in Brabant. Jan Boendale wrote that in Antwerp the moans of famished could almost move a stone to pity. In the streets lay their emaciated forms, groaning in heartrending fashion. Several chroniclers claimed that a third of the population perished, although modern historians tend to reduce their estimates. When normal harvests returned, it is estimated that France was missing a tenth of its population.

The terrible famines of the fourteenth century left a deep imprint on the European psyche. One of the most famous fairy tales begins like this. "Hard by a great forest dwelt a poor woodcutter with his wife and his two children. The boy was called Hansel and the girl Gretel. He had little to bite and to break, and once when great dearth fell on the land, he could no longer procure even daily bread. Now when he thought over this by night in his bed, and tossed about in his anxiety, he groaned and said to his wife: 'What is to become of us? How are we to feed our poor children, when we no longer have anything even for ourselves?'" Everybody knows what happened then. The children were abandoned in the forest and eventually found their way to a gingerbread house, where lived an old woman who wanted to cook and eat them.

THE NEXT DISASTER TO STRIKE WAS the arrival of the Black Death. In 1348–49 various regions of France lost between one quarter and a half, and in some cases up to 80 to 90 percent, of their population. The plague returned in 1361 and 1374, followed by smaller outbreaks roughly once every 10 years. By the end of the fourteenth century, the population of France was less than half of what it had been in 1300.

The Black Death was a tremendous shock to fourteenth-century Europe. In addition to its direct consequences, resulting from brutally killing between one third and one half of the population, it psychologically scarred the survivors. Yet it would be too facile to blame the troubles and miseries of the succeeding hundred years on the plague alone. A particularly naïve version of this explanation (which unfortunately is still found in some history books) is that the Black Death appeared seemingly from nowhere (the medieval Europeans thought it was sent by God as punishment for their sins) and changed the course of European history.

The bubonic plague was the most spectacular cause of the plunge in population, but by no means the only one. After all, the population decline began even before the plague struck in 1348. The other causes of population decline were famine, warfare, and falling birth rates. Furthermore, the Black Death was not a unique, unprecedented event in world history. Other spectacular epidemics, such as the Plague of Athens in 430 B.C., the Antonine plague (A.D. 165–180), and the plagues of Justinian (A.D. 542–546), always strike during the same phase of the secular cycle—at, or just past, the population peak. Less spectacularly, the bubonic plague staged a comeback during the next secular cycle in Europe, and played an important role in the population declines of the seventeenth century (for example, the Great Plague of London of A.D. 1665). In general, epidemics almost always play a role in secular population declines. The most important factor explaining the spread of epidemics during this phase of the cycle is increased mobility of people, resulting from the migration of

landless peasants to towns and cities, increased vagrancy, and the movement of rebel bands and troops. Additionally, large segments of population are undernourished, or on the brink of starvation, and therefore
become susceptible to disease agents. Thus, the conditions of overpopulation create a fertile ground for the spread of epidemics, and also ensure a
high death toll.

From the point of view of Western Europeans, the Black Death
appeared as an exogenous and inexplicable event. But Europe was not an
island; it was affected by Eurasia-wide processes. In the thirteenth century,
the huge core region of Eurasia was unified by the Mongol Empire of
Chinggis Khan. One consequence of the Mongol conquest was an
increased density and speed of traffic, trade, raids, and communications
across Central Asia. The increase in traffic made it possible for the plague
bacteria to survive and spread over large distances. In the 1330s and 1340s,
the Mongol dynasties ruling China, Turkestan, and Persia experienced
simultaneous political disintegration, throwing the great steppe into turmoil. Large numbers of people moved back and forth in a chaotic manner,
and thus spread the Black Death to both ends of the continent. The plague
appeared in China first (in 1331). Fifteen years later, the disease broke out
among the Tatar army besieging Caffa, and from there it spread to the rest
of Europe.

Just as the causes of the Black Death are complex, so were its consequences. By relieving population pressure, no matter in how horrific a
manner, the Black Death had a beneficial effect on the survivors. The drop
of population set in motion the Malthusian machinery, but now working
in reverse. When the short-term disruptive effects of the catastrophe
worked themselves out, food prices declined, real wages increased, and
land rents decreased. Formerly landless peasants inherited land from a
deceased relative, or took over vacant farms whose owners succumbed to
the plague. Landowners were suddenly confronted with a severe labor
shortage, and had to drastically lower rents. In some cases, landlords were
so desperate that they let land for free, simply asking that the tenant keep
land productive and maintain structures on it. Shortage of labor drove
wages up. In 1320, a building worker in Rouen earned 1.5 sou per day. In
1380, after the third visitation of the Black Death, he commanded a daily

wage of 4 sou. The real wage in England doubled or even tripled between the beginning of the fourteenth century and the middle of the fifteenth century. Except for periods of intensive warfare, real wages and consumption levels of ordinary people improved handsomely.

Lands of marginal value for growing crops were abandoned or turned to pasture, which resulted in an overall increase in agricultural productivity. Overall food production declined, but the population plunged even faster, so that there was suddenly more than enough food to go around. People ate more meat and drank more beer and wine. The relative importance of bread in a person's diet declined, and what bread was consumed was of higher quality. The French historian Emmanuel Le Roy Ladurie relates how in 1338 the Provençal drovers working on their lord's reserve ate a very crude kind of bread made mainly with barley. After the great plague, barley bread was considered to be good enough only for the sheepdogs, whereas the laborers were entitled to wheat bread.

Economic trends during the thirteenth and fourteenth centuries provide a brilliant confirmation of one aspect of the Malthusian theory—the effect of population pressure on food prices, real wages, and land rents. The population increase to 1300 and then decline, especially after 1348, brought about precisely the trends predicted by the theory. But the theory of Malthus makes another prediction, that when the economic situation experienced a drastic improvement after the Black Death, population numbers should respond by increasing. By 1380, a generation since the arrival of the Black Death, the economic indicators suggest greatly improved conditions of life for the lower classes. Yet population stagnated, and even declined further, contrary to what the Malthusian theory predicts. In France, the first signs of population increase appear only after 1450, and in England only toward 1500. What caused this prolonged— century-long—period of depression? It was not disease. Although the plague outbreaks continued throughout the fifteenth century, they were less frequent and milder than the outbreaks during the sixteenth century, when population again resumed growth. It is clear that something is wrong with the simple-minded version of the Malthusian theory. We need to look elsewhere to understand the hundred years between 1350 and 1450—to the dynamics of the ruling class and its relations with the state.

WHO COMPRISED THE RULING CLASS OF medieval France? In agrarian societies, where most economic activity is concerned with growing crops and raising livestock, land is the chief means of production, and therefore the main form of wealth. Distribution of landed wealth within the society usually correlates very well with the distribution of political power, because wealth and power are akin to potential and kinetic kinds of energy in physics. Wealth, or rather income derived from it, is readily converted into power by buying influence or hiring retainers. Vice versa, political power brings with it the ability to acquire land, thus storing power for future use.

At the top of the power hierarchy of France stood the great territorial magnates—lay lords (the king, dukes, counts, and barons) and prelates (abbots, bishops, and archbishops). Below them were a multitude of nobles, from the more substantial knights to relatively poor country squires. There were between 60,000 and 100,000 noble households in France, or just under 2 percent of the total population. The differences in wealth within the second estate (that is, the nobility; the first estate were the clergy, and the third estate the commoners) were enormous. Consider the county of Forez in south-central France in the late thirteenth century. At the top of the local hierarchy stood the count of Forez with 12,000 livres of annual income. Below him were two or three barons with incomes of between 1,000 and 2,000 livres per year. Twenty or so substantial knights, each with a castle, enjoyed incomes between 100 and 500 livres. The holders of fortified houses were worse off, with incomes of 50 to 100 livres per year. At the bottom of the noble hierarchy were about 100 lesser gentry whose income varied between 25 and 50 livres per year. To put this income in perspective, the basic minimum on which a single person could live in modest comfort at the time was 5 livres (this was, the typical allowance provided to a young nobleman attending university, or a pension to a widow of the lesser gentry). In other words, 25 livres per year was enough to maintain a family of four or five, but left no surplus for status seeking.

Below the lesser gentry was a stratum of free peasants who owned the land that they worked. Finally, the great majority of the population did not own any land beyond, at best, a cottage with an attached vegetable garden. Some of these people were serfs, who worked fields owned by a feudal lord; others rented land, or hired out as agricultural laborers. In the late thirteenth century, a large and growing number were indigent, vagabonds, or criminals. The distribution of wealth in towns was similarly unequal, with a few great merchants on top and the impoverished majority at the bottom.

Medieval England had similar social structure. At the top were around 200 great barons whose incomes were measured in hundreds or thousands of pounds. Below them were the middle ranks of 3,000 knights and esquires earning between £20 and £100. (The English pound was equivalent to 5 livres, and so this group corresponded to the French knights with 100 to 500 livres.) The lesser gentry with £5 to £20 pounds per year (equivalent to 25 to 100 livres) numbered perhaps 10,000 households. Below the gentry was a group of free peasant landowners—yeomen. A laborer at that time earned on the order of £1 to £2 per year (assuming he could get full employment).

The boundary between the nobility and the commons was not sharp, because some yeomen enjoyed incomes substantially greater than £5 per annum. At the same time, a member of lesser gentry with the borderline annual income of £5 (or 25 livres in France) could not afford to properly equip himself for war, the supposed raison-d'être of his estate. A horse together with armor and weapons cost in the neighborhood of £20, or four times as much as his annual income! Trained warhorses capable of bearing a knight in plate armor were sold in the late thirteenth century for astronomical sums in the range of £40 to £80.

The population surge of the High Middle Ages, as discussed earlier, brought impoverishment and increasing hardship to the great majority of the population. But the noble landowners, unlike the poor, generally profited from the economic trends of the thirteenth century. The value of their main product, grain, increased as a result of price inflation, while their costs, wages to agricultural workers, declined. Alternatively, they could rent their land at the greatly inflated rates of the late thirteenth century. Furthermore, whereas the price of such basic consumption items as food and fuel, without which humans cannot survive, increased enormously, the price of manufactured goods increased much less, or even declined. This happened because demographic growth reduced the cost of human labor, which was a major part of the price of manufactured goods. Suddenly, the nobility found themselves flush with money, which they could spend on luxuries and conspicuous consumption. Merchants responded to the increase in noble purchasing power by importing more luxuries from overseas, while urban entrepreneurs, employing the cheap labor migrating from the country to towns, greatly expanded production. As a result, the thirteenth century saw a great expansion of trade, the rise of arts and crafts, and urbanization. A class of wealthy merchants and entrepreneurs, catering to the noble needs, arose in towns. The great boom of Gothic architecture was also an indirect result of these economic trends— the lay and ecclesiastical landowners had a lot of money to burn, and conspicuous consumption could take the form of buying gorgeous clothes, or of building the most magnificent church in Christendom.

The thirteenth century, thus, saw two contradictory trends. On one hand the demographic pressure was rising, the standard of living of the great majority of the population was falling, and an ever-increasing proportion of people were pushed to the brink of disaster. On the other hand, the wealthy and powerful were enjoying a golden age. The warning signs of the troubles to come were there, but were not perceived. Who cares what happens to the great unwashed multitudes? Because the texts in the thirteenth century were written for the elite, and in a large degree by the elite, it is also easy for modern historians to miss the signs of the impending disaster.

THE WHEEL OF FORTUNE TURNS, and those who were recently on top, suddenly find themselves sliding to disaster. Noble prosperity led to expansion of their numbers, which after a while had a negative effect on their incomes.

The general demographic upturn of the thirteenth century did not bypass the nobility. Their numbers increased, and because their economic position was better than that of the commoners, nobility numbers increased even faster than that of the general population. During the age of increasing incomes, some nobles found that division of their estate between two or more heirs could allow all of them to have enough income to maintain noble status. Magnates with far-flung possessions would use some inconveniently located property to set up a younger son as a middle-rank noble.

Additionally, nobility was never a closed estate, despite the propaganda then or now. There was a constant movement of lineages into and out of the noble estate. Rich merchants never missed an opportunity to convert some of their wealth into landed property. After they had enough land, they moved to the country, severing their connection with the "ignoble" pursuits such as trading. After that, it was a simple matter of entering into the second estate by, for example, purchasing an ennobling patent from the king. Other routes to nobility were via royal service or an ecclesiastical career.

Peasants also could move into nobility, as long as they were willing to take the long view. A well-to-do peasant would increase his land by buying a sliver here and there, and by lending money to poor neighbors and then taking over their land when they became insolvent. His son would stop working the land himself, instead farming it with hired hands, and continue the process of augmenting his possessions. The grandson would rent his land out, join the retinue of the local lord, when it was periodically called by the king for military service, and perhaps marry a daughter of gentle but impoverished lineage. The great-grandson would continue rendering periodic military service, socialize with other local nobles, and live in a noble manner. After three generations of maintaining noble status, nobody would question the nobility of a descendant of the original peasant. As a sixteenth century English nobleman put it, he "who can live idly and without manual labor and will bear the port, charge, and countenance of a gentleman … shall be taken for a gentleman." Alternatively, transition into the second estate could be accomplished at any point by purchasing an ennobling patent. Or a noble genealogy might be invented. In short, there were innumerable ways of moving into the second estate. The main requirement was accumulation of enough landed property.

There was also a constant movement of individuals and lineages out of the noble estate. An impoverished noble lineage might find its income insufficient for maintaining the level of expenditures necessary for "noble living," and quietly sink into the class of small farmers working their own land. However, during the times of general noble prosperity, downward mobility was minimized, because even lesser gentry, holding small amounts of land, found that it could support them in the style necessary for maintaining their noble status. In sum, economic trends of the later thirteenth century that favored landowners resulted in the splitting up of noble estates, increased upward mobility by commoners into the second estate, and decreased downward mobility. The numbers of nobles grew at the time when general population has already ceased to expand and the social pyramid was becoming increasingly top-heavy.

We can trace this process of elite overproduction in medieval England using the records of inquiries undertaken by the crown after the death of a tenant-in-chief. Tenants-in-chief were feudal landowners who were direct vassals of the English king. Their origin goes back to the Norman conquest, when William the Conqueror divided the English lands among his followers. The original tenants-in-chief included both the territorial magnates—the barons—and lesser landholders. The barons, in turn, gave land in return for service to their own knights, who were called subtenants (they were, thus, vassals of a vassal of the king). During the two centuries following the conquest, many tenancies-in-chief were split between co-heirs, and the number of direct tenants of the crown grew. By 1250, this segment of population included both earls, with annual incomes running into thousands of pounds, and yeomen living on £5 per year, giving us a fairly good sample of the entire landowning class. When a tenant-in-chief died, the government conducted an inquiry (called an inquisition post mortem) to discover whatever income and rights were due to the crown. For example, if the heir was under age, the crown administered his estates to its own advantage. The marriage of an heiress was also in the king's hands, and could be sold for a tidy sum of money, or given as a reward to a loyal retainer. If there were no heir, the lands were taken over by the crown. All of these were lucrative sources of income, and the government wanted to keep close tabs on the proceedings associated with the inheritance of a tenancy-in-chief. Many thousands of the records of investigations post mortem are preserved in the National Archives of the United Kingdom. The information below is based on the analysis by the historical demographer Josiah Cox Russell of more than 8,800 inquisitions for the period 1250 through 1500.

We are interested in one particular piece of information provided by inquisitions post mortem—the total number of male heirs alive at the death of a tenant-in-chief. When averaged over hundreds of individuals, this number, called the *replacement rate*, tells us what were the numeric dynamics of this population group for any given period of time. When the replacement rate was greater than one, the numbers of noblemen were increasing. On the other hand, if the replacement rate is less than one—that is, each dying father leaves, on average, fewer than one son—the overall numbers must be shrinking.

The story that inquisitions post mortem tell us is quite striking. During the last half of the thirteenth century, the English nobility did very well indeed—each tenant-in-chief left on average 1.48 sons. As a result of this demographic growth, the nobility numbers between 1250 and 1300 should have almost doubled. The bulk of the commoner population increase, however, was pretty much over by the middle of the thirteenth century; certainly the numbers of commoners did not increase at anywhere near the rate of the nobility. With the numeric ratio of nobles to commoners increasing, by 1300 the social pyramid was noticeably more top-heavy than 50 years before. Things got even worse after 1300. As noted previously, in the early fourteenth century the commoner population was actually decreasing, losing perhaps 10 percent even before the arrival of the Black Death. By contrast, the nobility's replacement rate was a healthy 1.23, implying a 40 percent increase in their total numbers during the first half of the fourteenth century.

The dramatic increase in the numbers of nobles in relation to the productive class had the same consequences as the increase of general population beyond the means of production—the economic position of nobility suffered. Put simply, when there are more people dividing the same pie, each gets a smaller slice. Many nobles found that their revenues were insufficient to support them in the style to which the previous generation was accustomed. Decreasing the level of consumption was unthinkable because it meant losing the elite status, and nobles responded by extracting a greater proportion of resources from peasants, by seeking supplemental sources of income with the state, and by going in debt. None of these strategies was sustainable in the long run. The state could not employ all impoverished nobles—there were too many of them, and the crown itself was sliding into financial insolvency, as discussed later in this chapter. Extracting greater revenues from peasants meant that the landlords went beyond skimming the surplus and started cutting into the resources that peasants needed to survive. Landlord oppression was undermining their own economic basis, as peasants declined by flight, starvation, or even death in futile rebellions.

"Ye nobles are like ravening wolves," wrote Jacques de Vitry in the thirteenth century. "Therefore shall ye howl in hell ... who despoil your subjects and live on the blood and sweat of the poor." Whatever a peasant amasses in a year, "the knight, the noble devours in an hour." De Vitry warned not to take the poor lightly. "If they can aid us, they can also do us harm. You know that many serfs have killed their masters or burned their houses." De Vitry's words were prophetic. In 1320, a mass peasant movement called the *Pastoureaux* (the "Shepherds") swept the kingdom of France. An unfrocked priest and an apostate monk preaching the crusade to a crowd of peasants was the catalyst. A great army of the rural poor joined by vagabonds and felons marched on Paris, where they liberated the prisoners in the Châtelet and defied the king, who shut himself up in the palace of the Cité. From Paris, they went south toward Saintonge and Aquitaine, storming castles, burning town halls, pillaging the countryside, and slaughtering Jews and lepers. At some point, their numbers reached 40,000, but eventually they broke up in a number of smaller bands. The nobles organized themselves and hunted them down, hanging thousands of the Pastoureaux from trees.

The arrival of the Black Death completed the process of thinning the base of the social pyramid. In general, epidemics always cause a higher mortality among the poor, who suffer from malnutrition, greater crowding, and a lack of bedcare and medicines. In the case of the plague, however, the best way to avoid it was flight. Whereas the urban poor died in droves, the rich had their country estates to escape to, like the young aristocrats in the *Decameron* who left Florence for a pastoral palace "removed on every side from the roads" with "wells of cool water and vaults of rare wines." It is generally estimated that the first outbreak of plague in 1348–49 carried away some 40 percent of the English population. Monks who ministered to the dying suffered an even greater mortality. The mortality of tenants-in-chief, on the other hand, was only 27 percent. At the top of the social pyramid, the peers lost barely 8 percent of their number. The only reigning monarch who died from the pestilence was King Alfonso XI of Castile.

The post-Black Death increase of wages and decline of land rents was an unmitigated economic disaster for landowners. The worst hit were the lesser- and middle-rank landowners who relied on hired labor to farm substantial properties. As landless peasants took over the land made vacant by pestilence, the numbers of agricultural laborers shrunk, and they began demanding higher wages. The landowners responded by passing in 1351 the Statute of Laborers in an attempt to fix wages and prices and to compel able-bodied unemployed to accept work when offered. The statute was vigorously enforced, but was ultimately economically ineffective. It foundered on the free-rider problem: It was to the benefit of each individual employer that others would be limited to lower wages, so that he could attract sufficient labor by offering a slightly better wage. Because everybody felt the same way, the limits on wages quickly unraveled. Characteristically, the employers (the gentry) were not prosecuted for offering illegal wages, although many laborers were punished for accepting them. The labor legislation, in general, was the focus of much popular hatred, and its enforcement was one of the most important causes of the peasant revolts of 1381. Manorial courts increased their revenues after the Black Death, a remarkable achievement considering that the numbers of tenants had fallen drastically.

The magnates did better than the middle-rank and lesser elites, at least to 1380. The large landowners employed numerous armed retainers who intimidated peasants into accepting the high rents and low wages that prevailed before 1348. The magnates also had a longer reach, especially in counties where they had a lot of property. They could more easily locate runaway serfs and return them to their land, or punish them as an example to others. In short, they were able to use extra-economic—coercive—means to stabilize their incomes, at least temporarily. In a few cases, as on the Welsh marches, lords were even able to increase their incomes by intensifying peasant oppression. The Arundels increased their income from the lordship of Chirk in North Wales from £300 to £500 between 1320 and 1380. Henry the Bolingbroke used the occasion of his succession after the death of his father John of Gaunt to force the people of Cydweli to pay £1,575. Such unpredictable and arbitrary exactions contributed to the Welsh uprising lead by Glyn Dŵr in 1400.

The same forces were operating in post-Black Death France. Desperate to maintain their revenues from a shrinking productive base, the nobles increased the press on the peasants, which triggered in 1358 the violent peasant reaction, known as the *Jacquerie*. Although rebellions of French and English peasants were speedily suppressed, they shocked the ruling classes, and forced them to somewhat relax their grip on the productive segment of the society. An even more important factor than armed rebellion, however, was a quiet and gradual process by which peasants simply moved away from lords or territories where they were getting a poor deal. Lords persisting in peasant oppression eventually found themselves without peasants to oppress.

A generation after the Black Death, it was clear that the lords lost their struggle against the law of supply and demand. In the estimate of the French medievalist Guy Bois, most seigneurs lost a half to three quarters of their revenues. The revenues of Jeanne de Navarre from her Champaign and Brie properties fell from 23,000 to 10,000 livres. The income of the abbey of Saint-Denis declined by half in nominal terms and by two thirds in real terms—from 72,000 to 24,000 *setiers* (a measure of volume) of grain. At the same time that seigneurial revenues declined, prices of manufactured goods increased driven by growing wages. The same dynamic that created the age of noble prosperity in the late thirteenth century now ran in reverse a hundred years later.

As the amount of surplus produced by peasants shrank, the numbers of landowning elites who were supported by the surplus were increasing. The plunge in their income meant that the nobles had to either adjust to a lower level of consumption or try to do something about it. The lesser gentry, whose incomes around 1300 were 25 to 50 livres per year, found themselves faced with an awful dilemma of losing their noble status, because their incomes no longer permitted them to maintain it. "To preserve caste, the lord was compelled to draw more, on peasant production, and by other means," concludes Guy Bois. "On the other hand, any additional drain endangered the ability for self-subsistence of the peasant holding. The contradiction was insoluble and disruptive." As their incomes declined, nobles began looking to "other means" to preserve their caste. Because overall amount of resources was limited, one noble could get ahead only at the expense of another, leading to intensification of the intra-elite conflict.

Between 1300 and 1350, the social fabric of the French society began unraveling, first in the frontier regions, and later in the center. In Gascony, the houses of Armagnac and Foix clashed over the succession of the viscounty of Béarn. This feud was to go over the next two and a half centuries, and end only after the complete extinction of one of the houses. While the magnates fought over large stakes, private wars between lesser nobility proliferated in Gascony. Between 1290 and 1327, for example, at least 12 outbreaks of intra-elite violence are recorded in surviving sources.

At the opposite end of the kingdom, in the urbanized Flanders, tensions increased between the established urban patriciate, who were allied to the French crown, and the newly enriched bourgeoisie, who used the proletariat as shock troops in their struggle for power and status. In 1302, the struggle for power led to a full-blown rebellion in Bruges that spread to the whole of western Flanders. When Philip the Fair sent an army to pacify them, the Flemish infantry crushed the French aristocratic cavalry in the battle of Courtrai. In 1325–26, the urban communities of Flanders rose against their ruler, Count Louis of Nevers. In 1328, the French knights massacred the burgers at the field of Cassel, in a payback for the Courtrai debacle, and established French administration in Flanders. However, in 1337, the weavers of Ghent revolted yet again, and under the leadership of Jan van Arteveldt expelled Louis of Nevers. The Flemish made a commercial treaty with England and in 1340 recognized Edward III as their sovereign. The Flemish rebellion opened the northern route for the English invasion under Edward III, and was the first step in the sequence that lead directly to the battle of Crécy.

The north and east of France (the provinces of Picardy and Burgundy) were sites of the baronial movement against royal taxation during the reign of Louis X (1314–16). In the county of Artois, the revolt against the central power became complicated by internecine fighting between the adherents of Robert of Artois and those of his aunt Mahaut, who both claimed the county. Robert of Artois lost the struggle and eventually ended up in exile in England, where he joined his voice to those urging Edward III to war against France.

In 1341, Brittany descended into civil war when its duke John III died without direct heirs. The succession was disputed between two factions, Blois and Monfort. In the ensuing civil war the lesser nobles and the Celtic west supported the Monforts, while the great lords and French-speaking bourgeois of the east rallied to the Blois faction. The English supported the Monfort faction by launching a *chevauchée* (a "mounted raid" whose purpose was to lay country to waste) and besieging the important Breton strongholds of Rennes, Vannes, and Nantes.

The clear pattern here is that in each region the conflict began as civil war, and then one of the factions—the Monforts, the Arteveldts, or Robert d'Artois—invited Edward III to intervene on their side. It was reportedly Jan van Arteveldt who suggested that Edward III should declare himself the king of France, to legitimize the Flemish support.

In 1354, violent intra-elite conflicts spread to the very heart of the kingdom, Ile-de-France and Normandy. The pervasive air of conflict begins to sound like a Clint Eastwood spaghetti western, such as *The Good, the Bad, and the Ugly*. The key player in these events was Charles of Navarre, whom later historians called the Bad. Charles the Bad was a natural focus around which aristocratic opposition crystallized because of his close dynastic connections to the royal family. When the last son of Philip the Fair died without male heir in 1328, the crown went to the nephew of Philip the Fair, Philip VI Valois. There were two other potential claimants: the English king Edward III, who was the son of Philip's daughter Isabel, the "She-Wolf of France"; and Philip of Évreux, the son of Philip the Fair's half-brother. Philip of Évreux married Joan of France (the granddaughter of Philip the Fair) and was compensated with the kingdom of Navarre in return for renouncing any claim to the crown. His son Charles of Navarre, thus, was a descendant of Capetian kings through both his father and mother. From his father, Charles also inherited very substantial landholdings in Normandy and Ile-de-France. The dissident factions of the impoverished and turbulent nobility of these two provinces looked to Charles of Navarre as their natural leader.

The second protagonist in the story was John II, called the Good, who succeeded to the French throne in 1350. John the Good precipitated the conflict when he made his favorite, Charles d'Espagne, the constable (the chief military officer of France). To make matters worse, the king gave Charles d'Espagne (who, thus, found himself in the role of the Ugly) the county of Angoulême, which belonged to the house of Navarre. The loss of his territory infuriated Charles the Bad, and he struck back at John the

Good through his constable. In January 1354, when the constable was on a visit in Normandy, a group of Norman nobles led by Charles the Bad's brother, Philip of Navarre, broke into the room where he was sleeping and dragged him from the bed. The naked constable fell on his knees and begged Philip of Navarre for mercy, crying "he would be his serf, he would ransom himself for gold, he would yield the land claimed, he would go overseas and never return." But the pleas of the unfortunate favorite were to no avail, and the enraged assassins hacked him to death, leaving his body pierced with eighty wounds, according to the chronicler's report.

The office of the constable was a very lucrative one—he was paid 2,000 francs (livres) per month in peace, and upon the outbreak of hostilities a sum equal to one day's pay of all men at arms under contract. He was also a source of extensive patronage, because he controlled recruitment, provisioning, and other arrangements for war. Multitudes of nobles, whose landed income was insufficient to support themselves, depended on income that it was in the power of the constable to bestow on them. Conversely, all those who were excluded from the trough hated the constable and wished for his downfall. By striking the blow that removed the favorite, Charles the Bad instantly made himself the leader of the growing dissident faction, who blamed the Valois kings for misgovernment and military reverses. Normandy, where Charles the Bad had extensive properties and close connections to the local nobility, was virtually in rebellion, refusing to pay taxes and contribute men to the army. The inability of the crown to get any funds from this wealthy province was a significant contribution to the collapse of the royal finances.

The assassination of the constable was just the first act in the play of revenge tragedy. One murder led to another in a spiraling pattern of revenge and counter-revenge. In April 1356, the dauphin was entertaining Charles of Navarre and the leading Norman nobles at a banquet in Rouen (the capital of Normandy), when John II with many armed followers burst in. Despite the dauphin begging his father not to dishonor him by committing violence upon his guests, the king ordered the arrest of Charles of Navarre and all others present who participated in the murder of the constable. He himself handled Jean d'Harcourt, one of the chief assassins, so roughly that he tore his doublet from collar to belt. The next morning, Jean d'Harcourt and three other Norman nobles were taken to their execution, when the king, who apparently could not wait any longer to assuage his thirst for vengeance, suddenly halted the procession in the open field and ordered the prisoners to be beheaded on the spot. Harcourt's death was particularly painful, because the substitute executioner was very inept, and took six blows to sever his neck.

The execution of Jean d'Harcourt and others was not a particularly intelligent thing to do, because Jean had three brothers and nine children married to various noble families of northern France. The King alienated a whole segment of nobility, without eliminating the main malefactor—Charles of Navarre, who was imprisoned in the Châtelet in Paris, and later played his typically disruptive Bad role in the collapse of 1356–60.

The erratic and violent behavior of the king during this episode is symptomatic of another social trend—the late medieval crime wave. Brutal and senseless bursts of violence were particularly frequent during this age. In 1358, Francesco Ordelaffi, the ruler of Forli in northern Italy, was defending his city against the besieging papal forces, when his son Ludovico begged him to yield rather than persist in a futile defense. "You are either bastard or a changeling!" roared the enraged father, drew a dagger, and stabbed his son "so that he died before the midnight." The count of Foix killed his only legitimate son in a similar fit of ungovernable rage. In England, every other generation of feudal lords revolted against the king, but before the fourteenth century they always stopped at committing regicide. Between 1327 and 1485, however, they murdered five kings.

The wave of violence was not limited to the great lords, but affected all levels of the society. The rate of homicides per 100,000 in rural Northamptonshire tripled between 1300 and 1380. Court records preserved in the Officialty of Cerisy in Normandy indicate that there were on average 1.2 assaults per year during the first half of the fourteenth century, and only 2 percent of these involved the use of deadly weapons. By contrast, around 1400 there were 4.9 assaults per year of which 25 percent were with weapons. In the 1450s, the number of assaults was still 4.3 per year (40 percent with weapons), but by the end of the fifteenth century, the assaults fell to 0.7 per year, and only 8 percent employed deadly weapons. Scattered statistics from Italy and Germany paint the same picture. Violent crimes rose to a peak between 1350 and 1450 and subsided thereafter.

The causes of rising violence included the desperate economic situation of the peasants and disruption of the social fabric due to plague and war. However, the primary reason of the collapse of law and order was the failure of the ruling class. There were huge numbers of destitute, but armed and dangerous, nobles. Individuals fought duels or ambushed each other, and families and clans conducted multigenerational feuds. Increased levels of aggression were self-feeding. A murder was followed by revenge in a cycle of violence familiar to fans of Mafia crime stories. Moreover, frequent and brutal assaults and homicides undermined the social and psychological barriers against interpersonal violence. It was really the nobles who were the "criminal underclass" during the late Middle Ages. In fourteenth-century Gloucestershire, more than half of resident knights and esquires committed at least one felony. When the state went into financial collapse and lost the control of the army, the last remaining restraints were removed from the throngs of "noble thugs," and the whole fabric of the society disintegrated.

KINGS OF FRANCE HAD TWO KINDS of income. The first kind, ordinary revenues, was seigneurial or feudal in nature, and included rental income from the crown estates, fines and fees for administering justice, tolls on commerce, and profits from minting of currency (the so-called seigniorage). Ordinary revenues were meant to be used for regular maintenance of the state. The second kind, extraordinary levies, was collected in case of emergency and for such national projects as crusades and war. When Louis IX was captured in 1250 while on crusade in Egypt, the money needed to ransom him was raised by means of an extraordinary levy.

The ordinary income of the French crown quadrupled between 1180, the beginning of the reign of Philip II Augustus, and 1250. When Philip's grandson Louis IX went on his ill-fated crusade, he controlled the ordinary revenues of 250,000 livres. Inflation was mild during this period (the price of wheat increased by 20 to 30 percent), and did not cut in a substantial way into the financial health of the state. The expansion of royal revenues was partly due to the territorial conquests of Philip and his successors, and partly the result of demographic growth. In fact, these two processes interacted in a synergistic fashion. The initial phase of medieval population growth, before population pressure reduced per-capita rate of production, resulted in an increased flow of taxes into royal coffers. Simply put, more peasants meant more taxes. Increased revenues were used by the French kings to fund territorial expansion, which in turn brought in more taxpayers. A kind of a virtuous cycle between growing revenue and war success is how the Capetians managed the explosive growth of their domain during this period.

However, population growth continued during the thirteenth century, and after 1250 the number of people began approaching the maximum that could be fed given the medieval level of agricultural technology. The surplus produced by the peasants, which is the difference between how much food they grow and how much of the product they need to survive and produce replacements for themselves, shrank. The revenues of the state suffered because it lived off the surplus. Even today it is possible to forcibly deprive the agricultural laborer of more than the surplus, but peasants might rebel or starve to death in great numbers, neither of which is a desirable consequence from the point of view of the state—as the totalitarian regimes in Russia and China witnessed. The state in thirteenth century France competed with the landowning elites for the peasant-produced surplus. As noble incomes shrank, they found a great number of ways to redirect the flow of taxes in their own favor. The combined effect of these economic and social trends meant that around 1300, and especially during the early fourteenth century, the royal finances came under an increasing amount of pressure.

Between 1250 and 1300, the ordinary revenues of the crown doubled in nominal terms to 500,000 livres. But the price of wheat during this period also doubled, meaning that the revenues of Philip IV the Fair (1285–1314) stagnated in real terms. In the fourteenth century, the revenues started falling. The last Capetian king, Philip's son Charles IV (1322–28), received ordinary revenues of 280,000 livres, which in real terms amounted to only half of what his father had enjoyed 30 years earlier. The royal finances got a much needed help when the accession of the first Valois king, Philip VI (1328–1350), brought the vast appanage of the Valois family into the royal domain. However, Philip VI's ordinary revenues (in real terms) amounted to only 80 percent of those available to Philip the Fair.

Until the reign of Philip the Fair, the crown had no difficulty living on its ordinary revenues, and occasionally collecting extraordinary levies (for periods of particularly intense war effort). By the end of the thirteenth century, however, when the ordinary revenues stagnated in real terms, expenses, especially for military operations, soared. To raise his income, Philip began using extraordinary taxes in a regular manner. He also imposed forced loans on the bourgeois and manipulated the currency. In one of the best-known events of his reign, Philip the Fair destroyed and looted the Order of the Templars.

The Templars originated as an order of monastic knights during the crusades. Unlike the Knights of St. John, who were also called the Hospitallers, the Templars were not known for charity and did not support hospitals, but set out to create a wealthy and powerful "transnational corporation." Profiting from the tax-exempt status that the pope conferred on them during their crusading period, they lent money at lower interest rates than the Italian or Jewish bankers. They also served as bankers for the popes and lent large sums of money to Philip the Fair. On October 13, 1307, Philip ordered all Templars in France arrested and the order's property seized. The Templars were accused of heresy, sorcery, and sodomy, and were subjected to the most-horrible tortures—racking, thumbscrews, and starvation. Their teeth and fingernails were pulled one by one, bones broken by the wedge, and feet roasted over flames. After 36 died in torture chambers and several by their own hand, the Grand Master Jacques de Molay and 122 other knights confessed to all the crimes. "And he would have confessed that he had slain God himself if they had asked him that," wrote a chronicler. When Jacques de Molay was burned at the stake, he proclaimed his innocence and called down a terrible curse on the king and his descendants to the thirteenth generation. Within a year, Philip the Fair was dead. All of his 3 male heirs died, one after another, without leaving descendants, during the next 14 years. As one disaster after another fell on France during the fourteenth century, the legend of the Templar's curse was remembered by people and grew in the retelling.

The methods used by Philip the Fair to fill his treasury, especially the recurrent use of war subsidies, incurred much resentment among the landowning and urban elites. The basic and essentially irresolvable problem was that the state competed with the elites for the shrinking surplus. In the first half of the fourteenth century, the kings began experiencing increasing resistance to taxation. For example, in 1314 Philip the Fair required a war subsidy for a campaign in Flanders. When last-minute negotiations averted the conflict, but the Royal officials nevertheless continued collecting a subsidy, a widespread rebellion erupted.

The lack of consensus on the need for national taxation had a direct effect on the ability of the state to wage the war against the English during the Hundred Years' War. Philip VI (1328–50) and John II (1350–64) were unable to collect subsidies except in the time of outright conflict, and as a result faced increasing financial distress. As a result, France was always unprepared whenever military operations resumed after a truce. The military disasters of 1346 and 1347 (the defeat at Crécy, the loss of Calais) finally persuaded the Estates General in 1355 to 1356 to authorize necessary taxation, but now their attempts to impose taxes ran into resistance at the local level. In the end, the Estates were unable to produce the money they promised, and royal finances collapsed.

THE ECONOMIC AND SOCIAL TRENDS OF medieval France suggest the reasons for its fourteenth century collapse. Before examining the actual sequence of events leading to the fall, however, it is necessary to dispel one common myth: that France's troubles were brought by the persistent conflict with the English, known as the Hundred Years' War (1338–1453). First, the dates 1338 and 1453 are completely arbitrary. During this period, France and England were not at war continuously. There were several breaks in fighting, the longest of which was during 1389–1411. Before 1338, the French and the English fought a war as recently as in 1324–1327, and before that in 1294–1298. After 1453, there were wars in 1475 and 1489–1492. In fact, almost every generation of the French and the English fought against each other during their "Thousand Year War" between 1066 and 1815. Second, with only one quarter of the French population, England was simply not in the same league as far as military power is concerned. The English won several spectacular battles, but as we will shortly see, they were able to conquer and hold territory only when the French were mired in internecine fighting. As soon as the French got some semblance of internal unity, they immediately reconquered their territory. This happened twice; it was no fluke. Today historians emphasize that the main cause of the protracted warfare during 1338–1453 was not a dynastic conflict between the English and French kings, but rather the struggle between the great territorial magnates of France—the French king; the dukes of Brittany, Burgundy, and Guyenne (the latter was also the king of England); the counts of Flanders and Armagnac; and so on. While the magnates fought at the national level, noble factions slaughtered each other at the regional level, and peasants murdered lords and each other at the local level. As the great French historian Fernand Braudel said once, the Hundred Years' War should more properly be called the "Hundred Years of Hostility."

The first phase of the Hundred Years' War, from the outbreak of hostilities in 1338 to the Peace of Bretigny in 1361, was disastrous for France. There were four major actions, all French debacles—the naval battle of Sluys (1340), the land battles of Crécy (1346) and Poitiers (1356), and the siege and capture of Calais by the English (1347). Contemporaries were astonished by the repeated defeats that mighty France suffered at the hands of relatively puny England. (The fourteenth-century Florentine historian Mateo Villani called Edward III *"il piccolo re d'Inghelterra"*—the "little king of England.") The number of troops who fought in the battle of Crécy illustrates this disparity in power—there were 12,000 English facing between 30,000 and 40,000 French. The standard explanation of English victories is their effective use of archers. There is no question that the longbow is a fearsome weapon, but there was another factor in the French failure—their lack of cohesion, their inability to cooperate.

By the early 1340s, elite overproduction undermined the prosperity and unity of the France's ruling class. Large numbers of nobles had hardly any more land than a well-to-do peasant; they were what the French historian Marc Bloch called the *"seigneurs sans terre"*—"lords lackland." The wages paid to a man at arms varied between 7 sou 6 denier for a squire and 15 sou for a knight banneret. A typical campaign of one to two months could yield 25 to 50 livres, equivalent to an annual income of the lesser nobleman. And there was the prospect of loot and ransoms. When the crown issued summons for the fighting men of France, in preparation for the campaigns against the English, literally tens of thousands of knights responded. "Everything happened", wrote the medieval military historian

Philippe Contamine, "as if the king and his lieutenants ... were surprised, even nonplussed, by the number of men at arms who responded to their order. Perhaps hesitations Philip VI displayed in the course of the military operations may be partially explained by the perplexity, if not confusion, of his entourage, in the presence of the incessant flow of disorganized crowds flocking to join his person." Whereas before the campaign the royal officers expected to get 10,000 cavalry troops, they would get two or even three times the number. Moreover, the nobles brought with them the enmities and feuds that multiplied over the previous decades, and now divided them. The French army was not a cohesive force, as its behavior on the field of Crécy amply demonstrated. Despite the king's order not to attack, because the time was late and the forces were not properly arrayed, the vanguard charged the English in their well-defended positions. Later, one part of the French army fought another, when the knights decided to slaughter the Genoese crossbowmen. "Slay these rascals who get in our way," somebody shouted as the knights cut their way through. Wave after wave of attack was launched from the disorganized French ranks, and the English defeated each one. The day after the battle, several French levies who did not even know that the battle was already lost, marched toward Crécy and were cut down by the English knights. In short, it is hard to avoid the impression that the French army defeated itself, with a very little help from the English.

Although the French hosts were completely ineffective against the English, and lost one battle after another, they nevertheless had to be paid. But the declining royal revenues were increasingly inadequate to cover the spiraling costs of war. Remembering the baronial revolts of 1314–1316, during the 1340s and 1350s the Crown sought the help of the ruling elites (urban patricians and rural nobility) in collecting additional taxes. The disaster of Crécy and the loss of Calais the next year brought home to the nobility the seriousness of the situation, and the Estates General endorsed the royal plan for raising revenues at the end of 1347. The arrival of the Black Death the next year, however, disrupted tax collection, and no significant revenue materialized. Large-scale hostilities resumed in 1355, when Edward III landed in Calais and marched his army into Artois and Picardy. John II the Good chose not to seek battle, but to burn or carry off anything the countryside might offer an invading army. This scorched-earth policy succeeded in driving the English back to the Channel, but at the cost of leaving the local populace to starve. In December 1355, the Estates General met in Paris and authorized taxation for prosecuting war, but the attempts to collect the taxes ran into the resistance of local assemblies. The Estates met again in 1356 and through 1357, but their focus shifted from securing means of fighting the war to a more political agenda.

On September 19, 1356, the French army met near Poitiers the English army led by the Black Prince. The outcome was another disaster for the French. John the Good, 18 counts and viscounts, 21 barons and bannerets, and 2,000 knights and squires were captured. The debacle triggered the collapse of the state that manifested itself as urban revolution, aristocratic rebellion, and peasant uprising, all at once.

The government led by the dauphin (future Charles V) was confronted with two related problems. First, it had to come up with a huge ransom of 3 million livres for John II even though the state was bankrupt, and could not even pay the army. The government had no recourse but to convene the Estates General to make its appeal for money directly to the representatives of the elites. The second problem, however, was that the string of defeats, despite heavy taxation, had completely destroyed the credibility of the government. Additionally, the nobility itself was suffering from collapsing revenues and the need to raise money for their own ransoms. Here is how the contemporary chronicler Jean Froissart describes the mood of the country.

"So all the prelates of the Church, bishops and abbots, all the nobility, lords and kings, the provost of the merchants of Paris and the burgesses, and the councillors of the French towns, met together in Paris to consider how the realm should be governed until their king should be set free. They also wanted to find out what happened to the vast sums which had been raised in the past through tithes, levies on capital, forced loans, coinings of new money and all other extortionate measures by which the population had been tormented and oppressed while the soldiers remained underpaid and the country inadequately protected, but of these matters no one was able to give an account."

The assembly elected 12 representatives from each of the 3 estates. "It was then decided by common consent that these 36 persons should meet frequently in Paris to discuss the affairs of the realm and put them in order.... As a first measure, the Three Estates stopped the coining of the money then being minted and took possession of the dies. Secondly, they required the dauphin to arrest his father's chancellor, with Sir Robert de Lorris, Sir Simon de Bucy, Jean Poillevillain and other financial officers and former counselors of the king, in order that they should render a true account of all the funds which had been levied and collected on their advice. When these high officials heard of this, they completely disappeared and were wise to do so. They left the kingdom of France as quickly as they could and went to live in other countries until the situation should have changed. Next they appointed on their own authority officials with the duty of raising and collecting all the levies, taxes, tithes, loans, and other duties payable to the crown and they had new coinage of fine gold minted, called *moutons*." By taking over the functions that were always the prerogative of the crown, the Council of Thirty-Six has accomplished what amounts to a coup-d'etat.

The key leader from the third estate to emerge in the revolutionary ferment of 1356–1358 was Etienne Marcel, the provost of merchants (basically, the mayor of Paris). Marcel was a member of the class of urban merchants and businessmen who had achieved great wealth during the previous century and now wanted to translate it into power and status. Several of Marcel's relatives had already achieved noble rank. A cousin bought a patent of nobility for 500 livres; Marcel's father-in-law and brother-in-law, starting as wealthy merchants in Rouen, became ennobled in the royal service. The tactics that Marcel used was mobilization of the urban masses of Paris as shock troops in wringing concessions from the dauphin-regent.

The confrontation between Marcel and the dauphin reached the climax in January 1358. The triggering event was, as usual, a spiral of violence and counter-violence. A citizen named Perrin Marc assassinated the dauphin's treasurer. The murderer was forcibly taken from the sanctuary in a church by the dauphin's marshall and hung. Etienne Marcel, assembling a crowd of 3,000 armed artisans and tradesmen, wearing the red-and-blue hoods of the popular party, marched to the royal palace. One of the dauphin's councillors, who had the misfortune of encountering the throng, was recognized and, before he could flee, struck down by so many blows that he expired on the spot. Reaching the palace, the crowd burst into the dauphin's chamber. As the terrified dauphin cowered in his bed, the provost's men fell upon his two marshals (including the one who had hung Perrin Marc) and butchered them before his very eyes. The dauphin, "grieving and dumbfounded," prayed to Marcel that the people of Paris might be his good friends as he was theirs, and accepted from Marcel two lengths of red-and-blue cloth to make hoods for himself and his officers. But the dauphin Charles, despite his sickly and nonmartial appearance, had a core of steel in him and a good head on his shoulders (he was later to be called Charles *le Sage*—the Wise). As soon as he could, Charles escaped from Paris to a nearby town of Senlis, where he set out to gather the support of the nobles.

While the government was deadlocked between the dauphin's and Marcel's factions, all remaining structures of law and order in the countryside disintegrated. "At that time a knight called Sir Regnault de Cervoles, commonly known as the Archpriest," relates Froissart, "took command of a large company of men at arms assembled from many countries. These found that their pay had ceased with the capture of King John and could see no way of making a living in France. They therefore went toward Provence, where they took a number of fortified towns and castles by assault and plundered the whole country as far as Avignon under the sole leadership of Sir Regnault. Pope Innocent VI and his cardinals who were at Avignon at that date were in such a fear of them that they hardly knew where to turn and kept their household servants armed day and night. After the archpriest and his men had pillaged the whole region, the pope and his college opened negotiations with him. He entered Avignon with most of his followers by friendly agreement, was received with as much respect as if he had been the king of France's son, and dined several times at the palace with the pope and the cardinals. All his sins were remitted him and when he left he was given 40,000 crowns to distribute among his companions. The company left the district but still remained under the command of the archpriest."

There were many other *routier* bands, in addition to the archpriest's. The area around Paris was devastated by demobilized French men at arms, by the English, and by the partisans of Charles of Navarre, who was freed from Châtelet, where John II had imprisoned him. After paying heavy taxes for many years, and having been forced to pay for ransoms for their masters captured at Poitiers, the harrying by the free companies was the last straw for the peasants of Ile-de-France.

BY THE SUMMER OF 1358, France rode the Wheel of Fortune to the bottom. The king and the flower of the French nobility were captive of the English. The legitimate government, headed by the dauphin-regent, was chased out of the capital by the Parisian mob under the leadership of Etienne Marcel and faced a rebellion of a large segment of the French nobility, led by Charles of Navarre. A peasant revolt was raging in Ile de France, Picardy, and Champagne. And, finally, the country was overrun by numerous companies of unemployed soldiers and impoverished nobles, turned brigands. Although the Black Death, the courage of the English, the bad weather, and various other circumstances were factors in this decline, the critical one, the one that marks all declines and all ascents of the wheel of historical fortune, is cooperation (whether it seems to be failing because of class warfare or regional warfare).

Chapter 9

A New Idea of Renaissance

Why Human Conflict Is Like a Forest Fire and an Epidemic

The nobility and urban elites were shocked by the military and social crises of the 1350s. The violence of the Jacquerie and urban riots terrified them. The Three Estates, or what was left of them, because by 1358 the nobles had largely withdrawn their support, demonstrated its inability to turn things around. The elites began withdrawing their support from various anti-Valois factions and consolidating around the dauphin Charles.

Etienne Marcel turned the nobility against himself when he led Paris mobs in murdering royal marshals and terrorizing the dauphin. Marcel's populist tactics and his intrigues with the "Jacks" and the English also cost him the support of the urban magnates. Increasingly isolated, the provost attempted to obtain aid from the Flemish towns, but on July 31, 1358, he and several other members of his faction were killed in street fighting with Parisian supporters of the dauphin.

About the same time, the nobles again demonstrated that a peasant uprising has no chance against a prepared and organized nobility. The turning point was the battle between thousands of peasant insurgents (9,000 according to the chronicler) and a company of 40 lances (120 men at arms) led by the Captal de Buch and Gaston of Foix in the town of Meaux. "The count of Foix and the Captal de Buch and their men, who were ready armed, formed up in the marketplace and then moved to the gates of the market and flung them open. There they faced the villeins, small and dark and very poorly armed.... When those evil men saw them [the knights] drawn up in this warlike order—although their numbers were comparatively small—they became less resolute than before. The foremost began to fall back and the noblemen to come after them, striking at them with their lances and swords and beating them down. Those who felt the blows, or feared to feel them, turned back in such panic that they fell over each other. Then men at arms of every kind burst out of the gates and ran into the square to attack those evil men. They mowed them down in heaps and slaughtered them like cattle; and they drove all the rest out of the town, for none of the villeins attempted to take up any sort of fighting order. They went on killing them until they were stiff and weary and they flung many into the River Marne. In all, they exterminated more than seven thousand Jacks on that day.... After that route at Meaux, there were no assemblies of the Jacks, for the young Lord de Coucy placed himself at the head of a large company of knights and squires who wiped them out wherever they found them, without pity or mercy." By the end of August 1358, the Jacquerie was over.

The next year, the English again invaded the French heartland. Edward III's aim was Reims, where he planned to crown himself the king of France. (Reims was where French coronations were traditionally held.) The dauphin wisely avoided battle and practiced a scorched-earth policy, thereby preventing the English from sustaining their siege of Reims. Edward then attempted to take Paris, but again was frustrated. His troops exhausted and treasury depleted, Edward negotiated a peace treaty at Brétigny (1360). In return for Edward's renouncing his claim to the French throne, Charles yielded large amounts of territory in the southwest and north, and promised to pay an enormous ransom—three million livres—for his father.

In 1359, the dauphin called for a meeting of the estates of the whole kingdom. This time the elites were able to bury their differences. After lengthy consultations, they hammered out a permanent solution for financing the state. The ordinance of December 5, 1360 became a landmark in French fiscal history by establishing the basic tax framework of the kingdom that was to last until the French Revolution. It imposed two kinds of taxes: the hearth tax and sales taxes, including an important tax on salt consumption, called the *gabelle*. This system of taxation represented a compromise between the landed and urban elites. The main burden of the hearth tax was on rural lordships, whereas sales taxes primarily affected the urban population. The salt *gabelle* was a highly regressive tax, the main burden on which had to be borne by the poor (who, as usual, got shafted because they were not represented in the Estates General).

There was very little opposition to the new taxes. The evident need to ransom the king was clearly one factor, although in the end the whole amount of ransom was never paid; instead, the government of the dauphin Charles wisely used the money to build a new army. Perhaps even more important was the collective realization that something had to be done or France was lost. Another contributing factor was the massive "pruning" of the French nobility administered by the war. The worst disaster, that of Crécy, wiped out 10,000 of the "flower of the French nobility" and Poitiers accounted for another 2,500. Thousands died at the naval battle of Sluys (1340), in the local civil wars such as that raging in Brittany, and at the hands of the Jacks and *routiers*. In short, by 1360 there were fewer "noble thugs" to cause trouble—some were killed off, others inherited property of their slain relatives, and the rest were simply fed up with perpetual violence and chaos. The swing in the public opinion in favor of peace and stability was evident in the new tone of literature on warfare and chivalry. Whereas the emphasis before the collapse of 1358 was on the right to private war and the pursuit of honor and glory, now it addressed questions of discipline and public order. In a motet (a polyphonic choral composition sung in Latin), Philippe Royllart praised Charles's victories over the English: "Thou hast vanquished the enemy that plagued our innocent people," but then added, "now bring the peace to us. Listen to us and make it happen." This new social consensus, however, was still quite fragile and, as we shall see shortly, France was to experience a relapse into chaos during the early fifteenth century, but for now the nobility had circled its wagons around the government led by Charles.

The most important use of the regular tax income was building a permanent army. Unlike the vast and chaotic throngs of knights of the previous reign, the army of Charles the Wise had only 2,400 men at arms and 1,000 crossbowmen, of which 60 percent were mounted. These troops were permanently employed and regularly paid. The permanent forces were joined during the periods of particularly intense activity by supplementary retinues of men at arms, bringing the total to the maximum of 5,200. The first military success of the new army in the spring of 1364 was to crush the forces of the Navarrese faction in Normandy, led by Charles the Bad. In 1369, the war with the English resumed as a result of the appeal to the king by the count of Armagnac against the Black Prince. During the next decade, the French conducted systematic, if unspectacular military operations directed by such decidedly unchivalric leaders as Bertrand du Guesclin. By the end of Charles V's reign in 1380, almost all French territory was regained. The English clung to a few towns and fortresses on the Atlantic coast and the territory immediately surrounding these strongholds. The last *chevauchée* (a raid in force deep into the French territory with the purpose of causing as much destruction as possible) was conducted by the English in 1380. All hostilities ceased in 1388, and were not to resume until 1411.

AS DISCUSSED IN THE PRECEDING CHAPTER, the fourteenth-century state collapse in France was brought on by a combined action of popular immiseration resulting from excessive population growth, elite overproduction, and the state's insolvency. By the end of the fourteenth century, general overpopulation had been "dealt with" by the Great Famine of 1315–22 and the Black Death from 1348 on. The bloodletting of Crécy and Poitiers, coupled with losses during the intra-elite civil wars and the popular uprisings, made inroads into the numbers of the nobility. Unfortunately, it was not enough to solve the problem of elite overproduction. There were still too many nobles around, and, moreover, their numbers were replenished by vigorous upward mobility from the ranks of commoners.

The early fourteenth century saw the rise of a large social group of "elite aspirants"—well-to-do commoners who wanted to translate their wealth into power and status, people such as Etienne Marcel, Jan van Arteveldt, and members of their factions. During the troubled times of the fourteenth century, these individuals were entering the second estate in large numbers. Some were ennobled in return for military service by the king and other magnates; others capitalized on the financial troubles of the crown by simply purchasing ennobling patents. We can trace the rise of these new elites by looking at the numbers of ennobling patents issued by the French kings. Between 1307 and 1328, Philip the Fair and his sons issued on average four patents per year. Under Philip VI (1328–50), this number increased to 10, then to 14 under John II (1350–64), finally reaching the peak under Charles V (1364–80)—20 per year. During the fifteenth century, the rate of ennoblement gradually fell, and Charles VIII (1483–98) issued only 6 patents per year.

Additionally, the disasters of the 1340s and 1350s primarily affected noblemen of military age. A generation later another crop of young noble males was raised and ready for action. The new generation did not experience at first hand the military disasters of Crécy and Poitiers, the state collapse, and the Jacquerie that shocked those of their fathers (who survived) and made them close the ranks around the government of Charles the Wise. The new generation was going to repeat the mistakes that led to the previous collapse.

When we look at the history of France during the Hundred Years of Hostility, we notice that good reigns alternated with bad ones. The reign of John II (1350–64) was the period of social dissolution and state collapse, whereas that of his son Charles V (1364–1380) was the time of national consolidation and territorial reconquest. The next reign, that of Charles VI (1380–1422), was another period of social disintegration and collapse. It was followed by the period of internal consolidation and national resurgence under Charles VII (1422–61), which finally lifted France out of the late medieval depression. This is a general dynamical pattern of alternation between very turbulent and relatively peaceful spells that is observed again and again during the secular disintegrative phases. The explanation of such swings in the collective mood lies in the social psychology.

Every episode of internal warfare develops like an epidemic or a forest fire. In the beginning of the conflict, each act of violence triggers chains of revenge and counter-revenge. With time, participants lose all restraint, atrocities become common, and conflict escalates in an accelerating, explosive fashion. After the initial explosion, however, violence drags on and on, for years and sometimes even for decades. Sooner or later most people begin to yearn for the return of stability and an end to fighting. The most psychopathic and violent leaders get killed off or lose their supporters. Violence, like an epidemic or a forest fire, "burns out." Even though the fundamental causes that brought the conflict on in the first place might still be operating, the prevailing social mood swings in favor of cessation of conflict at all costs, and an uneasy truce gradually takes hold. Those people, like the generation of Charles the Wise, who directly experienced the period of civil warfare, become "immunized" against it, and while they are in charge, they keep things stable. The peaceful period lasts for a human generation—between 20 and 30 years. Eventually, however, the conflict-scarred generation dies off or retires, and a new cohort arises, people who did not experience the horrors of civil war, and are not immunized against it. If the long-term social forces, which brought about the first outbreak of internal hostilities, are still operating, the society will slide into the second civil war.

It is amazing how closely the events leading to the second crisis reproduced those that ended in the crisis of the 1350s. As before, the first sign of the impending disaster was the appearance of vast mobs of impoverished nobles looking for military employment. In the fall of 1386, between 10,000 and 20,000 nobles flocked to L'Écluse, where preparations to invade England were under way. (The invasion never took place.) In 1396, thousands of French knights went on a crusade against the Turks, only to perish at the battle of Nicopolis. The nobility again started fragmenting into feuding factions. During the minority of Charles VI in the 1380s, factions began crystallizing around his uncles, the "princes of the lilies"—the dukes of Anjou, Burgundy, and Berry (the same one who commissioned the beautiful illustrated manuscript *The Very Rich Hours of the Duke of Berry*). These princes impoverished the treasury by pocketing the taxes collected in the territories over which they had control (their appanages) and by diverting government funds for personal projects. The political program of the duke of Burgundy was to use the resources of France to build an independent principality in Burgundy and the Low Countries. Louis of Anjou had dynastic ambitions in Italy and tried to get the treasury to underwrite the costs of his Italian expedition. Another faction was the "Marmousets" (grotesques, gargoyles—so called by their enemies because of their bourgeois origins), a group that included high civil officials and military leaders close to the previous king, Charles the Wise. This faction was the only one that worried about the common good. The Marmousets' objectives were relieving the burden on the taxpayers while building up the resources in the royal coffers.

During the 1390s, the various groupings of the power elites gradually consolidated into two opposing factions: one led by the power-hungry duke of Burgundy, the other by the brother of the king, Louis of Orléans, when he came of age. Few realized at the time that this factional rivalry would plunge France into an extremely bloody civil war that would last for 30 years.

Consistent state policy was impossible while various factions contended for power. The central government was also weakened by the intermittent insanity of the king. When the king was incapacitated, the Burgundian faction was ascendant. During his more lucid periods, the Orléanists held the power. The fragile consensus on taxation, achieved in 1360, was lost. Some taxes were repealed, such as the hearth tax that so displeased the landowning nobility. Others (sale taxes, the salt *gabelle*) were first annulled, but then immediately re-imposed, causing discontent and even brief rebellions that had to be crushed by force.

While Philip of Burgundy (Charles the Wise's generation) was alive, the rivalry between the Burgundian and Orléanist factions did not escalate into open conflict. In 1404, however, Philip died and was succeeded by his son John the Fearless. The French historian Edouard Perroy famously characterized John as possessing "a strong and unpleasant character. Small and ugly, and with a long nose, a wry mouth, and an undershot jaw, even more ambitious than Philip ... he was harsh, cynical, crafty, imperious, gloomy, and a kill-joy." In a fit of murderous rage against Louis of Orléans (as he confessed later, "the Devil tempted me"), which was so typical of the late Middle Ages, he ordered the assassination of his cousin. On a dark November night in 1407, Louis was ambushed and butchered as he was returning home from a visit to the queen.

This murder, just as the murder of the constable by the Navarrese faction 50 years before, touched off an escalating wave of violence. The French elites divided into two armed camps. The anti-Burgundian faction was now led by the count of Armagnac, father-in-law of Charles, the new duke of Orléans, and therefore were called the "Armagnacs." The Armagnacs were the party of the greater royal officials and high nobility, with much following in the south and southeast. The Burgundians drew their strength from John's territories in the northeast and north, and from the Parisian bourgeoisie and academics.

From 1407 to 1414, the two factions battled for the capital and both appealed for the English aid at various stages of the struggle. In 1413, the royal council summoned the Estates to obtain consent for taxation, but the

Estates refused to act until officials guilty of misappropriations were punished and certain reforms of government undertaken. The government was forced to yield to these demands, and suspended all financial officers and appointed a commission of inquiry to prepare reforms.

It seems as though the French were determined to replay the drama of the 1350s. Just as before, the country was without an effective king (this time, due to his insanity rather than capture). John the Fearless played the role of Charles the Bad to perfection. There was even a new Etienne Marcel.

On April 27, 1413, a Parisian mob led by the butcher Simon Caboche broke into the residence of the king and the dauphin. They killed three from the kings' retinue and imprisoned 15 others. They also besieged the Bastille and massacred the hated Armagnacs throughout the city. The next month was one of continuous riots. The crowd terrorized the king and almost daily exacted fresh victims from him and demanded reforms. The rioters imprisoned suspects and carried out summary executions.

Finally, the revolutionary excesses of Caboche's butchers turned the moderate burghers against them (as they turned against Marcel two generations ago). They approached the dauphin Charles (the future Charles VII and the grandson of Charles the Wise) who called for help from the Armagnacs. The Armagnacs entered Paris on August 4. The balance of power swung against the faction of Caboche and John the Fearless, who was pulling the strings from the background. The butchers attempted to storm the town hall, but were repulsed. The Burgundians then made an attempt to kidnap the king, which was also frustrated, and John the Fearless left the capital in defeat. Caboche survived by also fleeing Paris.

By 1414, the Armagnacs won control of most of France. But there was a new king in England, young and ambitious, who was keenly observing the anarchy in France—Henry V. After allying himself with John the Fearless, Henry V invaded France in 1415 and met the French forces at Agincourt. The battle of Agincourt was a close replay of Crécy. A small army of 10,000 English won a resounding victory over a chaotic throng of three times as many French knights. At the end of the day, 10,000 corpses of the French nobility lay in heaps on the field of battle.

As the English leisurely completed the conquest of Normandy, the Burgundian forces besieged Paris held by the count of Armagnac. The Armagnac hold on the capital was broken when the Burgundian partisans rose in Paris and killed thousands of Armagnacs. When the Burgundians entered the capital in May 1418, it was littered with Armagnac corpses "piled up like pigs in the mud," as reported by an eyewitness. The dauphin and the surviving Armagnacs had to abandon Paris to the Burgundians.

The following year (1419), Rouen surrendered to Henry V and the English conquest of Normandy was complete. The English successes gave John the Fearless second thoughts, and he attempted to negotiate with the dauphin and the Armagnacs. But during the meeting between the dauphin and the duke of Burgundy at the bridge of Montereau, intended to cement the treaty of friendship, the Armagnacs treacherously killed John in revenge for the murder of Louis of Orléans 12 years earlier. The new duke, Philip the Good, swore vengeance and returned to the English alliance. Working with the Burgundians, the English overran northern France and installed themselves in Paris. By the treaty of Troyes (1421), Henry V married the daughter of Charles VI and was named the heir to the French throne, while the dauphin was disinherited. In 1422 both Charles VI and Henry V died. The infant Henry VI of England was recognized as king of France in the north, supported by the Burgundians, and later crowned in Paris.

The position of the Dauphinists (formerly Armagnacs) continued to deteriorate during the 1420s. In 1424, they lost the battle of Verneuil, and in 1428 the English began the siege of Orléans. Meanwhile, the Lancastrian France had become a wilderness laid waste by its English garrisons, by Dauphinist raiders, by deserters, and by *écorcheurs*. The *écorcheurs* or "flayers" were the heirs of *routiers* of the previous century. They took their name from their custom of stripping their victims to the skin, although many would not stop at that, and stripped the skin itself from the unfortunates who fell in their hands.

THE PREVIOUS CHAPTER ASKED WHY the population of France did not increase during the second half of the fourteenth century. After the Malthusian pressure was relieved by the Great Famine and, especially, the Black Death, the population rate should have responded. In reality, it did not. For the next hundred years, there were some episodes of tentative recovery, which were reversed by new declines. By the middle of the fifteenth century, the population of France was still half of what it was at the peak of 1300. A sustained period of population growth began only after 1450.

To explain this prolonged period of the "late medieval depression," which puzzled historians for a long time, we need to go beyond the strict Malthusian theory. As we have just seen, the condition of elite overproduction that started to afflict the French society in the early fourteenth century, and was exacerbated by the general population collapse of 1315–50, was still not abated by 1400. A direct result of that was a series of civil wars, peaking first in the 1350s and then in the 1410s. The internal fighting was exacerbated by popular uprisings, foreign invasions, and by the general collapse of law and order in the countryside. The whole period of 1350–1440 was the "golden age" of *routiers* and *écorcheurs*.

The most obvious effect of prolonged political and social instability on the general population was in causing elevated mortality. Peasants were killed directly by royal armies, by the free companies, by bandits and other criminals, and by deadly quarrels. (As discussed before, crime rates exploded during this period all across Europe.) The movement of armies, mercenary bands, and vagabonds also spread around epidemics, thus indirectly contributing to high mortalities. The late Middle Ages were a time when all became intimately acquainted with the Grim Reaper. The cultural reflection of this fascination was the bizarre cult of death that arose in the late fourteenth century and reached a peak during the fifteenth. A new kind of processional play came into vogue—the *danse macabre*.

General instability also affected birth rates. Women married later and had fewer children. Unwanted babies were abandoned or killed. Populations also declined as a result of emigration. Peasants ran away from harsh and grasping lords and from war-torn areas. All of the main demographic forces—mortality, natality, and emigration—were affected by heightened sociopolitical stability and acted to reduce the population.

Even more importantly, internal warfare damaged productive capacity of the society. Successful practice of agriculture requires at least a minimal degree of stability, but that is precisely what French peasants did not get during the Hundred Years of Hostilities. Some areas of France, such as Normandy, were fought over repeatedly and suffered extensive damage. A contemporary observer, the Norman bishop Thomas Basin, described the situation in northwestern France during the 1420s as "a state of devastation such that from the Loire to the Seine, and from there to the Somme, the peasants having been killed or run off, almost all fields were left for a number of years not only uncultivated, but without people ... All that could be cultivated at that time in that region was only around and inside towns or castles, close enough so that, from the top of the tower or watchtower the eye of the lookout could perceive the attacking brigands. Then, with the sound of a bell, or horn, or some other instrument, he gave all those working in the fields or vineyards the signal to withdraw to the fortified place."

What Basin was observing was that warfare and brigandage not only cause direct mortality and damage to agriculture, but that they also impose a kind of the "landscape of fear." Only land near fortified places can be worked; the rest of agriculturally suitable land is abandoned.

The Paris region was another area where fighting was prolonged, and as noted previously, its rural population might have decreased fourfold! The region suffered both because it was close to Flanders and Normandy, which were the sources of the English *chevauchées*, and because it was the national capital, over which the Armagnac and Burgundian factions fought. The south (especially southwest) was similarly devastated. Philippe de la Boissière wrote in the fifteenth century that "this land of Saintonge, except for the towns and fortresses, was deserted and uninhabited ... Where there had once been fine manors, domains, and heritages, towering bushes grew." Some areas escaped devastation for a while, but not for long. When the English under the Black Prince marched through the Massif Central in 1356, according to Froissart, they found "the land of Auvergne which they had never before entered ... so prosperous and so full of all manner of goods that it was a marvel to see." Needless to say, the prosperity of Auvergne did not survive the Black Prince and his troops.

Paradoxically, although France possessed plenty of wonderful agricultural land, more than enough to feed its greatly diminished population, there was a serious deficit of land that could be cultivated in peace. Peasants abandoned villages for the relative safety of fortified towns. Around such Alsatian towns as Colmar, there were whole "belts" of dead villages. The abandoned land was allowed to turn fallow, or was lightly grazed by cattle. Incessant warfare also destroyed infrastructure. For example, in the area of Langle (modern Pas-de-Calais) the drainage system was abandoned, and the land was first flooded and then deserted. The French historian Emmanuel Le Roy Ladurie estimates that a minimum of 10 million acres of land was abandoned between 1350 and 1440.

As a result, famine became endemic in France during the first half of the fifteenth century. There were crises in food supplies around Paris and Rouen in 1421, 1432, 1433, and particularly 1437–39. The fundamental problem was not overpopulation, as in 1315–22, but lack of security. This can be seen most clearly by looking at how real wages fluctuated during the fifteenth century. The fourteenth-century population decline translated into excellent real wages for working people. In the first decade of the fifteenth century (before the second crisis), a building worker in Paris could buy 25 kilograms of grain with his daily wage. During the war decades of the 1420s and 1430s, by contrast, the laborer's wage collapsed to 10 kilograms of grain. As soon as the area around Paris was pacified, however, the wages jumped back up. From 1440 to the end of the century, the daily wage was again equivalent to 25 kilograms of grain. The second half of the fifteenth century was deservedly called the golden age of the common people.

THE DISINTEGRATIVE PHASE OF THE secular cycle could not end until the surplus nobility were somehow removed from the scene. This problem was solved during the first half of the fifteenth century—not by a conscious design, but as a result of operation of impersonal social forces. The numbers of nobility diminished because of increased mortality and downward mobility, and decreased upward mobility.

The hecatombs inflicted on the French nobility during the second stage of the Hundred Years' War were even greater than those of the first, especially when considered in proportional terms. The worst disaster was undoubtedly Agincourt, where 10,000 French nobles perished. Among the fallen were more than 10 dukes and counts, 120 barons, and 1,500 knights. Earlier, several thousands of French nobles participated in the crusade to free Hungary from the Turks, where they perished at the battle of Nicopolis (1396). The Dauphinist casualties at the battle of Verneuil (1424) were about 7,000, although only a part of them were French. (There was a big Scot contingent fighting on the French side.) And casualties in large battles were only a part of the total drain on the French nobility. Untold thousands lost their lives in the civil wars and small-scale military operations (sieges, skirmishes) against the English. Massacres, such as that of Armagnacs in Paris (1418), became commonplace. King Henry V of England (as well as other military leaders of the time) was notorious for the atrocities that he routinely committed. The best known one is the killing of the prisoners that he ordered on the field of Agincourt, but there were many others. For example, when he took the Armagnac castle of Rougemont (1421), he hanged the entire garrison. Those defenders, who escaped and were caught later, were drowned. (Did he run out of rope?) When dispossessed nobles in Normandy persisted in using guerilla tactics, the English called them "brigands" and hanged them when they caught them. Other atrocities include the cold-blooded butchering of 2,000 men, women, and children in Caen in 1417, and Henry's refusal to allow 12,000 poor folk driven out of the besieged and starving Rouen to leave. He forced them to stay in the city ditch, where most of them died of inclement climate (it was winter) and starvation. The last two examples refer to commoners, but they illustrate how callous the fighting men were about taking life, and the nobility were often treated in the same way as commoners (except when there was a hope of ransom). Both commoners and nobles suffered from the casual attitude to taking life, but because the nobles were the military class, they paid a disproportionate price.

The study of Lyon wills by the French medievalist Marie-Thérèse Lorcin provides us with a unique glimpse at the difference between noble and commoner mortality rates. The wills list all surviving sons and daughters at the time of death of a testator. Lorcin found that in commoner families males outnumbered females by 13 percent. This pattern is just what we expect in a pre-industrial society where a substantial proportion of women died in childbirth. In noble families, however, the pattern was reversed—there were only 85 males per 100 females. In other words, there were 28 percent fewer noble males than we would expect if their mortality patterns were the same as commoners. Actually, the disparity between the noble and non-noble sex ratios was due not only to the differential mortality, which was real enough, but also to the higher proportion of noble-women going to nunneries, and thus being spared the dangers of childbirth. But this observation reminds us that any population group could decline as a result of either higher mortality, or lower birth rate, or both. Removal of a large proportion of noble daughters to cloisters, thus, was another mechanism by which the numbers of nobility declined. The wills studied by Lorcin allowed her to calculate that during the second half of the fourteenth century and the first half of the fifteenth, the proportions of noble girls becoming nuns were 40 and 30 percent, respectively. Only in the second half of the fifteenth century did this proportion decline to 14 percent. At the same time that fewer nobles married, the average family size also experienced a decline. In the preceding chapter, I used the data from investigations post mortem to show that the replacement rate of the landowning elites was well above one all the way up until 1350. After that date, it abruptly fell—to 0.82 in the second half of the fourteenth century and 0.87 in the first half of the fifteenth century. The replacement rate went back above one (to 1.27) only after 1450.

In summary, demographic forces—death and birth rates—were gradually reducing noble numbers. Patterns of social mobility worked in the same direction. Above I have already mentioned that during the fifteenth century ennoblements fell from 20 to 6 per year. At the same time, rates of downward mobility increased. During the first half of the fifteenth century, the noble incomes continued on the downward spiral that began in the fourteenth century. Even during peaceful times, landlords suffered from the unfavorable (to them) economic trends of high wages, low rents, and depressed grain prices. The periods of warfare brought complete ruin to them. An example of a more extreme collapse is provided by the seigneury of Sully (in the Orléans region), whose revenue between 1383 and 1455 fell from 700 to 143 livres! Data from other regions suggest less-extreme but still substantial declines of revenues. In war-torn Normandy income declines between 1400 and 1450 were on the order of 50 percent.

The severe depression of landed incomes did not affect all noble families uniformly. Rather, it imposed a selection regime in which the weak and unlucky declined and eventually succumbed, whereas the strong and lucky held their own, or even got ahead. The impoverished nobles who attempted to maintain the levels of consumption necessary for preserving their status rapidly ran up debt, and eventually had to sell their lands. Thus, the majority of the lesser gentry, those families with 25–50 livres per year, who already were on the brink by 1350, were plunged beyond the point of no return. On the other hand, many magnate families during this period were buying up lands. It was easier for a great lord to reduce consumption without crossing the line between nobility and commonality. Furthermore, magnates were better positioned to profit from the royal patronage (even though the total flow of royal favors was greatly diminished during this era due to the persistent insolvency of the crown), and land was cheap.

Another group that profited from the economic situation were certain bourgeois, particularly those who provided administrators and financiers for the state. But these individuals were a numerically small group, and their ennoblement could not reverse the overall trend of thinning the ranks of nobility. Thus, the old nobility shrank in numbers, but largely remained in control. This process can be illustrated with the situation in the Sologne (within the county of Blois). The Sologne contained nine fiefs possessing the right of high justice. Five of these fiefs remained within the hands of the old nobility without interruption. Of the remaining four, one was seized by the duke of Orléans for its debts, one was sold to another old noble family, and the last two were acquired by new nobility—the d'Étamps family, originating in the late fourteenth century. Thus, the total number of old nobility families shrank appreciably, but there was only one *parvenu* family to plug the resulting gap. Similar developments occurred at the opposite end of France, in the county of Bigorre, where there were 40 fiefs in 1313 but only 18 in 1429. Twelve fiefs disappeared as a result of depopulation and village abandonment. The other 10 fiefs were acquired by the surviving seigneurs. Thus, there were fewer lords in the county, but the surviving ones had, on average, more land than in 1300.

Economic difficulties, elevated mortality due to conflicts, and declining replacement rates had a measurable effect on the rate of noble family and lineage extinction. Although the county of Forez in south-central France escaped the worst excesses of the Hundred Years' War, the rate of extinction of noble lineages in this region increased almost twofold from 31 percent during the thirteenth century to 54 percent and 55 percent in the fourteenth and fifteenth centuries, respectively.

We lack direct information about the overall numbers of nobles in medieval France, but scattered data indicate that in the early fourteenth century nobles constituted between 1.3 and 3.4 percent of the population, depending on province, for an average of 2.4 percent. One hundred fifty years later, the nobles were between 1 and 1.6 percent of the general population. In other words, because the total population halved over this period, the numbers of nobles declined by a factor of four. The declining tendency was particularly obvious with respect to the middle ranks—the knights—whose number decreased over the 150 years from 5,000–10,000 to just 1,000.

The press that the nobility exerted on the commoners was declining not only because there were relatively fewer landlords per peasant, but also because nobles were forced to adjust their consumption levels to match their diminished incomes. Gone were the opulence and conspicuous consumption of the High Middle Ages. The royal courts of the late fifteenth century were small and drab affairs. Louis X (1461–83) of France was a man of simple, even bourgeois, habits. In England, the first Tudor, Henry VII (1485–1509), was a tight purse. What a contrast between the courts of these two kings and those of Francis I and Henry VIII during the next century! The cultural change is evident in the arts. Portraits of that time show that somber gowns were in, ostentation out. In architecture, there is a change from a flamboyant style of late Gothic to the elegant and simple Renaissance.

BY THE LATE 1420s, the severe pruning of the nobility abated the social pressures that had fueled the intra-elite competition and conflict. At the same time, after two decades of civil war and foreign invasions, everybody, from the magnate to the peasant, was heartily sick of chaos and unending turmoil and wanted stability at almost any cost. The problem was that the position of Charles VII was so weak after the disaster of Verneuil (1424) that for a while it was not even clear around whom the forces for order could consolidate. Charles was not even formally invested with the French crown (he could not get to Reims, which was in the English hands), and he was reduced to holding his court at a provincial town of Bourges (hence the disparaging nickname the *roi de Bourges*). In an incredible development, making one think that societies can act almost like living organisms, in 1428 France produced Jeanne d'Arc. The lifting of the siege of Orléans by Jeanne followed by the coronation Charles VII in Reims in 1429 was the turning point. The conclusion of a treaty with the duke of Burgundy (1435) brought the civil war to an end, and the French reconquest slowly gathered steam. Paris was recovered in 1436, Gascony (except Bordeaux and Bayonne) was reconqured in 1442, Normandy in 1450, and finally Bordeaux fell in 1453.

The decade after 1435 saw a permanent establishment of state finance in France, essentially along the lines hammered out in 1360. By 1460, the restored fiscal system was producing 1.8 million livres a year. Solid fiscal foundation was a factor of critical importance in ending the Hundred Years' War, but it itself was a consequence of the new-found feeling of national unity among the elites, which was widely shared by the lower classes, as the dynastic conflict between the Valois and Plantagentes became gradually transmuted into a national war of liberation against the English.

WHEREAS FRANCE BEGAN ITS CLIMB out of the medieval depression c.1450, in England the time of troubles dragged on for another half century. In fact, in the second half of the fifteenth century, England saw the worst period of instability in its history. The period opened with Cade's rebellion of 30,000 men in Kent and Sussex in 1450. A dreary civil war between the Lancastrians and Yorkists dragged on between 1455 and 1485. Henry VII Tudor (1485–1509) had to deal with a series of revolts, conspiracies, and pretenders. Only after the last pretender, Perkin Warbeck, was defeated in 1497 had England finally become pacified.

The divergence between the French and English trajectories can be traced to the middle of the fourteenth century. The Great Famine and the Black Death had the same effect on both countries: a disproportionate die-off of the producing population leading to a dangerous disbalance between too few peasants and too many lords. However, in 1356, the English won the victory at Poitiers and captured the French king. On the eve of the battle, the finances of the English crown were on the verge of collapse. Edward III imposed heavy taxes, causing widespread resentment, and borrowed like a fiend. His default on the loans from the Lombards caused the collapse of several Italian banks. The great victory at Poitiers brought with it increased legitimacy, which helped to quiet the grumbling over taxation, and, more importantly, a windfall of ransoms from the French king and nobles. Thus, precisely the same event that tipped France into the tailspin allowed the English a respite from their own troubles. During the next century, England continued shipping off the excess of its nobility to France, where they plundered with the free companies, or carved temporary domains for themselves, or simply were killed. The surplus noble thugs contributed to the chaos in France, but their absence from England allowed preservation of fragile balance within the island. This export of instability, however, did not solve the root causes that generated it. England experienced a great peasant rebellion and a change of dynasty at the end of the fourteenth century. But these upheavals were not enough to solve the problem of elite overproduction.

As soon as the French regained their social cohesion, England lost its outlet for venting steam. In 1453, the English were expelled from France, and practically immediately, just two years later, England went into its own tailspin. The struggle during the Wars of the Roses was extremely bitter and bloody. Kings were deposed and quietly murdered in prison or killed on the battlefield. Princes were strangled in the Tower of London. After a battle, the peers of the realm from the losing faction were made to kneel in the mud, and their heads were lopped off. Lesser nobility and gentry enthusiastically slaughtered each other in a host of small-scale feuds that broke out all over the country. Toward the end of the fifteenth century, the English ruling class was pruned to the point where stability could gradually begin to reassert itself.

It is interesting that after the English and French trajectories diverged during the fourteenth century, these two societies continued to oscillate with a phase shift. For example, the next period of instability in France began with the religious wars and ended with the Fronde. In England, instability began with the Great Revolution, continued with the Glorious Revolution, and ended with two aftershocks of Jacobite rebellions in Scotland. Therefore, the instability phase in France was a century between 1560 and 1660, whereas in England it occurred later, roughly between 1640 and 1740. This observation drives the final nail in the coffin of the climatic explanation of secular cycles. The cores of the two states, southern England and northern France, have very similar climates, and if it was climate change that was responsible for decline and collapse, then the two societies should have experienced it at the same time. Yet they did not. On the other hand, if cycles are generated internally, preservation of phase shift is precisely what we should expect.

WE HAVE THUS SEEN THAT THE very stability and internal peace that strong empires impose contain within it the seeds of chaos. Stability and internal peace bring prosperity; prosperity causes population increase. Demographic growth leads to overpopulation; overpopulation causes lower wages, higher land rents, and falling per-capita incomes for the commoners. At first, low wages and high rents bring unparalleled wealth to the upper classes, but as their numbers and appetites grow, they too begin to suffer from falling incomes. Declining standards of life breed discontent and strife. The elites turn to the state for employment and additional income, and drive up its expenditures at the same time that the tax revenues decline because of the impoverished state of the population. When the state's finances collapse, it loses control of the army and police. Freed from all restraints, strife among the upper classes escalates into civil war, and the discontent among the lower classes explodes into popular rebellions.

The collapse of order brings in its wake the four horsemen of apocalypse—famine, war, pestilence, and death. Population declines, and wages increase, while rents decrease. As incomes of commoners recover, the fortunes of the upper classes hit the bottom. Economic distress of the elites and lack of effective government feed the continuing internecine wars. But civil wars thin the ranks of the elites. Some die in factional fighting, others succumb to feuds with neighbors, and many just give up on trying to maintain their noble status and quietly slip into the ranks of commoners. Intra-elite competition subsides, allowing order to be restored. Stability and internal peace bring prosperity, and another secular cycle begins. "So peace brings warre and warre brings peace."

Empires, therefore, go through an alternation of roughly century-long integrative and disintegrative phases as a result of their inner workings. But this does not mean that external factors are unimportant—as noted previously, although they do not cause secular cycles, they can influence them. Suppose that the population has already grown to the point where all potentially cultivable lands are cultivated, so that the capacity of land to feed the people is already under strain. A global cooling of the climate, causing a decline in crop production, will tip the society over the edge of sustainability. The resulting population decline will mainly affect the lower classes, making for a top-heavy society and that, as we know, rapidly leads to increasing social instability and collapse. If not for the temperature change, this society would enjoy internal peace for a while longer (although disintegration phase cannot be postponed forever).

In this theoretical example, the onset of instability was still due to internal causes (elite-commoner balance getting out of whack, causing intense intra-elite competition, and so on), but the timing of collapse was advanced by inclement climate. Again, external factors do not explain the secular cycle, but can influence it. Suppose the global cooling occurs earlier, when the population is sparse, and there is plenty of uncultivated land. A decline in crop productivity will impose some hardship, because peasants will need to increase the amount of land they cultivate to make up for poorer harvests. Perhaps population growth will be slower because of harsh winters. But there will be no population decline, no elite-commoner disbalance, and stability will be preserved. Climate worsening, thus, may or may not bring about the society collapse, depending on what stage of the cycle the society is in when it hits. This is why no strong association exists between climatic change and decentralization phases.

Other external factors can advance or delay the onset of crisis. States do not exist in isolation; they are surrounded by potential enemies or prey. External warfare can have a large effect on how the secular cycle develops. We saw how the loss of French territories in 1453 immediately precipitated crisis in England. Territorial gain, on the other hand, can postpone the crisis very substantially. During the Romanov dynasty (1613–1917), Russia enormously expanded its territory. The newly conquered steppe regions were sparsely populated and could accept massive inflows of colonizers, which relieved population pressure in the core regions. Nobles also profited from this colonization, by acquiring estates in the new lands. The nobility numbers expanded, but slower than the numbers of peasants. As a result, during the seventeenth and eighteenth century, the Russian society had a tiny ruling class—only about 1 percent of the total population, which explains the extremely long period, over two centuries, of internal stability. There were peasant uprisings, which were handily suppressed, and palace coups when the upper nobility wanted to change an emperor, but nothing like the time of troubles before the Romanov era. Only in the nineteenth century, after the colonization of the new lands was over, did the usual trends toward overpopulation and, particularly, elite overproduction assert themselves again. The result was the revolutions of 1905 and 1917, the civil war, and Stalin's purges.

When cycles are generated internally within a dynamical system, we should not expect rises and falls to succeed each other with a high degree of regularity, for the same reason that weather systems—and forest fires—are so difficult to predict. First, there is the curious property of nonlinear dynamical systems that mathematicians call chaos. Chaotic systems oscillate in a seemingly erratic but nevertheless completely deterministic fashion. Second, and more important, is that societies are not closed systems—they are affected and afflicted with a variety of external forces, such as climatic change, the arrival of a pandemic, or the invasion of an army. As a result, some cycles will take longer to complete, and others will run their course faster. Sometimes a cycle might even be completely aborted, if a Chinggis Khan or a Timur arrives with a huge army and piles the heads, of commoner and noble alike, in a huge pyramid.

Chapter 10

The Matthew Principle

Why the Rich Get Richer and the Poor Get Poorer

Secular cycles are one of the most pervasive rhythms of history. They affect practically all facets of social life, from homicide rates to the styles of architecture. The phase of the secular cycle also determines the trend in social and economic inequality—whether it increases or decreases. This aspect is of particular interest because of the corrosive effect that glaring inequality has on the willingness of people to cooperate, which in turn underlies the capacity of societies for collective action. The effect of growing inequality is not limited to the escalation of "class warfare" between the poor and the rich. Increasing inequality within classes also leads to intense conflict of commoner versus commoner and aristocrat versus aristocrat. Growing inequality, thus, is an important part of *imperiopathosis*—the process by which imperial nations lose their high asabiya. What are the social forces that cause inequality to grow, and how does inequality affect societies?

Social scientists have debated this question for centuries, indeed for millennia. (The great Greek philosophers Plato and Aristotle, for example, devoted much thought to inequality and its effect on politics.) One interesting idea is that increased wealth inequality can result from just economic exchange—trade. This was theoretically demonstrated by Robert Axtell and Joshua Epstein of the Brookings Institution. Axtell and Epstein devised a complex computer model that they call Sugarscape. Sugarscape is a virtual landscape within which certain resources are distributed, such as "sugar" and "spice." Agents run around within this landscape, collecting, storing, and consuming sugar and spice. When Epstein and Axtell added to their model an ability to trade, agents immediately began exchanging sugar for spice and vice versa, and learned to set exchange rates (prices) for these two commodities depending on their supply and demand. What is particularly interesting to us is that, as time went by, wealth (stores of sugar or spice controlled by an agent) began to be distributed more and more unequally. Soon the great majority of the agents became very poor, while a small minority accumulated great riches.

Although the model of Axtell and Epstein might seem to have little relation to reality (it is not much more than a computer game), its results illustrate a profound principle. The poorer agents are at a disadvantage, compared to the richer ones, and, as a result, tend to lose ground. By contrast, the richer agents tend to increase their stores of resources with time. In the language of dynamical sciences, this is called a "positive feedback loop"— the rich get richer, and the poor get poorer. Social scientists came up with another name for it, the "Matthew principle," because the New Testament says: "For whosoever hath, to him shall be given, and he shall have more abundance: but whosoever hath not, from him shall be taken away even that he hath" (Mathew 13:12).

The Matthew principle operates not only on wealth distribution among the merchants, it is also a general mechanism by which all kinds of inequality can arise. In fact, the name for this principle was coined by the sociologist Robert K. Merton in the context of "accumulation" of peer recognition by scientists, as measured for example, by who gets cited. All this is very interesting, but how does it relate to premodern agrarian societies, which is the main subject of interest to us? The main form of wealth in agrarian societies is land, because one needs land to grow crops and raise livestock, the chief products in agrarian economy. How does inequality of land ownership develop?

A COUPLE OF YEARS AGO I decided to answer this question. I wanted to gain a very detailed, intimate understanding of this process. This meant that I needed an explicit mathematical model.

Models are simplified descriptions of reality that strip away all of its complexity except for a few features thought to be critical to the understanding of the phenomenon under study. Mathematical models are such descriptions translated into a very precise language that, unlike natural human languages, does not allow for any double (or triple) meanings. The great strength of mathematics is that, after we have framed a problem in mathematical language, we can deduce precisely what are the consequences of the assumptions we made—no more, no less. Mathematics, thus, is an indispensable tool in true science; a branch of science can lay a claim to theoretical maturity only after it has developed a body of mathematical theory, which typically consists of an interrelated set of specific, narrowly focused models.

Although mathematics is indispensable in developing theory, it does not mean that here I have to inflict the equations on the reader to explain what the theory tells us. The Princeton economist Paul Krugman once wrote, "The equations and diagrams of formal economics are, more often than not, no more than the scaffolding used to help construct an intellectual edifice. Once that edifice has been built to a certain point, the scaffolding can be stripped away, leaving only plain English behind." Here is the story in plain English.

As is usual with such investigations, I started with a simple model. Imagine an idealized society, in which peace and the rule of law reign—there is no violence or theft. Property can only be inherited or sold and bought. Because we are interested in agrarian societies, land is the main type of property. Initially, each family has the same amount of it. You might wonder why I bothered with such a simple model. Surely it has nothing in common with any real society? The point of this model, however, was not to provide a description of any specific situation, but to lay bare the logic of how inequality develops. The connection to the messy reality comes later, after we have finished building the theoretical framework within which this reality can be conceptualized.

So we start with an absolutely egalitarian distribution of wealth. Will this equality persist into the next generation? For one thing, different families will have different numbers of children. Children from larger families will inherit smaller portions, whereas in a family with a single child, that child will get the whole inheritance. In one generation, the wealth distribution will cease to be egalitarian. In the next generation, things will become worse, because again there will be variation in the number of children, and some of the already small plots will be subdivided further. As a result, inequality will grow with time. Ironically, the very conditions of social peace and lawful transmission of property between generations create the conditions under which the society gradually separates into the poor and the rich.

In this first-cut model, I assumed that property is divided equally among all children. How do other methods of inheritance affect the results? If only one child inherits, for example, the oldest son (this rule of inheritance is called "primogeniture"), all the rest of his brothers and sisters are dispossessed. In one generation, a whole class of propertyless people is suddenly created. Primogeniture, therefore, creates inequality even faster than equal division. If the first son gets half, and the other half is divided equally among the rest of the heirs, inequality will grow at the rate that is intermediate between that for equal division and primogeniture. Thus, unequal division of property only makes things worse.

We also need to consider what happens when a man and a woman form a family, and join their inheritances together. In my simple model, I assumed that couples are formed without paying attention to the wealth of the partner (the "love conquers all" assumption). However, it is more likely that wealthier men will tend to choose as brides wealthier women (or their parents will arrange such unions). When I added such a "materialistic" tendency to the model, I saw, as expected, a much faster rate of inequality increase.

So far I have focused exclusively on the distribution of wealth. Another important aspect of the model is income. Does wealth inequality translate into income inequality? To answer this question, I had to add to the model a productive component. Land by itself does not generate income; it has to be worked by somebody to produce food (one also needs seed, agricultural implements, and so on; but let's ignore such complications—again, progress in theory building is made by adding one thing at a time, not by jumping into the messy reality with all of its glorious complexities). It turns out that whether wealth inequality gets translated into income inequality, or not, depends on the population density—the size of potential workforce in relation to the amount of land that can be cultivated.

For a rich family to translate its large wealth into extra income, it must hire the poor ones to work its land, because there is a limit to how much land the family members can cultivate themselves. If there is more land than available workers can cultivate, some land will lie fallow and not generate any income. But even the land for which hired help can be found will also bring only a minimal profit to the landowner, because the wages will be high (because of a labor shortage). Alternatively, rather than hire workers to work their land, the rich might rent it to them—let them cultivate it in return for a fee. Again, however, because land is in greater supply than potential renters, the landowners will be forced to rent it at a very low rate. As a result, the distribution of income will be less extreme than that of wealth. The rich will not be able to fully use their wealth. The poor will be able to retain the bulk of what they produce with their labor, even though they do not own the land.

The situation changes dramatically when the population grows to the point where there is an oversupply of labor. Now wealthy landowners can get away with paying low wages, just enough to make sure that their hired help does not starve. The poor, who do not own enough land to feed their families, are forced to work for minimal wages (or rent the lands of the rich at usurious rates). Furthermore, because there are more people than are needed to work the land, some of the poor will be unemployed. They will face a stark choice of gradually selling what land remains in their hands to feed their families or starving. Thus, the process of wealth concentration will accelerate. Not only will the rich now get huge incomes from their property, they will be able to use some of this income to augment their wealth even further. Overpopulation is a mighty force driving economic inequality.

In the model, the poor lost their remaining land by being forced to sell it to the rich, parcel by parcel, to stave off starvation. What actually happened in most historical societies was that the poor did not sell their land outright, but used it as a collateral for loans to tide over a bad patch (a year of poor harvest, or temporary inability to obtain extra work). In the end, however, the land was still lost, when the debtors found themselves unable to repay the loans.

IF WE START WITH COMPLETELY EQUITABLE distribution of property, in just one generation the society will stratify into those who have more, and those who have less. The only way to stop this process constantly breeding inequality is by either abolishing private property altogether or by abolishing the right to inherit it. A milder form of keeping inequality in check is a steeply progressive tax on inheritance. In other words, some sort of redistributive scheme could be used. Also, a variable number of heirs is only one, although very powerful, mechanism of inequality production. Some people are hardworking, others not so; some are smart, others dumb; some are lucky, others not. Such differences between people result in different rates at which they accumulate wealth. The institution of private property then stores the wealth differences, and the institution of inheritance transmits it across generations.

The mathematical model I developed, however, tells us that this mechanism by itself will not produce a vast gulf between the rich and the poor. When land becomes a scarce commodity, however, another process begins to operate. Human beings need to consume a certain amount of goods to survive. Most basically, they have to get enough food. Those who do not have enough land to feed themselves will have to start selling what they have to make up the difference. As a result, they become poorer. By contrast, those who have more land than they need to feed themselves will have a surplus income that they can use to acquire even more land. Thus, the rich get richer. The positive feedback of the Matthew principle arises as a result of threshold of the minimum consumption level. The Matthew principle ensures that all people whose land holdings are below the threshold—the poor—gradually lose their remaining property, which ends up in the hands of the rich. Finally, the population is divided into a tiny minority of wealthy landowners and a huge majority of landless proletarians.

I ran various versions of my model. (Different inheritance rules and other tweaks affected the results.) I came to believe that I understood how inequality arises *in the model*. But any model is a simplified description of reality. Is this one a good description? Does it really capture some essential features of the real world? We need to see how the dynamics, postulated by the model, work in some real historical society. Fortunately, as a result of decades of excellent research by the historians of medieval England, we have enough information for this particular society to enable our testing of the model.

It is possible to trace the hypothetical trajectories of two peasant families—call them the Atwoods and the Harcombs—across three generations during the second half of the thirteenth century. The families themselves are imaginary, but the data on various economic aspects of their life is real. This is another kind of modeling, in which we use data to set the boundary conditions within which the model trajectory can develop. Both the Atwoods and the Harcombs start with 30 acres of land (the great-grandfather generation), but the Atwoods consistently have two heirs, whereas the Harcombs produce only one in each generation.

SOMETIME IN THE SECOND HALF OF the thirteenth century, Jack Atwood's grandfather inherited half of his father's land, 15 acres. According to the calculations of economic historians, this was just sufficient to feed his family, even after paying off the priest, the lord, and the king. Grandfather Atwood would be considered as a middling sort in his village, neither rich nor poor. During bad years, he would have to borrow to make ends meet, but then he would be able to repay his debts during good years. When he died, the land was divided between his two sons, Jack Atwood's father and uncle.

Seven and half acres was not enough to feed the family, and Jack's father had to supplement his income from the crops by hiring out to help with plowing and harvesting. Each spring, the Atwoods bought several piglets, raised them during summer, and sold them for bacon in the fall. Jack's mother made some additional pennies by spinning wool. In good years, the Atwoods just managed to make the ends meet, and perhaps in really good years they could even afford to eat one of their pigs at Christmas. But there were also bad years, when Jack's father fell behind on the dues he owed to the tithe and tax collectors.

The only recourse was to borrow money from his wealthier neighbor, a Mr. Harcomb, using his land as collateral. Unfortunately, no matter what the Atwoods did, the debt never went away; it just kept getting bigger and bigger. When Jack's father died, the lord took as heriot (death duty) their only bull, which they used for plowing. The parish priest was entitled to the next-best beast, and took the pig. There was not enough money to pay off the debt to the Harcombs, and they took possession of most of the Atwood land, leaving the heirs with a cottage and a small plot that was only good for growing kitchen vegetables.

Being the only child in the family, Grandfather Harcomb inherited the whole 30 acres. This amount of land allowed him to make a cash surplus in a normal year. He also had the luck of being appointed as the village headman, which provided him with extra opportunities to buy an acre here and there. His only son, Matthew's father, inherited 35 acres of land. Matthew's father was the neighbor who loaned money to Jack's father, so when the latter died, the Harcomb's lands were augmented by an additional 5 acres. Matthew inherited the whole Harcomb land and married the sole daughter of another substantial peasant in the village, who brought in a handsome dowry. He now had more than 50 acres of land, which he could not work all by himself.

But in the early fourteenth century, there was plenty of surplus labor in the village, and they could be hired at quite reasonable wages from Matthew's point of view. Over the last several generations, grain prices kept climbing, and Matthew was making big profits from managing his land. Like his father, he invested a portion of his gains into purchasing more land. He could also build himself a larger house, begin drinking expensive wine imported from Bordeaux (other villagers drank beer), and wear new and colorful clothes (instead of wearing homespun like every-body else). The Harcombs and the Atwoods both started as middling peasant families, but after three generations they were rapidly drifting into different social classes.

While Matthew Harcomb was plotting about how to get his family accepted by the local gentry, Jack Atwood did not know whether he would be able to survive the coming winter. He and his younger brother, Will, were left to share the Atwood cottage. Their only source of income at this point was to hire out as field laborers to wealthier peasants, such as Matthew, or work on the local lord's demesnes. Unfortunately, by this point in the secular cycle half of the villagers did not have enough land to support themselves, and the competition for jobs was fierce.

Jack could seek employment elsewhere, and that's what hundreds of thousands of rural Englishmen were doing at that time. During the thir-teenth century, the population of London increased from 30,000 to 80,000. An unskilled worker, such as a mason's helper, could earn a penny per day, assuming work was available. They were paid only for the days they worked, and given that there were many religious holidays when no work was done, unskilled workers could hardly earn more than a pound a year. Most of this salary would go to pay for food, the rest for dwellings (unheated in winter, because wood was very expensive in the cities). Poor people could not afford to buy new clothes, but there were many second-hand clothing dealers. There was no question of starting a family.

A skilled worker made three pence per day, or close to two pounds sterling per year. This salary allowed him to support a family, although life in big cities was so unhealthy that few children survived to maturity.

THE SPECIFIC TRAJECTORIES OF THE Atwoods and the Harcombs are hypothetical, but the wealth stratification in the English villages c. 1300 was very real. Around 3 percent of villagers were wealthy like Matthew. Twenty percent were substantial peasants (with 30 acres of land) who enjoyed a cash surplus in a normal year. Another 30 percent had just enough land (15 acres) to balance on the edge of survival. And half of peasants did not have even that.

Interestingly enough, the Matthew effect also was at work among the aristocracy. The wealthiest Englishman in the early fourteenth century was Thomas, earl of Lancaster. His annual income was £11,000—5,000 times greater than that of a skilled mason! Furthermore, the huge fortunes, such as the earl's, were a comparative novelty in England. A hundred years earlier, the largest income in England was enjoyed by Roger de Lacy, constable of Chester. It was only £800 per year. Very few lords at that time had incomes exceeding £500. Around A.D. 1300, however, six earls (including Lancaster) had annual incomes of more than £3,000. Sure there was inflation during the thirteenth century, but even taking it into account the incomes of the richest nobles increased manifold compared to a century earlier. At the same time, the inflation ate into the incomes of the middling sorts. Two generations before, masons were also paid 3 pence per day, but this money then bought more bread than at the overpopulation peak of the cycle. And skilled masons were not badly off. (They constituted the middle class of medieval England, such as it was.) There were many more destitute folk in England of 1300 than a century before. Thus, the poor became poorer, while the rich grew richer.

By no stretch of imagination could England of 1200 be called an egalitarian society. Medieval people were quite aware of great disparities in wealth and power, and accepted it as ordained by God. The commons and the lords found some kind of accommodation, a form of social equilibrium. However, in the early fourteenth century, the disparity between the rich and the poor reached alarming proportions, putting the social consensus under strain. And the distribution of wealth was becoming very uneven, not only among the English as a whole, but also within each social class. Thus, the Atwoods were sinking into poverty at the same time that the Harcombs were waxing in wealth. Within the nobility, at the same time that the earls of Lancaster were growing increasingly wealthy and power-ful, the great majority of the country gentry struggled to retain the stan-dard of living they had become accustomed to. The growing within-class inequalities undermined the foundations of the social order. Landless peasants saw other peasants, who were intrinsically no better than them, grow rich and "put on airs." Impoverished gentry, who now could not afford their bottle of French claret with dinner and were forced to drink beer like commoners, saw others of their class rolling in the lap of luxury. This was patently unfair. Even worse, some of their peasant neighbors were avid to better their social standing. The friction between upwardly mobile commoners and backsliding gentry was generating heat and sparks, and later contributed to the lengthy and bitter civil wars. The growth of inequality undermined social solidarity.

ALL IN ALL, THE MODEL DID NOT do too poorly. As always, there is no per-fect mapping of the virtual reality in the model to the "real" reality. However, the two main processes that it identified as the engine of growing inequality appear to have counterparts in the data, at least as far as medieval England is concerned. But there is one problem. In the model, inequality always grows with time. Is this reasonable?

If the Matthew principle operated all the time, over the past 10,000 years or so that humans have had property, status inequality, and complex societies, we should have converged to the "inequality extreme," in which one individual held all the property, and everybody else was destitute. Such an outcome is possible in the model (when inheritance is modeled accord-ing to the primogeniture rule), but obviously it did not happen in the real world. Moreover, looking at the historical record, we observe not only periods when inequality increased (as in thirteenth-century England), but also periods when it decreased. In the United States, for example, during the twentieth century economic inequality decreased from a peak of the "roaring twenties" to a trough in the sixties. Since the 1960s, however, wealth disparity has been increasing again, making great strides during the "greed decade" of the 1980s.

What social forces could bring about the decrease in inequality? Perhaps we can answer this question by tracing the social and economic trends in England after the population peak c. 1300. As we have seen, the fourteenth century was a period of catastrophic mortality and population decline. By 1400, half of the population was gone. Population decline dramatically lowered the peasant-land ratio. Suddenly, there were not enough hands to work the land. The laws of economics decreed that wages should go up. The English parliament, dominated by landowners, passed legislation requiring workers to accept the same wages as were current before 1349, but this law (unlike the law of supply and demand) was completely ineffectual.

Not only did the wages go up, but the problem of landlessness was greatly alleviated by the plague. Formerly poor peasants inherited land when richer relatives died or married widows with land. They also now could rent the land from the gentry at very cheap rates. What happened was that when the aftershocks of the bubonic plague died out, fewer people meant lower demand for grain, and grain prices declined. Squeezed between higher wages and collapsing grain prices, the lords saw their profits from direct management of the demesne evaporate. As they despaired of trying to make a profit, they gradually abandoned direct cultivation with hired labor and began letting the land out to peasants. Because land was in abundance, they could often get only nominal rents, but it was better than nothing.

For more than a century after the Black Death, population numbers in England stayed low, and the economic conditions continued to favor peasants. Unlike their forebears in the decades around 1300, fifteenth-century peasants drank as much ale as they wanted. They ate a lot of meat (mainly pork and mutton), cheese, and fish (during Lent). They wore new, if homemade, clothing, sometimes made from the wool of their own sheep.

In the fifteenth century, a stonemason in London earned twice as much as a century before, but the price of food was less. In real terms, worker incomes tripled. Life of commoners in fifteenth-century England was not by any means idyllic, because there was too much death. People died from the recurrent bouts of epidemic, from robbing brigands and murderous knights, from childbirth (women), and alehouse brawls (men). But for those who survived, life was much, much better than a century earlier.

This great reduction of poverty was one of the factors ensuring that economic inequality was much diminished in the fifteenth century. At the same time that the numbers of destitute declined, the super rich also started disappearing, although this process took most of the fifteenth, and part of the sixteenth century. How did this happen?

The richest man in England in the late fourteenth century was John of Gaunt, the duke of Lancaster and the son of Edward III and uncle to Richard II. Gaunt married Blanche of Lancaster, grand-niece of Earl Thomas and the sole heiress to the Lancaster fortune. The annual income of the duke of Lancaster was close to £15,000. In 1399, John of Gaunt's son Henry Bolingbroke overthrew Richard II, and became the new king. As a result, the Lancaster inheritance was merged into the crown. In the next generation, the largest fortune belonged to Richard of York, another descendant of Edward III. His annual income in 1436 was assessed as £3,230. The only other income of more than £3,000 was that of the earl of Warwick—compared to six such incomes a century before. In fact, even these two large fortunes were soon to disappear. The York inheritance was added to the crown in the same way as Lancaster's, when Richard of York's son deposed Henry VI Lancaster and was crowned as Edward IV in 1461. The Warwick fortune was absorbed by the crown after 1471, when Richard Neville, the earl of Warwick, was killed in battle fighting against Edward IV.

Destruction of the great fortunes continued under the Tudors, who had it in for their over-rich and over-mighty subjects. The first two Tudors, Henry VII and Henry VIII, employed judicial murder with great effect, systematically exterminating all potential claimants to the English throne, who also happened to be among the richest landowners. Elizabeth I crafted a gentler method—a kind of "progressive taxation" scheme. When one of her subjects became too wealthy, she invited herself to his castle along with her whole court. After some weeks of dining and wining the queen and hundreds of her followers, the unfortunate host was financially ruined for many years to come, and was too busy paying off his debts to contemplate rebellion.

THE TWO FORCES THAT REDUCED economic inequality in England after the Black Death were low population and high social instability. Low population resulted in good wages and a high employment rates, meaning land-less peasants and urban workers could generate comfortable incomes to feed their families. The same conditions made it difficult for the rich to generate high incomes from their property. Chaotic conditions reduced inequality by hitting particularly strongly both the very poor and the very rich; the middling sorts suffered relatively less. The impoverished died in droves during the recurrent epidemics and periodic food shortages brought on by civil war. They were also exterminated without pity when caught in the factional fighting. The wealthy and powerful magnates were also vulnerable because they were the natural foci around which political power crystallized. Having already much power, they wanted more and aimed for the throne, or set themselves up as kingmakers. If they personally were not ambitious, their retinues pushed them to reach for greater power so that they could participate in the division of spoils. Those of the magnates who resisted such pressures fell afoul of the rulers, who could never trust them, and executed them on trumped-up charges. Being at the top of the power pyramid in fifteenth-century England was lethal. If in 1300 there were 200 great baronial families, who were summoned to the House of Lords, in 1500 there were only 60, and half of them were of recent origin. The king himself, Henry VII, was a grandson of the Welsh adventurer Owen Tudor. The house of Plantagenet, with all of its numerous branches, was exterminated.

Toward the end of Henry VII's reign (he died in 1509), England was at peace, internally and externally. This was the best time for the little people, their true golden age. Wages were good, food prices low, epidemics declined, and the strong state suppressed banditry and put a lid on noble violence. The four apocalyptic horsemen were in retreat—but not beaten once and for all. Their time would come again, because peace and prosperity in pre-industrial times contained the seeds of future war and misery.

Just as three centuries before, the population began increasing, first slowly, but then at an accelerating rate. During the next 150 years, the numbers of people in England doubled and approached the level of 1300, with the same consequences. The poverty of the lower classes began increasing again. The purchasing power of a worker's daily wage was halved toward the end of the sixteenth century.

The increasing difficulties for the commons underwrote another golden age of the aristocracy. Their newly won prosperity rapidly became reflected in what they wore. "In 1485, most English people, even well to do, wore similar dress," noted the historian Ronald Berger in *The Most Necessary Luxuries.* "Women wore plain, loose-fitting garments, and men did likewise. Fine but simple linen was as acceptable in formal costume as ornate silk. The third and fourth decades of the sixteenth century, however, saw an explosive growth in the consumption of expensive and ornate costume. Demand rose enormously, especially among the wealthy, who purchased expensive brocades, velvets, and silks for new and splendid costumes. During the reign of Elizabeth, men changed their fashions entirely; their clothes became more elaborate and distinctive. Women matched male attire with exquisitely decorated farthingales and fine damask gowns. The sixteenth century closed with a 'wild orgy of extravagance,' as the provincial gentry attempted to emulate the London *haute monde* by wearing extravagant costumes and hats with 12-inch crowns."

The new prosperity of the ruling classes reversed the trend to the diminution of their numbers, which predominated during the fifteenth century. In 1500, there were only 60 peers—great lords who were summoned to parliament by a personal writ from the king, and who sat in the House of the Lords. In 1640, on the eve of the English Revolution, there were 160. In 1500, there were between 5,000 and 6,000 gentry families, but in 1640 there were 18,500 of them. Whereas the population of commoners increased twofold over the 140-year period, the aristocracy increased threefold. Just as happened three centuries before, the society became top-heavy.

Because the historical record gets better as we travel toward the present, we can trace more precisely the trends of increased intra-elite competition. The historical sociologist Jack Goldstone noted in *Revolution and Rebellion in the Early Modern World* that there was a great explosion in enrollments at the Oxford and Cambridge universities during the second half of the sixteenth century, which reached the peak in 1640, just on the eve of the Great Revolution. This was not because English gentlemen suddenly conceived a love of letters and learning—no, they needed a university diploma to better compete in the job market. By the middle of the eighteenth century, when the intra-elite competition for jobs greatly subsided, the enrollments at Oxford and Cambridge declined to their pre-1600 levels. The problem was, however, that the university credentials did not guarantee a job anymore, because most of the competition also had them. As the historian Lawrence Stone wrote, "The universities were turning out an educated clergy and laity in excess of suitable job opportunities, and were thus creating a large and influential group of discontented 'Outs.'"

Intra-elite competition also spilled into the courts. "In 1640, there was probably more litigation per head of population going through the central courts at Westminster than at any time before or since. But one hundred years later in 1750, the common law hit what appears to have been a spectacular all-time low." And many gentlemen took a more direct approach to settling scores with rivals. In the late sixteenth century, a veritable epidemic of dueling swept the English aristocracy. Historians traced this epidemic by counting how often duels and challenges were mentioned in newsletters and private correspondence. In the 1580s, there were only 5 such mentions, the next decade there were nearly 20, and at the peak, during the 1610s, 39. This might not represent the most accurate method for tracing social trends, but the eightfold increase in duel incidence, occurring over the span of one generation, speaks for itself.

THE SEVENTEENTH WAS ANOTHER "calamitous century," the time of trouble comparable in many respects to the fourteenth century. All European states were affected. France went into collapse first. The civil war between the Catholics and Huguenots began in the 1560s and was raging full force during the 1580s and 1590s. After a relative quiet under Louis XIII and Richelieu, there was another state collapse during the Fronde (1648–53). The civil wars in Germany began in 1618 with the Bohemian revolt against the Habsburgs, and dragged on for 30 years (which is why this period is known as the Thirty Years' War). The Spanish Habsburgs fought an 80-year war against the Dutch rebels, which ended in 1648 when Spain finally recognized the independence of Holland. In the 1640s, the Spanish also had to deal with simultaneous uprisings in Catalonia, Portugal, and Italy. Russia went through its own "time of troubles" (1604–13). Finally, there were two revolutions and an extended civil war in England during 1640–90.

Troubled times are not fun to live through, but they make a great setting for historical novels. One of the best adventure novels of all times (some would even say *the* best) is the book *The Three Musketeers* and its sequels by Alexandre Dumas. The main character of the novel is based on a real person, Charles de Batz-Castelmore, count d'Artagnan, whose career started during the times of Richelieu, and ended under Louis XIV, "the Sun King." By following the historical d'Artagnan's career, we can obtain a glimpse of the calamitous seventeenth century from the point of view of a French nobleman.

The real d'Artagnan (actually, he was usually referred to as Chevalier de Batz-Castelmore, but it is easier to continue calling him d'Artagnan) was born in 1611, the third son of a Gascon nobleman. He had three brothers and two sisters. d'Artagnan and his brothers were the typical surplus elites. The amount of surplus that could be wrung from the peasants stagnated and even declined in the early seventeenth century, and therefore impoverished aristocrats had to seek employment with the state, church, or great lords. Certainly, the revenues of the family were insufficient to support the four de Batz-Castelmore brothers. One of them went into the church, and the other three pursued military careers. By the time d'Artagnan arrived in Paris, his oldest brother was already dead in battle; the second oldest, Paul, made an illustrious career (and had served in the Musketeers). d'Artagnan had an excellent political clout with de Treville, the captain of the Musketeers, because of the previous distinguished service by his father, uncle, and two older brothers. However, he could not join the ranks of the Musketeers right away, because they only accepted veteran soldiers. So he was placed in another prestigious regiment, the King's Guards of Monsieur des Essarts (and became a Musketeer in 1645).

We do not know whether the real d'Artagnan fought as many duels as the fictional one, but he probably fought his share, because France of his time was at the crest of the wave of a dueling epidemic. Dueling had almost disappeared in France during the fifteenth and early sixteenth centuries. Under François I and Henri II, a handful of judicial duels took place with royal sanction. As the numbers of surplus elites increased, however, so did their propensity to resolve their quarrels by murdering each other. After 1560, dueling for personal honor and without royal sanction became so common that contemporary commentators believed more noblemen died from it than in combat. One estimate was that 7,000 to 8,000 were killed in the two decades after 1588. It was said that Henri IV granted more than

6,000 pardons for the killing of gentlemen in duels during the first 10 years of the seventeenth century. Dueling was effectively eliminated only during the reign of Louis XIV, at the very end of d'Artagnan's life. (He was killed in battle in 1673.)

Violence was rampant not only between individual nobles, but also between noble factions. (This is reflected in the Dumas novel, in which the Musketeers battle it out with the cardinal's guardsmen, in a manner of the gang warfare between the Bloods and the Crips of modern Los Angeles.) The problem was that d'Artagnan was not the only noblemen seeking to supplement his income by serving the king. There were many thousands of impoverished aristocrats in Paris, while employment opportunities could not keep pace with the growing numbers of such job seekers. As Jack Goldstone noted, "Limits on available land, civil and ecclesiastical offices, and royal patronage led to increasingly polarized factional battles between patron-client groups for available spoils."

When one aristocratic faction won, it attempted to completely exclude its rivals. One of the notorious examples of this was the situation in England between 1617 and 1628, when the faction led by George Villiers, the duke of Buckingham, managed to monopolize the court's patronage. In his novel, Dumas paints a fairly favorable portrait of Buckingham, but in real life this royal favorite was a pretty unsavory character who used his power to unscrupulously enrich himself and his cohorts. In the words of the historian David Loades, "The ascendancy of Buckingham transformed abuse into a scandal of systematic exploitation."

We have already seen how declining economic fortunes of aristocrats create the climate conducive to interpersonal and interfactional conflict. It is important to stress that the purely materialistic calculation—"I lack sufficient funds to support the life style to which I am entitled by birth, and I will obtain this money by force if necessary"—is just one possible motive driving violence, and not necessarily the most powerful. The "knaves" might act on this calculation, especially if they deem that they are likely to get away with it. But for many other kinds of people, such as the moralists, the purely materialistic motive could be only a part, and a small one at that, of what drives them to become troublemakers. When an aristocratic faction, such as that led by Buckingham in the early seventeenth century, monopolizes all largesse flowing from the state, they offend not only against the pocketbook of those excluded, but also against their moral feeling. It is not fair, it is not *right* that a small clique is rolling in luxury while everybody else suffers. The moralistic impulse is to punish the offender. John Felton, who assassinated Buckingham in 1628, might have been a fanatic, or perhaps he was a moralist with a highly developed sense of right and wrong. When presented with glaring injustice, moralists also self-organize in action groups. Such faction formation is the usual stage before the full-blown revolution.

In France, rival factions formed around two powerful magnates, the constable of Montmorency and the duke de Guise, during the 1550s. When the French king Henry II died in 1559, the Guise faction succeeded in virtually monopolizing the patronage of the young king, Francis II. The success of the duke de Guise and his Catholic party provoked an anti-Guise plot by several thousand Huguenot nobles in 1560, which was brutally suppressed. Intra-elite conflict then rapidly escalated into the French Wars of Religion. Duke de Guise was assassinated by a Huguenot nobleman in 1563, triggering a spiral of revenge and counter-revenge killings that decimated the top ranks of the French nobility during the next three decades.

The rise and fall of the dukes of Buckingham and de Guise graphically illustrates the dangers of extreme inequality for the social order. Rampant inequality feeds into the perception of the extant social order as unjust and illegitimate, and creates excellent breeding conditions for the rise of revolutionary ideologies. In the early modern period, these ideologies took the religious form. Later, the dominant revolutionary ideologies were nationalistic and Marxist. Today, we are seeing the rise of religious-based revolutionary ideologies again, such as the Wahhabism. There are huge differences between the English Puritans, the French Jacobins, the Russian Bolsheviks, and the Islamic Al Qaida, but there is at least one common thread running through all these ideologies and movements associated with them—a burning desire for social justice.

THE WARS OF RELIGION WERE OVER before d'Artagnan was born. When he began his career in the 1630s, the French nobility still retained the collective memory of the bloodbath of the Wars of Religion. So the young bloods killed each other with gusto, but the older statesmen did not allow this dueling and factional infighting to grow into a full-scale civil war. It was only when all those who had direct memory of the Wars of Religion died out or retired that the d'Artagnan generation became free to repeat the mistakes that led to the previous civil war.

When d'Artagnan arrived in Paris to seek service with the king, the wealthiest man in France was Armand du Plessis, cardinal-duke of Richelieu. The annual income of Richelieu was several million livres, and over his 18 years of service as prime minister he accumulated a staggering fortune of 22 million livres. For comparison, the majority of French nobility at this time "enjoyed" incomes of 1,000 livres per year or less. And these were among the richest 2 percent of the population of France! Urban workers, except for the skilled ones, earned less than 100 livres per year.

In 1642, Richelieu died, followed soon by Louis XIII. Louis XIV, who was five years old at the time, ascended the French throne. His mother, Anne of Austria, served as regent, while the government of France was entrusted to Cardinal Mazarin (an Italian of modest origins, and reputedly the queen's lover). Mazarin disbanded the Musketeers of de Treville in 1646, but retained the service of d'Artagnan as his confidential agent. d'Artagnan served his patron ably and loyally, even during the turbulent years of the Fronde (1648–53), when the popular revolt, aided and abetted by the anti-Mazarin faction of powerful nobles, forced the king and his court to flee Paris. In 1651, Anne of Austria, under the pressure from the rebelling nobles, was forced to dismiss Mazarin, and he left the country. In 1653, however, the civil war died out, and Anne was able to recall Mazarin, who served as prime minister until his death in 1661. The loyalty of d'Artagnan was eventually rewarded with the captain-lieutenancy of Musketeers.

The fortunes made by Richelieu and his second-echelon ministers pale into insignificance when compared to the rapacity of state officers during the Mazarin era (which contributed in no small manner to the outbreak of the civil war). Mazarin himself lost all of his fortune in 1651, when he was forced out of office, and had to start from scratch after he regained his position as prime minister in 1653. Yet, when he died in 1661, he left 37 million livres to his heirs! That is, his fortune grew at the rate of nearly 5 million livres per year—50,000 times the annual income of a simple laborer.

The growth of private fortunes, however, reached the peak during the Mazarin era. After Mazarin died, Louis XIV assumed direct control of his government. After a century-long period of discord, which saw two major civil wars and a host of lesser noble revolts and popular uprisings, the French ruling class was ready to close the ranks around the central government. From this point on, for more than a century until the Great Revolution, France saw no significant intra-elite conflict. All energies of the nobility were channeled into external wars, which were practically continuous during the reign of the Sun King. (Louis XIV died in 1715.) d'Artgnan was to die in one of these wars, when during a battle in Holland a musket ball hit him in the throat. Internal consolidation was accompanied by more equitable distribution of wealth (at least among the nobility). The peasants got loaded with heavy taxes to support the aggressive external policy of Louis XIV, and when they rebelled against the crushing burden, this time there were no dissident nobles to weaken the state's repressive apparatus, and all such rebellions were easily suppressed.

One of the first things that Louis XIV did after assuming the reins of government was to rid himself of one of his over-mighty subjects. The superintendent of finance, Nicolas Fouquet, had accumulated a fortune evaluated at 15.4 million livres—a far cry from Mazarin's, but nothing to sneer at. Fouquet made a mistake by throwing a great party at his opulent Chateau of Vaux-le-Vicomte to which he invited the king. The palace and the party were so magnificent that they outdid the king's. (This was before Versailles was built.) In his *Memoirs*, Louis XIV wrote about Fouquet: "The sight of the vast establishment that that man built, and the insolent acquisitions that he had made, could only convince me of the unbounded level of his ambition; and the general calamity of all my people solicited constantly my justice against him." Two weeks after the party, Louis summoned d'Artagnan (whose services he inherited after Mazarin's death) and ordered Fouquet's arrest. d'Artagnan had the distasteful duty of guarding Fouquet for the next four years, until the latter was tried, stripped of his wealth, and sentenced to life imprisonment.

During the reign of Louis XIV, the excesses of government officials were gradually brought under control. The wealth of the chief minister of Louis XIV, Jean-Baptiste Colbert, was estimated at between 5 and 6 million. The minister of war, Louvois, gained a fortune of some 8 million in a career spanning 20 years (1672–91). In the early eighteenth century, the fortunes of ministers declined even further. As the finance and taxation historian Richard Bonney noted, "After 1720, ministerial gains from office were small beer indeed compared to the situation before 1661." At the same time that the high-end fortunes were disappearing, noble poverty also declined, primarily by means of forcing impoverished nobles out of the second estate into the third. For example, in 1640, two thirds of noble families in rural Normandy had incomes of less than 1,000 livres. By 1700, this proportion declined to 40 percent, and half a century later only 10–15 percent of the nobles were in such impoverished conditions.

WHEN RICH GET RICHER AND POOR get poorer, cooperation between social classes is undermined. But the same process is operating within each class. When some nobles are growing conspicuously more wealthy, while the majority of nobility is increasingly impoverished, the elites become riven by factional conflicts. Within the secular cycle, as the disintegrative phase follows the integrative one, inequality rises and falls. A life cycle of an imperial nation usually extends over the course of two, three, or even four secular cycles. Every time the empire enters a disintegrative secular phase, the asabiya of its core nation is significantly degraded. Eventually, this process of imperiopathosis reaches its terminal phase—the imperial nation loses its ability to cooperate, and the empire collapses. Most empires, therefore, fall for internal reasons. Paraphrasing Arnold Toynbee, great empires die not by murder, but by suicide.

Chapter 11

Wheels Within Wheels

The Many Declines of the Roman Empire

F
ew topics in history have generated so much heated controversy and so little enlightenment as the decline and fall of the Roman Empire. Much of the blame for the confusion should be placed squarely on the English historian Edward Gibbon (1737–94). Between 1776 and 1788, Gibbon published a long and rambling account of Rome's decline and fall in six volumes and a million and a half words. ("Another damned, thick, square book! Always scribble, scribble, scribble! Eh, Mr. Gibbon?"— the duke of Gloucester, upon being presented with the second volume of *The Decline and Fall*.) The story begins with the Antonine age in the second century A.D., which Gibbon believed was the peak of the empire, and ends in the fifteenth century, when Constantinople fell to the Ottoman Turks. As noted previously, a "decline" of more than 12 centuries in duration does not strike me as a useful concept in the analysis of historical dynamics. And Gibbon never makes it clear just when did the Roman Empire fall. Certainly, it does not make sense to postpone this date until 1453, the year of Constantinople's fall, because it marks the end of an entirely separate empire, the one we now call the Byzantine. Today, the official date of Rome's collapse is A.D. 476, when the last puppet emperor in the West, Romulus Augustus, was deposed by Odovacar, the Germanic king of Italy. But modern historians would be quick to point out that this is an artificial breakpoint. The barbarian chieftains wielded the real power in Italy at least for two decades before the deposition of Romulus Augustus. Many historians would go even further back in time, and point to the third century as the "collapse," a time of internal disintegration, civil war, and relentless barbarian invasions. And some have argued that Rome began its long decline in the first century B.C., when the Republic disintegrated and was replaced by the autocratic rule of the emperors.

So how do we make sense of how and why (and when!) Rome fell? A general theory could tell us which processes are crucial to the collapse of empires, and which are incidental. In the absence of such theoretical guidance, we are at the mercy of correlations. For example, the Roman Empire adopted Christianity during the fourth century, and then collapsed in the fifth. So is there a causal relationship here? Gibbon thought so. But if that's the case, we should expect to see the same causal connections elsewhere, and there is simply no empirical evidence supporting such a proposition. Both the Franks and the Byzantines adopted Christianity, and it only strengthened their asabiya and enabled them to expand their empires. Why should the same religion play a destructive role in one case (Rome) and a constructive role in another (Byzantium)?

Many things went on in Rome, and an aspiring theorist who wants to launch a new theory has plenty of material to pick from. Was it the Christianity? Or the decline of the "bourgeoisie," as another historian of Rome thought? Or imperial bureaucratization? Or lead poisoning? Latching on any particular correlation in the rich history of the Roman Empire, and basing on it a grand theory that explains its collapse is easy, but ultimately unsatisfying. Dozens, perhaps even hundreds, of such theories have been proposed over the centuries. This is not the way to do science.

A good scientific theory is parsimonious, which means that it has to be very ruthless about choosing what data to use, and what to ignore. Take the theory of classical mechanics, which explains planetary motions. It could not care less that Mars is red, or Venus is blue. Or that Saturn has rings, but Mercury does not. If one wants to understand why a planet within the solar system follows any particular trajectory, one should completely ignore 99 percent of the huge mass of data the astronomers collected. To a very good approximation, all one needs to know is how far the planet is from the Sun. How do we know that the distance from the Sun is crucial, whereas a planet's color is irrelevant? Because there is a general theory, based on Newton's laws of motion, which tells us what kinds of data we need. If we want to have a science of history, we should proceed in exactly the same way. Of course, human societies are much more complex entities than planetary systems, and therefore we should not expect the same level of precision (nor parsimony) as achieved in celestial mechanics.

A general theory for the rise and decline of empires we have. The crucial variable in it is the collective capacity for action, the society's asabiya. Competition between societies leads to asabiya increase, whereas competition within a society causes its asabiya to decline. As we have seen in Part I of this book, metaethnic frontiers, where groups and civilizations clash, are the crucibles within which high-asabiya societies are forged. The almost inevitable consequence of high capacity for collective action, however, is territorial expansion that pushes the frontiers away from the center and removes the very forces that fostered high asabiya in the first place. Thus, success breeds eventual failure; the rise carries within it the seeds of the fall—peace brings war, and war brings peace. In the language of nonlinear dynamics, rise-and-fall phenomena are explained by negative feedback loops.

Decline of asabiya is not a linear process. As we now know, empires go through long—secular—cycles of alternating integrative-disintegrative phases. Within-society competition wanes during the integrative phase and waxes during the disintegrative phase. It is during disintegrative phases when the asabiya of the society takes a big hit. Furthermore, one disintegrative phase is usually not enough to completely degrade the cohesion of a high-asabiya society. It typically takes two or three secular cycles for an imperial nation to lose its capacity for concerted action.

However, even this portrayal is an oversimplification. Disintegrative phases are also not uniformly bad. Because people get fed up with constant instability and insecurity, civil warfare during an instability phase tends to skip a generation—the children of revolutionaries want to avoid disorder at any cost, but the grandchildren are ready to repeat the mistakes of their grandparents all over again. As a result, disintegration phases tend to go through two or three "fathers-and-sons" cycles before a renaissance can take hold and the society can enter a secular integrative phase.

The dynamics of imperial rise and decline, therefore, are like a mechanism with wheels within wheels within wheels. The waxing and waning of asabiya is the slowest process, taking many centuries—often a millennium—for a complete cycle. Secular cycles occur on a faster time scale. A typical imperial nation goes through two or three, and sometimes even four secular cycles during the course of its life. Finally, the disintegrative phase of each secular cycle will see two or three waves of political instability and civil warfare, separated by periods of fragile peace. The characteristic time scales, therefore, are a millennium for the asabiya cycle, 2 to 3 centuries for a secular cycle, and 40 to 60 years (two generations) for fathers-and-sons cycles. These are just orders of magnitude; there is no exact periodicity in any of these processes. Human societies are highly complex systems, much more complex than solar systems. External factors, such as gradual changes of the global climate, can speed up or slow down any of the key processes that drive historical dynamics. Even more importantly, nonlinear interactions between various processes can produce internally driven irregular behavior—mathematical chaos. Mathematicians have proven that a dynamical system affected by two sources of cyclic behaviors will, under certain conditions, behave chaotically—in an erratic manner that looks random, but in reality is completely internally generated. Finally, neighboring societies interact with each other, and this is another source of irregularity. In a previous chapter we saw how the collapse of France during the fourteenth century allowed England to postpone its own collapse by almost a century. So when I say "cycle," I do not mean something that is strictly periodic, like an hour arm sweeping the clock face, but a rise-and-fall dynamic, which has a *characteristic time scale*, a period that can vary within certain bounds.

We now see why it is so hard to determine just when the Roman Empire achieved its peak and switched to its decline. Cliodynamics predicts complex dynamical behavior for historical empires, with shorter cycles embedded within longer cycles, and so on. Let's observe the wheels within wheels of ancient Rome.

AS DISCUSSED IN CHAPTER 6, the first secular cycle of Rome began in the seventh century B.C. and ended in the middle of the fourth century B.C. The centralizing, integrative tendency dominated the first half of this period (up to 500 B.C.), and the disintegrative, centrifugal tendency predominated during the second half. The important landmarks in Roman history were the sack of Rome in 390 B.C. by the barbarian Gauls, which signaled the arrival of a new metaethnic frontier, and the Licino-Sextian Laws of 367 B.C., which transformed the political structure of the Roman state. By the second half of the fourth century, patricians and noble plebeians merged into a new social and political elite, the senatorial class. Their new cohesion was sorely needed for the struggle against the Gauls. It also bred success in the external wars of conquest, which brought in booty and land. Increased resources reduced competition within the society, strengthening its asabiya, which bred military success, in a kind of a virtuous cycle. The reorganized Roman state easily turned back a new Gallic invasion in 349 B.C. and began a long period of conquest of first central Italy, then all of the peninsula, and eventually the whole Mediterranean.

The integrative phase of the second secular cycle was unusually long. It lasted for two centuries and ended around 140 B.C. During the two centuries that followed the Licino-Sextian compromise, Rome maintained unity at home, while fighting a series of ferocious wars abroad. Some of these external conflicts, especially the war with Hannibal, imposed horrific casualties on the Roman citizenry, thus setting back population increase. This was one of the reasons for an unusually long integrative phase. The second reason was the very success of Rome's expansionist program. Conquests brought in booty, tribute, and lands that underwrote the expansion of the elites without making the society top-heavy (or, rather, it postponed the inevitable day of reckoning). Common citizens also participated in the division of the spoils. During the period 334 to 263 B.C. alone, an estimated 70,000 citizens left Rome for the colonies established within the conquered territories. As a general rule, territorial expansion prolongs integrative phases. The integrative phase during the third Roman cycle was also unusually long, lasting from 27 B.C. to A.D. 180.

Eventually, however, the social forces driving the secular cycle caught up with the Roman Republic. The important threshold was crossed in 203–175 B.C., when the Romans successfully subjugated Cisalpine Gaul, thus pushing the metaethnic frontier away from the core of the Roman state. In the aftermath of the war with Hannibal (218–201 B.C.), Roman census figures indicate that there were around 200,000 citizens (free adult males). During the next century, the number of citizens more than doubled. The population of the city of Rome increased even faster, from 150,000 to 450,000. (This estimate includes women, children, slaves, and resident foreigners.)

Massive population growth, coupled with the Roman custom of equal division of property among the heirs, resulted in rapidly increasing economic inequality. Several generations of property division among multiple heirs resulted in each heir's share being grossly insufficient for feeding the family. The history was repeating itself, again. Some impoverished landholders were forced to sell their land to the aristocrats flush with the spoils of Rome's conquests and eager to invest their fortune in land. Others tried to go on, ran up unsustainable debt levels, and also lost their land (or even freedom). The end result of this process was the gradual disappearance of the class of small landowners, which had been the backbone of the Roman state and army. Some citizens, unable to repay their debts, were turned into slaves. Others sold themselves into slavery because they were unable to feed themselves. The majority became landless proletarians and either worked the land of aristocratic landowners or drifted to Rome and other large cities in search of work. Finally, a few—those with few children, the thrifty and hardworking, or simply the lucky ones—grew in wealth and aspired to better their social standing.

The diminution of the class of small landowners was easily perceptible to the contemporary observers because these people were the ones who manned the Roman legions. Various authors decried what they perceived as "depopulation." In reality, the overall population was expanding rapidly. What was declining was the numbers of the "middle classes," the citizens with enough property to qualify them for the army service. To expand the pool of recruits, the authorities gradually reduced the minimum amount of property that qualified a citizen for army service, and finally abolished it altogether in 107 B.C. Despite these measures, the proportion of citizens in the Roman army kept declining, and the missing numbers had to be made up by using noncitizen Italian allies. By the end of the second century, there were two allies for each Roman serving in the army.

Whereas in fourth century B.C. the majority of Roman citizens were in the "middle class"—they owned enough land to feed themselves and their families—two centuries later few of such free smallholders remained. The upper and lower classes of the Roman society had drifted apart. At the bottom were the vast multitudes of slaves, freedmen, and proletarians; at the top, all wealth and power was concentrated in the hands of a small group of aristocrats. Inequality was further exacerbated by the Roman institution of slavery. Millions of slaves, captured during the wars of conquest, flooded Italy during the second century B.C. Because slaves had no human rights, and legally could hold no property (in practice, some masters allowed them to accumulate funds to buy themselves out of slavery), their presence in massive numbers made the Roman society during the late Republic even more unequal than is usual in pre-industrial states.

One of the most striking developments in the second century B.C. was the growth of both the numbers and wealth of the Roman elites. The scale of senatorial fortunes grew at an astronomical rate. One of the foremost members of the Roman aristocracy, L. Aemilius Paullus, who put an end to the kingdom of Macedon in 167, left a fortune of a measly 1.44 million sesterces upon death. A century later, the fortune of the famous orator Cicero was 13 million sesterces. And Cicero was a "new man." (He was born in a provincial town and was the first of his clan to enter the senate and gain the consulship.) His wealth is indicative of the "run of the mill" of the Roman elite (the senatorial class), not the super wealthy. At least five senators had fortunes greater than 100 million sesterces, and those of Crassus and Pompey were on the order of 200 million. For comparison, a soldier in the legions was paid 500 sesterces per year.

A huge influx of wealth from the conquests and the exposure to the "decadent Orient" drove conspicuous consumption by the Roman upper crust to levels that would have appalled Cincinnatus or Camillus. The degree of luxury enjoyed by the wealthy and powerful Romans is even surprising to us, the moderns. Just listen to Cicero:

> *Here you have the other coming down from his fine house*
> *on the Palatine [one of the seven hills of Rome, a fashion-*
> *able neighborhood for the wealthy]: He has for his enjoy-*
> *ment a pleasant suburban country seat, besides a number of*
> *farms all of them excellent and near the city; a house*
> *crammed with Delian and Corinthian vessels [made of gold,*
> *silver, and bronze, famous for their workmanship], among*
> *them a self-cooker [a utensil for boiling, resembling a tea*
> *urn], which he recently bought at so high a price that*
> *passers-by, hearing the auctioneer crying out the bids,*
> *thought that an estate was being sold. What quantities*

besides of embossed silver, of coverlets, pictures, statues,
marbles can you imagine he possesses? As much of course as
could be heaped in a single house, taken from many illustri-
ous families during the times of disturbance and rapine. But
what am I to say about his vast household of slaves and the
variety of their technical skill? I say nothing about such
common trades, such as those of cooks, bakers, litter-bear-
ers: To charm his mind and ears, he has so many artists, that
the whole neighborhood rings daily with the sound of vocal
music, stringed instruments, and flutes, and with the noise
of banquets by night. When a man leads such life, gentle-
men, can you imagine his daily expenses, his lavish displays,
his banquets? Quite respectable, I suppose in such a house, if
that can be called a house rather than manufactory of
wickedness and lodging-house of every sort of crime. And
look at the man himself, gentlemen; you see how, with hair
carefully arranged and reeking with perfume, he struts
about all over the forum accompanied by a crowd of wearers
of the toga; you see what contempt he has for everyone, how
he considers no one a human being compared with himself,
and believes that he alone is wealthy and powerful.

The target of Cicero's attack is Chrysogonus, a powerful freedman and a favorite of the dictator Sulla. As we all know, Sulla instituted "proscriptions" that identified certain individuals as enemies of the state that could be killed with impunity. The property of the proscribed was sold at auction, and the proceeds replenished Sulla's treasury. Chrysogonus supervised this process, and used it to enrich himself. For example, Cicero charges that the property of Sextus Roscius, valued at 6 million, was sold for a mere 2,000 sesterces to Chrysogonus and his cronies.

Chrysogonus, being a freedman, was not a typical member of the ruling class. But his ostentatious habits were not simply the excesses of a *nouveau rich*. The hereditary members of the senatorial aristocracy wallowed in luxury even more. Think of how much one had to spend just to organize a decent banquet. It would not do to serve the guests with the produce grown on the local farm. No, one needed to import at great expense peacocks from Samos, oysters from Lake Lucrino, and snails from Africa. The guests could be treated to a performance of the exotic dancers from Gades (modern Cadiz) and a recitation of bawdy verses by a Greek poet from Alexandria. The works of art and silver plate had to be exhibited prominently—let the guests die from envy! Never mind that the censors of 275 B.C. removed P. Cornelius Rufinus from the senate because he owned vessels to the weight of 10 pounds. During the late Republic, you had to own hundreds of pounds just "to keep up with the Joneses." The younger Drusus reveled in the possession of 10,000 pounds of silver, but that was perhaps overdoing it.

It should not be surprising, then, that the cost of a banquet could easily run into tens of thousands of sesterces. Just one peacock cost 200 sesterces—half a year's pay for a soldier. Plutarch reports that on one occasion, when Lucullus gave a banquet for Cicero and Pompey, the meal cost him 200,000 sesterces—the equivalent of annual pay of a cohort of legionnaires!

ROMAN LITERATURE OF THE FIRST CENTURY B.C. is full of diatribes against the dissolute habits of the contemporary aristocracy. The moralist writers saw direct connections between the rise of luxury and the moral decline of Rome. "No country has ever been greater or purer than ours or richer in good citizens and noble deeds; none has been free for so many generation from the vices of avarice and luxury; nowhere have thrift and plain living been held so long in such esteem," wrote Livy at the beginning of his history. Livy began writing his great work in 29 B.C., precisely at the end of the century-long disintegrative phase, the period "in which the might of an imperial people is beginning to work its own ruin." Livy's aim was to educate the character through the study of history: "I invite the reader's attention to the serious consideration of the kinds of lives our ancestors lived, of who were the men, and what the means in both politics and war by which Rome's power was first acquired and subsequently expanded; I would have him trace the process of our moral decline, to watch, first, the sinking foundations of morality as the old teaching was allowed to lapse, then the rapidly increasing disintegration, then the final collapse of the whole edifice, and the dark dawning of the modern age." This assessment was echoed by other Roman historians. Sallust (86–34 B.C.) blamed the momentous events of 146 B.C.—the destruction of Carthage and the conquest of Greece—for the start of decline, because the first removed the external enemy who kept the Romans unified, and the second introduced to Rome the enervating vices and luxuries of the Greek world. It was in the time of Sulla (138–78 B.C.), argued Sallust, that *luxuria* ("luxury") and *licentia* ("licentiousness") began to infect Roman citizens.

The contemporaries perceived clearly the onset of Rome's imperiopathosis, listed its symptoms, and provided a diagnosis. In fact, Sallust's diagnosis is not too far from the explanation of Rome's decline offered by cliodynamics. The first part of the diagnosis, the removal of the external enemy, is basically correct. However, as we saw in an earlier chapter, the external enemy, the struggle with whom forged Roman nation, was the Gauls. There is no question that the Carthaginians added significant pressure to the metaethnic cauldron from which Rome arose, especially during the Second Punic War (although even during that conflict, the majority of Hannibal's army were the Gauls). But the Carthaginians, even though speaking a Semitic language and worshipping a somewhat different pantheon, were still part of the same Mediterranean civilization to which the Romans also belonged. It is doubtful that Rome would rise as a world empire if it were only subjected to the pressure form Carthage. Here is where a general and empirically grounded theory becomes invaluable. Because all world empires arose from metaethnic frontiers (so far as we know), the key factor in the rise of Rome must have been its metaethnic frontier with the barbarian Gauls. The pushing away of this frontier, which occurred when Cisapline Gaul was definitively conquered in the early second century B.C., was thus the first precondition of the ensuing decline.

The second part of Sallust's diagnosis needs greater modification. The ancients were fond of inveighing against the "enervating" effect of luxury. Now *luxury* has two components, one physical—creature comforts—and the other social—conspicuous consumption. It is clear that the first aspect of luxury, personal comfort, should have no effect on the collective solidarity. For example, the wealthy Romans spent even more money on beautifying their dwellings than on the banquets. They constructed private baths, complete with warm, hot, and cold pools, and lavished money on formal gardens. Why should baths and gardens be "enervating"? One could actually argue the opposite, by pointing to the health benefits of such "luxuries." Why should cultivating asparagus—a monstrous piece of gluttony, according to Pliny—soften the moral fiber of the Roman aristocracy?

If we redefine "luxury" as conspicuous consumption, however, the argument begins to make much more sense. The main point of conspicuous consumption is to signal to others high status, power, or wealth. Thus, having a hot bath at home is not conspicuous consumption today in the United States, because pretty much anybody can afford it. But a private bath in the republican Rome was most certainly a form of conspicuous consumption, because only the wealthiest could afford it. A modern visitor is struck by the opulence of private baths in Roman villas adorned with the elaborate and beautiful mosaics. It was not just about soaking in hot water, it was a social statement.

Conspicuous consumption is inherently divisive because it draws boundaries between the haves and the have-nots. It elicits envy and weakens solidarity. But it is even more important as a symptom of deeper processes—growing inequality and within-group competition for resources and power that gradually undermine group solidarity.

A TURNING POINT WAS THUS CROSSED during the second century B.C. Whereas the Roman aristocrats of the early Republic competed in who could die for *patria* in the most glorious way, in the late Republic they competed in who could throw the most sumptuous banquet. In 275 B.C., possession of 10 pounds of silver plate was considered as "anti-social behavior," two centuries later possession of 10,000 pounds of silver was a source of pride for the owner.

Socially disintegrative forces were also affecting the commoners. A small minority of them grew in wealth and aspired to join the ranks of the elite; whereas the majority lost their land holdings and were forced to work the land of the rich, to drift to the cities, where they swelled the urban proletariat, or to join the legions. The huge pool of potential recruits, destitute and desperate, was later one of the main factors driving the civil wars of the first century.

Finally, and perhaps most importantly, we need to factor in the effect of slavery. The Roman conquest of the Mediterranean during the second century B.C. flooded Italy with slaves, so that their numbers approached (and at times could have even exceeded) the numbers of free Italians. Slaves were employed in mines and as rowers of galleys, as domestic servants, and as agricultural laborers. At the same time that the small farm was disappearing, the slave plantation was taking over the peninsula and Sicily.

The distinction between slaves and freemen is perhaps the most extreme form of social inequality. Thus, widespread slavery must be a very corrosive influence on the society's asabiya. In fact, empirical evidence shows slavery has a deep, and lasting, negative impact on "social capital." (Social capital, as discussed in Chapter 13, is the equivalent of asabiya in modern societies.) For example, recently the political scientist Robert Putnam mapped the distribution of social capital among the American states. He found that the zone of high social capital is centered on the northern Midwest and extends east and west along the Canadian border. The zone of low social capital is centered over the Mississippi delta and extends outward in rising concentric circles through the former Confederacy. This north–south gradient in social capital has deep historical roots. Alexis de Tocqueville observed precisely the same pattern when he traveled in America in the 1830s: "As one goes farther south, one finds less active municipal life; the township has fewer officials, rights, and duties; the population does not exercise such a direct influence on affairs; the town meetings are less frequent and deal with fewer matters."

What is the explanation for this pattern? Putnam points to a "striking correlation between low social capital at the end of the twentieth century and slavery in the first half of the nineteenth century. The more virulent the system of slavery then, the less civic the state today. Slavery was, in fact, a social system *designed* to destroy social capital among the slaves and freemen. Well-established networks of reciprocity among the oppressed would have raised the risk of rebellion, and egalitarian bonds of sympathy between the slave and free would have undermined the very legitimacy of the system. After emancipation the dominant classes in the South continued to have a strong interest in inhibiting horizontal social networks. It is not happenstance that the lowest levels of community-based social capital are found where a century of plantation slavery was followed by a century of Jim Crowe politics. Inequality and social solidarity are deeply incompatible."

It was, thus, the rise of inequality and especially of its ugliest form, slavery, that began corroding Roman asabiya during the second century B.C. If social solidarity began its decline during this period, however, it does not mean that the Roman state declined in all other ways at the same time. "Decline" is not only nonlinear, it is also multidimensional. For example, under a different measure of decline, the territorial extent of the empire, the peak was achieved under the emperor Trajan (A.D. 98–117). In other words, the territorial decline followed asabiya decline with a lag of three centuries. There is no contradiction in this. The capacity of a state to expand depends on the product of its asabiya and geopolitical resources— population numbers and the ability of economy to generate surplus. Thus, there is nothing paradoxical in the fact that territorial expansion proceeded at the same time that asabiya was declining. Furthermore, the decline of collective solidarity is an extremely lengthy process that occurs over many centuries, and it comes in spurts and stops. Asabiya is degraded by within-group competition and growing inequality (which are really two sides of the same coin), and these forces wax and wane together with the secular cycle. This is why, after the troubled period of late Republic was over, the Roman Empire was able to reconstitute itself under the Principate. It took yet another time of troubles, the calamitous third century, to kill the Roman asabiya for good. But we are running ahead of ourselves, so let's return to tracing the social trends responsible for the Republic-Principate transition.

THE FIRST SIGNS OF THE LATE republican crisis were the slave revolts, which began breaking out all over the Roman world in 138 B.C.—in Italy (where it was suppressed with the crucifixion of over 4,500 slaves at Rome and surrounding towns), at the great slave market of Delos, and at the silver mines of Laurium (near Athens). The worst one was the revolt of 70,000 slaves in Sicily (135–132 B.C.). This so-called First Servile War was followed by the Second (104–101), also in Sicily, and then the Third (73–71), led by Spartacus.

Peasant rebellions rarely succeed in agrarian societies when the elites maintain their unity, and slave revolts in late republican Rome were not an exception to this rule. A much more dangerous threat to the state arises when the elites become splintered, and certain factions begin to mobilize popular support to be used in their quest for power. Tiberius Sempronius Gracchus (163–132 B.C.) was a politically ambitious young noble from a very prominent family. His father achieved the pinnacle of political success, having served as consul (twice) and censor. But the nobles of the Tiberius Gracchus generation faced a much stiffer competition for the top offices than was true of their fathers. It was natural for one of them to use the swelling popular discontent for political advancement. Furthermore, Tiberius's motivations needed not be wholly self-serving—the great polarization of wealth, resulting in a few controlling immense fortunes while most of citizens were landless, was patently unfair.

In 133 B.C. Tiberius Gracchus was elected as the tribune of the people and immediately introduced a law designed to break up the large private estates created out of public land and distribute them among the landless citizens. This bill divided the Roman aristocracy into two factions: the populists, led by Tiberius Gracchus, and the *optimates* ("the best ones"), who opposed him. In many ways, the populist-optimate split mirrored the struggle of the orders between the patricians and the wealthy plebeians three centuries before.

After increasingly bitter struggle over this bill, Tiberius and 300 of his supporters were murdered by a group of optimates and their clients in the Forum. However, the land commission set up to administer the Gracchan land law continued to function after his death. During the next 6 years, it allotted land to more than 75,000 citizens, alleviating the worst of the social pressure. The next leader of the populist faction was Tiberius's brother Gaius Gracchus, who was elected the tribune of the people in 123 and again in 122 B.C. Gaius continued to support his brother's program of land distribution and introduced *lex Frumentarium*, which provided grain to the citizens of Rome at subsidized prices (and later evolved into the dole). Like his brother, Gaius was eventually brought down by his optimate enemies, and died in street fighting. With him 3,000 of his partisans were killed.

After two turbulent decades (the 130s and 120s B.C.), a new generation of leaders came to power who managed to preserve fragile internal peace for almost 30 years. A populist politician Lucius Apuleius Saturninus tried to push a program of radical legislation down the throats of the optimates in 100 B.C., but the optimates murdered him and suppressed the populist party, preserving the equilibrium for another decade. However, below the surface, pressures were building up. The main issues that dominated the political arena were the demand for land by impoverished citizens, and the demand for citizenship by the Italian allies. The optimates stubbornly resisted both of these demands.

In 91 B.C. the allies revolted (this civil war is misleadingly known as the Social War, a better translation from Latin would be "the war with allies"), and the next two decades were those of almost continuous internal warfare. The Social War ended in 87, when Rome extended citizenship to all Italians, but was immediately succeeded by the civil war between the populist and optimate factions, led respectively by Marius and Sulla. During this conflict, first Marius and then Sulla used the proscriptions to exterminate their opponents in their hundreds and thousands. There was the rebellion of the Marian leader Sertorius in Spain. The slave rebellion led by Spartacus (73–71 B.C.) was the final straw that shocked the ruling class into some semblance of consensus.

Another fragile equilibrium was achieved in 70 B.C. under the consulships of Gnaeus Pompeius Magnus (Pompey the Great) and Marcus Licinius Crassus. This peaceful interlude lasted for another 20 years, and was marred only by the Conspiracy of Catiline (63 B.C.), a rebellion that was rather easily suppressed by the consul Marcus Tullius Cicero, the famous orator.

The equilibrium was shattered when Caesar crossed the Rubicon in 49 B.C. The next two decades were another period of continuous civil war. First, it was Julius Caesar against Pompey the Great, then Caesar against Pompey's partisans after the Great One's death in Egypt in 48 B.C. After the assassination of Caesar, the struggle was between Caesar's assassins, Brutus and Cassius, and Caesar's successors, Mark Anthony, Lepidus, and Octavian (44–42). The period of 41 to 31 saw confused struggle between Octavian, Mark Anthony, and Sextus Pompey (the son of the Great One) in various combinations. Eventually, Sextus Pompey was defeated in Sicily, but escaped to Greece, where he was executed; Mark Anthony was defeated in the battle of Actium, and committed suicide in Egypt in 30 B.C. This, finally, left Octavian, or Augustus as he was now styled, the last one standing. In 27 B.C. he established the new political regime, which we call the Principate (from the title he used, the *princeps*, because the emperor was in theory merely the first among equals).

The disintegrative phase of the republican cycle, thus, is almost a textbook example of the fathers-and-sons type of dynamics. The first two decades, 140 to 120 (all dates B.C.) were a time of contention, the next three decades relatively peaceful. The period 90 to 70 was another civil war, the succeeding two decades, 70 to 50, peaceful. The last period of civil war was 50 to 30, following which the disintegrative phase ended to the general relief of all those who were still alive.

THE DISINTEGRATIVE PHASE OF THE late Roman Republic ended for the same reason that it did in the French and English cases—the long period of internal instability "solved" the elite overproduction problem. The extent of carnage during the civil wars of the first century B.C. was truly awesome. In just one decade, 91 to 82 B.C., as many as 200,000 men lost their lives. The Spartacus rebellion accounted for another 100,000. Yet another 100,000 men were killed between 49 and 42 B.C. As one wit said, a hundred thousand here, a hundred thousand there, and soon we are talking about really big numbers.

Most of the casualties in the civil wars were commoners—landless citizens, noncitizen Italians, noncombatants caught in the fighting. But even if only 1 percent of these casualties came from the aristocracy, it would represent a significant drain on their numbers. At least as important was the mortality during the street rioting—it is reported that 3,000 supporters of Gaius Gracchus died when he was murdered. Finally, and perhaps most importantly, every time a winning faction gained control of the state, it enthusiastically slaughtered its opponents. The most famous (or infamous) were the proscriptions under Sulla. His victims included 15 men of consular rank, 90 senators, and 2,600 knights. (The Roman knights—equestrians—were the middle rank aristocrats, just below the senators in status and wealth.) Because the senate membership before Sulla was 300, he managed to obliterate a cool third of the Roman magnates. And the proscriptions of Sulla were just a single episode in the bloody struggles of the first century B.C. Before Sulla, there was "the reign of terror" by Marius and his partisans. The later proscriptions, following Caesar's death in 44 B.C., resulted in the executions of 300 senators and 2,000 knights. Caesar had increased senate membership to 900 (thus satisfying the pent-up demand for upward mobility), so this round of proscriptions carried away yet another third of Rome's top aristocracy.

The pruning of the elites and elite aspirants, thus, was one factor in the return of stability. The second factor was the resumption of external conquests. For almost a century after the lucrative sacks of Carthage and Corinth in 146 B.C., Roman external wars brought little in terms of booty, because they were wars of defense (as against the Germanic Cimbri and Teutones) or revolt suppression (as in the interminable partisan warfare in Spain). The situation began to change during the lull between the two civil wars, with the eastern conquests of Pompey the Great in the 60s and Gallic conquests of Caesar in the 50s. When the last civil war was over in 30 B.C., expansion was resumed. The conquered territories were reorganized to yield an enormous amount of taxes. If the state revenues in late second century B.C. were on average 80 million sesterces, a century later they grew to half a billion sesterces. In other words, not only did the top of the social pyramid shrink, its supportive base simultaneously expanded.

The third important trend during the last days of the Republic was the shift in the social mood. The society was exhausted and ready to welcome a regime that restored internal peace and order. These yearnings were reflected in the contemporary literature—the poet Tibullus exclaims: "I don't want to die young and for nothing!" Vergil's *Georgics* are filled with longing for peace: "so many wars throughout the world ... the fields going to waste in the farmer's absence." When Octavian Augustus emerged as the winner of the civil war, he found it relatively easy to impose a new political regime of the Principate. The rule of Augustus rested on a broad popular consensus. For example, when in 23 B.C. Augustus gave up the annual consulship he held since 31, the people of Rome, fearing the diminution of his authority and return of political instability, rioted trying to force him to accept the office.

The return of political stability under Augustus was accompanied by a gradual reversal of the previous trend of growing economic inequality. The basic precondition of reduced inequality was the population decline that occurred during the preceding disintegrative phase, which created space where landless peasants (mainly, veterans) could be settled. During the civil wars, Octavian simply seized land from Italian towns, and divided it among his veterans. After the end of the wars, he spent 860 million sesterces to purchase more land to settle veterans. Large numbers of landless citizens also emigrated to the provinces, further decreasing the population pressure on the resources within Italy. The government of Augustus, thus, was able to restore, to a certain degree, a class of relatively prosperous small landowners.

There were also forces acting on the other end of the wealth distribution, but the reduction of the super-rich fortunes got under way only after the reign of Augustus. The fortune of Gnaeus Cornelius Lentulus, consul in 14 B.C., topped those of Pompey or Crassus—he reputedly owned property worth 400 million sesterces. The scale of private fortunes declined during the first century A.D. The only exception was the fortune acquired by the freedman of emperor Claudius (A.D. 41–54), Narcissus, which was also 400 million sesterces. However, Narcissus did not live to enjoy his ill-gotten wealth—after Claudius died, Narcissus was poisoned by Agrippina (the mother of the emperor Nero).

The top of the wealth pyramid was whittled down by a variety of means. Augustus practiced a sort of a "progressive inheritance tax"—he forced the richest people of his time to include him in their wills. By this means, big chunks of private fortunes were siphoned into the state's coffers. The second way of cutting down to size the over-mighty subjects was more direct—execution on the charges of treason, sometimes real, sometimes trumped up. The emperor Claudius condemned to death 35 senators and many knights; a substantial part of their fortunes must have gone into the imperial treasury. Nero is said to have executed six of the largest landowners in Africa Proconsularis and thus gained possession of the rich Bragadas Valley. When a number of plots against Nero proliferated (toward the end of his reign), he forced a great number of senators and knights to commit suicide, including such well-known persons as the moralist Seneca and the poet Lucan. More magnates lost their lives after the overthrow of Nero, as a result of coup-d'états during the "year of three emperors" (A.D. 69). By the reign of Vespasian (A.D. 69–79), the ranks of Roman senators had become depleted to about 200—from a peak of over 1,000 under the late Republic. In other words, the elite pruning had continued during the first century of the Principate. This trend resembles in many ways the downfall of the "over-mighty subject" under the Tudors in the early modern England.

The end result was that during the first century of the Principate the relative power of the most powerful and wealthy private individuals declined substantially with respect to that of the state. At the same time, small landholders enjoyed a period of relative economic prosperity, which was not marred by sociopolitical instability. The conflicts, described above, took the form of elite purges or palace coups, and had little effect on common people. There was only one year of civil warfare, A.D. 69, before the return of instability at the end of the second century.

Peace and prosperity in agrarian societies, however, contain the seeds of the troubles to come. The Wheel of Fortune can slow down or speed up, but it never ceases to operate. However, it becomes tedious to read about one secular cycle after another, because with all their variations due to different times, geography, and national character, the basic mechanism is still the same. For this reason, I only hit the highlights of the Principate cycle (27 B.C.– A.D. 284), and then return to the main theme of interest to us—the causes of the decline of Roman asabiya.

INTERNAL PEACE AND ECONOMIC PROSPERITY after 27 B.C. brought about rapid population growth. By A.D. 100, Italy was again suffering from overpopulation. With the resumption of population growth, the Matthew principle began operating with a vengeance. By A.D. 100, the impoverishment of small farmers reached such proportions that the authorities took note. Under the emperor Trajan (A.D. 98–117), they instituted a system of public assistance for freeborn children. This program was prompted by the decline in the numbers of small farmers, especially in central Italy, resulting in a reduction of the numbers of Italian recruits to the legions. Indeed, in the beginning of the first century, Italians supplied two thirds of recruits for the imperial legions, but by the end of the century this proportion fell to below one fourth. Unfortunately, the measures taken by the authorities were completely ineffectual. During the second and third centuries, the proportion of legion recruits from Italy fell to just 3 percent.

At the same time that the smallholder class was disappearing, the core of the Roman Empire—peninsular Italy, including Sicily—was taken over by the *latifundia* ("large estates") and villas of the rich. With the cessations of external conquests, the supply of slaves diminished, and the agricultural labor forces became dominated by the *coloni*, tenants of the great landowners.

A.D. 96 to 180, known as the reigns of the "five good emperors" (Nerva, Trajan, Hadrian, Antonius Pius, and Marcus Aurelius), was the period of internal peace and stability, during which the empire reached and stabilized at its maximum territorial extent. It was also the golden age of the aristocracy. The elites did very well economically and their numbers grew. Social and economic indicators of aristocratic well-being—building activity and marble production, the number of inscriptions and documents, and so on—peaked toward the middle of the second century.

By A.D. 150, the social system was growing dangerously top-heavy, but it still managed to preserve its internal stability. This equilibrium was destroyed with the arrival of an epidemic that reached the Roman Empire in 165, the "Antonine plague." The Antonine plague was probably smallpox, or a combination of measles and smallpox. Its impact on the Roman population during the first visitation of 165–9 was probably comparable to the impact of the Black Death on the European population. After the first shock, the epidemics recurred, often causing catastrophic losses, during the 170s and 180s. Another wave of epidemics hit the empire in the 250s and 260s.

Things unraveled very rapidly in the wake of the epidemic. Sensing weakness, the Germanic and Sarmatic tribes pressed across the Rhine and Danube frontiers. From 167 on, the empire was repeatedly invaded by the barbarians. The imperial finances rapidly collapsed. Marcus Aurelius was the first (but not last) emperor to sell the gold vessels and artistic treasures of the imperial palace to finance his campaigns. The main coin of the realm, *denarius*, was debased again and again over the next century, until its silver content fell to just 2.5 percent. Even debased currency was in short supply, and the empire lost its ability to control the legions, because it could not pay them anymore. A popular uprising flared up in Egypt, and there were hunger riots in Rome herself.

The last of the "good emperors," Marcus Aurelius was able to hold the ruling class of the empire together for a while, but his heir Commodus (180–192) could not. (Commodus is the main villain in the very popular but historically inaccurate movie *The Gladiator* with Russell Crowe in the main role.) The first plot against him was hatched in 182, when a number of senators conspired with Commodus's sister Lucilla to assassinate him. The plot failed and was followed by the execution of the conspirators and, later, a number of other senators whom Commodus suspected of treason. Commodus was then poisoned during the end-of-the-year celebration, survived the attempt (probably due to vomiting most of the poison as a result of excessive drinking), and was assassinated the next day when he was recovering in the bath. He was strangled by his wrestling partner, Narcissius, who joined the plot against Commodus. The next two emperors, Pertinax and Julianus, lasted only 87 and 66 days, respectively, and the full-blown many-sided civil war was on.

The first civil war was won in 197 by Septimus Severus, the commander of the Danube legions. As usual, it was followed by a relatively peaceful generation—the reigns of Septimus himself and then his son Caracalla. In 217, however, Caracalla was murdered. His demise unleashed a veritable epidemic of emperor assassinations. (Four emperors were killed one after another between 217 and 235.) The last assassination triggered a general civil war, which was to drag on for 50 years. The imperiopathosis of the Roman nation went into its acute phase, and sometime during this period the patient died.

SEPARATING CONTINUOUS PROCESSES INTO discrete phases is always arbitrary, but if I were pressed to say just when did the Roman Empire end, I would choose A.D. 268. This was the year when a cabal of officers from the Danubian frontier assassinated the emperor Gallienus, and took the business of the empire into their own hands. They produced a string of ruthless and capable rulers, known as the "Illyrian soldier-emperors." One of them, Diocletian, reunited the empire in 285. Another, Constantine, moved the capital to Constantinople in 330. They continued to call themselves "Romans," but they and their soldiers were the germ of a new imperial nation, not the one that was born on the banks of Tiber a millennium before—the new nation that would eventually build the Byzantine empire. These "Illyrians" did not trust Italians. (That is probably why they killed Gallienus, who seemed to be a good sort and tried hard—but he was not one of them.) And they had a good reason not to, because the Italians had clearly lost any remaining asabiya by this point.

The cohesive nation of citizen-soldiers was gone. Instead of them, the core region of the Roman Empire was inhabited by an atomized society, characterized by extreme degrees of social and economic inequality, and an almost total lack of solidarity bonds between individuals. This state of affairs was a product of several centuries of operation of the Matthew principle. Slave plantations began spreading in Italy during the second century B.C. and largely displaced freeholds during the next century. Under the Principate, the numbers of slaves employed in agriculture gradually diminished and eventually they were replaced with *coloni*—tenant farmers of the great landowners. Although slavery disappeared, the gap between the peasants and the aristocrats continued to grow. As in the post-Civil War southern American states, the magnates of the later Roman Empire continued to have a strong interest in inhibiting horizontal social networks among their tenants. They were also making a concerted effort to tie peasants to the land. By A.D. 400, the legal codes refer to tenants as "slaves of the land."

Wealth inequality in the Roman Empire reached its peak during the fourth century, but its growth was not linear. As discussed earlier in the chapter, the first leap in economic inequality occurred during the disintegrative phase of the republican cycle (second and first century B.C.), when the typical wealth of a Roman senator increased to 10–20 million sesterces. During the integrative phase of the Dominate, senatorial wealth apparently did not grow. For example, Pliny the Younger, a senator of middling wealth at the end of the first century, had an annual income of 1.1 million sesterces. Because the typical yield on capital in agrarian societies is around 6 percent, an income of 1.1 million implies a total wealth of 15–20 million, or about the same as under the late Republic. But during the disintegrative phase of the Principate, wealth inequality jumped again. Middling aristocrats in the western empire in the late fourth century had incomes of 1,333 to 2,000 Roman pounds of gold. Translating this number into total wealth, we have 100–150 million sesterces. In other words, the personal fortunes of aristocrats increased by another order of magnitude, and that at a time when the empire was shrinking and the total amount of wealth was diminishing. This increase in the wealth of the elites had to come at the expense of the pauperization of the commoners. Everything we know about the late empire supports this view.

By the fifth century, the Italian society, if we can still call it that, had lost any remnants of ability to act in a concerted manner. Italians did not serve in the legions or as government officials. Central authorities could not collect taxes. The magnates ignored any orders issued by the imperial government, and began raising private armies. These private forces, however, were completely ineffectual against the barbarians who invaded Italy during the fifth century.

The millions of inhabitants of the Italian Peninsula outnumbered the invaders by orders of magnitude—modern historians estimate that most of these barbarian nations numbered in tens of thousands, and even the largest hordes could not have much more than a hundred thousand people. Yet they could move through Italy at will, sacking Rome on numerous occasions—all of this without eliciting any collective response from the population. The only reason that Italy enjoyed a relatively prosperous period during the fourth century, it seems, was the imposition of peace and order by the authority, located outside the asabiya black hole that developed in the core of the Roman state—the eastern Roman Empire based in Constantinople. But even the rulers of the western half of the empire abandoned Rome, and moved their headquarters closer to the frontier. Within Italy, the center of gravity shifted from Rome north to Milan and then to Ravenna. This development reflects an important difference between the northern (trans-Apennine) and peninsular Italies, a difference that has persisted to the modern days.

The northern segment of the Apennine Mountains, which separate the peninsula from the Po Valley, was a metaethnic frontier between the Mediterranean civilization and the Celtic "barbarism" during the first millennium B.C. After Rome won its centuries-long struggle against the Gauls, the peninsula and Sicily became the core region of the Roman Empire. It was within this region where the ruling class had its country villas; it was here that slave plantations displaced freeholds, and where all the major slave uprisings raged during the late Republic. Trans-Apennine Italy (or Cisalpine Gaul, as it was known during the Republic) developed on a diverging trajectory. When the Romans conquered this region, they ethnically cleansed the majority of its Gallic inhabitants, and encouraged colonization by small-scale farmers. As far as we know, the large slave plantations never spread into the trans-Apennine Italy. Even as late as A.D.100, according to Pliny the Younger, slave agricultural labor was not used in the Po Valley. Thus, trans-Apennine Italy did not experience the corrosive effects of the most extreme form of inequality, slavery. The western emperors moved their capital to this region probably because its population retained a certain degree of social solidarity, unlike the imperial core region south of the Apennines.

In the fifth and sixth century, trans-Apennine Italy received another influx of free farmers, these coming from across the Alps. The largest group of immigrants was the Longobards or Lombards, as they became known in Italy. In A.D. 568, the whole Longobard nation left the Hungarian plain (which was promptly taken over by the Avars; probably it was the pressure from these steppe warriors that induced the Longobards to migrate), and invaded northern Italy. The Longobards eventually assimilated to the Romance language, but they also gave their name to the region where they settled most densely—Lombardy.

As a result of staying outside the imperial core region, and because of several influxes of relatively solidary groups of free farmers, trans-Apennine Italy did not lose all of its asabiya, and its geopolitical trajectory was different from that of the old imperial core. Peninsular Italy, including Sicily, remained an asabiya black hole from the collapse of the Roman Empire to this very day. Its fate was determined entirely by the interplay of external forces. First, it was part of the Gothic kingdom, and then it was reconquered by the Byzantium. Toward the end of the first millennium, Sicily fell into the hands of Muslims, while the area around Rome was organized as a papal state. In the eleventh century, Sicily and southern Italy were conquered by the Normans. The Norman rulers were replaced by the German Hohenzollerns, then by the French Angevins, and then by the Iberian Aragonese and Castilians. Not a single internally generated attempt at state building occurred.

In northern Italy, by contrast, several medium-sized states developed across the centuries. Venice created a Mediterranean trading empire, and conquered a substantial chunk of continental Italy. During the fourteenth century, the duchy of Milan managed to conquer most of the Po Valley. On the other hand, no true metaethnic frontier developed in trans-Apennine region after the collapse of the Roman Empire. The various Germanic invaders settled among the natives and rapidly assimilated to Christianity (if they were not yet Christian) and the Romance language. Thus, the asabiya of northern Italians was only sufficient for building small or medium-sized states. When great imperial powers—France, Spain, Austria—intruded into Italy, even the strongest Italian states, such as Milan, were reduced to choosing (at best) which of the external empires to submit to. In the nineteenth century Italy was unified, characteristically, by northerners—the Piedmontese of what is misleadingly called "the kingdom of Sardinia," a state that actually originated on the other side of the Alps in what is now French Savoy. Nevertheless, it was remarkable that Italy managed to become unified at all—in fact, the Italian unification is a rare exception to the rule that large states can arise only on metaethnic frontiers. The state built by the Piedmontese was neither particularly large, nor particularly good at the game of empire, but it still constitutes a counterexample, or an anomaly from the point of view of the metaethnic frontier theory. This exception to the rule underlines the point made earlier in the book, that historical dynamics is much more complex than, say, planetary motions around the sun. The associations between metaethnic frontiers and aggressive empires is a powerful historical generalization, but it is not without some exceptions, even if the exception cases are borderline, like nineteenth century Italy.

After the unification, Italy attempted to join the club of the great powers, but its imperial career in modern times was short and inglorious. The performance of the Italian army during the two world wars was, to state it most generously, lackluster. Italy also holds the dubious distinction of being the only European state that was defeated by an African country (Ethiopia) in the nineteenth-century scramble for colonies.

I do not want, however, to give an impression that military success is the only measure of social solidarity. Furthermore, the wars in which the post-unification Italy was involved were conducted overseas. A true meas-ure of solidarity is the ability of a country to defend itself when invaded, and even defense of the *patria* is not the only purpose to which social soli-darity could be put. Economic growth also requires a certain degree of social capital, and northern Italians have done very well by this measure. This is a theme to which I will return in Part III.

Part III

CLIODYNAMICS

A New Kind of History

Chapter 12

War and Peace and Particles

The Science of History

War *and Peace* by Leo Tolstoy is not only one of the most revered novels ever written, it is also a treatise on the science of history. Leo Tolstoy (1828–1910) lived during the golden age of classical physics, when it seemed that a complete understanding of the physical world was almost in sight. (The discovery of relativity and quantum mechanics in the early twentieth century showed that this was an illusion.) Tolstoy must have asked himself whether the methods that worked so well in physics could be applied to the study of history—precisely the premise with which we started on our search for a new kind of theoretical history.

Two triumphs of classical physics inspired Tolstoy to think about how mathematical history could be conceived. One was the invention of differential and integral calculus, which allowed Isaac Newton (1642–1727) and others to develop the equations of planetary motion. The second was the statistical mechanics developed by, among others, Pierre-Simon Laplace (1749–1827). Laplace saw the universe as a huge collection of bodies and particles, all obeying Newton's laws of motion. He argued that if we only could determine the positions and velocities of all these bodies at one point in time, then in principle we could calculate their trajectories as far in the future as we wanted. From this, Laplace deduced that the universe is completely deterministic. There was no place for anything like free will in his vision of how the world worked.

We now know that this notion of determinism is wrong. For one thing, particles at the subatomic level behave in a stochastic—completely erratic and unpredictable—manner, and modern physics has been unable to reduce their behavior to the action of deterministic laws. It is quite possible that the universe, at some very basic level, is not deterministic at all.

Second, complex systems, and the universe is certainly a complex system, can behave in a *chaotic* manner. When a system behaves chaotically, tiny perturbations make its future trajectory completely unpredictable. A little electron deciding to jump from one orbit to another will completely change the course of a chaotic dynamical system.

Although Laplace's vision of the deterministic universe turned out to be mistaken, it does not diminish the achievements of statistical physics in other, less-cosmic applications. For example, the methods of statistical mechanics were able to explain very well such things as temperature, or gas pressure. Pressure, for instance, is the force exerted by gas on the walls of the container, and it results from the action of myriads of gas molecules constantly hitting the container walls. Pressure is not a property of any particular molecule (a molecule is characterized by its mass, position, and velocity), it is a characteristic of the whole ensemble of molecules. However, the amount of pressure can be calculated by averaging over the actions of the myriad of molecules. Statistical physics can even predict how increasing the temperature of the gas will affect the pressure. (Molecules run around faster and hit the walls harder, so that pressure increases.)

Now a society also consists of a number of "particles"—individuals. Is it possible to somehow average over individual actions to understand what the society will do, by analogy with statistical physics? Tolstoy thought yes. "Only by taking infinitesimally small units for observation (the differential of history, that is, the individual tendencies of men) and attaining to the art of integrating them (that is, finding the sum of these infinitesimals) can we hope to arrive at the laws of history.

"To study the laws of history we must completely change the subject of our observation, must leave aside kings, ministers, and generals, and the common, infinitesimally small elements by which the masses are moved. No one can say in how far it is possible for man to advance in this way toward an understanding of the laws of history; but it is evident that only along that path does the possibility of discovering the laws of history lie, and that as yet not a millionth part as much mental effort has been applied in this direction by historians as has been devoted to describing the actions of various kings, commanders, and ministers and propounding the historians' own reflections concerning these actions."

Tolstoy found particularly objectionable the view, held by many nineteenth-century historians, that history is made by the great men. "The first

15 years of the nineteenth century in Europe present an extraordinary movement of millions of people. Men leave their customary pursuits, hasten from one side of Europe to the other, plunder and slaughter one another, triumph and are plunged in despair, and for some years the whole course of life is altered and presents an intensive movement which first increases and then slackens. What was the cause of this movement, by what laws was it governed? asks the mind of man. The historians, replying to this question, lay before us the sayings and doings of a few dozen men in a building in the city of Paris, calling these sayings and doings 'the Revolution'; then they give a detailed biography of Napoleon and of certain people favorable or hostile to him; tell of the influence some of these people had on others, and say: That is why this movement took place and those are its laws. But the mind of man not only refuses to believe this explanation, but plainly says that this method of explanation is fallacious, because in it a weaker phenomenon is taken as the cause of a stronger. The sum of human wills produced the Revolution and Napoleon, and only the sum of those wills first tolerated and then destroyed them."

Today the idea that history is moved solely by actions of great men is thoroughly discredited, but we continue to overestimate the influence of an individual on the course of history. Why else was there so much hope pinned on capturing Saddam Hussein by the occupying powers in Iraq? Yet the deaths of Saddam's sons and his capture accomplished precisely what Tolstoy would have predicted—nothing.

We do not have to accept all ideas of Tolstoy—after all, he wrote *War and Peace* more than a century ago. But his argument that a science of history can be constructed only by integrating over the actions of myriads of individuals is, I think, valid. It is also accepted by modern sociologists. How we can deduce macro-social dynamics from the micro-actions of individuals is one of the central questions in sociology. The analogy with statistical physics, which deduced macro-properties, such as pressure and temperature, from micro-characteristics of molecules, is compelling.

The theoretical framework for understanding the rise and fall of imperial nations came from the same tradition. Take asabiya, the capacity for collective action. It is impossible to say that "Napoleon had great asabiya." That would be as ridiculous as saying that "the temperature of this oxygen molecule is 10 degrees centigrade." Asabiya is a property of a group, not an individual. Collective solidarity, of course, is not the only factor that influences the fates of empires, but other factors (population numbers, economic inequality, sociopolitical instability, and so on) have the same nature of being characteristics of groups or societies, rather than specific actions by kings, generals, and ministers. The explanations that I proposed in the course of this book are consistent with the logic argued by Tolstoy.

This is not necessarily a good thing, because under certain conditions actions of some individuals *do* matter. Constantine the Great established the Byzantine capital at a particularly auspicious place—on a crossing of trading routes, but also in a highly defensible location. Some historians argued that the situation of Constantinople was a big factor in the subsequent survival of the Byzantine Empire. I do not think it was the definitive factor, but, on the other hand, I would not want to deny that it played an important positive role in increasing the empire's longevity.

A better example is the influence of Napoleon on obtaining victory on the battlefield. When describing Napoleon's actions at the field of Borodino (the major battle of the 1812 invasion of Russia by Napoleon, which was marginally won by the French), Tolstoy stresses how ineffectual Napoleon's orders were in directing his troops. Consistently with his conception of history, Tolstoy argues that Napoleon was simply deluding himself that he directed anything. In actuality, each army fought on its own, because officers and soldiers themselves knew what had to be done, and orders arriving from Napoleon were outdated or simply wrong. The Russian commander Kutuzov does not meddle in this natural process, and gains Tolstoy's approval for that.

Is Tolstoy correct in pushing his logic to this extreme? This is a question into which we can actually sink our scientific teeth. During the Napoleonic wars, the French army fought scores of battles, some under the leadership of Napoleon, others led by his generals. Using the methods developed by military historians, which I discuss shortly, it is possible to do a statistical analysis of the battle outcomes. Taking into account various factors, such as the numbers of men on each side, the armaments, position, and tactical surprise (if any), the analysis shows that Napoleon as commander acted as a multiplier, estimated as 1.3. In other words, the presence of Napoleon was equivalent to the French having an extra 30 percent of troops. This is strong evidence that the extreme position advocated by

Tolstoy cannot be right. Of course, we still do not know whether Napoleon's dispositions before the engagement or directions during the battle were instrumental in increasing the chance of the French victory. It is also possible that the "Napoleon effect" was entirely due to his mystique or charisma, which elevated the courage and determination of soldiers. Most likely, all of these factors were operating together, and we cannot distinguish between them with data. We do know, however, that the presence of Napoleon had a measurable effect on the outcome. Here we have one clear-cut example of the importance of an individual in history.

The problem, however, is that it does not help us in building a better theory. Napoleons, Alexanders, Caesars, and so on probably influenced the course of history during their lifetimes. It does not mean that they could do whatever they wanted—Caesar did not manage to end the disintegrative phase of the republican cycle; he did not even manage to survive to an old age. But it is likely that without him the Gaul would be conquered a generation later, and this is a substantial perturbation of the Roman trajectory. But where did Caesar come from? What kind of theory could tell us when to expect an appearance of a hero, and when not? I do not know of such a theory. Until we have it, the knowledge that extraordinary people appear once in a while and that they influence the course of events is useless to us. It cannot be meaningfully fitted within the theoretical framework.

Think about it from a different angle. Suppose all I proposed in this book would be to say that different nations have different asabiya and therefore that is why some rise and others decline. Would that qualify as a scientific theory? Not at all, because asabiya would be just a different name for the fact that some empires grow and others fall. Just coining a term does not explain anything. If I can tell you why asabiya grows and why it declines, however, we have the beginnings of a theory. We can then work on turning such beginnings into a mature scientific theory by testing the theory's predictions with empirical data.

So we end up in a situation where we know that a certain factor—actions of certain individuals, the "great men"—has an effect, but choose not to include it in the theory. This is a frustrating, but quite typical situation in science. As I said before, a good scientific theory does not need to include everything we know about the subject. It needs to include only the stuff that is necessary for getting the job done; the rest must be ruthlessly expunged. A slightly more sophisticated approach than completely omitting such factors from the theory is to include them as stochastic influences, or random effects. Randomness is a general model that scientists use for things they do not understand.

THE SCIENCE OF HISTORICAL DYNAMICS—cliodynamics—offers insights not about certain individual people, but about all individuals in a group—call them societies, states, or empires. The basic premise of the discipline is that history is shaped by great impersonal forces—not by actions of single individuals, but by actions of whole collectives of them. This does not mean that I personally think that individuals do not matter; in fact, we sometimes can measure the effect of a remarkable individual (such as Napoleon) using standard scientific methods. The theory ignores the action of individual wills (or treats them as stochastic factors), but it also ignores many other influences that affect the course of history—this is what good scientific theories are supposed to do, after all. A good theory is not necessarily the absolutely correct theory. In fact, in science we do not have absolutely correct theories. All scientific knowledge is tentative and subject to revision, as was shown by the Einsteinian revolution that overturned Newtonian physics. Just because it was later shown that Newtonian classical mechanics was wrong does not mean that it was a bad scientific theory. On the contrary, it was an extremely productive scientific enterprise, which explained certain natural phenomena with a degree of accuracy hitherto unprecedented. It allowed physicists to ask a lot of interesting and profound questions about the universe. Eventually it collapsed under the weight of accumulated anomalies and was replaced with Einstein's theory of relativity. Thus, Newtonian theory was good science, because it was *productive*, not because it was right (which it was not).

In my opinion, cliodynamics is a productive framework. The mass of empirical material that we have ploughed through suggests so. However, I would be the last to argue that cliodynamics is the final word in our understanding of the rise and fall of states, or even that it is a mature theory like Newtonian classical mechanics. A lot more work needs to be done to bring the science of history to the same stage of scientific maturity that was enjoyed by classical mechanics in the eighteenth and nineteenth centuries.

So what about the role of individual in history? At present, I do not know how to include individuals in the theoretical framework of cliody-namics, so we must, by necessity ignore their role. If somebody can figure out how to modify the theory to include the individuals in it (or any other factor that is currently left out), I would be the first to applaud such a development. Again, a good scientific theory is the one that offers a pro-ductive paradigm. Even if it stimulates somebody to come with a com-pletely alternative theory that explains the empirical world better than the one we have now, I would be thrilled. There is no penalty in science for being wrong, as long as you do it in an interesting and productive way. Newton turned out to be wrong, but he is one of the greatest scientists ever.

"MEN MAKE THEIR OWN HISTORY, but not of their own free will; not under circumstances they themselves have chosen but under the given and inher-ited circumstance with which they are directly confronted." These words, belonging to a contemporary of Tolstoy, Karl Marx, express very well why a theory that completely ignores individuals could do quite well in explain-ing historical dynamics. I would, however, do away with the "not of their own free will" part, because it seems to deny that people have free will. I am not sure whether this was Marx's intention, but I want to stress that the issue of free will in this context is a complete red herring. Whether people have free will or not (I happen to believe that we do) has nothing to do with our ability to understand and predict historical dynamics. No contra-diction exists between exercising free will to choose one's actions at the micro level, and lacking the ability to influence events at the macrosocial level.

Laplacian determinism is dead. When we heat gas in a container by so many degrees, we can predict practically exactly just how far the pressure will increase. But it does not mean that all particles within the container behave in a completely deterministic way. Gas molecules follow completely chaotic, unpredictable trajectories. At a lower level, quantum physics tells us that the behavior of subatomic particles cannot be predicted; that is, they have a kind of "free will." However, randomness at the quantum—micro—level is completely averaged out when we get to the macro level of the gas container. There are zillions of particles in the container, all behaving randomly, but when we average over them (by measuring pressure, for instance, which is an average property) we get extremely precise measurements.

To give an analogy in sociology, consider suicide, one of the most drastic and personal decisions that a person can make. The fact that people kill themselves, to me is the ultimate proof that the free will exists. Yet at the macro level, the annual numbers of suicide in a large country is a highly predictable statistic. This year's number will be very similar to the last ones. Moreover, at times of social stress, the suicide rates go up in a predictable way. Other factors also affect this property of a society, and they provided the basis for *Suicide*, a classic study by one of the founders of modern sociology, Emile Durkheim (1857–1917).

Here's then an example of how an exercise of free choice at the micro level can have a vanishingly small effect at the macro level. But at least a person contemplating suicide can affect the statistics of suicide rate by one death. There are many structural situations in social life in which even such a tiny effect is denied us.

I live in Connecticut, a state where during the 2004 elections John Kerry was projected to win over George Bush by 10 percent. Such a large gap meant that Kerry victory was a foregone conclusion. Certainly both the Democratic and Republican campaigns treated it this way—both spent hardly any money on political advertising in Connecticut. When I got up on that second Tuesday of November 2004, the exercise of my free will—whether I would vote for Bush, Kerry, or Ralph Nader, or simply would not vote at all—was completely irrelevant to the final outcome. The effect of my single vote was not simply tiny, it was exactly nil. Kerry would get his 7 electoral votes, not 7.00001 nor 6.99999, no matter what I did. When a dynamical system dampens out small perturbations, we call it stable. The electoral process in Connecticut was stable to small perturbations such as my vote, so the only "rational" action for me would be to skip voting that day. (I voted anyway—think of it as exercising my free will.)

For Connecticut to swing for Bush, about 100,000 people would have had to switch their votes to him from Kerry. In New Mexico, on the other hand, the gap between Bush and Kerry was only about 6,000 votes, so if only 3,000 had switched, the outcome of the state election would be different. Now we are getting closer to the scale at which individuals can operate.

It is at least conceivable that a committed and charismatic person could build an organization that would persuade 3,000 people to switch their votes from one candidate to another. If one individual could amplify his or her will to sway a few thousand other people, their change of heart would then be amplified at the level of the state of New Mexico. About 750,000 people voted in New Mexico in the 2004 elections, and because in the American system the winner takes all, all their votes would be added to Kerry's total. Unfortunately, the effect of this perturbation would be dampened out at the next level, because New Mexico's five electoral votes would have been insufficient to give the presidency to Kerry. As we all know, the main suspense of the last election was centered on the battleground state of Ohio. If Ohio had gone to Kerry, he would have won, and we would finally get a macro-level effect.

What this example shows is, among other things, the value of bringing the perspective of nonlinear dynamical science to the thinking about social phenomena. The society is a complex system, and we know that complex systems, in general, are affected by a variety of positive and negative feedbacks. Let us think of an act of a single free will (whether it is a subatomic particle or a human being) as a "perturbation." Negative feedbacks counteract the effect of a perturbation; they dampen it out. Positive feedbacks, by contrast, amplify the effect of a perturbation; they blow it all out of proportion. In different places of a complex system, and at different times, feedbacks act in different ways, so that a few thousand people changing their minds in Connecticut could be immediately dampened out, but in New Mexico amplified (but then dampened out at the next level). Perhaps in Ohio a perturbation could travel all the way and flip the end result. The situation when a dynamical system acts in a way that amplifies perturbations is known in nonlinear dynamics as *sensitive dependence*. It is sensitive dependence that makes systems behave in a chaotic, apparently erratic manner.

Tolstoy's concept of history as a result of the sum of myriads of human wills is, therefore, valid but overly simplistic (which is not surprising because science in the nineteenth century had not yet discovered sensitive dependence and chaos). Actions by many individuals are not simply added together, in the same manner that we calculate the statistics of suicide rate by adding together all suicides in a year. Things are more complex. Some micro actions, by most people most of the time, have no effect whatsoever on the behavior of the system as a whole—they are completely dampened out at the macro level. But sometimes an individual acts in a place and at a time where the macrosystem is extremely sensitive to small perturbations. Then a little act of a little individual can trigger an avalanche of consequences, and result in a complete change of the course of events. The childhood rhyme "For want of a nail" illustrates this idea perfectly.

This is an optimistic conclusion, because it suggests that not all individual action is doomed to be futile at the macro level of social systems. There is no excuse in not trying to do good, because even if most of such actions would probably dissipate without any lasting effect, once in a while a small action will have a large effect. We can really amplify the effects of our efforts by organizing or joining a group.

But the optimism should be tempered by humility. Small acts can cause large effects, but people performing these acts usually have no idea whether there will be an effect at all, and if there is, what it will be. It is in the nature of dynamical systems to behave in seemingly capricious ways, so that an action aimed at achieving one objective might end up doing precisely the opposite. The French nobles, clergy, and third-estate notables, who in 1789 stopped obeying the king and took the government in their own hands, certainly had no intention of starting a bloody revolution in which most of them would lose their heads to the guillotine. Yet this is precisely what happened.

TOLSTOY'S DISCUSSIONS OF THE SCIENCE of history were not limited to his thoughts on the role played by individuals versus large impersonal social forces. He also made it very clear that the theory of history should be expressed in mathematical terms. In one remarkable passage, dealing with the guerilla war by the Russians against Napoleon's troops, he actually used mathematical equations.

"In military affairs the strength of an army is the product of its mass and some unknown x," he writes. "That unknown quantity is the spirit of the army, that is to say, the greater or lesser readiness to fight and face danger felt by all the men composing an army, quite independently of whether they are, or are not, fighting under the command of a genius, in two- or three-line formation, with cudgels or with rifles that repeat 30 times a minute. Men who want to fight will always put themselves in the most advantageous conditions for fighting.

"The spirit of an army is the factor which multiplied by the mass gives the resulting force. To define and express the significance of this unknown factor—the spirit of an army—is a problem for science.

"This problem is only solvable if we cease arbitrarily to substitute for the unknown x itself the conditions under which that force becomes apparent—such as the commands of the general, the equipment employed, and so on—mistaking these for the real significance of the factor, and if we recognize this unknown quantity in its entirety as being the greater or lesser desire to fight and to face danger. Only then, expressing known historic facts by equations and comparing the relative significance of this factor, can we hope to define the unknown.

"Ten men, battalions, or divisions, fighting fifteen men, battalions, or divisions, conquer—that is, kill or take captive—all the others, while themselves losing four, so that on the one side four and on the other fifteen were lost. Consequently the four were equal to the fifteen, and therefore $4x = 15y$. Consequently $x/y = 15/4$. This equation does not give us the value of the unknown factor but gives us a ratio between two unknowns. And by bringing variously selected historic units (battles, campaigns, periods of war) into such equations, a series of numbers could be obtained in which certain laws should exist and might be discovered."

The exact details of this calculation are not important (in fact, Tolstoy did not get it quite right); what is important is the intent to express ideas about such historical phenomena as battles in mathematical language, and the suggestion that coefficients in equations can be estimated empirically. Tolstoy goes a bit overboard when he dismisses the importance of armament, leadership, and other factors that all affect combat. But his basic point—that there is a certain factor x that cannot be reduced to numbers, armament, and so on—is completely valid. The factor x, which Tolstoy identifies as the spirit of an army, is of great interest to us, because it is clearly related to asabiya. The fighting spirit is one component of asabiya—the capacity for collective action in battle. It is an important part of the overall capacity for collective action, but not the whole of it. After all, Romans lost most of their battles against Hannibal, yet won the war.

There is more to winning wars than being good at fighting battles. And war is not the only way to expand and keep territory.

Returning to the more narrow issue of battle performance, is Tolstoy's idea about estimating it from data workable? It turns out yes. Here I turn to the work of the American military historian, Col. Trevor N. Dupuy (1916–1995), *Understanding War: History and Theory of Combat.* Dupuy assumed that the combat power of an army could be represented as a product of three quantities. The first one is force strength, which is basically the number of troops, but modified by the quality and quantity of their equipment. Generally speaking, a horseman has an advantage over an infantryman. A heavy tank with thick armor and a large gun has an advantage over a light tank.

The second quantity is operational and environmental factor modifiers. Clearly, terrain will affect the outcome. It is extremely difficult for an infantry force to resist a cavalry (or tank) attack when they are caught in the open plains, but they have a much better chance in the woods, or in an urban environment. Whether a force is on the offensive or defensive also makes a big difference. (It is easier to defend, especially in a well-prepared position.) Other factors, such as weather, fatigue, and so on also need to be taken into account.

The third quantity is combat effectiveness, which is the same as Tolstoy's factor x. This is the one that we are primarily interested in.

The best data set, analyzed by Dupuy, was 81 engagements between the Allied (Anglo-American) and German forces in 1943–44. For each battle, Dupuy calculated force strengths, taking into account the numbers of tanks, artillery pieces, air support, and so forth. He then estimated the factor modifiers, such as the posture (defensive versus offensive). Finally, he evaluated the outcome of engagement, using such factors as the casualties on both sides, the achievement (or not) of the objective, and the loss of territory (when the defeated army was forced to retreat). The measured outcome of the battle gives us an estimate of the ratio of combat powers of the two armies, because we expect that an army with a greater battle power will win, and the greater is its power in relation to the opponent, the more favorable will the outcome be to the winner.

Dupuy now has an equation with three known quantities (the ratios of combat powers, of force strengths, and of modifying factors) and one unknown (the ratio of combat efficiencies). It is a simple matter to solve it for the unknown quantity, and we have our estimate of the relative combat efficiency (relative to the enemy, because we can only estimate the ratio of the two quantities—this is Tolstoy's x/y).

The results are striking. The Germans consistently outperformed the Allies in the ability to wage combat. If we assign 1 to the average combat efficiency of the British, the American efficiency was 1.1 and German 1.45. In other words, if the British wanted to get an even chance at winning a battle against the Germans, they had to bring 45 percent more troops (or arm them more heavily in the same proportion). Americans had to mass a third as many troops as Germans to have a 50:50 chance of victory. Dupuy also calculated average estimated efficiencies for all the U.S., British, and German divisions that participated in multiple engagements. There was a significant amount of variation between individual divisions. For example, the best German division, Herman-Hoering Panzer-Parachute, was almost twice as good as the worst, the 29th Panzer. Despite this variation, the overall difference between the American and German combat efficiencies was very clear. If we remove the worst German division and the best American division, there would be no overlap. Apart from these two outliers, each German division was better than any American one.

This result is very believable, because anybody who read on the history of World War II knows that the Germans fought very well in it. However, it is one thing to have a qualitative impression of something, and a very different thing to have a quantitative estimate of the same thing, based on cold, hard numbers. Science thrives on numbers.

But it is not just quantification that is interesting about Dupuy's work. During the last several decades, history has been rapidly quantified (there is even a new scientific branch of history, called *cliometrics*—from *Clio*, Muse of history, and *metrikos*, "measure"), and many kinds of numeric data are now available. What's interesting is the particular quantity that Dupuy succeeded in measuring. Many people would probably think that "fighting spirit" is somehow soft and "squishy." We've already seen that most mainstream philosophers of history rejected theories such as that of Ibn Khaldun as "softening of the fiber" or "mystical explanations." Fighting spirit would surely fall under the same category, in the thinking of these scholars. The best rebuttal to such criticisms is to show that you can measure the quantity by applying standard statistical methods to data. The success of Dupuy in quantifying combat efficiencies of Germans, Americans, and British during World War II shows that the critics are wrong. Consistency among national estimates of combat efficiencies for different divisions shows that the statistically derived measures reflect some real property of the societies that produced these divisions. Also, I have only discussed the best data set analyzed by Dupuy. But he and others looked at other time periods and combatants. For example, it turns out that the Germans show a marked superiority over the Allies during World War I. The analysis of the Arab-Israeli wars indicates that the Israelis enjoyed a twofold advantage in combat efficiency ratings over the Egyptians, Syrians, and Jordanians. Remember that when Dupuy estimated combat efficiency he took into account any differences in weapon superiority, so it reflects the seemingly intangible qualities of these nations—such as the asabiyas of their armies.

This is very encouraging, but combat efficiency is only one aspect—the military one—of the overall asabiya of a society. Can we use scientific methods to quantify nonmilitary facets of the capacity for collective action? A very interesting and quite recent development in political science says yes. I now turn to the work of Robert Putnam and others on something they call "social capital."

Chapter 13

The Bowling Alley in History

Measuring the Decline of Social Capital

In 1993, Robert Putnam published *Making Democracy Work: Civic Traditions in Modern Italy.* "Social capital," as Putnam explains, "refers to features of social organization, such as trust, norms, and networks that can improve the efficiency of society by facilitating coordinated actions." Putnam's social capital is asabiya for modern democratic societies, with an emphasis on its nonmilitary aspects. Along with a growing number of professional scientists and lay readers, I applaud Putnam's work, but I prefer Ibn Khaldun's term *asabiya*, acknowledging as it does the long history of this particular approach to the understanding of human affairs.

In the 1970s, the Italian political system was reformed, with the center delegating unprecedented powers and resources to the new regional governments. The reform gave political scientists, such as Putnam, a wonderful opportunity to study how the political culture of a region affects the institutional performance of the regional government. What we have here is a kind of political experiment. The same structure of regional government is imposed in all different provinces of Italy, from Piemonte in the north to Calabria in the south. All regional governments are given similar amounts of funds. Political scientists then observe how well each government operates during the next two decades. Any differences they detect should be due to the political culture of the region.

How can one measure "institutional performance," that is, how well regions are governed? Asabiya (or social capital) is the key. However, capacity for collective action is a complex, multifaceted property of society, and therefore we cannot expect a single way to measure it perfectly.

Putnam and his co-workers, however, came beautifully close. They chose 12 indicators, ranging from measures of operation efficiency such as bureaucratic responsiveness and budget promptness to a quantification of services provided to the public, such as the number of daycare centers and family clinics. The researchers at first had doubts about whether these very different indicators would add up to a coherent set, in the sense that they would measure the same underlying property of the regional society. After they analyzed their data, however, they saw that different indicators were all telling pretty much the same story—if a region was high in one indicator, it was likely to be high in others. It seemed to them that the indicators were getting at some basic feature of social life, which meant that they could be combined into a single measure of institutional performance. Another indication that the combined measure got at something real was its temporal stability. Relative rankings of regions stayed pretty much the same for the period studied, from the early 1970s to the mid-1980s.

When Putnam and co-workers finished estimating the institutional performance for each Italian region, they saw a remarkable pattern. There was very strong north-south gradient in how well regions were governed. The regions in the Po Valley such as Emilia-Romagna and Lombardia were consistently at the top of rankings in institutional performance, whereas southern regions, such as Campania (the region around Naples), Calabria (the "toe" of the Italian boot), and Sicily were at the bottom.

Well before Putnam, and even before the Italian experiment in devolution of powers to regional governments, anthropologists knew that something was wrong with the society of the Italian south—the *Mezzogiorno*, as it is known in Italian. A particularly interesting study is that by the American anthropologist Edward Banfield, who spent a number of years in a southern Italian village during the 1950s and 1960s. In 1967, he published a book detailing his findings, *The Moral Basis of the Backward Society*. Banfield describes the extreme atomization of the southern Italian society, in which all cooperative efforts are limited to the smallest possible societal unit, the family. Relations even to such kin as cousins, and sometimes even grown-up siblings, are rife with distrust and lack of cooperation. Community-level cooperative efforts are virtually impossible. Banfield called this type of society "amoral familism," and defined its basic philosophy as this: "Maximize the material, short-run advantage of the nuclear family; assume that all others will do likewise." This is the philoso-phy of the knave, in the technical sense of the term that I introduced in Part I. No wonder, then, that the Mezzogiorno society cannot function as a society. Even calling it a *society* is misleading; it is really a conglomerate of atomized nuclear families.

Putnam's and other recent studies support and extend the anthropo-logical, locally focused observations of Banfield. Big differences exist between the Italian north and south in the degree of interpersonal trust and solidarity. Northern Italians are much more networked. The density of civic associations such as choral societies, hiking clubs, literary circles, and hunting clubs is much higher in the north than in Mezzogiorno. Interest in public issues and devotion to public causes follow the same pattern. In other words, the performance of regional governments is a part of a whole bundle of social variables, at the root of which lies the variation in social capital, in asabiya among the regions.

Institutional performance is, thus, not a cause, but an effect of the quantity of asabiya. Social capital sounds like something made of bricks and mortar, some kind of plant machinery, but insofar as it is analogous to asabiya it is something profoundly human.

What about that other familiar social phenomenon in southern Italy? The existence of criminal organizations in the region preceded Marlon Brando. Sicilian Mafia and its sister organizations, Neapolitan camorra and Calabrian 'ndrangheta, have been a continuous presence in Mezzogiorno, whereas the north does not have anything similar. Where did these criminal organizations come from and why do they persist? Social scientists (for example, Diego Gambetta) have argued that Mafia arises as a social response to the pervasive lack of trust. Where public trust is scarce, there is a high demand for protection. Mafiosi are private entre-preneurs who supply protection, no matter how inefficiently.

The disparity in economic development between the Italian north and south is striking. Today the south is rural and poor, whereas the north is urban, industrialized, and wealthy. Few people realize just how well off the Italian north is, because when we see economic statistics for Western Europe, they are typically broken down by country, rather than by regions. Italy as a whole is in the middle of the pack, but its northern regions, such as Lombardia and Emilia-Romagna, are at the very top of the list. The overall rank for Italy is pulled down by its poor Mezzogiorno. Yet only a century ago there was practically no wealth differential between the north and south.

What is particularly interesting is that the asabiya matrix was already in place in the north, even a century ago. Following Italian unification in 1860 and until 1920, big differences existed between the north and south in Putnam's measures of social capital such as membership in mutual-aid societies and cooperatives, and strength of national political parties. But there were no comparable differences in economic development. The economic trajectories of the north and south began diverging only after 1920. This observation suggests that the difference in social capital today is not simply a result of the north being wealthier and more developed. The causation actually goes the other way: The north is more economically developed *because* it has more social capital.

How is social capital translated into economic capital? Francis Fukuyama (of *The End of History* fame) argued recently in *Trust: The Social Virtues and the Creation of Prosperity* that social trust is a key factor in economic growth. The importance of the rise of the modern corporation for economic growth is rarely disputed. So too, few would doubt that when it comes to surviving in the highly competitive global economy, it is the large-scale business organizations—the giant international corporations—that do best. But the large size of these business entities is also a liability.

A corporation is in many ways organized as a specialized society. The larger the corporation, the harder it is to monitor the performance, and the more the management must rely on trust and norms. Giant companies, thus, cannot rely only on self-interest and coercion to motivate their members (that is, employees) to give their best performance. Fukuyama studied how corporations are organized in several different societies, such as the United States, Japan, Germany, Italy, and China, and how the country's culture, and following Putnam, particularly its social capital, affects the functioning of its business organizations. Fukuyama showed that only high-trust societies, such as the United States and Japan, provide the cultural matrix within which huge corporations could arise and prosper. For such companies to be viable, it is necessary that their employees share a high degree of generalized trust (that is, not only trust toward their immediate co-workers, bosses, and underlings, but general trust that employees they do not know will do the right thing). Ironically enough, although externally corporations brutally compete in the free market, their internal workings rely not on market forces, but on group solidarity! This is one of the best-kept secrets in the economic sciences.

Just as you cannot construct a viable society, so you cannot put together a viable company from knaves alone. Asabiya is as important in large multinational corporations today as it was in Virginia in 1700 or North Africa in the fourteenth century. In modern Mezzogiorno, a business corporation could never get going, because potential partners knew that they would get cheated at the first opportunity—so what's the point of exposing oneself to it in the first place? Of course, a businessman could rely on the Mafia for contract enforcement, and the Mafia has in fact played this role. But the solution is imperfect because of large transaction costs. Fundamentally, the Mafia is a very inefficient organization that makes the societies in which it operates poorer. The Mafia itself suffers from the mutual distrust among its members. That is why police have long had the chore of fishing out the Mafiosi corpses from the Bay of Naples and quiet spots in New Jersey's Meadowlands.

Northern Italians have been much more successful in cooperating in business ventures. But here is a very interesting observation. Italian economic success came entirely from small and medium-sized companies, typically family owned and operated. Italy has not a single publicly held international corporation on the model of General Electric or Mitsubishi. The largest Italian company, Fiat, is still family owned. The typical successful Italian company is a family-owned business with perhaps a hundred employees in Milan or Bologna. They occupy a variety of niches from fashion to high-precision machinery, and they are extremely successful at what they do. But they cannot break into certain international markets because they lack the advantage of size. And they cannot grow to a large size, because the Italians, even northern ones, can cooperate only in medium-sized groups. Is this why northern Italians historically could not get beyond medium-sized states?

WHEN TRYING TO UNDERSTAND THE amoral familism of the Italian south, Edward Banfield drew an explicit contrast with the vibrant civic culture of a small Midwestern American town in the 1950s, a social group with which he was intimately familiar. Banfield's observations echo in a remarkable way those of Alexis de Tocqueville. We have already had a chance to consult Tocqueville's study of the civic life in America. But Tocqueville also traveled in Naples and Sicily as a young man, before he went to America, and in the long essay he wrote describing the trip he remarked on the culture of distrust and duplicity that pervaded the southern Italian society. It is remarkable how stable this particular manifestation of asabiya (or, rather, lack of it) has been in that region.

Two hundred years ago, both America and the Mezzogiorno were pretty much in the same position with respect to each other as they are today—the first flowing with an abundance of asabiya or social capital in the form of a myriad functioning national and local institutions, the other suffering from an almost complete lack of such networking. Both places industrialized and modernized in the intervening two centuries. The economic and social changes have been enormous. Yet, at a certain basic level, that of social cohesion and capacity for collective action, neither society changed that much. This is not to say that the asabiya of a society is set in stone; just that it changes very slowly, on the time scale of centuries.

The roots of the Italian north-south divide must go back a long time. Robert Putnam sees it going back to the eleventh century, when a centralized Norman kingdom was established in southern Italy and when independent communes began organizing themselves in the north. In the north, the more democratic governments of the city communes in Florence, Venice, Bologna, and Milan nurtured civic spirit. In the south, according to Putnam, a succession of authoritarian governments stifled social capital.

Putnam is correct that the north-south divide existed at least a thousand years ago. To locate the actual point when the divide arose, however, it is necessary to go another millennium back in time, to the Roman Empire. In Chapter 11 we saw how an asabiya black hole developed in the core region of the Roman Empire—the Italian Peninsula and Sicily—but not in the Po Valley. After the collapse of the empire, northern Italy was settled by several waves of Germanic immigrants, most notably the Langobards/Lombards during the sixth century. These immigrants came from high-asabiya societies, and their influx reinforced the north-south divide that formed under the empire. Because no metaethnic frontier formed in northern Italy, its inhabitants never developed high asabiya necessary for building a large state (before the Italian unification of the nineteenth century, which was discussed in Chapter 11). As a result, only medium-sized states developed there, starting with the Lombard kingdom in the seventh century, and then the states built by Milan, Florence, and Venice during the Middle Ages. But even such medium levels of asabiya were much more than what was available in the south, where no internal attempts at state building have developed since the fall of the Roman Empire. The Norman kingdom in southern Italy, after all, was kept cohesive by the high asabiya of the Norman invaders. When they assimilated and lost their group solidarity, other influxes of asabiya were necessary to maintain centralized government in the region.

IT IS A STARTLING IDEA THAT certain cultural differences between Lombardians and Calabrians of the twenty-first century might actually be due to events that occurred two thousand years ago. Yet we know that asabiya changes very slowly. Two or three centuries on a very intense metaethnic frontier seems to be the minimum time needed to nurture high asabiya. World empires often last a millennium, so the decline of asabiya is equally slow. Asabiya black holes can persist for centuries, and why not for millennia, if no frontier happens to hit upon it?

This raises an important problem, perhaps the most important: Is understanding the life cycle of imperial nations any real use to us now? I have developed the theory of cliodynamics explicitly for agrarian societies and tested it with historical data—but can the theory be extended to modern times we live in? Can it help us understand the politics of today, and even perhaps help us avoid some of the mistakes that our predecessors committed? Let us look at one specific attempt to apply one of the theories that we discussed to our present social problems.

In his book *The Great Wave*, David Hackett Fischer traces four secular waves of the European history in the last millennium. We have already discussed the first two waves. The first one is the high Middle Ages (the integrative phase) followed by the crisis of the fourteenth century (the disintegrative phase). The second one is the Renaissance (integrative phase), followed by the crisis of the seventeenth century (disintegrative phase).

The third wave is the Enlightenment (integrative phase) followed by the age of revolution (disintegrative phase).

The fourth wave, argued Fischer, is what we are living through now. The integrative phase started with the equilibrium of the Victorian era (second half of the nineteenth century) and continued through most of the twentieth century. The last half of this phase, and especially since 1960, was characterized by persistent price inflation, something that occurred in every cycle. The disintegrative phase has begun in the late twentieth century.

Fischer holds that the same majestic rhythm Western societies marched to continues to resonate to this very day. His critics were harsh. Paul Krugman was one of them. His critique acknowledged that Fischer is on to something—the empirical evidence for secular cycles is unassailable. But Krugman rightly criticized Fischer for his overly cavalier treatment of modernity. One cannot assume that the social and economic forces that operated in agrarian societies to produce secular cycles would continue behaving in the same way today. One cannot disregard the seismic changes that have occurred during the last century or two. We live in a very different world from that inhabited by the Romans or the Normans, or even the Europeans of the Napoleonic era.

Food production typically employed 90 percent of the population of agrarian societies. Before the industrial revolution, population growth during every secular cycle was stopped when people ran out of things to eat. Today, however, England's population is 10 times greater than at the peaks of the fourteenth and seventeenth centuries, and this population is fed from a fraction of the area that was cultivated during those peaks. The English, like Americans, get some of their food from abroad, but the main reason there is no famine in England or any developed nation today is that the productivity of an acre of cropland is now more than ten times what it was in the Middle Ages.

The green revolution, which increased crop yields in temperate countries, is not over yet. We are now seeing a similar change in the tropics. Brazil is poised to flood world markets with cheap food. However, whole regions in modern equatorial Africa continue to experience widespread famines.

The same imbalance exists with epidemics. AIDS had the potential to be another Black Death, if not for the advances in molecular biology and medicine. If not for molecular genetics, we would not even know why we are dying. But just knowing the cause (even without a cure) allowed societies to control the spread of the epidemic. In Africa, AIDS did result in a pandemic—that is still growing. In fact, several African countries have experienced during the late twentieth century what appears to be a classical demographic-structural collapse, in which overpopulation led to state breakdown and bloody, even genocidal civil wars (for instance, Somalia and Rwanda).

The prevalence of liberal democracy today also distinguishes us from the agrarian societies studied by historians. At least in theory, democracy should channel intra-elite competition into less-violent forms. By allowing orderly and peaceful transfer of power, modern democratic societies should prove to be more resistant to state collapse. However, because true liberal democracies have been around only for a century or so (it is only in the early twentieth century that the suffrage began encompassing more than 50 percent of the adult population), they have not yet been around long enough to experience a secular cycle.

The world has changed. Several cause-effect chains, operating in agrarian societies, have been completely ruptured, or at least transformed in a big way by the industrial revolution. On the other hand, many of the economic and social trends during the last half-century or so have been moving together in highly suggestive ways. For example, we know that twentieth century was an era of inflation, which came after a period of relatively stable prices (Fischer's equilibrium of the Victorian era). Most people tend to explain persistent inflation as just another characteristic of modernity, but every previous secular wave, without exceptions, saw a "price revolution" that ended up in crisis.

A rise in crime rates has afflicted Western countries since 1960. It has been observed not only in America, but also in Great Britain, Germany, Italy, and the Scandinavian countries. This rising trend is especially baffling to the experts because for at least a century before 1960, crime statistics in all of these countries had been declining. Could it be that crime statistics reflect an increase of some sort of social pressure? In past secular cycles, we typically see a rise in crime rates in the pre-crisis period.

Another important indicator is the degree of economic inequality. Again, the 1960s is a breakpoint: Before that date, inequality was declining in the United States; after that date, it started increasing. In the decades right after World War II, a huge gap did not exist between the salaries of common workers and the compensation of CEOs. Adjusted for inflation, the incomes of the lowest 20 percent of workers have been stagnating and actually declining since 1970. The Matthew principle is in full operation.

Moreover, the official inflation rate, calculated by Bureau of Labor Statistics, does not tell the whole story. Many big-item purchases, most notably the prices of homes and the cost of education and health care, have been growing much faster than inflation.

The trends in education are particularly revealing because it is one of the best indicators of intra-elite competition. During the twentieth century, ever-increasing numbers of school graduates in America went to college. By the late twentieth century, just finishing college was not enough to enter the increasingly more competitive job market, and the number of college graduates earning Ph.D.s started increasing. The "price" of a Ph.D. in terms of years necessary for completion has been growing even faster. Between 1967 and 1995, the average length of time until finishing a Ph.D. increased in physical science from 6 to 8.4 years, and in social sciences from 7.7 to 10.5 years. In the humanities, the average time to a Ph.D. is 12 years, and in education 19.9 years!

These trends are signs of a credentialing crisis, which reflects increased intra-elite competition—more and more is required of adults to maintain familiar standards of comfort. Similar trends have been observed during pre-crisis phases of previous secular cycles. At the University of Paris, it took eight years to earn a Doctorate degree in the thirteenth century (five years to obtain a Bachelor degree, then three more to achieve the Doctorate). In the fourteenth century, it took 16 years to earn a Doctorate. The cost of education increased much faster than inflation in sixteenth-century France. Enrollments in Oxford and Cambridge peaked just before the Great Revolution, and then declined during the eighteenth century.

Finally, there has been a troubling trend in the American asabiya. Robert Putnam asserts in *Bowling Alone* that at least since the times of Tocqueville, the American society has always enjoyed large stocks of social capital. But, beginning in 1960, several indicators of social capital started declining. Putnam writes, "We have become increasingly disconnected from family, friends, neighbors, and social structures, whether PTA, church, recreation clubs, political parties, or bowling leagues." Thirty years ago, people invited friends for dinner twice as often as today. Social trust also seems to be declining. Certainly, the proportion of people saying that they trust the government in Washington has been steadily declining—from between 70 and 80 percent in the late 1950s to between 30 and 40 percent in the 1990s. Forty-five percent of Americans believe little or nothing in their daily newspapers, up from 16 percent two decades ago. The message of *Bowling Alone* is one of the increasing isolation of individuals, alone in cars, alone at work, divorced, bowling under fluorescent lights alone. Surely that is a sign of impending danger for any society.

If this trend of social disintegration does not correctly foretell more trouble, it will be because new kinds of integration are now at work. My last chapter is a hopeful one about how the trend toward greater communication and interconnectedness might affect our secular cycle, might change what asabiya means geographically, and might indeed change the very idea of what empire is.

Chapter 14

The End of Empire?

How the Mobile Phone Is Changing Cliodynamics

In 1918, as the victors of the First World War were dismantling the Habsburg and Ottoman empires, while revolutions were tearing apart Russia and Germany, many thought that the age of empires was over. The death of imperialism was next proclaimed in the 1960s when England, France and other European colonial powers shed their overseas empires. When the Soviet Union collapsed in 1991, commentators of international affairs held another wake for empire. Is this the end of history? Or at least the end of the cycles of empires? Or are rumors of empire demise exaggerated? Will the insights from cliodynamics about historical empires remain as purely academic knowledge, fit to be enjoyed only by armchair historians, sitting snug by the fire and sipping an after-dinner cognac? Or do these insights have relevance to international politics today?

Recently, there has been much discussion of whether the United States today is an empire that can and should be compared with imperial powers of the past. Empire seems to be in fashion, even if some (generally those with left-leaning politics) hate the idea, whereas others (such as neoconservatives) love it. According to Charles Krauthammer, a frequent contributor to the neoconservative *Weekly Standard*, "We are not just any hegemon. We run a uniquely benign imperium."

In 2001, a team of scholars, led by former U.S. House of Representatives Speaker Newt Gingrich (who was trained as a historian), was commissioned by the Pentagon to write a report on historical empires, and make recommendations on how the U.S. could sustain its military and political predominance in the world. Fundamental issues were addressed such as whether the U.S. even was an empire; and if so, is that good or bad? And, most interestingly, the question was raised whether history offers useful lessons for America. The report concluded, "If we can take lessons from history it is this: For the U.S. to sustain its predominance it must remain militarily dominant, but it must also maintain its preeminence across other pillars of power." Not everybody agrees. A classical scholar, Bernard Knoz, told Maureen Dowd of the *New York Times*, "Empires are pretty well dead; their day is gone." The British historian Niall Fergusson, author of the 2003 book *Empire*, said, "The technological and economic differences between modernity and premodernity are colossal." Finally, officials of the George W. Bush administration insist that America is not an empire.

According to my definition, an empire is a large multiethnic territorial state with complex power structure. Nobody would dispute that the U.S. is a large territorial state. As to its multiethnic composition, Chapter 2 discussed that the American melting pot had definite racial boundaries. As a result, the modern U.S. includes many minorities—Native Americans, African Americans, and Latinos, to name only three. Certain political scientists have recently argued that some large minorities, most notably the Latinos, are resistant to the assimilation of the formerly dominant WASP (White Anglo-Saxon Protestant) culture. A particularly interesting case is the Chicanos (Mexican Americans), a growing and fairly cohesive subculture. Chicanos do not consider themselves to be immigrants to the U.S., because the areas where they are numerically strong were conquered by the U.S. from Mexico in the mid-nineteenth century. Chicanos, it is claimed, have different values, stressing more the extended family and less freedom and democracy than would be the case for the mainstream U.S. culture. Such claims might be overstated, and have been vociferously disputed. Nevertheless, they serve to remind us of the limits of the melting pot metaphor—the U.S. is not a monoethnic nation, even if we discount recent immigrants.

The U.S. also has complex power structure, especially when we consider it as a global power. Although the internal arrangements of the U.S. are reasonably simple—it directly controls the 50 states, the District of Columbia, and dependent territories (such as Puerto Rico and a number of Pacific islands), its external influence reaches across the globe. It militarily occupies Kosovo, Afghanistan, and Iraq. It has a strong degree of indirect control via heavy military presence (for example, in South Korea) or economic subsidies (Israel). Given the economic and diplomatic help that Israel gets from the U.S., it is essentially an American client state. The U.S. wields a great deal of political control by means of such organizations as NATO. Finally, using a variety of overt and covert means, the U.S. has been largely successful in installing friendly governments, traditionally in Latin America, more recently in countries such as Georgia and Ukraine. As one Latin American joke goes, "Do you know why there are no coup d'états in America? Because they don't have American embassies."

Such a complex structure of power is a hallmark of a typical empire, especially during its expansion phase. Republican Rome, for example, had its core territory inhabited by voting citizens, colonies peopled with Romans and Latins, territories inhabited by nonvoting citizens, allied cities, and client states such as Massilia in southern Gaul. The degree of political control declined from the center to the periphery. With time, however, the periphery was more closely integrated with the center.

Some might object that the U.S. cannot be an empire because it is democratically governed. However, not all empires have emperors. There were democratically governed empires such as the Athenian and the British. The Roman Empire under the Republic was governed collectively by several hundred noble and wealthy senatorial families. The political arrangements by which a state is governed are irrelevant to the definition of empire.

Retired Lt. Gen. William E. Odom, who headed the National Security Agency in the 1980s, and Robert Dujarric, a Council on Foreign Relations Hitachi fellow, estimate in their book, *America's Inadvertent Empire*, that the American empire "comprises 17 percent of the world's population but controls about 70 percent of the gross world product. Because nearly all of the developed countries are included, the network's share of science, technology, and corporate resources is closer to 90 percent of the world's total."

So what can the theories that we discussed in this book tell us about the dynamics of the world's current hegemonic empire? As we have seen, what makes empires function are the qualities of their core nations, of which the most important is asabiya. American asabiya might be on a decline, if recent trends in social capital are good indicators, but the U.S. still has an abundance when compared to other large contemporary countries. The response of the American nation to the terrorist attacks of September 11, 2001 is clear evidence that the U.S. is highly capable of collective action. Most tellingly, there was no attempt by the mainstream opposition party, the Democrats, to use the events of 9/11 and the subsequent course of military operations in Afghanistan and Iraq as a means of political infighting against the ruling Republicans, even though the Bush administration arguably committed a number of grave errors.

The obverse side of internal cohesion, in fact one of the important factors sustaining it, is the "us versus them" mentality. Observers of current American politics, especially those from outside the U.S. (from where such matters are easier to see), have commented frequently on what they often characterize as the nationalistic, even xenophobic, strain in America, which has become particularly apparent in the post-9/11 era, but was discernible even before. The British journalist and writer Anatol Lieven, now at Washington's Carnegie Endowment for International Peace, recently argued that American patriotism has two faces. The first is the "American Creed," a civic ideology that espouses liberty, democracy, and the rule of law. A powerful integrative ideology with elements of messianism has always been extremely important in the success of world empires. The Byzantines had their Orthodox Christianity, the Arabs had Islam, the French had *la mission civilisatrice*, and the Soviets had Marxism-Leninism. The American Creed impels its adherents to extend the Western values and Western democracy to the whole of the world. Much is admirable in this ideology, but there is also a dark side. Many nations (not just their rulers, but the population at large), most notably in the Muslim world (but not only there), do not desire to be "civilized" in this way. They have their own culture and traditions and would prefer to be in control over which elements of Western civilization they adopt and integrate into their own, and which they reject.

The second aspect of the American patriotism is what Lieven calls "Jacksonian nationalism." President Andrew Jackson (1767–1845) is best known for his victory against the British at New Orleans in 1815. But he achieved prominence as an Indian fighter and leader of local militias on the Tennessee frontier. Most of his campaigns were against the Cherokee, Creek, and other Indians. Lieven argues that "although 'Jacksonian nationalism' contains other important elements, including nativism, anti-elitism, anti-intellectualism, and dislike of the Northeast, a strong sense of White identity, and violent hostility to other races, was long at its core."

In 1831, during Jackson's presidency, the Cherokee Nation appealed to the U.S. Supreme Court against new laws passed by the state of Georgia, which laid the basis for the Indians' expulsion from the lands they held long before European settlers appeared in America. These laws were in violation of several treaties with U.S. governments, and a majority of the Supreme Court, led by Chief Justice John Marshall, ruled in favor of Cherokees.

As Lieven relates, "To this Jackson reputedly replied, 'John Marshall has made his decision; now let him enforce it.' Although the president may not actually have said this, these words certainly reflected the spirit in which he acted. The U.S. government refused to defend the Cherokees against Georgia, Jackson warned them that they had no choice but to leave, and within a few years (although after Jackson himself left the office) they were driven out of their ancestral lands onto the 'Trail of Tears' to Oklahoma, on which a great many died of disease and malnutrition."

Fast forward to the twenty-first century. In the aftermath of the terrorist attack of September 11, 2001, the radio show host Michael Savage, after referring to Arabs as "nonhumans," said "conversion to Christianity is the only thing that probably can turn them into human beings." As Lieven reports, he then declared: "Smallpox in a blanket, which the U.S. Army gave to the Cherokee Indians on their long march to the West, was nothing to what I'd like to see done to these people."

The comparison that Lieven draws between the struggle of settlers against Indians on the American frontier and the clash between U.S.-led Western and Muslim civilizations fits with the principles of cliodynamics. I have argued in Chapter 2 that the origins of the American nation and the source of its high asabiya are found in the settler-Indian frontier during the seventeenth, eighteenth, and nineteenth centuries. The frontier is long gone, but cultural idioms and techniques of dealing with challenges are being adapted to the new challenges and adversaries.

ON MARCH 25, 1957, in a spectacular Renaissance palazzo in Rome, six European nations—France, West Germany, Italy, Belgium, the Netherlands, and Luxembourg—signed the treaty establishing the

European Economic Community, the precursor of the European Union. A glance at maps of Europe in 1957 and A.D. 800 shows that the combined territory of the six founding members traces almost precisely the empire of Charlemagne. The symbolism is heavy. It was in Rome, on Christmas Day of A.D. 800, that the pope crowned Charlemagne as emperor. Is the E.U. a new kind of empire?

In terms of its size, multiethnic population, and complex power structure the E.U. fits my definition. Furthermore, during the half century of its existence, the E.U. has been aggressively expanding, adding most recently six central European and two Mediterranean countries during the writing of this book. The core state of the E.U., Germany, meanwhile gobbled up former East Germany in 1990. However, all expansion to date was accomplished entirely by peaceful and consensual means. Historical empires do not always need to conquer new territories. As discussed previously, there were voluntary admissions to the Roman and Russian empires. Many medieval European states grew by dynastic unions. Still, the entirely peaceful expansion of the E.U. is unprecedented in world history—ultimately, all historical empires had to counter external or internal threats with force. Member states have used armed force, as the United Kingdom in its 1982 war with Argentina over the Falkland Islands, but the E.U. as a whole has not done it—so far? The Europeans are moving in the direction of creating a unified military force, but we will have to wait and see whether the E.U. will prove capable of using the force when threatened. More importantly, how strong is the European asabiya? Will it motivate people to sacrifice their comforts, treasure, or blood for the sake of the unified Europe? So far, the main financial burden of empire has been borne largely by the Germans. It is customary for core nations of empires to bear the main brunt of its costs, but how long will the Germans consent to this state of affairs? Will the years of slow economic growth and high unemployment, which as of the time of this writing show no signs of ending, eventually sap the willingness of the Germans to sacrifice for the sake of the dream of a powerful united Europe?

Unlike the E.U., China fits the definition of empire perfectly. Its conquest of Tibet and willingness to indefinitely suppress Uigur separatism in Xinjang suggest no aversion to the use of force. Having regained Hong Kong, the Chinese are now bending all their efforts to bringing Taiwan into the fold. It also seems that the Chinese are currently extending their economic influence all over the globe—buying ore from Australia and oil from Sudan and Venezuela. China has begun throwing its considerable weight around in ASEAN, the Association of Southeast Asian Nations. North Korea is essentially a client state of China.

Between 1978, when the Chinese leadership began implementing economic reforms, and 2003, China has quadrupled its gross domestic product and is now the second largest economy in the world (measured on a purchasing power parity basis). If China can maintain economic growth at the same rate for another decade, it will surpass the U.S. and become the largest world economy. Economic power inevitably brings in its wake political and military power. If current trends continue, China will become the next world hegemon—a prospect that must be of concern to the American political and military establishment.

Then there is the core state of the former Soviet Empire, Russia—down but perhaps not yet out. The place to watch as an indicator of what will happen to Russia as a great power is Chechnya.

In 1996, after two years of conflict, Russia signed a peace treaty with the Chechen separatists. The so-called Khasavyurt Agreement was essentially an admission of Russian defeat that gave Chechnya de-facto independence. The Russians were sick and tired of the conflict, and basically wished Chechnya and the Chechens to go away and leave them alone. However, internal developments within Chechnya made such a course of events impossible. First, the victors started fighting among themselves. The nationalist faction lost to the Islamists, who included many Al Qaida immigrants from outside Chechnya, such as the notorious Jordanian warlord Khattab. Later, after the second war began, several nationalist leaders went over to the Russian side. Islamists were primarily interested in Chechnya as a bridgehead for building an Islamic caliphate that would stretch from the Black to Caspian Sea and up to the Middle Volga.

The economics of the newly independent republic could not support the large Chechen population even before the conflict (which was one of the important causes of the war); and even that meager economic base was greatly damaged by the war. Fund transfers from the outside, both from Russia (bizarrely, the Russian government continued to transmit pensions to elderly Chechens!) and from the Islamic foundations from the Arab world and elsewhere, were not enough. Soon bands of armed Chechens began raiding southern Russia for cattle. Others siphoned oil from the Baku-Novorossiysk pipeline, until the Russians built a spur bypassing Chechnya. Yet others robbed trains. A particularly repulsive business was slavery. Non-Chechens were captured outside the bandit republic and transported to Chechnya. Those who had wealthy relatives were held for ransom, whereas most were put to work in agriculture and construction. Some people were lured into North Caucuses from as far away as St. Petersburg and Moscow with promises of a lucrative job. It is not known how many people were enslaved, but the count is in the many thousands.

In 1999, as a first step in expanding their bridgehead, the Islamists invaded Daghestan, a North Caucasian republic within the Russian Federation situated to the east of Chechnya. At the same time, the leaders of the new jihad, the Chechen Basayev and the Jordanian Khattab, organized several explosions in Russia that targeted multi-apartment buildings. Four buildings were blown up, including two in Moscow, killing nearly 300 men, women, and children. The Islamists' intent was apparently to terrify the Russians and break their will to resist. If so, they miscalculated.

The Chechens pushed all the wrong buttons. It is remarkable how closely they made themselves fit the image of that "other," in the struggle against whom the Russian nation was forged in the sixteenth and seventeenth centuries—the Tatars. The Chechens were not bow-wielding horse riders, true—they rode Jeeps, and wielded Kalashnikovs and rocket-propelled grenades. But they were the Muslim threat from the south, and professed a particularly aggressive brand of Islam, the Wahhabism (the sect to which Bin Laden belongs). They raided the Russians with the purpose of robbing them, and they turned Russians into slaves. Several captives of the Chechens managed to escape the mountains, and millions of Russians watched stories about their tribulations on television.

Across the centuries, as discussed in Chapter 2, the collective response by Russians to military pressure was to strike back and conquer the source of trouble. Ermak and his Cossacks went across the Urals to stop the Tatar raiding at the source. In fact, Chechnya was conquered by Russia in the nineteenth century precisely for the same reason. Russians did not care to rule impoverished mountains inhabited by barbarous and disagreeable highlanders. But when the Orthodox Christian Kingdom of Georgia, pressed by the Turks, asked to be admitted within the Russian Empire, the Chechens found themselves sitting on top of the communications highway between central Russia and Georgia. It was natural that the tribal high-landers would turn to robbing passing caravans and kidnapping people for ransom. One of the best novels by the Russian writer Alexander Pushkin, *The Prisoner of Caucases*, relates the story of a Russian officer, captured and held for ransom by the highlanders, and how he escaped. Almost two centuries later, a Russian movie of the same title retold the story, but with modern characters.

I am not saying that the Russian reaction in 1999 could have been accurately predicted ahead of time. On one hand, culture is conservative, and a social group tends to respond the same way they always have, just as Anatol Lieven suggested today's Americans react the same way toward Arabs as early American settlers did toward Native Americans. It is as if such behaviors are written into cultural genes. A more extreme case is the apparent inability of southern Italians to cooperate ever since the fall of the Roman Empire. On the other hand, cultures change. Between the thirteenth and sixteenth centuries, the Tatars lost their asabiya, while the asabiya of the Russians in contrast increased.

Here then is why I consider Chechnya such an important indicator of the future trajectory of the Russian state—and an empirical test of the asabiya theory. If the Russians succeed in reincorporating the Chechens within the Russian federation, my guess is that Russia will regain its status as world empire. If not, and a Caucasian caliphate expands to the Middle Volga, it will most likely mean the end of Russia as we know it. There is a third possibility—the collapse of the old Muscovite core and the rise of a new imperial nation in the southern borderlands of Russia. Interestingly enough, there has been a rejuvenation of the Cossack subculture since the Soviet Union collapsed. New Cossack movements are particularly active in the southern region of Russia just north of the Caucases. Will the twenty-first century see another Ermak, crossing the Caucases with an army of trusty companions, on his way to conquest and riches?

The age of empires is not over—although the age of emperors may be. Even the least democratic empire, China, is governed collectively rather than by a monarch. The trajectories of two of the potential empires, the E.U. and Russia, are very hard to predict. Unfortunately, the trajectories of the U.S. and China are all too predictable. Most serious political scientists expect an escalating geopolitical competition between the two. We can only hope that this competition will take the relatively benign route of a cold war.

WHEN GHAITH ABDUL-AHAD, a reporter with the U.K. newspaper *Guardian*, met the Yemeni *jihadi* ("Islamic holy warrior"), the jihadi was praying in a room in one of Fallujah's safe houses. It was early November 2004, during the street battles in Fallujah between coalition forces and rebels led by Abu-Musab al Zarqawi.

"The room was half-lit, the walls were bare except for one picture of Mecca. The only piece of furniture was a prayer mat in the middle of the room twisted at an angle to face the south. A Kalashnikov rifle and an ammunition pouch were laid against the wall.... On the mattress sat a man with a small Qur'an in one hand and a set of prayer beads in the other. Sometimes his voice would be drowned out by the sounds of explosions rocking the city. As he finished his prayers he stood up, held his hands high and started praying: 'Oh God, you who made the Prophet come out victorious in his wars against the infidels, make us come out victorious in our war against America. Oh God, defeat America and its allies everywhere. Oh God, make us worthy of your religion.'

"The man—tall, thin with a dark complexion, black eyes and a thin beard—arrived in Fallujah six weeks ago. He spent a few days sharing a room with other fighters until they were distributed among the mujahideen units in the city. He was with a group of the Tawhid and Jihad stationed in the west of Fallujah in the Jolan district where heavy fighting has been raging for the last two days.... Anxiously waiting for the Americans outside a makeshift bunker, he told his story. He said he was not here because he loved death as death but because he perceived martyrdom as the most pure way in which to worship God."

The jihadi was a Yemeni religious student, who had been studying Islamic law for six years, while working as a minibus driver to support a pregnant wife and five children. He first tried to come to Iraq to fight the Americans in 2003, but was turned back at the airport, by the Yemeni police.

"For a year he went back to his studies and his family, forgetting Iraq and jihad. But the scandal of prisoner abuse at Abu Ghraib woke him up, he said. His wife, a religious student working on her Master's thesis, urged him to leave everything and go for jihad in Iraq. 'She told me they are doing this to the men, imagine what is happening to the women now. Imagine your sisters and me being raped by the infidel American pigs.' He suddenly realized his mistake, he said, and spent the night crying.

"The next day he borrowed money for another journey—one that he described as his last. He was given a contact name in Aleppo, a city in the north of Syria, who would arrange for him to be smuggled across the border. 'I didn't tell anyone, I just told my wife. I borrowed a car from a friend and we went out to do some shopping. She bought me two trousers and a shirt. We went then to my father's house. I told my mother, forgive me if I had done anything wrong. She said, why? I told her nothing, I just want forgiveness from you and dad. She asked me if I was going to Baghdad. I said no. She hugged me and cried.'

"The fighter told how he went back home and sat with his wife and children, who had no idea that this was their last dinner with their father. 'My favorite daughter came and sat in my lap and slept there. She opened her eyes and said, 'Daddy, I love you.' Weeping as he spoke, he said: 'You know these memories are the work of the devil trying to soften my heart and bring me back home. The only place I am going from here is heaven.'"

TODAY THE MOST VIOLENT CLASH of civilizations occurs on the metaethnic frontiers of Islam with the Western, Orthodox, Hindu, and Sinic civilizations. Previously, I took a brief look at how this civilizational conflict is influencing the internal cohesion of the core states of the Western and Orthodox civilizations, the U.S. and Russia. But a metaethnic frontier exerts its transformative role on the asabiyas of people on both sides of the fault line. Just as the Americans and Russians feel the pressure from aggressive Islamist groups, the Muslim societies are also under enormous stress from other World metaethnic communities. It is not surprising that the metaethnic frontiers in Kashmir, the Balkans, Northern Caucasus, and Xinjang are a constant source of conflict. As the story of the Yemeni in Fallujah reminds us, however, the hottest spot of trouble is in the Middle East.

Until the nineteenth century, the metaethnic frontiers between the West and Islam were situated far from the core of the Muslim world. But when the Ottoman Empire began crumbling, the Western great powers started encroaching on this core. Egypt became a protectorate of Britain in 1882, and Iraq and Syria became the British and French zones in the aftermath of World War I. From 1920, hundreds of thousands of Jewish immigrants flowed into Palestine. In 1948, the state of Israel was established by the U.N.

Although Israel is not a Christian nation, the Arabs and other Muslims perceive it as a solid part of the West and, even more narrowly, an outpost of American imperialism in the Middle East. This perception is fed by the massive economic aid to Israel, the powerful pro-Israeli lobby in the American politics, and the heavy diplomatic and symbolic assistance that Israel gets from the U.S. The invasion of Iraq by the American and British troops in 2003 further solidified Arab identification of Israel as a part of the West.

The Arabs in Palestine have, thus, been subjected to the transforming influence of a metaethnic frontier for about a century. The results are easy to see. There is now a distinct Palestinian identity, where there was none prior to the massive immigration of European Jews into Palestine. The asabiya of Palestinians has increased enormously.

During the first Arab-Israeli war of 1947–48, Palestinians were unable to cooperate effectively against the Jews. In fact, on several occasions Palestinian factions fought battles with each other. Despite their advantage of numbers, the Arabs lost the war.

Some two generations later, the situation has radically changed. In 2000, the Arabs won their first war against Israel, when the Shiite fighters of Hezbollah forced the withdrawal of Israeli forces from Lebanon. But an even more striking development is the rise of the suicide bomber. Martyrdom as the most pure way in which to worship God, using the words of the Yemeni fighter in Fallujah, has been in the cultural repertoire of Islam for centuries. So it is not surprising that the struggle of the Arabs against "Jews and Crusaders" takes this form. But the massive numbers of volunteers for suicide missions is new. It is also a phenomenon largely restricted to the Middle East. Suicide bombing elsewhere is nowhere near on the same massive scale. In the North Caucases, where Islamists have attempted to imitate the Palestinian suicide bombing campaign, they found that they do not have a source of ready volunteers, after they ran out of the "black widows," the wives of slain mujahideen fighters. The Chechen architects of the suicide bombing campaign started using unwitting accomplices (bombs were exploded by handlers using remotes), and coerced women into "volunteering," as the interviews with a failed suicide bomber Zarema Mujakhoeva indicate. The interviews with failed bombers in Palestine, or mujahideen fighters in Iraq, like the Yemeni interviewed by Ghaith Abdul-Ahad, indicate a very different kind of commitment (although, no doubt, some suicide bombers in Palestine were also victims of coercion).

The rise of suicide bombing is not due to some sort of fanaticism supposedly inherent in Islam. The Arab societies in the vicinity of Israel have been transformed by a century-long exposure to the metaethnic frontier. Militant organizations such as the Hezbollah or Hamas are a direct result of the frontier pressures. As the interview with the Yemeni fighter shows, not all jihad warriors are driven by the thirst for death—the portrayal of Islam as a religion of death is misleading. The Yemeni did not want to die; he wanted to go back home to see his newly born daughter. But a more powerful motive compelled him to fight the Americans. So strong was his thirst for justice, that he was willing to sacrifice his life. The Yemeni was a moralistic punisher, if a rather extreme version of the type.

The occupation of Iraq by the U.S. and allied forces expanded the zone of direct contact/conflict between the Western and Islamic metaethnic communities. It is now Americans who have to deal with Islamic martyrs, homegrown in Iraq as well as flocking from all over the Muslim world. Was the invasion wise? The theory—the American Creed—is that bringing democracy and the rule of law to the Middle East will transform the Arab societies there and place them on the road to freedom and prosperity. It might work.

The metaethnic frontier theory, however, predicts that the Western intrusion will eventually generate a counter-response, possibly in the form of a new theocratic caliphate, because that is the traditional way in which Islamic societies have responded to challenges from other civilizations. Such a response is not going to happen next year. Last time the West intruded in the Middle East was during the Age of Crusades. Two centuries passed from the First Crusade, which arrived in the Holy Land in 1099, to the rise of Saladin's Ayyubid dynasty in 1174. The Crusaders were expelled from their last stronghold of Acre in 1291.

On the other hand, the Western pressure on the Islamic societies of the Middle East dates at least to the occupation of Egypt by the British troops in 1882. The establishment of Israel in 1948 merely elevated it to new heights, and the second Iraq war increased the pressure to what might be an unbearable pitch for the Arabs. It is possible that the world changed so much from the days of Ibn Khaldun that his law of asabiya does not operate any longer. But is it wise to bet on it?

In *Pattern and Repertoire in History*, Bertrand Roehner and Tony Syme suggest that human societies have memories. When presented with challenges, they tend to reach into their collective memories for a response that worked before in similar situations, and then adapt it to the new challenge. They illustrate their idea with what they call the building blocks of the French revolution. It turns out that certain elements of the Great Revolution of 1789—the confrontation between the king and the Estates General, or the intervention of the Parisian population—recurred in the fourteenth, fifteenth, sixteenth, seventeenth, and eighteenth centuries. I commented on this recurrence in Chapters 8 and 9, when discussing how Parisian mobs intimidated the dauphins in 1358 and again in 1413. The parallels between the attitudes of Americans to the Cherokees in the nineteenth century, and Arabs in the twenty-first century, or the Russian response to the Chechen challenge evoking their interaction with the Tatars many centuries before, are other examples of the idea of social memory—cultural genes.

Surely history does have insights to offer us in understanding contemporary politics—this is after all not a new idea. On the other hand, there is no question that the world changed dramatically in the past two centuries, so any lessons that cliodynamic principles offer must be scrutinized in the light of specific significant events. As noted previously, modern societies have been freed from the fear of hunger. However, the Yemeni in Fallujah story illustrate another profound difference between the modern and agrarian societies.

When he heard about the events in Iraq, this jihadi was in Yemen more than a thousand miles away. In the agrarian era, a Yemeni would hear only confused rumors about the doings in Mesopotamia; today, he gets his news, blood and all, delivered into his living room, courtesy of modern technology and Al Jazeera.

Pre-industrial societies had their own "mass media." A face of the king on a coin was a powerful visual image that reached all his subjects who handled money, and played an important role in creating a national identity. The primate of a national church could instruct parish priests to deliver sermons on a specific topic, thus reaching multitudes of illiterate peasants. Still, important landmarks were passed when political pamphlets became common in the sixteenth century, broadsheet newspapers in the nineteenth century, and the TV became ubiquitous in the twentieth. Having your president talk to you in your home is a powerful method for mobilizing mass support for the state's policies. Modern nationalism is orders of magnitude more efficient at reaching citizens than what was possible in premodern times. A tightly integrated premodern nation, such as the Romans of the early Republic, could number tens of thousands of citizens, perhaps a hundred thousand. In empires that encompassed millions or tens of millions of subjects, it was inevitable that only the elites would be able to share in a common identity. Modern technology changed that and made possible the integration of tens and even hundreds of millions people into cohesive nations. It has also decoupled geographic and information/symbolic spaces. One does not need to be physically close to a metaethnic frontier to be under its influence. An Arab community in Detroit might now be more closely integrated with their coreligionists thousands of miles away in Lebanon than with a Polish working-class neighborhood a mile away.

Mass media has been with us for some time, and social scientists have constructed theories of its effects on the dynamics of modern societies. Techniques for polling public attitudes and, on the darker side, manipulating public opinion are becoming increasingly sophisticated. Because communications technology continues to develop at such a fast pace, however, these theories have had short shelf life.

Mass media can be viewed as having simple hierarchical structure. There is a center, where news, opinions, and entertainment are produced;

and then there are the masses who consume the information products. The reality is at least a bit more complicated because typically, there are several centers—national TV channels, major newspapers, and wire services. This alone, however, does not change the hierarchical nature of the system. Different information providers influence each other in complex nonlinear ways, but they still constitute a tiny information elite. The huge majority of citizens even in the most democratic countries are merely passive recipients. Or, rather, have been passive recipients, because the structure of the world's information space is undergoing a radical change.

Before the 1990s, even a person living in the relative communication freedom of the U.S. had little alternative to the American mass media. Today, all the major newspapers in the world have Web sites, and one's ability to get news and opinion is limited only by the number of languages one can read. Actually, many non-English language news providers now post English translations of their texts on the Web. A Chinese view can be garnered from the *People's Daily*, an Arab view from the Cairo weekly *Al Ahram*. As anybody who has routinely read newspapers in two different countries knows, the range of opinions, and even of events deemed important to be reported, that one can get from the mass media of a single country is blinkered. This is apparent even when comparing, say, the American and French presses—although both countries are part of the same Western civilization.

But the Internet has done more than just broaden the spectrum of news sources. The truly revolutionary change is that the Internet is beginning to blur the difference between news providers and news consumers. One group of new players in the information space are the "bloggers" (from *Web log*, which was shortened to blog). It is relatively easy for an individual to set up his or her own Web site, and periodically post on it interesting news items, gleaned from other sources, links to interesting sites (including other bloggers), and personal commentary on, for example, politics and violence in the Muslim world. One blog is titled "Friends of Democracy: Ground-level views from the people and bloggers of Iraq," another "Jihad Watch," and another "Global Guerrillas: Networked tribes, infrastructure disruption, and the emerging bazaar of violence." There were millions of such bloggers in the U.S. alone in 2004, and their numbers have been growing exponentially, doubling every half a year. Collectively, they are known as the blogosphere.

In a remarkable test of strength, the blogosphere challenged a news report, run by a mainstream television channel during the 2004 presidential election. Dan Rather, now former anchor of CBS News, presented allegations on *60 Minutes* that friends in high places had ushered young George W. Bush into the Texas Air National Guard in 1968, as his way of evading military service in Vietnam. Four memos, supposedly written by Lt. Col. Jerry Killian in 1972–73, substantiated the allegations. In these memos, Killian expressed frustration that then-subordinate Lt. Bush was shirking his guard obligations. Killian purportedly complained that he was under pressure to "sugarcoat" Bush's record. The day after the broadcast many newspapers, including the *New York Times,* followed up on the story.

The blogosphere encompasses the whole political spectrum, but the bloggers on the right had long charged that Rather was biased in favor of Democrats. Some bloggers noted that the memos were suspiciously well formatted—something that we expect now in the age of word processors and laser printers, but not the way a document produced on a typewriter in the 1970s is likely to look. After a frenetic keyboard-clacking debate, a consensus emerged in the blogosphere that the documents must be fakes. Within a week of the original broadcast, Dan Rather and CBS were in retreat. They were forced to admit that they were too eager to accept the documents as genuine and retracted the story. Dan Rather retired. The blogosphere demonstrated its power, no doubt not for the last time.

Myriad unpaid activists acting without any central direction were able to humble a mighty multi-billion-dollar corporation. It was a victory of heterarchy over hierarchy. A *heterarchy* is a kind of network structure, in which no discernible centers of control are apparent. Information flows back and forth between the nodes, rather than solely from the center. The blogosphere is a heterarchical structure; its host, the World Wide Web is, too; so, too, is Al Qaida.

The problem for social theorists is that it is much easier to understand and model hierarchies. Linear cause-effect relationships are easy to make sense of. In heterarchies, nonlinear feedbacks reign. What one node does might affect other nodes, thus changing what they do, and in turn affecting the original node where the signal originated. As a result, heterarchical networks behave in highly complex ways, and are difficult to predict. Emergence (or not) of consensus is one example of such a complex self-organizing behavior. Other examples include the mysterious synchrony achieved by fireflies that flash in unison by the thousands, rhythmic synchronized clapping by European audiences at music concerts, and coalescence of global terrorist networks. Our understanding of the dynamics of heterarchical networks is in its infancy.

ALTHOUGH THE RISE OF THE World Wide Web, and the various phenomena that it made possible (such as the blogosphere), is a striking sign of how the world is changing, the Internet is still the province of a minority of the world's population. The blogosphere provides an integrative technological matrix only for the wealthier and more intellectual segment of the world population, the information-savvy elites who are comfortable with reading, evaluating, and writing. The device that will probably have the greatest impact on social dynamics is the mobile phone.

Mobile phones are cheap and easy to use, and they are spreading well beyond the "golden billion." In fact, in the poorest areas in the world, the mobile phone is the main device for long-distance communications, because telephone lines were never installed in such areas. In 2003, in the Philippines, where GDP per capita was only $4,600 (based on purchasing power parity), 1 person in 10 owned a cell phone.

Handheld multipurpose devices today are not just phones; they may also include a computer, a GPS unit, and a camera—all in a tiny fist-sized package. The technology writer and futurist Howard Rheingold writes in *Smart Mobs: The Next Social Revolution*, "They enable people to act together in new ways and in situations where collective action was not possible before." Mobile phones "will help people coordinate actions with others around the world—and, perhaps, more importantly with people nearby." They enable smart mobs—"people who are able to act in concert even if they don't know one another."

As the devices become smaller and more powerful, they turn a person wearing it into a potential TV reporter. Rheingold reports how in 2000 technology researcher and innovator Steve Mann launched "ENGwear, an experiment in wearable news-gathering systems." In the spring of 2000, Mann together with his students, all wearing their experimental devices, went to an anti-poverty demonstration in Toronto. When violence broke out, Mann reported, "We, along with the journalists and various television crews, ran for cover. However, unlike the reporters, my students and I were still broadcasting, capturing almost by accident the entire event. Whatever we saw before us was captured and sent instantly in real time to the World Wide Web, without our conscious thought or effort."

When the bloggers bashed CBS, the only tools they had were their analytical and communications abilities. They could not get at raw data, for which they relied on the traditional news agencies; they could only analyze them. How will our society change when bloggers begin wearing Steve Mann's devices?

Peer-to-peer journalism (or to seem younger than I am, I should say p2p journalism) is still a matter of the future (at least as of the time of this writing, although perhaps not when this book is actually read). However, the mobile phone has already been responsible for the fall of at least one government.

As Rheingold describes: "On January 20, 2001, President Joseph Estrada of the Philippines became the first head of state in history to lose power to a smart mob. More than 1 million of Manila residents, mobilized and coordinated by waves of text messages, assembled at the site of the 1986 'People Power' peaceful demonstration that had toppled the Marcos regime. Tens of thousands of Filipinos converged on Epifanio de los Santos Avenue, known as 'Edsa,' within an hour of the first text message volleys: 'Go 2EDSA, Wear blck.' Estrada fell."

IS THE E.U. A NEW KIND OF EMPIRE? Will the emerging competition between the U.S. and China take the same forms as the struggles of great powers in history? Has the Russian imperial nation exhausted its asabiya? Will another mighty caliphate emerge in the Middle East during the twenty-first century? What does the recent decline of asabiya in the U.S., discussed in Chapter 13, portend for the future of the American empire? This chapter offers more questions than answers.

It is important not to overestimate our understanding even of simple agrarian societies. Applying history's lessons to the present day presents even more difficulties because we live in a different world from the one of the Assyrians, the Romans, and the Mongols. Abundant food and energy, rapidly developing technology and science, mass media, the World Wide Web, and the mobile phone make any direct comparisons between historical agrarian empires and the modern industrial states problematic. On the other hand, modernity did not remake human nature. We still make babies the old-fashioned way, we kill each other in individual and collective conflicts, and feelings of group loyalty, as well as intolerance toward strangers, continue to hold sway over us.

Is it possible to design institutions that will enhance asabiya—the social capital of which Putnam has written? Or, at least, can we design societies in such a way that asabiya is not constantly being degraded? Do humans always need the threat of imminent danger from some outside enemy to cooperate effectively? Some might conclude from my book that the principle of asabiya implies that for all humans to cooperate we would need to be attacked by extraterrestrials.

Even though modern societies have solved the problem of feeding the population, they are still susceptible to the elite overproduction problem. Will intra-elite competition escalate into violence and cause Western states to collapse even in the presence of democratic institutions, designed to channel conflict into peaceful forms? Can we find a middle way between redistributive state socialism and letting the Matthew principle run amok, creating inequality and undermining cooperation?

The life cycles of imperial nations as I believe the science of cliodynamics defines them have not preordained what will happen tomorrow to the dominant empires of our time, but they do map the critical factors of their past and guide us toward the critical choices we will have in the next generation, century, and millennium. I hope that the description I have provided of these life cycles and the research that attends them will make the importance of cooperation to the long-term prosperity of humanity clear. *E pluribus unum.*

Notes

Y ou can find the technical account of the major theories discussed in *War and Peace and War* in two books: Turchin, P. 2003. *Historical Dynamics: Why States Rise and Fall* (Princeton University Press); and Turchin, P., and S. A. Nefedov. 2006. *Secular Cycles* (not yet published). Beware! These books are not light reading—they have lots of equations, data graphs, and statistical analyses.

Many recent books have addressed the possibility of reshaping social sciences in the image of natural sciences. I enjoyed reading and recommend the following:

Gladwell, M. 2000. *The Tipping Point: How Little Things Can Make a Big Difference*. Little, Brown, and Co, Boston.

Roehner, B., and T. Symes. 2002. *Pattern and Repertoire in History*. Harvard University Press, Cambridge, MA.

Ball, P. 2004. *Critical Mass: How One Thing Leads to Another*. Farrar, Strauss, and Giroux, New York.

Seabright, P. 2004. *The Company of Strangers*. Princeton University Press, Princeton, NJ.

Surowiecki, J. 2004. *The Wisdom of Crowds*. Doubleday, New York.

Diamond, J. 1997. *Guns, Germs, and Steel: The Fates of Human Societies*. W. W. Norton, New York. (Jared Diamond's Pulitzer Prize winning book is a must-read. See also his new book *Collapse*.)

There are also a number of books on world history that I found very useful and edifying:

Christian, D. 1998. A *History of Russia, Central Asia, and Mongolia*. Blackwell, Oxford.

Christian, D. 2004. *Maps of Time: An Introduction to Big History*. University of California Press, Berkeley.

Kennedy, P. 1987. *The Rise and Fall of the Great Powers: Economic Change and Military Conflict from 1500 to 2000*. Random House, New York.

Mann, M. 1986. *The Sources of Social Power. Volume I. A history of power from the beginning to A.D. 1760*. Cambridge University Press, Cambridge, UK.

McNeill, W. H. 1976. *Plagues and peoples*. Anchor Books, New York.

McNeill, W. H. 1982. *The Pursuit of Power*. University of Chicago Press, Chicago, IL.

I have checked the basic historical facts, such as dates and battle locations, with Stearns, P. N. 2001. *The Encyclopedia of World History, 6th Edition*. Houghton Mifflin, Boston. (The CD-ROM version).

Note that throughout the text, the years in parentheses for rulers indicate the reigning years; for other people they are the year of birth and death.

Introduction

"I thank Asimov for raising it again." The idea of "laws of history" predates Asimov's trilogy by many centuries. Perhaps the best known is the conception of Karl Marx. Leo Tolstoy thought that laws of history could be discovered by understanding how individual human wills are combined in collective action. I discuss these issues more fully in Chapter 12.

"the behavior of a group is determined by the actions of individuals who are its members" The issue of how we can deduce the behavior of a group from knowledge about individuals is known in sociology as the micro-to-macro problem. Coleman, J. S. 1990. *Foundations of Social Theory*. Belknap Press, Cambridge, MA, pp. 5–23. See also Hechter, M. 1987. *Principles of Group Solidarity*. University of California Press, Berkeley, CA. Goldstone, J. A. 1994. Is revolution individually rational? Groups and individuals in revolutionary collective action. *Rationality and Society* 6:139–166.

My definition of ethnicity follows that of Brass, P. R. 1991. *Ethnicity and Nationalism: Theory and Comparison*. Sage Publications, New Delhi, p. 18. See also the discussion of ethnicity in Turchin 2003:33ff.

"Domination, however, is made possible only because groups are integrated at the micro level by cooperation among their members." Collins, R. 1992. *Sociological Insight*. Oxford University Press, New York, p. 8.

"so peace brings warre and warre brings peace" George Puttenham in 1589.

"The demographic-structural theory" was proposed by Jack Goldstone. See Goldstone, J. A. 1991. *Revolution and Rebellion in the Early Modern World*. University of California Press, Berkeley, CA. Goldstone's theory focused on the link between population increase and state collapse. Later I added the feedback connection from sociopolitical instability to population decline (Turchin 2003: Chapter 7). See also Nefedov, S. 1999. "The method of demographic cycles in a study of socioeconomic history of preindustrial society." Ph.D. dissertation (in Russian), Ekaterinburg University, Ekaterinburg, Russia, and the forthcoming book *Secular Cycles* by Turchin and Nefedov.

"These theories are part of a new science of historical dynamics." Cliodynamics is a general theoretical framework not limited to any specific number of theories. Presently, in addition to the three theories discussed in this book, it also includes two other theories: ethnokinetics, the study of ethnic assimilation and religious conversion; and geopolitics, the study of how space affects the ability of state to project power. See my technical book *Historical Dynamics: Why States Rise and Fall* (Turchin 2003).

Chapter 1

The description of Ermak's conquest was taken from the nineteenth-century Russian historian N. M. Karamzin (Book III of the *History of the Russian State*). For the English translation, see Soloviev, S. M. 2002. *History of Russia*. Volume 11. Academic International Press, Gulf Breeze, FL. An excellent general treatment of Russian history is Riazanovsky, N. V. 2000. *A History of Russia, 6th Edition*. Oxford University Press, New York.

The long quote from the *Stroganov Chronicle* is from Dmytryshyn, B., E. A. P. Crownhart-Vaughn, and T. Vaughan. 1985. *Russia's Conquest of Siberia.* Western Imprints, Portland, OR.

One of the most readable sources about the history of the steppe nomads, including the Mongols, is still Grousset, R. 1970. *The Empire of the Steppes: A History of Central Asia.* Rutgers University Press, New Brunswick, NJ. The Rubruck quotation is from Barfield, T. J. 1994. "The Devil's Horsemen." In S. P. Reyna and R. E. Downs, editors. *Studying War: Anthropological Perspectives.* Gordon and Breach, Langhorn, PA.

On the Mongol organization, see Note 16 on p. 492 of McNeill, W. H. 1963. *The Rise of the West.* New American Library, New York.

Chapter 2

The early sixteenth century was a key period in the formation of the Muscovite state and in Russian ethnogenesis. Unfortunately, it is the period that many histories of Russia treat meagerly (for example, Riazanovsky). My description of the Muscovite struggle against the Crimean Tatars is taken from Kargalov, V. V. 1974. *On the Steppe Frontier.* Nauka, Moscow. Unfortunately, this text is available only in Russian. A good English-language description of the steppe frontier in Eastern Europe is McNeill, W. H. 1964. *Europe's Steppe Frontier.* University of Chicago Press, Chicago. For successive defense lines, see p. 174ff in Hellie, R. 1971. *Enserfment and Military Change in Muscovy.* University of Chicago Press, Chicago.

On the economic costs of Crimean raids, see Khodarkovsky, M. 2002. *Russia's Steppe Frontier.* Indiana University Press, Bloomington, IN, p.223. Khodarkovsky conservatively estimates the total amount that Russia poured into Crimea (the bulk of it spent redeeming the captives) as 6 million rubles. For comparison, the annual salary of a Cossack was around 5 rubles.

The quotes from Beauplan are from the English translation; see Beauplan, Guillaume Le Vasseur. 1993. *A Description of Ukraine.* Introduction, Translation, and Notes by Andrew B. Pernal and Dennis F. Essar. Harvard University Press, Cambridge, MA.

Ukrainian frontier experiences are described in Subtelny, O. 1988. *Ukraine: A History*. University of Toronto Press, Toronto. On the differences in the organization of the Russian and Ukrainian frontiers, see Sanin, G. A. 1992. The southern border of Russia in the second half of the seventeenth—first half of the eighteenth centuries (in Russian). *Russian History* 19:433–457.

"Russian history continued to suffer from observer biases in the twentieth century." The traditional, Cold War era view of Russian history is presented by Pipes, R. 1974. *Russia Under the Old Regime*. Scribner, New York. Recently Pipes's interpretations and scholarship has been criticized; see, for example, Weickhardt, G. G. 1993. The pre-Petrine law of property. *Slavic Review* 52:663–679. A much more balanced treatment of the relations between state and society in early modern Russia can be found in Kollmann, N. S. 1987. *Kinship and Politics: The Making of the Muscovite Political System, 1345–1547*. Stanford University, Stanford, CA; Kollmann, N. S. 1999. *By Honor Bound: State and Society in Early Modern Russia*. Cornell University Press, Ithaca, NY; and Kivelson, V. A. 1996. *Autocracy in the Provinces: The Muscovite Gentry and Political Culture in the Seventeenth Century*. Stanford University Press, Stanford, CA. Ostrowski, D. 1998. *Muscovy and the Mongols: Cross-Cultural Influences on the Steppe Frontier, 1304–1589*. Cambridge University Press, Cambridge, UK.

"cooperative spirit in the frontier territories" McNeill on the cooperation between commoners and elites in early modern Russia: "The peasants, although compelled to accept a burdensome serfdom, saw a rude sort of justice in the service state, which required landowners to serve the tsar just as the peasants were compelled to serve their masters, the landowners." McNeill, W. H. 1964. *Europe's Steppe Frontier*. University of Chicago Press, Chicago, IL. p. 64.

For the social composition of the Russian frontier, see Stevens, C. B. 1995. *Soldiers on the Steppe*. Northern Illinois University Press, DeKalb. See also Mironov, B. N. 2000. *A Social History of Imperial Russia, 1700–1917*. Westview Press, Boulder, CO.

"The pressure from the steppe nomads molded Muscovy's institutions and culture." In fact, Muscovy directly imported a number of institutions, such as the postal service and tax administrative methods from the Golden

Horde. See Halperin, C. J. 1985. *Russia and the Golden Horde: The Mongol Impact on Medieval Russian History*. Indiana University Press, Bloomington, IN.

"instead of challenging you to a duel, they would sue you in court" See Kollmann, *By Honor Bound*, p. 153.

"During the 1640s, the authorities confiscated the magnate-owned land within the frontier, freed the peasants, and enlisted them in dragoon regiments for garrison service." See Davies, B. 1992. Village into garrison: the militarized peasant communities of southern Moscovy. *Russian Review* 51:481–501.

"tragedy of the commons" Hardin, G. 1968. The tragedy of the commons. *Science* 162:1243–1248.

"The frontier was a true fault line, on which two very different civilizations came in contact, soon to became conflict." Nancy Shoemaker has recently showed that the intensity of metaethnic hostility between Europeans and Indians developed gradually. By the end of the eighteenth century, Europeans and Indians abandoned an initial willingness to recognize in each other a common humanity. Instead, both sides developed new stereotypes of the "other" rooted in conviction that they were peoples fundamentally at odds, by custom, and even by nature. Shoemaker, N. 2004. *A Strange Likeness: Becoming Red and White in Eighteenth-Century America*. Oxford University Press, New York.

"Modern histories do not emphasize this aspect of the conflict, but it was very intense, at times genocidal." On the genocidal conflict between settlers and Indians in North America, see Osborn, W. M. 2000. *The Wild Frontier: Atrocities During the American-Indian War from Jamestown Colony to Wounded Knee*. Random House, New York. A useful article about King Philip's War is W. G. Giersbach "King Philip's War: America's Most Devastating Conflict," which you can find online at www.militaryhistory-online.com.

Mary Rowlandson's account has been recently reprinted in Slotkin, R., and J. K. Folsom, editors. 1978. *So Dreadful a Judgment: Puritan Responses to King Philip's War, 1676–1677*. Wesleyan University Press, Hanover.

"A recent compilation counted more than 16,000 recorded atrocities." Osborn, *The Wild Frontier.*

"Another characteristic of the Americans, which was commented upon at length by that astute Frenchman" Tocqueville, Alexis de. 1984. *Democracy in America.* Anchor Books, Garden City, NJ.

On the attitudes of Euro-Americans toward mixed European-Indian marriages, see West, E. 1999. *The Contested Plains: Indians, Goldseekers, and the Rush to Colorado.* University Press of Kansas, Lawrence, KS.

Chapter 3

For the battle of Teutoburg Forest, see Wells, P. S. 2003. *The Battle That Stopped Rome: Emperor Augustus, Arminius, and the Slaughter of Legions in the Teutoburg Forest.* W. W. Norton, New York.

On the early Germans, in addition to Wells 2003, see Wells, P. S. 1999. *The Barbarians Speak: How the Conquered Peoples Shaped Roman Europe.* Princeton University Press, Princeton, NJ. See also Wolfram, H. 1997. *The Roman Empire and Its Germanic Peoples.* University of California Press, Berkeley; Musset, L. 1975. *The Germanic Invasions: The Making of Europe AD 400–600.* Pennsylvania State University Press, University Park, PA; Geary, P. J. 1988. *Before France and Germany: The Creation and Transformation of the Merovingian World.* Oxford University Press, New York. Todd, M. 1992. *The Early Germans.* Blackwell, Oxford.

"a highly conflict-prone band of territory extending a hundred miles from the frontier" Geary 1988:57.

"the god Tiwaz, the head of the German pantheon" Geary 1988.

On the rise of the cult of Odin, see Miller, D. H. 1993. Ethnogenesis and religious revitalization beyond the roman frontier: The case of Frankish origins. *Journal of World History* 4:277–285.

"I know that I hung" Cited from Lindow, J. 2002. *Norse Mythology: A Guide to the Gods, Heroes, Rituals, and Beliefs.* Oxford University Press, p. 248. For more on Odin, see Munch, P. A. 1926. *Norse Mythology.* Oxford University Press, London.

"The new warlords worshipped Odin … and legitimated their political power by claiming direct descent from him." For the genealogies of Anglo-Saxon kings, tracing their descent from Odin, see Grimm, J. 1880. *Teutonic Mythology*. W. Swann Sonnenschein & Allen, London, p. 165.

"cooperation between Germanic chieftains … their frequent meetings with each other in the capitals of frontier provinces, such as Cologne, Mainz, or Augsburg" Wolfram 1997:41.

"the Vandals … backed the Goths and the Burgundians deployed behind the Alamanni" Wolfram 1997:43.

"Attila means 'daddy' in Gothic." Wolfram 1997:143.

"masses of farmers quietly colonizing frontier regions" Musset 1975:67.

On the relationship between Franks and Alamanni, see Hummer, H. J. 1998. "Franks and Alamanni: A Discontinuous Ethnogenesis." Pages 9–32 in I. Wood, editor. *Franks and Alamanni in the Merovingian Period: an Ethnographic Perspective*. Boydell Press, San Marino, RSM.

"The name for the other great confederation, the Franks" Hummer 1998. Same source for the name *Alamanni*.

"the Romans were unable to subdue the Alamanni" Hummer 1998.

"in 260 Gallienus controlled only the middle third of the empire" Southern, P. 2001. *The Roman Empire from Severus to Constantine*. Routledge, London.

"northern Italy was settled by several waves of Germanic immigrants, most notably the Langobards/Lombards" Musset 1975.

"the geographic origin of recruits for the Roman legions" see Figure 13 in MacMullen, R. 1988. *Corruption and the Decline of Rome*. Yale University Press, New Haven, CT.

An excellent and detailed treatment of Byzantine history is Treadgold, W. 1997. *A History of the Byzantine State and Society*. Stanford University Press, Stanford, CA.

"Gibbon raced through this period in one chapter, and devoted the rest of his three fat volumes to the 'decadent' periods." Treadgold, W. 1988. *The Byzantine Revival, 782–842*. Stanford University Press, Stanford, CA.

For the population of Constantinople, see Modelski, G. 2003. *World Cities: -3000 to 2000*. Faros 2000, Washington.

"In *Chronicle of the First Crusade* Fulcher of Chartres wrote quoted from Collins, J. B. 2002. *From Tribes to Nation: The Making of France 500–1799*. Wadsworth, Toronto, p. 94.

Chapter 4

The source of quotes from Ibn Khaldun is Ibn Khaldun. 1958. *The Muqaddimah: An Introduction to History*. Translated from the Arabic by Franz Rosenthal. Pantheon Books, New York.

On Ibn Khaldun's life and times, read the introductory chapter in *Muqaddimah*, written by the translator Franz Rosenthal.

An assessment of Ibn Khaldun's theory: Inayatullah, S. 1997. "Ibn Khaldun: The Strengthening and Weakening of Asabiya." Pages 25–32 in J. Galtung and S. Inayatullah, editors. *Macrohistory and Macrohistorians*. Praeger, Westport, CT.

On Ibn Khladun as the world's first sociologist, see Gellner, E. 1981. *Muslim Society*. Cambridge University Press, Cambridge, UK.

For my account of the rise of Islam, I am heavily indebted to Donner, F. M. 1981. *The Early Islamic Conquests*. Princeton University Press, Princeton, NJ.

"The location of this frontier was determined almost entirely by environmental influences." Whittaker, C. R. 1994. *Frontiers of the Roman Empire*. Johns Hopkins University Press, Baltimore. It also has a good analysis of the transformative influence of the Roman frontier on the pre-Islamic Arab polities.

"the sinews of state" John Bartlett (1919) in *Familiar Quotations, 10th Edition*, p. 1002 traces the origin of this expression. "Diogenes Laertius, in his Life of Bion (lib. iv. c. 7, sect. 3), represents that philosopher as saying, [greek],—'Riches were the sinews of business,' or, as the phrase may mean, 'of the state.' Referring perhaps to this maxim of Bion, Plutarch says in his *Life of Cleomenes* (c. 27), 'He who first called money the sinews of the state seems to have said this with special reference to war.' Accordingly we find money called expressly [greek], 'the sinews of war,' in *Libanius*, Orat. xlvi. (vol. ii. p. 477, ed. Reiske), and by the scholiast on Pindar, Olymp. i. 4 (compare Photius, Lex. *s. v.* [greek]). So Cicero, Philipp. v. 2, 'nervos belli, infinitam pecuniam.'"

"the Ghassanids conducted successful military operations against powerful tribes located 500 miles or more away" Donner 1981.

"Ten years after experiencing the horror of civil war and genocide, many Rwandans are turning to Islam. " See Lacey, M. 2004. "Ten years after horror, Rwandans turn to Islam." In the *New York Times*: April 7, 2004.

"at least half a dozen of monotheistic prophets active in Arabia in the early seventh century" Korotayev, A. V. 2004. *The Origins of Islam: Political-Anthropological and Socio-Ecological Aspects*. United Humanitarian Press, Moscow. See also Kennedy, H. 1986. *The Prophet and the Age of the Caliphates*. Longman, Harlow, England, p. 47.

"the west-Arabian religio-political association" Korotayev 2004.

On the *umma* Donner 1981.

"We choose death, while you choose life" See Stalinsky, S. 2004. "The West is weak because it respects life? Too bad." *National Review*, May 24, 2004.

Chapter 5

On the First World War in England, see Ferguson, N. 1999. *The Pity of War*. Basic Books. On World War I in France: Smith, L. V. 2003. *France and the Great War*. Cambridge University Press, Cambridge, UK.

"It was cooperation that provided the basis of social life." Thomas Aquinas, for example, thought that men naturally cohere into society; see Boucher, D., and P. Kelly. 1994. *The Social Contract from Hobbes to Rawls*. Routledge, London, p. 10.

"eyewitness account by William Brooks" www.spartacus.schoolnet. co.uk/FWWbrooks.htm.

"the great Scottish philosopher David Hume (1711–76) wrote" In *Essays: Moral, Political, and Literary*.

St. Louis quotation is from Evans J. 1957. *Life in Medieval France*. Phaidon Press, London, p. 12. The sentiments he expressed were still current in the political thought of the fifteenth century. Writing a century before Machiavelli, Christine de Pisan said: "He [the prince] must singularly love the good and profit of his country and people, and this, rather than his private profit, ought to occupy all of his attention." *The Book of the Body Politic* (c. 1407). Quoted from Collins, J. B. 2002. *From Tribes to Nation: The Making of France 500–1799*. Wadsworth, Toronto, p. 144.

"largely due to the work of Adam Smith (1723–90)." To be fair to Adam Smith, he did not think that society could be based entirely on self-interest. For example, in his book *Theory of Moral Sentiments* Smith discussed at length the importance of empathy in human affairs.

"even divorce rates" In the United States divorce rates are higher in states that provide liberal welfare benefits. Frank, R. H., T. Gilovich, and D. T. Regan. 1993. Does studying economics inhibit cooperation? *Journal of Economic Perspectives* 7:159–171.

"Damn John Jay! Damn everyone who won't damn John Jay!!" From Jervis, R. 1997. *System Effects: Complexity in Political and Social Life*. Princeton University Press, Princeton, NJ, p. 212.

"by sacrificing one copy of itself in the defender bee it will produce three more copies in the new bees" Because each of new four bees shares three quarters of her genes with the sacrificial defender, on average there will be $0.75 \times 4 = 3$ copies of the altruistic gene among them.

"developed by the biologist Robert Trivers and the political scientist Robert Axelrod." For more on reciprocity, see Seabright, P. 2004. *The Company of Strangers*. Princeton University Press; and Bowles, S. 2004. *Microeconomics*. Princeton University Press.

"the theory of cultural group selection, advanced by the UCLA anthropologists Robert Boyd and Peter Richerson" The original statement of the theory is in Boyd, R., and P. J. Richerson. 1985. *Culture and the Evolutionary Process*. University of Chicago Press, Chicago. A less-technical description is in Richerson, P. J., and R. Boyd. 1998. "The Evolution of Human Ultrasociality." In I. Eibl-Eibesfeldt and F. K. Salter, editors. *Ethnic Conflict and Indoctrination*. Berghahn Books, Oxford. See also Richerson, P. J., and

R. Boyd. 2005. *Not by Genes Alone: How Culture Transformed Human Evolution*. University of Chicago Press, Chicago.

"Gladwell has cited many other examples" See Gladwell, M. 2000. *The Tipping Point: How Little Things Can Make a Big Difference*. Little, Brown, and Co, Boston, pp. 177–192.

"social life, in all its aspects and in every period of history, is made possible only by a vast symbolism." Durkheim, E. 1915. *The Elementary Forms of the Religious Life, A Study in Religious Sociology*. Macmillan, New York.

"Real people did not behave in the way predicted by the self-interest hypothesis" Fehr, E., and S. Gächter. 2002. Altruistic punishment in humans. *Nature* 415:137–140. See also Bowles, S., and H. Gintis. 2002. Homo reciprocans. *Nature* 415:125–128.

"In some studies stakes were very high—equivalent to three months of salary" Fehr, E., U. Fischbacher, and E. Tougareva. 2002. *Do high stakes and competition undermine fairness? Evidence from Russia*. Institute for Empirical Research in Economics, University of Zurich. Working Paper ISSN 1424–0459.

"Graduate students in economics, on the other hand, tend to behave more selfishly than students from other disciplines." The classic study on this is Marwell, G., and R. Ames. 1981. Economists free ride, does anyone else? *Journal of Public Economics* 15:295–310. See also Frank, R. H., T. Gilovich, and D. T. Regan. 1993. Does studying economics inhibit cooperation? *Journal of Economic Perspectives* 7:159–171.

"When the game is played with university students from industrial societies crosscultural variation is not huge, although detectable" Roth, A. E., V. Prasnikar, M. Okuno-Fujiwara, and S. Zamir. 1991. Bargaining and market behavior in Jerusalem, Ljubljana, Pittsburgh, and Tokyo: an experimental study. *American Economic Review* 81:1068–1095.

"The researchers went around the world and played the ultimatum game in fifteen small-scale traditional societies" Henrich, J., R. Boyd, S. Bowles, C. Camerer, E. Fehr, and H. Gintis. 2004. *Foundations of Human Sociality: Economic Experiments and Ethnographic Evidence from Fifteen Small-Scale Societies*. Oxford University Press, New York.

"A recent experiment, conducted at Zurich by Fehr and colleagues" Quervain, D. J., U. Fischbacher, V. Treyer, M. Schellhammer, U. Schnyder, A. Buck, and E. Fehr. 2004. The neural basis of altruistic punishment. *Science* 305:1254–1258. See also, Knutson, B. 2004. A sweet revenge? *Science* 305:1246–1247.

"A whole new hot discipline, called neuroeconomics, was born in the last few years." In addition to the paper by Quevrain et al. (2004), see Sanfey, A. G., J. K. Rilling, J. A. Aronson, L. E. Nystrom, and J. D. Cohen. 2003. The neural basis of economic decision-making in the ultimatum game. *Science* 300:1755–1758; and King-Casas, B., D. Tomlin, C. Anen, C. F. Camerer, S. R. Quartz, and P. R. Montague. 2005. Getting to know you: reputation and trust in a two-person economic exchange. *Science* 308:78–83.

"Wilson and colleagues were able to mount a successful attack on the individual-selectionist dogma" See Sober, E., and D. S. Wilson. 1991. *Unto Others: The Evolution and Psychology of Unselfish Behavior*. Harvard University Press, Cambridge, MA.

"The best current explanation of how human ultrasociality" Here I say "best" because not all details have yet been worked out, and for some aspects there are still alternative explanations being vigorously debated—explaining sociality in humans is still very much work in progress.

"Leda Cosmides and John Tooby argue that there are specialized 'cheater-detection circuits.'" Cosmides, L., and J. Tooby. 2005. *What Is Evolutionary Psychology? Explaining the New Science of the Mind*. Yale University Press, New Haven, CT.

"The anthropologist Lawrence H. Keeley presents evidence" Keely, L. H. 1997. *War Before Civilization: The Myth of the Peaceful Savage*. Oxford University Press, New York.

"our capacity for symbolic thinking" See Greenspan, S. I., and S. G. Shanker. 2004. *The First Idea: How Symbols, Language, and Intelligence Evolved from Our Primate Ancestors to Modern Humans*. Da Capo Press, Cambridge, MA.

"Two key adaptations enabled the evolution of ultrasociality." To be sure, there were many other adaptations that played an important role in the evolution of sociality. I have already referred several times to the importance of social institutions—the laws, informal rules, and conventions that give durable structure to social interactions (see Bowles S. 2004. *Microeconomics: Behavior, Institutions, and Evolution*. Princeton University Press, p.47-48).

Chapter 6

The caption of the chapter is borrowed from an article by Raaflaub, K. A. 1996. "Born to Be Wolves? Origins of Roman Imperialism." Pages 273–314 in R. W. Wallace and E. M. Harris, editors. *Transitions to Empire*. University of Oklahoma Press, Norman.

My account of the early history of Rome draws heavily on Cornell, T. J. 1995. *The Beginnings of Rome: Italy and Rome from the Bronze Age to the Punic Wars (c.1000–264 BC)*. Routledge, London. Another useful reference is Pallottino, M. 1991. *A History of Earliest Italy*. University of Michigan Press, Ann Arbor, MI. See also Toynbee, A. J. 1965. *Hannibal's Legacy: The Hannibalic War's Effects on Roman life*. Oxford University Press, London.

For an excellent general text on Roman history, see Ward, A. M., F. M. Heichelheim, and C. A. Yeo. 2003. *A History of The Roman People*, 4th Edition. Prentice Hall, Upper Saddle River, NJ.

A useful Web-based source is the *Illustrated History of the Roman Empire* at www.roman-empire.net.

"Dionysius writes that during the plague of 463 B.C." See Duncan-Jones, R. P. 1996. The impact of the Antonine plague. *Journal of Roman Archaeology* 9:108–136. According to Dionysius, the plague of 451 B.C. killed all the slaves and half the citizens. Annalist historians recorded 16 epidemics during the fifth century, declining to 9 in the fourth century. Subsistence crises also were frequent and severe. Roman annalists recorded eight famines in the fifth century, compared to only two in each of the fourth and third centuries (Toynbee 1965:93).

On the Gallic-Roman frontier, see Chapter 1 of Dyson, S. L. 1985. *The Creation of the Roman Frontier*. Princeton University Press, Princeton, NJ; and Williams, J. H. C. 2001. *Beyond the Rubicon: Romans and Gauls in Republican Italy*. Oxford University Press.

"The Latins were a real nation, and they themselves were aware of it." See Cornell 1995 for a discussion of the ethnic boundary between the Etruscans and Latins.

"A century later Rome expanded to cover an area six time the size" From 50 to 300 hectares (a hectare = 2.5 acres). Typical population densities in the ancient Mediterranean cities were 100 to 200 people per hectare. From Cornell 1995.

"Known areas of other Latin towns are an order of magnitude smaller than that of Rome" The largest are 40 hectares. Tarentium's size was 500 hectares.

"Another sign of Rome's importance is the treaty that it made with Carthage in 507" This is now accepted by all serious scholars as genuine.

"And the war against the Etruscans continued to flare up periodically" Rome fought three wars with Veii during this period: in 483–474, 437–435, and 406–396.

"overpopulation led to recurrent epidemics" Livy records eight great famines during the fifth century, compared to only two in each of the two succeeding centuries.

"The mere threat of a *tumultus Gallicus*" Cornell 1995:325

"the Veneti loyally soldiered on" See Toynbee, A. J. 1965. *Hannibal's Legacy: The Hannibalic War's Effects on Roman Life*. Oxford University Press, London, p. 266.

"Many Italian cities fought loyally for Rome" On the loyalty of Italians to Rome during the war with Hannibal, see p. 16 of the Introduction by Betty Radice to the Penguin edition of Livy's *The War with Hannibal*.

"Such treatment of the inhabitants of a conquered territory was exceptional in Roman practice" See Brunt, P. A. 1971. *Italian Manpower: 225 BC – AD 14*. Clarendon Press, Oxford, p. 538.

"Topics for graffiti have varied little over the millennia" Wells, C. M. 1992. *The Roman Empire, 2nd Edition*. Harvard University Press, Cambridge, p. 190. "Two pence" in the prostitute's ad is two *asses*.

"The early Romans developed a set of values, called *mos maiorum*" See Ward et al. 2003:57.

On Roman morals, see Barton, C. A. 2001. *Roman Honor: The Fire in the Bones.* University of California Press, Berkeley.

"Who with the prospect of death, envy, and punishment staring him in the face, does not hesitate to defend the Republic, he truly can be reckoned a *vir*" Cicero in *Pro Milone*, cited from Barton 2001:43.

"it is sweet and glorious to die for one's country" Horace, Ode II. "Against the degeneracy of the Roman youth." eBook *The Works of Horace.* www.authorama.com/works-of-horace-3.html.

"bonds that held the community together" On religion as bonds, see Barton 2001:35.

"life could only be ensured by willingness to die" and following quotes, from Barton 2001.

For a very readable introduction to Sparta, see Cartledge, P. 2002. *The Spartans: The World of the Warrior-Heroes of Ancient Greece.* Vintage Books, New York.

"Those who honor the gods most finely with choruses are best in war." Cited from Powell, A. 1989. *Classical Sparta: Techniques behind Her Success.* University of Oklahoma Press, Norman, OK, p. 142.

"declaring war on one's own work-force was an action quite unparalleled in history" De Ste. Croix, G. E. M. 1981. *The Class Struggle in the Ancient Greek World.* Cornell University Press, Ithaca, p. 149.

On Macedonian history, see Hammond, N. G. L. 1989. *The Macedonian State: Origins, Institutions, and History.* Clarendon Press, Oxford.

Chapter 7

An excellent overview of the role of frontiers in the medieval European history is Bartlett, R. 1993. *The Making of Europe: Conquest, Colonization and Cultural Change.* Princeton University Press, Princeton, NJ.

On the Iberian frontier between Muslims and Christians, see Powers, J. F. 1988. *A Society Organized for War: The Iberian Municipal Militias in the Central Middle Ages, 1000–1284*. University of California Press, Berkeley. and Collins, R. 1983. *Early Medieval Spain: Unity in Diversity, 400–1000*. St. Martin's Press, New York. Reilly, B. F. 1992. *The Contest of Christian and Muslim Spain: 1031–1157*. Blackwell, Cambridge, MA.

On the rise of Spain, see Elliot, J. H. 1963. *Imperial Spain, 1469–1716*. St. Martin's Press, New York. Kamen, H. 2003. *Empire: How Spain Became a World Power, 1492–1763*. HarperCollins, New York. Kamen (pp.16–17) also discussed the integrative role of the Muslim frontier on the Christian nations in Spain, Catalans, Valenicans, Aragonese, and Castilians.

"Its capital, Córdoba, was the largest city in Europe after Constantinople" Modelski (2003) estimates its size as 450,000 in A.D. 1000. The largest Christian cities in Spain had populations of a few thousand—two orders of magnitude less populous.

For a comparison between the Iberian frontier with Islam and the Russian steppe frontier, see Armstrong, J. A. 1982. *Nations Before Nationalism*. University of North Carolina Press, Chapel Hill, NC.

"The brotherhood patrolled the roads and suppressed brigandage." Elliott 1963:85

"On per capita basis they paid more taxes" Pollard, S. 1997. *Marginal Europe: The Contribution of Marginal Lands Since the Middle Ages*. Clarendon Press, Oxford, p. 94. It seems to be a general observation that core areas of empires carried heavier tax burdens: the province of Holland in the Dutch Republic, Castile in Spain, Northern France in the French kingdom, southern English counties in Great Britain, and the Russians within the Russian Empire.

"They have conquered the Indies, East and West, a whole New World" Messire Pierre de Bourdeille Seigneur de Brantome. *Vie des hommes illustres et grands capitaines étrangers de son temps*. 1594. (English translation from Kamen 2003:471.)

"The bands of adventurers led by Cortés and Pizarro who conquered the New World." Collins (2002:232) points out that "Bernal Diaz, companion of Cortez, repeatedly compared the *conquistadores* to the brave knights of *Reconquista* of Spain from the Muslims."

On the early history of France, see Dunbabin, J. 1985. *France in the Making, 843–1180*. Oxford University Press, Oxford.

Scherman, K. 1987. *The Birth of France: Warriors, Bishops and Long-Haired Kings*. Random House, New York; and Bates, D. 1995. "Western Francia: the northern principalities." Pages 398–419 in T. Reuter, editor. *The New Cambridge Medieval History. Volume III c.900–c.1024*. Cambridge University Press, Cambridge, UK.

My description of the rise of Normandy follows Searle, E. 1988. *Predatory Kinship and the Creation of Norman Power, 840–1066*. University of California Press, Berkeley.

"But the Franks were never able to sustain their political control over the Bretons" Galliou, P., and M. Jones. 1991. *The Bretons*. Blackwell, Oxford.

"a rather brutal attack on it [Breton language] by the Republican French government during the nineteenth century" See Weber, E. J. 1976. *Peasants into Frenchmen: The Modernization of Rural France, 1870–1914*. Stanford University Press, Stanford, CA.

On the metaethnic frontier between the English and the Norse, see Thomas, H. M. 2003. *The English and The Normans: Ethnic Hostility, Assimilation, and Identity, 1066–c.1220*. Oxford University Press, New York.

On the other Norman conquest, see Brown, G. S. 2003. *The Norman Conquest of Southern Italy and Sicily*. McFarland, Jefferson, NC. In addition to French, English, and southern Italian "Normandies," there was also Iceland. Iceland was an isolated island with no external enemies. The Norse who settled there evolved a society that got along without the social discipline of either lordship or coercive kin groups. They managed a successful survival with the nuclear family, a weak sense of obligation to an extended kin, and with next to no government at all—all because they had no external enemies (see Searle, 1988:162).

On the early history of Germany, see Barraclough, G. 1963. *The Origins of Modern Germany*. Capricorn Books, New York.

On the beginnings of the German-Slavic frontier, see Althoff, G. 1995. "Saxony and the Elbe Slavs in the Tenth Century." In T. Reuter, editor. *The New Cambridge Medieval History. Volume III c. 900–c. 1024.* Cambridge University Press, Cambridge.

On Margrave Gero's "friendship banquet," see Althoff 1995:282.

"The pagans are evil" Cited from Pollard 1997:150.

"The core area of Poland was further east, which gave the Poles enough of a respite to organize a state large enough to resist the German advance." For Poland (and Hungary) as tenth-century examples of state formation on the periphery of empire, see p. 119 in T. Reuter, editor. *The New Cambridge Medieval History. Volume III c. 900–c. 1024.* Cambridge University Press, Cambridge, UK.

On the Baltic frontier, see Christiansen, E. 1980. *The Northern Crusades: The Baltic and the Catholic Frontier, 1100–1525.* University of Minnesota Press. Murray, A. V. 2001. *Crusade and Conversion on the Baltic Frontier, 1150–1500.* Ashgate, Aldershot, UK.

Chapter 8

My description of the glorious thirteenth century in France follows Tuchman, B. W. 1978. *A Distant Mirror: The Calamitous Fourteenth Century.* Knopf, New York, pp. 19–21. Tuchman's book is one of the most readable histories of the fourteenth century.

Another excellent book is Sumption, J. 1991. *The Hundred Years War: Trial by Battle.* University of Pennsylvania Press, Philadelphia. See also Seward, D. 1978. *The Hundred Years War: the English in France, 1337–1453.* Atheneum, New York.

An excellent, but more scholarly study of the crisis of the fourteenth century is Bois, G. 1984. *The Crisis of Feudalism.* Cambridge University Press, Cambridge, UK. See also Braudel, F. 1988. *The Identity of France. Volume II. People and Production.* Harper Collins, New York.

"I am in Paris, in the royal city where abundance of natural wealth" Cited from Evans, J. 1957. *Life in Medieval France.* Phaidon, London, p. 14.

On the Wheel of Fortune, see Mâle, E. 1972. *The Gothic Image: Religious Art in France of the Thirteenth Century.* Harper and Row, New York, pp. 94–97.

"Crisis of the Seventeenth Century" Trevor-Roper, H. R. 1966. *The Crisis of the Seventeenth Century; Religion, the Reformation, and Social Change.* Harper & Row, New York. Parker, G., and L. M. Smith. 1997. *The General Crisis of the Seventeenth Century, 2nd edition.* Routledge, London.

"the Age of Revolution" Hobsbawm, E. J. 1962. *The Age of Revolution, 1789–1848.* New American Library, New York.

On the rhythm of history, see Fischer, D. H. 1996. *The Great Wave: Price Revolutions and the Rhythm Of History.* Oxford University Press, New York.

"the most popular explanation of why the fourteenth century was the time of decline and disintegration in Europe invokes climatic change" See Fagan, B. M. 2001. *The Little Ice Age: How Climate Made History, 1300–1850.* Basic Books, New York. Also Galloway, P. R. 1986. Long-term fluctuations in climate and population in the preindustrial era. *Population and Development Review* 12:1–24.

"climatologists made great strides in refining their estimates of how temperatures fluctuated over the last two millennia" See Jones, P. D., and M. E. Mann. 2004. Climate over past millennia. *Reviews of Geophysics* 42:1–42.

"Dynamical feedbacks between population growth and sociopolitical instability in agrarian states" This is a title of one of my papers, published in 2005 in the journal *Structure and Dynamics: eJournal of Anthropological and Related Sciences.*

"strip all the mathematical and statistical scaffolding away" Krugman, P. 1999. *The Return of Depression Economics.* W.W. Norton, New York, p. xii.

"how one thing led to another" from the title of the book by Philip Ball, *Critical Mass: How One Thing Leads to Another.*

"economic historians have calculated that the minimum amount of land" For details, see Turchin and Nefedov, *Secular Cycles,* forthcoming.

Description of the Great Famine is from Johannes de Trokelowe, *Annales,* H. T. Riley, ed., Rolls Series, No. 28, Vol. (London, 1866), pp. 92–95.

Translated by Brian Tierney. Other stories were taken from Lucas, H. S. 1930. The Great European Famine of 1315, 1316, and 1317. *Speculum* 5:343.

"When normal harvests returned, it is estimated that France was missing a tenth of its population." Dense population areas, including Flanders, suffered more. Périgueux, which was among the most densely populated towns in southern France, lost a third of its inhabitants during the famines of 1330s (Sumption 1991:12).

"Ye nobles are like ravening wolves" Cited from Evans 1957:34.

"the arrival of the Black Death" In addition to Tuchman 1978, see Collins 2002:138ff.

"Today historians emphasize that the main cause of the protracted warfare during 1338–1453 was not a dynastic conflict between the English and French kings, but rather the struggle between the great territorial magnates of France" See, for example, Collins 2002:152.

Passages from Froissart are cited from Froissart, J. 1968. *Chronicles*. Penguin, London.

On the disintegration of the royal power in the fourteenth-century France, see Caron, M. T. 1994. *Noblesse et Pouvoir Royal en France*. A. Colin, Paris.

On the social structure of England, see Dyer, C. 2000. *Everyday Life in Medieval England*. Hambledon and London, London, UK.

On investigations post mortem, see Russell, J. C. 1948. *British Medieval Population*. University of New Mexico Press, Albuquerque, NM. and Hollingsworth, T. H. 1969. *Historical Demography*. Cornell University Press, Ithaca, NY.

"if the replacement rate is less than one, that each dying father leaves, on average, fewer than one son, and the overall numbers must be shrinking" The total number of nobles would also be affected by social mobility, but here I ignore this aspect of the problem, focusing solely on the demographic processes.

The incomes and numbers of nobles in Forez were taken from Perroy, E. 1962. Social mobility among the French noblesse in the later Middle Ages. *Past and Present* 21:25–38.

The quote about the gentleman status is by Sir Thomas Smith in *De Republica Anglorum* (1583), taken from Coss, P. 2003. *The Origins of the English Gentry*. Cambridge University Press, Cambridge, UK, p. 6.

"Between 1327 and 1485, however, they murdered five kings" Edward II, Richard II, and Henry VI were deposed and later killed in prison, young Edward V was murdered in the Tower of London, and Richard III died on the field of Bosworth. The murder of Edward II in prison was performed in a particularly gruesome manner.

"Violent crimes rose to a peak between 1350 and 1450 and subsided thereafter." See the evidence compiled in Turchin and Nefedov, forthcoming.

"A cousin bought a patent of nobility for 500 livres" Tuchman 1978:165

Chapter 9

In this chapter I continue to rely on the accounts by Tuchman, Sumption, and Bois. See also Perroy, E. 1965. *The Hundred Years War*. Capricorn, New York. On the social and economic trends in Europe after the fourteenth century, see Huppert, G. 1986. *After the Black Death: A Social History of Early Modern Europe*. Indiana University Press, Bloomington, IN.

"The Count of Foix and the Captal de Buch and their men …." Froissart, pp. 153–155.

"The ordinance of 5 December 1360 became a landmark in French fiscal history" See Henneman, J. B. 1999. *France in the Middle Ages*. Pages 101–122 in R. Bonney, editor. *The Rise of the Fiscal State in Europe, c. 1200–1815*. Oxford University Press, Oxoford.

"Thou hast vanquished the enemy that plagued our innocent people" Potter, D. 2003. *France in the Later Middle Ages, 1200–1500*. Oxford University Press, New York, p.109.

"The English clung to the towns and fortresses on the Atlantic coast"— These were Bordeaux, Bayonne, Brest, Calais, and Cherbourg.

"the numbers of ennobling patents issued by the French kings" Schalk, E. 1982. Ennoblement in France from 1350 to 1660. *Journal of Social History* 16:101–110.

"Marmousets" were grotesque sculptures adorning church portals. Source: *Glossaire: histoire et l'architecture*, www.lesmoulins.com/fr/ju/g/M.htm.

"It seems as though the French were determined to replay the drama of the 1350s" As I discuss in Chapter 14, human societies seem to have memories, and tend to behave similarly in similar situations. More on this in Roehner, B., and T. Symes. 2002. *Pattern and Repertoire in History*. Harvard University Press, Cambridge, MA.

"piled up like pigs in the mud" Anonymous. 1968. *A Parisian Journal, 1405–1449*. Clarendon Press, Oxford.

"late medieval depression" See Bois, G. 2000. *La grande dépression médiévale: XIVe–XVe siècles*. Presses Universitaires de France, Paris.

"Philippe de la Boissière wrote in the fifteenth century" Cited from Braudel, F. 1988. *The Identity of France. Volume II. People and Production*. Harper Collins, New York, p. 160.

"The French historian Emmanuel Le Roy Ladurie estimates " In Le Roy Ladurie, E. 1987. *The French Peasantry: 1450–1660*. University of California Press, Berkeley, CA, p. 37.

"The hecatombs inflicted on the French nobility" Contamine, P. 1972. Guerre, "État et société à la fin du Moyen Age." *Études sur les armées des rois de France 1337–1494*. Mouton, Paris. See also Contamine, P. 1984. *War in the Middle Ages*. Blackwell, Oxford.

"The study of Lyon wills" Lorcin, M. T. 1981. *Vivre et mourir en Lyonnais à la fin du Moyen Age*. Editions du CNRS, Paris.

"In war-torn Normandy income declines between 1400 and 1450 were on the order of 50 percent" Bois 1984.

"in the early fourteenth century nobles constituted between 1.3 and 3.4 percent of population" Henneman, J. B. 1996. *Olivier de Clisson and Political Society of France Under Charles V and Charles VI*. University of Pennsylvania, Philadelphia.

"the rate of extinction of noble lineages in this region" Perroy, E. 1962. *Social mobility among the French noblesse in the later Middle Ages. Past and Present* 21:25–38.

"The decade after 1435 saw a permanent establishment of state finance in France" Henneman 1999.

"During the next century, England continued shipping off the excess of its nobility to France" Essentially the same argument was made by Bois, G. 1985. "Against the Neo-Malthusian Orthodoxy." Pages 107–118 in T. H. Aston and C. H. E. Philpin, editors. *The Brenner Debate: Agrarian Class Structure and Economic Development in Pre-Industrial Europe.* Cambridge University Press, Cambridge, UK.

On the Wars of the Roses, see Storey, R. L. 1966. *The End of the House of Lancaster.* Stein and Day, New York.

Chapter 10

"the corrosive effect that glaring inequality has on the willingness of people to cooperate." See Bowles, S. 2004. *Microeconomics: Behavior, Institutions, and Evolution.* Princeton University Press, Princeton, pp. 165–6. For example, a study of water management in Tamil Nadu, India, found lower levels of cooperation in villages with high levels of inequality in landholding.

On the Matthew principle, see James Surowiecki, *The Wisdom of Crowds,* especially p. 170. The term was used by Robert Merton, who showed that already eminent scientists are given disproportionate credit; see Merton, R. K. 1968. The Matthew effect in science. *Science* 159:56–63.

"This was theoretically demonstrated by Robert Axtell and Joshua Epstein of the Brookings Institution" A very readable exposition of Sugarscape results is in Philip Ball, *Critical Mass,* p. 347ff.

"as a result of decades of excellent research by the historians of medieval England" An excellent overview is in Dyer, C. 2002. *Making a Living in the Middle Ages: The People of Britain 850–1520.* Yale University Press, New Haven, CT.

"Sometime in the second half of the thirteenth century, Jack Atwood's grandfather" The description of the hypothetical trajectory follows the economic data compiled in Turchin and Nefedov.

"wealth stratification in the English villages c.1300" Kosminsky, E. A. 1956. *Studies in the Agrarian History of England in the Thirteenth Century.* Oxford University Press, Oxford.

"The wealthiest Englishman in the early fourteenth century was Thomas, earl of Lancaster." Dyer, c. 1989. *Standards of Living in the Later Middle Ages.* Cambridge University Press, Cambridge, UK, p. 29.

"A hundred years earlier, the largest income in England" Painter, S. 1943. *Studies in the History of the English Feudal Barony.* Johns Hopkins Press, Baltimore.

"the social and economic trends in England after the population peak c. 1300" In addition to Dyer 2002, see Fryde, E. B. 1991. "Peasant Rebellion and Peasant Discontents." Pages 744–819 in E. Miller, editor. *The Agrarian History of England and Wales. Volume III: 1348–1500.* Cambridge University Press, Cambridge, UK.

"His annual income in 1436" Gray, H. L. 1934. Incomes from land in England in 1436. *English History Review* 49:607–631.

"In 1500 there were between 5,000 and 6,000 gentry families, but in 1640 there were 18,500 of them" See Mingay, G. E. 1976. *The Gentry: The Rise and Fall of a Ruling Class.* Longman, London; Heal, F., and C. Holmes. 1994. *The Gentry of England and Wales.* Stanford University Press, Stanford, CA; and Stone, L. 1972. *The Causes of the English Revolution: 1529–1642.* Harper and Row, New York.

"Historians traced this epidemic by counting how often duels and challenges were mentioned in newsletters and private correspondence" Stone, L. 1965. *The Crisis of Aristocracy: 1558–1641.* Clarendon Press, Oxford.

"Crisis of the Seventeenth Century" Trevor-Roper, H. R. 1966. *The Crisis of the Seventeenth Century; Religion, the Reformation, and Social Change.* Harper & Row, New York. Parker, G., and L. M. Smith. 1997. *The General Crisis of the Seventeenth Century, 2nd Edition.* Routledge, London.

For historical d'Artagnan, see the French Web site "*Les Gentilshommes de la Brette*" at http://gentilshommesbrette.free.fr/article.php3?id_article=39. English language articles on the Web include www.therfcc.org/d'artagnan-89280.html and www.madamebonancieux.com/dartagnan.html.

"One estimate was that 7,000 to 8,000 were killed in the two decades after 1588" Harding, R. R. 1977. *Anatomy of a Power Elite: The Provincial Governors of Early Modern France.* Yale University Press, New Haven, CT. See also Collins, J. B. 1995. *The State in Early Modern France.* Cambridge University Press, Cambridge, UK.

On the fortune of Richelieu, see Bonney, R. 1999. "France, 1494–1815." Pages 123–176 in R. Bonney, editor. *The Rise of The Fiscal State in Europe, c. 1200–1815.* Oxford University Press, Oxford.

"In his *Memoirs* Louis XIV wrote about Fouquet" Quoted from Collins 2002:351.

Chapter 11

For my description of Roman history, I continue to use Ward, A. M., F. M. Heichelheim, and C. A. Yeo. 2003. *A History of the Roman people,* 4th edition. Prentice Hall, Upper Saddle River, NJ.

Other useful texts are Crawford, M. 1993. *The Roman Republic, 2nd edition.* Harvard University Press, Cambridge; Wells, C. M. 1992. *The Roman Empire. 2nd edition.* Harvard University Press, Cambridge; and Le Glay, M., J. L. Voisin, Y. Le Bohec, and D. Cherry. 1997. *A History of Rome.* Blackwell, Oxford, UK.

"During the period 334–263 B.C. alone, an estimated 70,000 citizens left Rome for the colonies" Cornell, T. J. 1995. *The Beginnings of Rome: Italy and Rome from the Bronze Age to the Punic Wars (c.1000–264 BC).* Routledge, London, p. 381

"During the next century, the numbers of citizens more than doubled." For Roman census numbers, see Brunt, P. A. 1971. *Italian Manpower: 225 BC– AD 14.* Clarendon Press, Oxford, UK.

"The population of the city of Rome increased even faster, from 150,000 to 450,000." Chandler, T. 1987. *Four Thousand Years of Urban Growth: An Historical Census*. St. Gavid's, Lewiston.

"the authorities gradually reduced the minimum amount of property that qualified a citizen for army service" In 107, Marius enrolled in the legions *capite censi*, those without property who were simply listed in the census (Crawford 1993:79, 125, 128).

"The scale of senatorial fortunes grew at an astronomic rate." See Crawford 1993:75 and Shatzman, I. 1975. *Senatorial Wealth and Roman Politics*. Latomus, Brussels. On the concentration of wealth in the late Republic, see also Ward et al. 2003:234–5.

"Here you have the other coming down from his fine house on the Palatine" Cited from Freese, J. H. 1930. *Cicero: The Speeches*. William Heinemann, London, pp.133–135.

"to organize a decent banquet" Robert, J. N. 1988. *Les Modes à Rome*. Les Belles Lettres, Paris, pp.1–3; and Friedländer, L. 1968. *Roman Life and Manners Under the Early Empire, Vol. II*. Barnes and Noble, New York, p.152.

"Sallust (86–34 B.C.) blamed the momentous events" See Edwards, C. 1993. *The Politics of Immorality in Ancient Rome*. Cambridge University Press, New York.

"a monstrous piece of gluttony" Cited from Friedländer 1968:142.

"Robert Putnam mapped the distribution of social capital among the American states" Putnam, R. D. 2000. *Bowling Alone: The Collapse and Revival of American Community*. Simon and Schuster, New York, pp. 292–295.

"the late republican crisis" Narrative follows Ward et al. 2003.

"The extent of carnage during the civil wars" See Stearns 2001, Crawford 1993:1, and Le Glay et al. 1997: 118.

"I don't want to die young and for nothing!" Quoted from Le Glay et al. 1997:171.

"so many wars throughout the world … the fields going to waste in the farmer's absence" Quoted from Wells 1992:15.

On the settlement of Octavian veterans, see Wells 1992:21–22.

"I will only hit the highlights of the Principate cycle" The full treatment will be published in Turchin and Nefedov, forthcoming.

"Trans-Apennine Italy (or Cisalpine Gaul, as it was known during the Republic) developed on a diverging trajectory." See Toynbee 1965: 182–3 and Wells 1992:183.

Chapter 12

The full text of Tolstoy's novel *War and Peace* can be found at www.funet.fi/pub/culture/russian/books/Tolstoy/War_and_peace.

On the probable influence of Newton and Laplace on Tolstoy, see Ivars Peterson's MathTrek, October 29, 2001. *Tolstoy's Calculus*. MAA Online. www.maa.org/mathland/mathtrek%5F10%5F29%5F01.html.

Another interesting discussion is: Vitányi, P. Preprint. "Tolstoy's Mathematics in War and Peace." Available at http://xxx.lanl.gov/abs/math.HO/0110197.

"It is also accepted by modern sociologists." See references in the Introduction relating to the micro-to-macro problem.

"Using the methods developed by military historians" See Dupuy, T. N. 1987. *Understanding War: History and Theory of Combat*. Nova, Falls Church, VA. See also Hartley, D. S. 2001. "Topics in Operations Research: Predicting Combat Effects." *INFORMS*, Linthicum, MD.

"Men make their own history, but not of their own free will; not under circumstances they themselves have chosen but under the given and inherited circumstance with which they are directly confronted." Karl Marx, "The Eighteenth of Brumaire of Louis Bonaparte," in *Surveys from Exile. Political Writings, Volume 2*, Penguin Books, London 1973, p. 146.

On sensitive dependence and mathematical chaos, see, for example, Gleick, J. 1987. *Chaos: Making a New Science*. Viking, New York.

Chapter 13

For social capital, see the following:

Putnam, R. D. 2000. *Bowling Alone: The Collapse and Revival of American Community*. Simon and Schuster, New York.

Putnam, R. D., R. Leonardi, and R. Y. Nanetti. 1993. *Making Democracy Work: Civic Traditions in Modern Italy*. Princeton University Press, Princeton, NJ.

Pharr, S. J., and R. D. Putnam. 2000. *Disaffected Democracies*. Princeton University Press, Princeton, NJ.

Fukuyama, F. 1995. *Trust: The Social Virtues and Creation of Prosperity*. Free Press, New York.

Bourdieu, P. 1980. Le capital social: notes provisoires. *Actes de la Recherches en Sciences Sociales* 3:2–3.

Lin, N., K. Cook, and R. S. Burt. 2001. *Social Capital: Theory and Research*. Aldine de Gruyter, New York.

"Social scientists (for example, Diego Gambetta)" Gambetta, D. 1988. *Trust: Making and Breaking Cooperative Relations*. Basil Blackwell, Oxford.

Gambetta, D. 1993. *The Sicilian Mafia: The Business of Private Protection*. Harvard University Press, Cambridge, MA.

"in the long essay he [Tocqueville] wrote describing the trip"

"In past secular cycles, we typically see a rise in crime rates in the pre-crisis period." See Fischer 1996.

"official inflation rate, calculated by Bureau of Labor Statistics, does not tell the whole story" See Jarret Wollstein. 2005. "2% Inflation and Other Official Lies." www.isil.org/towards-liberty/inflation-gov-lies.html.

"credentialing crisis" See Collins, R. 1979. *The Credential Society: An Historical Sociology of Education and Stratification*. Academic Press, New York.

"The proportion of people saying that they trust the government in Washington has been steadily declining from between 70 percent to 80 percent in the late 1950s to 30 percent 40 percent in the 1990s." From Pharr and Putnam *Disaffected Democracies.*

"45 percent of Americans believe little or nothing in their daily newspapers, up from 16 percent two decades ago" According to a recent report from the Pew Research Center, "Trends 2005." http://pewresearch.org/trends/.

Chapter 14

"According to Charles Krauthammer" From Bacevich, A. J. 2005. *The New American Militarism: How Americans Are Seduced by War.* Oxford University Press, New York.

"whether the United States today is an empire that can and should be compared with imperial powers of the past" See "History and Hyperpower" by Eliot A. Cohen in the July/August 2004 issue of *Foreign Affairs.*

"Empire seems to be in fashion" See "The Empire Strikes Back" by Anatol Lieven in the July 7, 2003 issue of *The New York Times,* where Lieven reviews six recent books on empire.

The Pentagon-commissioned report on empires: See the March 5, 2003 column by Maureen Dowd in the *New York Times.*

"Certain political scientists have recently argued" See Huntington, S. P. 2004. *Who Are We: The Challenges to America's National Identity.* Simon & Schuster, New York.

"The British journalist and writer Anatol Lieven" See Lieven, A. 2004. *America Right or Wrong: An Anatomy of American Nationalism.* Oxford University Press, New York.

"adding most recently six central European and two Mediterranean countries during the writing of this book" This event took place on May 1, 2004.

For the background to the Chechen-Russian conflict, see Chechnya: The White Book published by the Russian Information Centre and RIA Novosti (03 April 2000). http://www.globalsecurity.org/military/library/news/2000/04/white/

For slavery in Chechnya, see:

Dixon, R. 2000. Chechnya's Grimmest Industry. Los Angeles Times (September 18, 2000).

Frabchetti, M. 2002. Russian returns after 13 years of Chechen slavery. Sunday Times (31 March 2002).

"Most serious political scientists expect an escalating geopolitical competition between the two" see Mearscheimer, J. J. 2001. *The Tragedy of Great Power Politics.* Norton, New York.

"Today the most violent clash of civilizations occurs on the metaethnic frontiers of Islam with the Western, Orthodox, Hindu, and Sinic civilizations." This observation was made by Samuel Huntigton in his 1996 book *The Clash of Civilizations and the Remaking of World Order,* and his insight has been fully borne out by the events of the subsequent decade.

"the heavy diplomatic and symbolic assistance that Israel gets from the U.S.," such as vetoing anti-Israeli propositions in the U.N. There is also a very noticeable difference in the coverage of Israel between American and European mass media, with the latter providing more balanced, and in some cases even pro-Palestinian, coverage.

"It is also a phenomenon largely restricted to the Middle East." The only major exception is the conflict between Tamils and Sinhalese in Sri Lanka.

"But an even more striking development is the rise of the suicide bomber." See:

Atran, S. 2003. Genesis of suicide terrorism. *Science* 299:1534-1539.

Atran, S. 2004. A leaner, meaner jihad. *New York Times* (March 16, 2004).

"coalescence of global terrorist networks" as Anne Rueter reports in *Ann Arbor News,* (March 28, 2004) Scott Atran argued, "It's clear we have misunderstood the nature of global jihad. It's misguided to think that terrorist attacks—98 suicide attacks occurred globally last year—are orchestrated by a tightly organized network run by al-Qaida. Rather, it seems we face a set of largely autonomous groups and cells pursuing their own regional aims. He describes terrorist cells that share motivation and methods with al-Qaida but act in isolation, swarming on their own initiative—homing in from scattered locations on various targets and then dispersing, only to form new swarms."

"Estrada fell." More recently, anti-Japanese demonstrations in China became so widespread, that the Chinese authorities became worried that they could keep them under control. See Yarley, J. 2005. A Hundred Cellphones Bloom and Chineses Take to the Streets. *New York Times* (April 25, 2005).

"complex self-organizing behavior" see Strogatz, S. 2003. *SYNC: The Emerging Science of Spontaneous Order*. Hyperion, New York; and Barabasi, A. L. 2003. *Linked: How Everything Is Connected to Everything Else and What It Means*. Plume.

Acknowledgments

I'd like to start the pleasant labor of thanking various people for enabling me to finish this book with my parents, who not only gave me life, but also set me on the path of intellectual curiosity and life-long infatuation with science from a very early age—longer than I can remember. Later in life I learned a tremendous amount about how to do research from my teachers and colleagues in the biological sciences, too many to enumerate here. Most recently, my colleagues in the Department of Ecology and Evolutionary Biology were very supportive of the new directions my curiosity took me, even though it landed me well beyond the boundaries of biology.

In this age of scientific specialization crossing scientific boundaries is fraught with difficulties and dangers. This is why I feel an enormous debt of gratitude to my colleagues in the social sciences who gave me positive feedback during the early stages of my investigation into historical dynamics—Jack Goldstone, Tom Hall, Rob Boyd, Randall Collins, Sergey Nefedov, Andrey Korotayev, Chris Chase-Dunn, and many others.

I am grateful to the University of Connecticut for providing a nurturing and supportive environment for unconstrained intellectual discovery. My department head, Greg Anderson, encouraged me to strike out beyond disciplinary bounds and provided much needed release from teaching. The dean of the Colleage of Liberal Arts and Sciences, Ross MacKinnon, supported my work in a most tangible way, by funding half salary of my research assistant. The excellent and well-stocked library at the University of Connecticut was indispensable. Deborah Tyser provided essential research assistance; without her energetic and expert help this book would take twice as long to research and write.

My editor at Pi Press, Stephen Morrow, was involved in this project from the very beginning—guiding, inspiring, and shaping the final product at every step of the way. I have been exceptionally fortunate in linking up with Stephen at just the right time to begin working on the book. Michael Thurston and other members of the staff at Pi Press provided expert and cheerful assistance with the technical aspects of getting the book out. Virge Krask did an excellent job in preparing the maps. Many thanks to Andrey Astakhov for providing the electronic version of the Surikov painting, a fragment of which appears on the dust jacket.

Many people read parts or the whole of a preliminary draft of the book. I'd like to thank particularly Andrey Korotayev, Paul Seabright, David Christian, Pete Richerson, Herb Gintis, Tom Hall, Anatol Lieven, and James Powers for their extensive comments and positive critique.

My greatest gratitude goes to the most important person in my life without whose constant encouragement and support this book could never happen. I dedicate War and Peace and War to her.

Index